Strategies and Resources for Teaching Writing

with the

Prentice Hall Reference Guide

Sixth Edition

John Charles Goshert
Utah Valley State College

STRATEGIES AND RESOURCES FOR TEACHING WRITING

with the

PRENTICE HALL REFERENCE GUIDE

SIXTH EDITION

Muriel Harris
Purdue University

PEARSON

Prentice
Hall

Upper Saddle River, New Jersey 07458

Copyright © 2006 by Pearson Education, Inc.
Upper Saddle River, NJ 07458

10 9 8 7 6 5 4 3 2

ISBN 0-13-168039-0
Printed in the United States of America

Contents

■ **PART THREE: ESL WRITERS IN THE COMPOSITION CLASS BY** *Cynthia Myers* **161**

■ **PART FOUR: READING AND WRITING ABOUT LITERATURE: A PRIMER FOR STUDENTS BY** *Edgar V. Roberts* **195**

Preface

Beginning writing instructors quickly learn that teaching college writing is an incredibly difficult task. The expectations we, our departments, and our institutions have for our students are high, yet we often find ourselves teaching in the midst of popular and student cultures that do not value writing as highly as we do. If we wish to bridge, or at least lessen this divide, we should keep abreast of best practices in a rapidly evolving field, consider ways of applying theoretical work in our daily classroom practices, and become participants in shaping the academic conversation about teaching college writing.

That said, however, the quotidian demands of our jobs can impede even the most sincere desire to stay current in the field. Thus, the seven sections in this supplement, *Strategies and Resources for Teaching Writing with the Prentice Hall Reference Guide*, contain resources to help you think about each major component of teaching introductory writing to college students. Presented in a relatively compressed form, each section will help you situate yourself in current approaches to teaching, from planning a term to incorporating literature, academic research, and emergent technologies into your course; these sections also include substantial resources for further reading. Because this text's authors draw on their experiences of teaching in institutions across the country and through various emphases and levels of access to resources, every introductory writing teacher will find relevant information and practices that can be applied immediately to his or her particular goals and institutional situation.

Although the Sixth Edition of the *Prentice Hall Reference Guide* provides a common point of reference for each section of the supplement, you will find that the value and application of the discussions and approaches presented here exceed a single text. Indeed, we hope that this book, like the handbook, will be a long term reference, one which provides you with portable strategies and a foundation for future growth that you will use and modify over time as your teaching develops.

Acknowledgements

I am deeply indebted to my colleagues at Utah Valley State College, especially those who read and commented on various drafts of Part One: Brian Whaley, Steve Gibson, and Mark Crane. Bonnie Kyburz and Doug Downs have been very generous with their time for ongoing, and always fruitful, discussions on broader pedagogical questions. Kate McPherson and Steve Gibson kindly allowed me to use their class materials for examples which appear in this manual. Marge Bartelt, of Owens Community College, shared her worksheet which appears in Chapter 4 of this manual.

Numsiri Kunakemakorn read each draft and gave me constant support throughout the process. My students have been there for each test drive of a new idea or approach; they have been both my greatest advocates and most adamant critics.

Finally, thanks to Shannon Howard, who brought me to the project and listened to enough ideas to fill a number of textbooks, and to Jennifer Conklin, who shepherded the project to completion.

PART ONE:
Strategies for Teaching Writing
John Charles Goshert, *Utah Valley State College*

CHAPTER 1
Introduction

Few teaching experiences more clearly illustrate the great divide between the goals and expectations of instructors of first year composition and those of our students than the question that, almost without exception, will be asked on the first day of each writing course: "So what do I have to do to get an 'A' in this class?" Although this question may never cease to frustrate us, we should realize that it is asked from a specific context, and that it is often the product of our students' elementary and secondary educational experiences. The emphasis on high stakes testing and increasing standardization of instruction in public education (today, even preschoolers in Head Start programs are being given tests tied to high academic stakes for themselves and financial stakes for their schools) means that many of our students arrive in the composition class with expectations about writing that have been built from over a decade of training which has often led them to associate good writing with following the rules set out and constantly reinforced by the triumvirate of the instructor, the textbook, and the handbook. They may come to class believing that the key to success is discovering what the instructor wants them to write—a heavily guarded secret—and then producing, or perhaps better, reproducing, that writing. As instructors of introductory writing courses, we are poised to have a significant impact on our students. We have a valuable opportunity to challenge dominant perceptions about the role of writing and end-driven conceptions of education. Indeed, because the introductory writing course is, for the majority of students, the first class they have in college, their experiences with us will play a crucial role in setting the tone for the remainder of their careers in higher education.

The college composition classroom has undergone significant changes in recent years. Because higher education is seen in increasingly vocational terms, composition programs are often pressured to give college writing vocational significance; as instructors in our individual classes, we are expected, similarly, to articulate to our students the practical application of the set of skills they expect to receive at our hands. Although we can certainly transmit sets of skills, techniques of writing, and knowledge of conventions to our students, we should, at the same time, resist the temptation to see skill sets as the sum total of what we have to offer. In fact, in our courses we should pursue ways of teaching and modeling the notion that writing need not be for anything other than increasing and broadening our students' abilities to communicate. What we can do is encourage students' already existing abilities, skills, and interests to help them learn to think, read, and of course write, critically.

In concert with the teaching of skill sets, we can begin to engender positive attitudes about writing, encouraging students who have had positive experiences in past writing classes and inspiring students who have been less fortunate in their experiences; we can make learning and writing an intellectual adventure that does not end on the final day of our course (or even on the last day of college, for that matter). We need not drive students toward predetermined ends, but instead toward developing in them a more nuanced understanding of, and a newfound interest in, writing. If we can teach positive attitudes about writing, our work in turn becomes more rewarding and more pleasurable.

One of the most important ways we can change negative attitudes about writing is by transforming our students' conceptions of the goals of writing. It need not be end-driven—concluded once the paper is written and a grade received—but, instead, it can be seen as an ongoing conversation, embedded in a process of critical thinking, planning, composition, and revision. By teaching writing that is oriented in process, we can help students begin to move away from perceptions of writing as a series of high stakes attempts to meet unattainable standards of correctness and, instead, toward a lasting perception of writing as an open-ended series of possibilities, always subject to revision and rethinking. Process-oriented composition instruction will help students gain confidence in their critical thinking and in their abilities to express themselves.

The *Prentice Hall Reference Guide to Grammar and Usage* by Muriel Harris reflects this process-oriented approach to teaching writing in its contents and in its organization. This supplement, *Strategies and Resources for Teaching Writing*, is meant to aid both new and experienced teachers of college writing in using Harris's handbook in a variety of ways, depending on the objectives and methods of the course, the academic calendar structuring the course, and, most importantly, the needs of students. The handbook can provide writing teachers and students alike with resources for not only developing and refining first drafts, but also for revisiting specific issues of conventional mechanics, usage, style, and voice, throughout the revision process. In the remainder of this chapter, I introduce some strategies for getting started and outline the areas on which the supplement focuses.

■ FLEXIBILITY IN PLANNING

In the earliest stages of planning a college writing course, we must recognize that only rarely, if ever, can we march a class in lock step through a syllabus each term. In order to support the process-oriented class environment, we can model flexibility for our students; through our willingness to detour from the class schedule, we can take opportunities to pursue ideas in which our students show interest; we can also leave time for unexpected challenges. Certainly, we must strive to reach goals and outcomes which we expect to achieve, and those which are established by our departments. If we work in a department that has a two-course composition sequence, such as English 101 (introductory writing) and English 102 (an introduction to research writing), we need to forecast ways to help our students move smoothly from one course to the next. We may even have a department-wide syllabus that we are expected to follow; but, in concert with institutional goals and planning, we should be aware as well that each writing class will work best when we allow students to have some say in its pace and development over the term.

Just as we should not have an overly rigid class schedule in which every minute of every class period is planned in advance, neither should we abandon the syllabus as a necessary tool that situates students and helps us articulate the individual assignments and larger goals of the course. Chapter 3 of this supplement focuses on a number of possible strategies for organizing a writing course by day, by week, and by unit; it also suggests some models for organizing courses on accelerated and summer schedules. Regardless of our choices in planning, we need to expect interruptions in the schedule and to be flexible enough to accommodate a diverse range of student writers who may be more or less prepared—or both simultaneously—than we expect at the outset of a term. Our flexibility in planning is a critical way of communicating to our students an awareness of their importance in the day-to-day unfolding of the class. When we involve students in the planning and shaping of the writing class, they are better prepared to work collaboratively in their writing and to see their writing projects as the products of a similarly flexible, recursive process.

As you prepare for teaching introductory writing, carefully read your department's literature on the course. Most departments have clearly articulated outcomes statements that you will be expected to meet by the end of the term; many departments will archive sample syllabi, sample writing assignments, and activities that will help you achieve your goals. Also, you should consider speaking with a writing program coordinator or a seasoned teacher of writing in your department. Their experiences will help you shape your plans so that you can establish and meet reasonable goals for your course. Read course texts in advance, and pace the amount of reading and writing in the class so that your students will be challenged but not overwhelmed. Finally, be sure to familiarize yourself with institutional policies on grading standards, attendance, academic dishonesty, and so on.

■ PEER EVALUATION

Just as we involve students in the planning of, and the day to day work in, our classes, so too should we involve them with each other throughout the writing process. As students move from planning stages, through drafting, and toward the submission of a writing assignment, peer respondents can make sense of the often nebulous concept of audience. Sharing work with other members of the class encourages student writers to see their readers as actual people who both share and diverge from the writer's background, experiences, and set of commonplace assumptions about the world.

Likewise, students value the role the classroom community plays in the writing process, as the location of critical reading and response that helps them write their best work. If we plan and supervise peer review sessions effectively, student writers receive valuable feedback from other students; additionally, through their active participation in peer reviews, students learn to read their own drafts with critical eyes, and thus are better equipped to shape and revise their work throughout the writing process.

One of the ways in which we can set the tone for productive peer review sessions is in planning assignments, particularly early in the term, that have a local focus. For instance, we can assign a description of place essay that asks students to focus on a campus location, or a problem-solution paper that treats an issue on campus or in the local community. Through such assignments, students begin to see writing as the product of an ongoing conversation among members of and between discourse communities. Writers become more comfortable with sharing their writing and peer reviewers become more confident in their abilities to read critically and offer productive advice. See Chapter 6 for a discussion of specific peer review strategies you can bring to your writing classes.

■ THE TEXTS WE TEACH

In order to illustrate the communal nature of writing in locations outside the immediate classroom, we can introduce our students to the ways in which conversations unfold through writing in numerous professions. In addition to more traditional reader/rhetoric and handbook texts, we can provide students with numerous benefits and insights by choosing to introduce them to academic writing in our composition courses. By providing our students with a critical understanding of the conventions of academic discourses, we can also begin to situate them in the reading and writing techniques that are integral to their college careers.

Academic writing can model radically different methods of argument than those to which students have been trained to appeal. At first, the specialized language and dense rhetoric of an essay dealing with, for instance, a medical ethicist's examination of performance-enhancing drugs' impact on professional sports, are daunting to our students. Yet, because the coercive rhetoric of the newspaper/television editorial is rapidly becoming the dominant form of argument, and the one most familiar to our students, academic writing can actually be quite refreshing. Particularly when we work to choose texts dealing with topics already of interest to our students, the purpose of academic writing is to invite an audience to participate in academic conversations, rather than being passive consumers of polemic debates and testimonial discourses that surround them in their everyday lives. We can show students the ways that knowledge and truth are socially constructed within and by particular discourse communities; that knowledge and truth emerge not only from empirical research and quantitative analysis, but also—and just as importantly—from expert use of rhetorical conventions in which any given field of academic inquiry operates.

Additionally, we can use academic writing to decenter our classrooms; that is, we can use it to resist the historical model of agenda-driven, programmatic concepts of writing in which teachers direct students into uniform topics and forms. Because academics bring a wide range of disciplinary and rhetorical approaches to almost every conceivable question and topic, we can help students to learn the conventions of academic writing while they pursue their personal interests. In short, we can teach our students about the kinds of conventions and conversations that are valuable to them personally and in their majors, and at the same time, we can invite them to participate in those conversations. Teachers need not abandon a significant role in the classroom, because they bring their own expertise to student questions about locating sufficiently scholarly writing and negotiating complex arguments. Teachers must also present the tools and strategies students will employ in order to approximate and enter the conversations on which they have chosen to focus their writing.

Most importantly, academic writing, especially writing about pedagogy, the purpose and history of higher education, can offer students a glimpse behind the curtain that separates them from their instructors. They are able to see us as we see them and to enter into conversations about the purpose and value of writing, about academic debate, and about higher education as they simultaneously inhabit and shape it for students who will follow them. Finally, academic writing relates to students' everyday experiences in the classroom, on campus, and throughout their academic careers.

As writing teachers, we also have a responsibility to follow discussions among our peers regarding developments in college writing textbooks, debates about and innovations in pedagogical approaches, and changes in departmental and institutional structures that affect our classrooms and students. When we invite our students to join us in academic conversations about college writing, we keep abreast of current trends and developments in the conversation, and we receive valuable, concrete feedback from those who are the subjects of the conversation. Our classrooms might become the crucibles in which students and teachers together occupy any number of positions in the conversation; we are able to see ourselves as the audience of the conversation, as its subjects, and as participants in the conversation who will move it toward its future iterations.

■ INCORPORATING NEW TECHNOLOGIES IN OUR TEACHING

In addition to the types of writing we choose to incorporate in our classes, we must also familiarize ourselves and our students with new technologies that aid in the writing process and in the dissemination of student writing to audiences outside the boundaries of the college campus. We can teach our students to use computers effectively in the composition and revision process; we can help them become critical readers of and respondents to the variety of information on the internet; and, we can encourage our students to utilize internet technologies for sharing their work with each other in peer review sessions, in conversations with us and with other students on campus, in their local communities, and around the world.

New technologies can also aid us in the management of class time and material. Thanks to "wysiwyg" (what you see is what you get) software products, we can easily build and publish websites through which students can access handouts and web links to resources both on and off campus, and which we can update with changes in class schedule and assignments.

Students can communicate with us and with their classmates via email. Students can also build their own websites where they are able to share their work and to collaborate with students and communities outside their immediate classrooms.

The development of internet-based classroom management products, such as Blackboard and WebCT, facilitate discussions between students and teachers outside of class time, and, by promoting ongoing peer review and collaboration, they also reinforce the value of process-oriented writing practices. Additionally, internet-based services for teachers, such as mydropbox.com, can assist us in identifying and locating the sources of plagiarized work. See Chapter 7 (Evaluation) in this supplement for a discussion of plagiarism in the internet age and some strategies for identifying plagiarism, and for helping our students to avoid plagiarism in their papers.

As I will discuss in Chapter 8 (Writing Assignments), recent developments in computers and in other information technologies have opened a vast range of opportunities for writing instructors to communicate with colleagues at the nation's largest research universities and to share in the resources available to them. Because many smaller comprehensive institutions now have online delivery systems and access to other technologies that speed delivery of interlibrary loan materials, instructors at all levels of higher education can introduce their students to research writing.

As with strategies of incorporating texts in the classroom into which students and teachers alike are implicated, so too might teachers and students become co-learners and co-participants in discovering and applying emerging technologies to writing courses. Indeed, even relatively young and relatively technologically savvy writing teachers will discover that the knowledge many of their students have about types and uses of technology far exceeds their own. When we appeal to students to share their knowledge with the class and to incorporate it into discussions and writing assignments, they are encouraged to inhabit a position of authority, and, as a result, we can increase their ability and willingness to approach less familiar elements of the course and writing assignments with confidence.

■ ACCENTUATING THE POSITIVE

Writing teachers can reinforce student's confidence in areas in which they are already adept by positively encouraging them in their writing. We can adopt affirmative marking and commenting strategies that accentuate our students' successes and guide them to recognize and want to overcome their challenges. Although we certainly still have a responsibility to encourage our students to improve and to identify specific areas in which they can use improvement, we can temper overzealous identification of shortcomings. If we focus on errors or flawed logic alone, we risk losing the interest of our students and engendering or reinforcing negative attitudes toward writing. When our students focus on the positive rewards of writing, they will be more willing to overcome their challenges as well. See Chapter 7 for a more detailed discussion of evaluation strategies.

As you can see from this introduction, we conduct our college writing classes most effectively by interweaving a set of practices which involve students in planning the course; which encourage collaboration in each other's invention, writing, and revision; which teach students to employ new technologies in composing and sharing their work; which introduce students to broader discussions about college writing in the academic community and invite students to become participants in those discussions. These components are linked by instructors who respond affirmatively to their students while encouraging them to continually revisit and revise their topics, ideas, and writing. Teaching writing as a recursive process departs from the high stakes writing which strikes fear into our students; we can encourage our students to transform their fear into excitement about the possibilities of writing. In turn, we will have more confidence in and remain excited about the work we do in the writing class.

SUGGESTED READING

Adler Kassner, Linda. "Structure and Possibility: New Scholarship About Students Called Basic Writers." *College English* 63, no. 2 (Nov. 2000): 229-43.

Anson, Chris M., and Hildy Miller. "Journals in Composition: An Update." "A Progress Report from the CCCC Committee on Professional Standards." *College Composition and Communication* 42 (Oct. 1991) 330–44.

Austin, Kurt. *Trends & Issues in Postsecondary English Studies.* Urbana, IL: National Council of Teachers of English, 1999.

Badger, Richard, and Goodith White. "A Process Genre Approach to Teaching Writing." *ELT Journal* 45, no. 2 (Apr. 2000): 153-60.

Berlin, James. *Writing Instruction in American Colleges 1900–1985.* Carbondale, IL: Southern Illinois University Press, 1987.

Bloom, Lynn Z., Donald A. Daiker, and Edward M. White. *Composition in the Twenty-first Century: Crisis and Change.* Carbondale, IL: Southern Illinois UP, 1997.

Bowden, Darsie. "The Limits of Containment: Text-as-Container in Composition Studies." *College Composition and Communication* 44 (Oct. 1993): 364–79.

Bullock, Richard, and John Trimbur, eds. *The Politics of Writing Instruction: Postsecondary*. Portsmouth, NH: Boynton/Cook, 1991.

Elbow, Peter. "Reflections on Academic Discourse: How It Relates to Freshmen and Colleagues." *College English* 53 (Feb. 1991): 135–55.

——. "The War Between Reading and Writing—And How to End It." *Rhetoric Review* 12, no. 1 (Fall 1993): 5–24.

France, Alan A. "Assigning Places: The Function of Introductory Composition as a Cultural Discourse." *College English* 55, no. 6 (Oct. 1993): 593–609.

Gale, Fredric G., James L. Kinneavy, and Phillip Sipiora. *Ethical Issues in College Writing*. New York: Peter Lang, 1999.

Gale, Xin, and Fredric G. Gale. *(Re)visioning Composition Textbooks: Conflicts of Culture, Ideology and Pedagogy*. Albany: State UP of New York, 1999.

Hairston, Maxine. "Diversity, Ideology, and Teaching Writing." *College Composition and Communication* 43, no. 2 (May 1992): 179–93.

Horner, Bruce. "Resisting Traditions in Composing Composition." *Journal of Advanced Composition*. 14, no. 2 (Fall 1994): 495–519.

Indrisano, Roselmina, and James R. Squire. *Perspectives on Writing: Research, Theory and Practice*. Newark, DE: International Reading Association, 2000.

Jarratt, Susan Caroline Funderburgh. *Feminism and Composition Studies: In Other Words*. New York: Modern Language Association of America, 1998.

Kennedy, Mary Lynch. *Theorizing Composition: A Critical Sourcebook of Theory and Scholarship in Contemporary Composition Studies*. Westport, CT: Greenwood Press, 1998.

Kirsch, Gesa, and Patricia A. Sullivan, eds. *Methods and Methodology in Composition Research*. Carbondale, IL: Southern Illinois University Press, 1992.

Laurence, Patricia. "The Vanishing Site of Mina Shaughnessy's 'Error and Expectations.'" *Journal of Basic Writing* 12, no. 2 (Fall 1993): 18–28.

Lindemann, Erika. *A Rhetoric for Writing Teachers*. 3rd. ed. New York: Oxford University Press, 1995.

Lourey, Jessica. "Grease on the Keyboard: Making Composition Work in a Technical College." *Teaching English in the Two Year College* 28, no. 2 (Dec. 2000): 175-81.

Love, Michael. *A Resource Text for College Writing.* Boston: Houghton Mifflin Custom Pub. 2000.

McComiskey, Bruce. *Teaching Composition as a Social Process.* Loga, Utah: Utah State UP, 2000.

Miller, Richard E. "Composing English Studies: Towards a Social History of the Discipline." *College Composition and Communication* 45, no. 2 (May 1994): 164–79.

Miller, Susan. *Assuming the Positions: Cultural Pedagogy and the Politics of Commonplace Writing.* Pittsburgh: UP of Pittsburgh, 1998.

Moore, Sandy, and Michael Kleine. "Toward an Ethics of Teaching Writing in a Hazardous Context—The University." *Journal of Advanced Composition* 12, no. 2 (Fall 1992): 383–94.

Morgan, Dan. "Ethical Issues Raised by Students' Personal Writing." *College English* 60 (Mar. 1998): 318-25

Norton, L. S. "Essay Writing: What Really Counts?" *Higher Education* 20 (Dec. 1990): 411–42.

Nystrand, Martin, et al. "Where Did Composition Studies Come From? An Intellectual History." *Written Communication* 10, no. 3 (July 1993): 267–333.

Odell, Lee, ed. *Theory and Practice in the Teaching of Writing: Rethinking the Discipline.* Carbondale: Southern Illinois Press, 1993.

Penrod, Diane. *Miss Grundy Doesn't Teach Here Anymore: Popular Culture and the Composition Classroom.* Portsmouth, NH: Boynton/Cook, 1997.

Phillips, Donna Burns, et al. "'College Composition and Communication': Chronicling a Discipline's Genesis." *College Composition and Communication* 44, no. 4 (Dec. 1993): 443–65.

Qualley, Donna J. *Turns of Thought: Teaching Composition as Reflexive Inquiry.* Portsmouth, NH: Boynton/Cook, 1997.

Renard, Lisa. "Cut and Paste 101: Plagiarism and the Net." *Educational Leadership* 57, no. 4 (Jan. 2000): 38-42

Runciman, Lex. "Fun?" *College English* 53 (Feb. 1991): 156–63.

Saks, A. L., and Richard L. Larson. "Annotated Bibliography of Research in the Teaching of English." *Research in the Teaching of English* 28, no. 2 (May 1994): 208–23.

Schultz, Lucille M. "Elaborating on Our History: A Look at Mid-19th Century First Books of Composition." *College Composition and Communication* 45, no. 1 (Feb. 1994): 10–30.

Sommers, Nancy I. "The Need for Theory in Composition Research." *College Composition and Communication* 30 (Feb. 1979): 46–49.

Tate, Gary, and Edward P. J. Corbett, eds. *The Writing Teacher's Sourcebook.* 3rd. ed. New York: Oxford University Press, 1994.

"Teaching Writing [Symposium]." *College Teach* 39 (Spring 1991): 44–64.

Thomas, P.L. "The Struggle Itself: Teaching Writing as We Know We Should." *English Journal.* 90, no. 1 (Sept. 2000): 39-45.

Tobin, L. "Reading Students, Reading Ourselves: Revising The Teacher's Role in the Writing Class." *College English* 53 (March 91): 333–48.

Trimbur, John. "Composition and the Circulation of Writing." *College Composition and Communication* 52, no. 2 (Dec. 2000): 188-219

Troyka, Lynn Quitman, with Gerber, Lloyd-Jones, et al. *A Checklist and Guide for Reviewing Departments of English.* New York: Modern Language Association and Associated Departments of English, 1985.

——. "Perspectives on Legacies and Literacy in the 1980s." *College Composition and Communication* 33 (Oct. 1982): 252–62. Reprinted in *Sourcebook for Basic Writing Teachers,* edited by Theresa Enos. New York: Random House, 1987.

Wallace, Ray, Alan Jackson, and Susan Lewis Wallace. *Reforming College Composition: Writing the Wrongs.* Westport, CT: Greenwood Press, 2000.

Yagelski, Robert P. "The Ambivalence of Reflection: Critical Pedagogies, Identity, and the Writing Teacher." *College Composition and Communication* 51. no. 1 (Sept. 1999): 32-50.

CHAPTER 2

Setting Realistic Goals for Beginning College Writers

Especially when we are teaching our first introductory writing courses, we can often get lost in trying to present our students with everything we have learned throughout our own academic careers in a single semester. Such lofty and optimistic goals are certainly commendable, because they emerge from our excitement about writing and through significant reflection on what we have done to consider the approaches to writing that work for us and those that do not. Despite our best intentions, however, when our ambitions for what students should—or even can—be able to process and produce over the term far outstrip their abilities, they will quickly lose interest or feel inadequate. Rather than becoming dejected about what we cannot reasonably expect to accomplish in a term, we should remain excited about the importance of our role at the beginning of a writing process that our students will continue to practice throughout their college careers and on into their professions or graduate work, and in their everyday lives. Thus, we must carefully consider the work that we can reasonably expect to accomplish in any term, given the constraints of time and the backgrounds and attitudes of our students.

One of the best ways of situating ourselves in relation to student abilities and department expectations is to consult the guiding documents of our institution's writing program. Writing program administrators or committees of writing specialists in the department may have produced statements on the goals and outcomes of first year composition that guide writing instructors as they plan the term. In a program with a two-course writing sequence, we should familiarize ourselves with the goals for courses which lead to our own or follow from it. The more aware we are of the writing program in its entirety, the more effectively we see the role of our own courses. We should also meet with our colleagues regularly. In the weeks before the beginning of the term, speak with a colleague who teaches or administers remedial or pre-college level writing classes, who can give you a profile of students who will be moving into college level introductory writing courses. Join a writing program discussion group, or consider developing a series of brown bag meetings so that groups of writing instructors have the opportunity to share their experiences, as well as strategies and approaches for success in meeting program goals. By participating in periodic discussions, your experiences and ideas will play significant roles in the future growth and development of the writing program.

If your department does not have outcomes statements or other guiding documents, you should consider familiarizing yourself with those of professional bodies whose focus is on first year writing programs. Organizations such as the Council of Writing Program Administrators (WPA), the National Council of Teachers of English (NCTE), the Modern Language Association (MLA), and the Conference on College Composition and Communication (CCCC), have position statements and outcomes guidelines that have been developed through numerous studies and ongoing reflection. Their statements will help us ensure that our courses are consistent with nationally recognized best practices, and they provide us with a framework that we can eventually modify to meet the needs of students at our particular institutions, or to pursue additional goals we develop through personal experience and reflection on our methods.

The following list is not exhaustive, but most instructors will pursue these goals in their introductory writing courses.

1. We can help students see that the ability to write well is not inborn, but learned. We can help students build positive attitudes that will ensure an interest in writing and developing skills long after they have left our classes (see the preface, "Hints for Using this Book," in the *Prentice Hall Reference Guide*).

2. We can help students understand the importance of purposeful writing. Students become invested in each writing project, and in the course itself, when they see the value of writing beyond simply producing an assignment for a grade or fulfilling a college requirement (see Chapter 1a in the *Prentice Hall Reference Guide*).

3. We can help students see that writing plays an important role in their lives. Even in our (and especially our students') image-dominated culture, writing remains a key to learning and to succeeding in college and at work.

4. We can help students learn to use technology to empower them as writers. When we integrate word processing software, online collaboration, and electronic research techniques into our courses, we offer students ever-widening opportunities for designing, presenting, and sharing their writing (see Chapters 2 and 5 in the *Prentice Hall Reference Guide*).

5. We can help students to see writing as a tool for reflection about the world and their own experiences. Critical writing and reflection allow students to examine and, perhaps, to rethink their assumptions about themselves and the world. Likewise, a paper will often take a direction the students had not planned on, and we can show students that writing reflects not only the development of their ideas, but also the emergence of their own authority and voice.

6. We can help students recognize and value the notion that effective writing is the result of a recursive process. Contrary to many students' assumptions, "real" writers rarely—if ever—simply produce a finished piece of writing in a single sitting. We can show students that the writing process is comprised of interrelated stages and strategies, which include planning, drafting, organizing, collaborating, editing, and revising (see Chapter 2 in the *Prentice Hall Reference Guide*).

7. We can help students understand multiple approaches to brainstorming, and to recognize the ways that testing ideas and arguments through the drafting process can lead to new questions, ideas, and connections (see Chapter 2a in the *Prentice Hall Reference Guide*).

8. We can help students value revision as an integral component of the writing process. Through productive peer review by students and affirmative comments and evaluation by the instructor, students learn that revision is perhaps the most important stage in the writing process. By showing students the significance of higher order concerns as well as lower order concerns, we help them see revision as more than simply fixing mistakes in grammar and mechanics, and instead as a global revisiting of a draft which takes into account audience, purpose, and organization as well (see sections 2e and 2f in the *Prentice Hall Reference Guide*).

9. We can help students understand that a piece of writing is never entirely finished. Instead, writers let go of a piece of writing when they have revised it enough to satisfy the demands of the situation (time, conventions, genre, length, and so on). While careful revision helps writers move increasingly closer to the essay they envision, expert writers rarely think they have written something that defies further revision. Students can learn to accept final responsibility for their work while seeking and considering feedback.

10. We can help students see the importance of considering multiple approaches to organization and development. They should be able to consider and anticipate critically the effects of their decisions to write open form or closed form arguments, and to experiment with various kinds of paragraph structure in their writing projects. Students may not be able to apply every structural variant, but we can make them aware of many principles of organization (see Chapter 3e in the *Prentice Hall Reference Guide*).

11. We can help our students understand what a paragraph is and how to write an effective and coherent one. We can acquaint students with various means of developing paragraphs that suit a writing project's audience, topic, and purpose. We can also emphasize the importance of writing paragraphs that are unified and coherent. By teaching students to write effective paragraphs, we help them establish the firm foundation for writing essays which are similarly unified and coherent (see sections 3a, 3b, and 3c in the *Prentice Hall Reference Guide*).

12. We can help our students learn a variety of strategies to make effective and appropriate transitions between ideas and parts of an essay. The informed use of key transition words and phrases, and the ability to write extended resting place transitions, help students to effectively draw readers through the procession of ideas and the development of an argument (see Chapter 15 in the *Prentice Hall Reference Guide*).

13. We can help students understand the necessity of supporting generalizations with specific evidence. Convincing the audience of a claim depends on the effective incorporation of supporting evidence, and the effective selection of evidence depends on audience, purpose, and genre of the writing project (see Chapter 4d in the *Prentice Hall Reference Guide*).

14. We can help students understand the importance of considering the audience in their writing. Many students come to college believing that the instructor is the sole audience for their writing. Through critical consideration of audience (classmates, the academic community, newspaper readers, a business forum, and so on), students realize that they belong to multiple communities of readers and writers, and that many of the choices they make as writers depend on defining the audience for any particular project. In short, we can teach students that they do not write, nor do their ideas and arguments exist, in isolation or solely in relation to the writing instructor (see Chapter 1 in the *Prentice Hall Reference Guide*).

15. We can help students understand that good grammar is not the same thing as effective writing. While we should take opportunities to cover common or recurring shortcomings in grammar and mechanics throughout the term, students must be constantly reminded that even flawless grammar is far from the totality of the writing process.

16. We can help students understand that inflated or inappropriate diction is not the same thing as sophisticated thinking. We can encourage our students to develop ideas sufficiently rather than turning to the thesaurus for overloaded words and phrases. We can show students that the most effective writing is that which makes its arguments in a clear, coherent way. Similarly, we can help students avoid turning to clichés and encourage them, instead, to express themselves in unique and situation-appropriate ways (see Chapter 41 of the *Prentice Hall Reference Guide*).

17. We can help students understand what an essay is. Through effective modeling and class discussion, we can show students that essays are not found only in the English classroom, but are in fact a prominent mode of expression. We should expose students to a variety of contemporary essays, which are written for numerous audiences and a variety of purposes, throughout the semester.

18. We can help students understand how to use a dictionary. We should show them the differences between and uses of desk and unabridged dictionaries. We can acquaint them with the methods for using each dictionary and show them the value of the prefatory matter of a dictionary. We can help them locate and use specialized and discipline-specific dictionaries in their research writing or in preparation for the work they will do in their majors.

19. We can help students understand how to use a handbook to find answers to questions they have about writing. We can model ways of using the handbook and encourage students to use the book independently throughout the term.

20. We can help students see the place and value of reading in the recursive writing process. The more students read, the more they see patterns of organization and models for their own writing emerge, and the more they develop strategies for critically evaluating what they read. Particularly considering the emergence and growing ubiquity of the internet, we must teach students that every piece of writing that is published is not necessarily valuable. Through both positive and negative examples, students will expand their repertoire of strategies and approaches they will use in their own writing.

21. We can help students see the value of research in developing sophisticated and informed academic writing. We can teach students many ways of searching for and acquiring source material and for distinguishing between scholarship and popular writing and the relative values of each. We can help students incorporate material found in sources through conventional quotation, paraphrase, and summary strategies. We can teach one or more bibliographic styles.

When we come to our introductory writing courses with a sense of confidence in goals that are reasonable and attainable, students will also respond with confidence that they can meet our expectations. Even if we cannot attain all of our goals in any single term, we have nonetheless done the critical work of ushering our students into the conventions of academic thinking and writing. We have also provided them with the invaluable means to break conventions which at first seem overwhelming or impossible into manageable components, which they will continue to develop throughout their college careers.

SUGGESTED READING

Baines, Lawrence, Coleen Baines, and Gregory Kent Stanley. "Losing the Product in the Process." *English Journal* 88. No. 5 (May 1999): 67-72.

Bizzaro, Patrick. "What I Learned in Grad School, of Literary Training and the Theorizing of Composition." *College Composition and Communication* 50, no. 4 (June 1999): 722-42.

Bruffee, Kenneth A. "Academic Castes, Academic Authority, and the Educational Centrality of Writing." *College Composition and Communication* 50, no. 4 (June 1999): 722-42.

Connors, Robert J. "The Erasure of the Sentence." *College Composition and Communication* 52, no. 1 (Sept. 200): 96-128.

Devine, T. G. "Caveat Emptor: The Writing Process Approach to College Writing." *Journal of Developmental Education* 11 (Fall 1990): 2–4.

Dossin, Mary Mortimore. "Writing Across the Curriculum: Lessons from a Writing Teacher." *College Teaching* 45 (Winter 1997): 14-15.

Lardner, Ted. "What Works? Rethinking the Theory-Practice Relationship in Composition." *Writing Instructor* 15 (Fall 1995): 5-17.

——. "Locating the Boundaries of Composition and Creative Writing." *College Composition and Communication* 51, no. 1 (Sept. 1999): 72-77.

Mayers, Tim. "(Re)writing Craft." *College Composition and Communication* 51, no. 1 (Sept. 1999): 82-89.

Newkirk, Thomas, ed. *Nuts and Bolts: A Practical Guide to Teaching College Composition.* Portsmouth, NH: Boynton/Cook, 1993.

Reid, Joy M., and Patricia Byrd. *Grammar in the Composition Classroom.* New York: Heinle & Heinle Publishers, 1998.

Troyka, Lynn Quitman. "Closeness to Text: A Delineation of Reading Processes as They Affect Composing." in *Relating Writing and Reading in the College Years*, edited by Thomas Newkirk. Boynton/Cook, 1986.

Wallace, D. L., and J. R. Hayes. "Redefining Revision for Freshmen." *Research in the Teaching of English* 25 (Feb. 1991): 54–66.

Chapter 3
Guidelines for Syllabus Design

Most higher education institutions in the United States require that each course have a syllabus, a detailed plan of instruction that students receive early in the term, if not at the first class meeting. Course syllabi will at least provide students with a schedule of assignments, a list of course texts, grading methods, and final grade distribution. Typically, instructors will also include a detailed description of the course, a statement on course goals and outcomes, an attendance policy, a statement on plagiarism, one or more ways of contacting the instructor, and office hours. There may be a standard syllabus for all introductory writing courses that has been devised by the writing program administrator or a committee of composition specialists in your department. Even when you are provided with relatively rigid guidelines, however, you will have the ability to meet department-wide goals on your own terms and to devise class activities with some independence. Even in less centrally managed programs, though, your institution will likely have a set of particular items that must be included in the syllabus and more specific guidelines for scheduling, so be sure to meet with a writing program administrator as you prepare your course plans.

We should make the syllabus describe the course as specifically as possible; having clear statements on course policies and writing assignments will prevent misunderstandings that, in extreme cases, can result in lawsuits. Keep in mind that the syllabus is considered—legally as well as institutionally—a contract between students and the instructor, so the more detail we provide, the better prepared our students are to tackle the work of the course and the better protected we are from dissatisfied students who tend to appear toward the end of the term. Likewise, once students have agreed to participate by enrolling in the course, we can expect them to produce the written work and satisfactorily accomplish all of the requirements we have set out in the syllabus. Indeed, students have a right to know what we expect of them, in terms of written production, the amount of reading required, and class conduct, and they should be able to expect that requirements are not going to be changed drastically—or at least arbitrarily—during the term.

From the instructor's standpoint as well, the syllabus is a necessary teaching tool that establishes a plan for the entire term. Because it helps us visualize our expectations for each week of the course, or each writing assignment we plan to teach, the syllabus helps us ensure that the amount of material we intend to cover is both reasonable and manageable. Instructors who do not carefully prepare their courses may find themselves heading into the final weeks of the term, and yet still having to cover three writing genres in order to meet department, institutional, or their own goals and expectations. Thus, legality and student security aside, it makes good pedagogical sense to prepare a syllabus for each course we teach.

A syllabus should begin with information about the course and the instructor. You should include the title, catalogue number, and section of the course, and the time, days, and location of class meetings; in fact, you may want to read this information in the opening minutes of the first class meeting and encourage students to compare the syllabus to their class schedules to make sure that everyone is in the right course, in the right place, and at the right time. Include your name and contact information, such as your office location, phone number, and email address. If you expect students to address you with a title, such as Mr., Ms., Dr., and so on, include that information; as you go over the syllabus, you may consider pronouncing your name once or twice as well.

Provide a detailed description of materials required for the course. List each required text, such as a writing handbook, a reader/rhetoric, and a college dictionary, and include edition number or year of publication, especially if local bookstores carry multiple editions of the texts. If you list texts in the course's bibliographic style (MLA, Chicago, or the like), students will have a ready model of citation conventions. If you recommend certain texts, such as a thesaurus, in addition to the required texts, be sure to list them here as well. Clearly state any other materials students will need for the course, such as computer disks and composition books or binders for journals. You should also consider requiring students to purchase a wallet folder to store drafts of writing projects and other course materials.

Many instructors will also include a narrative component on their syllabi that contains course descriptions or outlines of course goals. Drawing on the catalogue description and department guidelines, describe the goals of the course and how you expect them to be met during the term. Even if you list projects at another point in the syllabus, consider including here brief summaries of major writing assignments, journals, presentations, and other course requirements. If you have a policy on revision, be sure to include it and describe the conditions of and timeline for revisions. If you will not accept late papers, say so here; if you do accept late papers, clearly state the stakes of late submission, such as one deducted grade for every late day. Describe your attendance policy; some institutions have rigid attendance requirements and impose specific penalties for missing more than a certain number of days, so check the course catalogue or see a writing program administrator to ensure that your policy is consistent with that of your institution or department. If student participation is a component of the final grade (for many instructors, attendance and partic-ipation are tied together) include a brief explanation of what counts as participation and how you will determine the grade.

Include an overview of the course's grade distribution as well. How will major writing assignments, journals, occasional writing, revisions, presenta-tions, attendance, and participation together determine the student's final grade? If you intend to use a portfolio grading system, be sure to describe the methods of collecting and evaluating portfolios throughout the term and the materials that must be included. Along with the grading system in your course, you may also want to either include or summarize your insti-tution's statement on grading policies or the institution's criteria for award-ing particular grades. One of the most important parts of this section will be your statement concerning plagiarism, which will clearly state the penal-ties of academic dishonesty and may include references to definitions and examples in course texts (such as section 56a in the *Prentice Hall Reference Guide*). Your department or institution may have policies in place and a template statement that you can copy into this section.

Among other elements to consider including in your course descrip-tion, a resources statement helps students feel less isolated in the class. If there is a writing lab or tutoring center available on campus, let students know where it is and how to set up appointments. You might also empha-size that your scheduled office hours are there for the students' benefit and encourage them to make wise use of your time outside of regular class hours. If your department or institution has a policy for assisting students with disabilities (in some states, a disability statement is required by law), be sure to include contact names and numbers. You may also include a brief statement on style guidelines for writing assignments. Because the wide range of typefaces and fonts on students' personal computers can tempt them to make stylistic choices which range from inappropriate to outright illegible, let them know what you expect at the outset, long before the first paper is due.

Finally, the syllabus will include a calendar of assignments and activ-ities. The calendar may be as specific as a day-by-day list of reading and writing assignments for the entire term, or it may be as general as a list of due dates. Both specific and general approaches have benefits, but each also comes with certain drawbacks. Beginning instructors will benefit from a day-by-day plan, which provides them with a guide to pacing the course and gives them the best chance of completing every required assign-ment and fulfilling the goals of the course. The department's senior instructors or writing program administrators may have a time-tested schedule template that will help ground beginning instructors in meeting outcomes within the term, or will offer some guidance to an instructor who is teaching a new course. Students also tend to appreciate a detailed schedule because it helps them place the introductory writing class in relation to their other responsibilities. Keep in mind, however, that when we make highly detailed class schedules, these benefits to students and ourselves only accrue if we are able to keep more or less on track for the duration of the term, in some cases as long as sixteen weeks. We may want to wait, then, until we have some experience with the students at our institution and with various methods of organizing the course before we commit to a daily schedule on our syllabus.

Conversely, the bare bones class schedule allows for the greatest flexibility and improvisation. If they list only due dates for major writing assignments, instructors can adjust the pace of the course as they feel necessary. While this structure can have great effects of liberating students and instructors alike and encouraging student-directed organization, students may be frustrated if reading, prewriting, and other assignments seem to be assigned arbitrarily (even if they are not). We may have more difficulty getting student participation at busier times in the term, if students have not had sufficient opportunity to plan in advance. More importantly, this sort of syllabus may be too vague to help instructors—particularly beginning instructors or instructors with heavy teaching or preparation loads— pace themselves over the long run.

In either case, the syllabus should not be seen as a cage, but as a guide. We must allow for flexibility in pacing the course, being prepared to bend or even change our plans as required by the idiosyncrasies of each individual class. Indeed, as we write the class schedule on the syllabus, it is a good idea to put that flexibility into writing, by titling the calendar "Tentative Schedule of Assignments" or the like, so that students are aware of their role in shaping the course, and your willingness to adjust the pace as necessary. A good mix of the specific and general approaches to scheduling is to organize the course by stating goals and assignments for each week of class. Students are able to plan well in advance for this class and place it in relation with their other courses and responsibilities, and instructors are assured that they have a plan that will allow them to cover required material and achieve desired goals. However, both students and instructors are able to shape the class as it unfolds without feeling pressured to keep to an overly rigid schedule.

Certainly we have to make certain choices about scheduling at the expense of others each term. We should always experiment with new approaches to organizing our schedules according to our own experiences and the practices of other,s which we learn about as we keep abreast of professional literature. Like our students, we benefit from ongoing reflection about what we expect to do in class and the results of our efforts. Consider spending a few minutes after each class meeting to take some notes on which uses of the time were most effective and which uses you would change in the future. Our ability to write effective schedules will increase with each year we spend both teaching and continuing to learn about what we teach through reflection and reading professional literature.

There is, however, no such thing as a generic introductory writing course, because each instructor, department, and institution collaborate on what will constitute best practices and approaches to teaching the course. Additionally, our individual and institutional goals and practices must be considered in light of the length and pace of the term. Although the number of contact hours in a term—typically, forty-five—will remain constant whether we are teaching over fifteen weeks in a semester, or compressing the semester into an eight week accelerated block, or a six week summer session, time spent in class and significant time for reflection are both necessary for the material—and, perhaps more importantly, the writing process itself—to take hold and for our students to begin to have confidence in their abilities to write and to tackle challenges independently. Thus, the closer together the class meetings are and the longer the class sessions are, the more difficulty students have assimilating the principles we are teaching. In more compressed schedules, we should keep in mind that requiring a smaller volume of written production can often result in more learning from our students. If we work in departments requiring a fixed number of assignments or pages written per term, we have less flexibility in structuring our courses, but we can think about limiting the range of topics we require or adjusting the length of writing assignments.

Among other possible approaches to organizing introductory writing courses, consider the following focus areas:

➤ *Integrating computers into the writing process.* Instructors should consider taking advantage of computer enhanced classrooms on campus. The integration of computers can help students not only learn the academic skills required of college writers, but also acquire many of the skills they will need when they enter the workforce.

➤ *The whole essay.* Writing assignments and model texts are chosen to focus on the essay form.

➤ *Research skills.* The class focuses on helping students learn to do research in a range of disciplines, with attention given to developing critical reading skills and writing to academic audiences.

➤ *Language skills.* Both proficient and developmental students benefit from attention to sentence forms, with attention to the development of language over time and situation-appropriate usage.

The following introductory college writing syllabus is structured for a typical fifteen week semester and focuses on moving students through various genres that they are likely to use throughout their college careers. You can find detailed descriptions of and suggestions for teaching these genres in Chapter 8 of this supplement. Additionally, instructors will find the *Prentice Hall Reference Guide* easy to include as a text in this course. The readings, assignments, and goals work on the assumption that students are preparing either for a second term composition course that focuses on research writing, or an introduction to research methods and discipline-specific writing in their majors. Finally, I have structured the course assuming that regular reading is integral to developing strategies of critical thinking and writing, so most weeks will include reading assignments, which should be sufficiently nuanced and complex to encourage student engagement and discussion during class meetings.

Both regular and occasional writing assignments can easily be incorporated into such a course plan as well. Consider assigning weekly writing, which may include invention activities, responses to the week's lessons, and reflection on the student's progress and development as a writer throughout the term. Many reader/rhetorics are designed with regular journal writing in mind, and will include prompts for reflection on the content and significance of both rhetorical content and sample readings. If you do plan to assign journals, be sure to indicate regular dates for collection on the syllabus. We should also encourage students to reflect in writing, either formally or informally, on supplemental readings that we use to generate class discussion about the genres we teach, topic development, and argument. Even ten minutes spent at the beginning of a class meeting can help students formulate questions for clarifying the reading or reactions to the content, and help avoid dull or unproductive discussion periods.

WEEK ONE

Goals   Spend sufficient time describing and clarifying any questions regarding assignments, texts, and class schedule.

Be sure that students can locate course materials in bookstore, supplements in the reserve reading room, and course resources, including the writing lab, instructor's office, and online apparatus.

Introduce process-oriented writing.

Assignments   Assessment essay: "Describe an event (such as a book you read, a conversation with parent or role model, or an unexpected experience) that prompted your decision to attend college."

Introduction activity (this is a good ice-breaker that will make peer reviewing less uncomfortable later): students spend 10 minutes each interviewing each other, and then introducing each other to the rest of the class.

Read introductory chapters in course text(s).

Write a paragraph or two on opening the handbook and speculating on its uses and usefulness.

WEEK TWO

Goals   Introduce features of Paper #1: Topic Analysis

Define and discuss topic selection.

Help students select sufficiently arguable, problematic topics.

Define and discuss subject matter and rhetorical components of argument.

Assignments   Read handbook Chapter 1: Audience and Purpose.

Read handbook Chapter 4: Argument.

Read model texts for discussion.

Select topic for brief writing assignment and write introductory paragraph(s): Define topic and provide background.

WEEK THREE

Goals Complete a draft of the first writing assignment.

Discussion of common errors in conventional mechanics and usage.

Assignments Read relevant sections of the handbook. Consider, for instance, run-on and fragment sentences (Chapters 6 and 8), subject-verb agreement (Chapter 7), pronoun case (Chapter 19), prepositions (Chapter 21) and apostrophe use (Chapter 28).

Read model texts for discussion.

Peer review: during the first session, readers produce written responses; authors discuss reader response for clarification and revise papers between class meetings; during the second session, a second reviewer reads the revised paper so that authors can test their choices for revision and receive suggestions for further revision.

WEEK FOUR

Goals Managing complexity, considering multiple positions and perspectives.

Define and discuss types of appeals.

Introduce features of Paper #2: Solving a Local Problem.

Assignments Write a brief reflective response to the first writing assignment.

Paper #1 due.

Brief writing assignment, comparison of appeals: find advertisements for two or more similar items (a sports car, a minivan, and a delivery van; designer jeans and work jeans, etc.), and describe the types of appeal(s) used by each.

WEEK FIVE

Goals Giving a thesis tension.

Adding significance and meaning to data.

Exploring strategies for development and organization: closed form/thesis driven or open form/thesis seeking.

Assignments   Read model texts for discussion.

Read handbook Chapter 3: Paragraphs.

Read handbook Chapter 2: Writing Processes and Strategies, focusing on collaboration.

Classroom observation activity: take objects or sensory descriptions of the classroom and explain their positive or negative value; recast description of objects to give them the opposite value.

Draft introductory paragraph(s): Identify topic, provide background, preliminary statement of solution.

Initial peer review: authors bring typed introductions to class; readers ensure that topics are clear, local, and introduction includes sufficient background. Discussion generates a range of possible solutions and speculates on methods of evaluation.

WEEK SIX

Goals   Building confidence in revision and the writing process.

Hold revision workshops for Paper #1 and in preparation for peer review of Paper #2. Focus on issues other than mechanics, such as voice and tense shifts, avoiding monotonous tone and development, and writing effective transitions.

Assignments   Read handbook Chapters 11, 15 and 16: Consistency, Transitions, and Sentence Variety.

Complete draft of Paper #2 for peer review.

Following peer review, authors and readers write brief reflective pieces on the role of review and revision in the writing process.

WEEK SEVEN

Goals   Scheduled conferences and formative evaluations. Students bring Paper #1 to the conference and have Paper #2 returned to them. Student and instructor discuss the papers: how is the student improving? Is she applying process-oriented writing strategies and using time effectively? Are peer reviews useful? This is also a time to solicit formative evaluations in a relatively non-threatening setting, because students have an opportunity to talk about the course in general, its successes and shortcomings, what the instructor can do to make the course as effective as possible, and so on.

Assignments   Read handbook Chapter 52: Searching for Information.

Students produce brief list of interests, topics relevant to academic majors, and/or issues important in anticipated professional field.

WEEK EIGHT

Goals   Research seminar and preparation for Paper #3: Summary/Rhetorical Analysis. Class meets in library for presentation by instructor and/or research librarian. Students learn to do research in campus libraries, and to use other resources for book and article delivery. Special attention given to electronic searching and delivery strategies. Students have significant time during the research seminar to perform test searches and ask questions about their own topics.

Assignments   Read handbook Chapter 54: Evaluating Sources.

Locate source for Paper #3.

Bring sample sources to class and test for appropriateness.

Clarify the categories of research material assigned; students evaluate source material using criteria in sections 54c and 54d in the *Prentice Hall Guide*.

WEEK NINE

Goals   Work on transitions from summary component to rhetorical analysis component of Paper #3. Discuss strategies for shifting from non-evaluative voice and tone in summary (30% of paper's content) to the evaluative tone of analysis (70% of paper's content).

Emphasize the role of informed critical response in building the academic conversation around each topic and field of inquiry.

Assignments   Read model texts for discussion.

Read handbook Chapter 55: Taking Notes.

Compose first draft of Paper #3.

WEEK TEN

Goals   Introduce quotation, summary, and paraphrase strategies.

Encourage students to practice strategies of integrating source material on Summary/Rhetorical analysis paper in preparation for paper #5 (Exploratory Research Project).

Assignments   Read handbook Chapter 56: Using Sources.

Peer review of Paper #3.

WEEK ELEVEN

Goals   Preparation for Paper #4: Proposal/Annotated Bibliography.

Focusing on the process outlined in Chapter 51 of the *Prentice Hall Reference Guide*, students either extend or recast their topics from previous assignment and develop a research question that will carry them through Paper #5.

Assignments   Paper #3 Due.

Read handbook Chapter 51: Finding a Topic.

Read model texts for discussion.

Locate three sources related to the research question.

Draft reflective proposal statement: How did you select the topic? How is the topic relevant to your interests, major, choice of profession, etc.? What is the nature of your current thinking about your research question? What do you intend/expect to find through the research process?

WEEK TWELVE

Goals	Introduce MLA (or other relevant) conventions for bibliographies.
	Describe various methods of annotating: description, summary, evaluation, and combination of methods.
Assignments	Read handbook Chapter 58: Documenting in MLA Style.
	Compose annotated bibliography, incorporating MLA style for each entry.
	Paper #4 due.

WEEK THIRTEEN

Goals	Troubleshooting challenges in research methods and source location.
	Emphasize collaborative learning and problem solving.
	Review of challenges in spelling and mechanics.
Assignments	Planning and drafting Paper #5
	Group presentations: either assigned by instructor or self-selected, small groups of students choose a set of grammar and mechanics issues that remain concerns in their work. Based on relevant sections of the *Prentice Hall Reference Guide*, groups prepare and make brief presentations to the class that describe focus issues and provide examples for identification and correction either in their own work or in course texts. Students may not simply restate handbook examples.

WEEK FOURTEEN

Goals	Review discussion of plagiarism focused on appropriate use(s) of source materials. Focus on student writing for models, either to compare and correct or to identify successful incorporation of strategies.
	Review discussion of quotations, attributive tags, and bibliographic conventions.
Assignments	Continue drafting Paper #5

WEEK FIFTEEN

Goals   Polishing Paper #5 for submission. Discussions and workshops are student-directed and emphasize independent motivation and problem solving strategies.

Assignments   Peer review of Paper #5

Reflective self-and course evaluation

Paper #5 due.

✓ *Organizing by Topic and Rhetorical Issue*

Developed by Steve Gibson, the following syllabus anticipates specific topics and skills to be the focus of each class meeting in the term. Like the handbook, many reader/rhetoric texts are organized by topic and rhetorical issue, so the topic-oriented calendar easily ties course texts together. Among other advantages, this approach to the course schedule establishes a daily structure for class meetings, but allows the instructor to employ specific practices, assign particular model texts, and organize each meeting according to the needs of the individual class as it unfolds over the term. This schedule includes a review day for a final exam, which is a course requirement at many institutions.

WEEK ONE

Monday   Introduction to the course and the instructor

Assessment assignment given: "My History as a Reader and Writer"

Wednesday   Pursuing Problems

Friday   Invention

WEEK TWO

Monday   Believing and Doubting

Assessment assignment due

Wednesday   Thesis

Friday   Holiday

WEEK THREE

Monday	Supporting a Thesis with Points and Particulars
Wednesday	Purpose, Audience, and Genre
Friday	Seeing Rhetorically and Rhetorical Analysis

WEEK FOUR

Monday	Strategies
Wednesday	Composing and Revising
Friday	Observation Essay Due to Peers

WEEK FIVE

Monday	Observation Essay Due
Wednesday	Introductions and Conclusions
Friday	Tattoos

WEEK SIX

Monday	Reading Rhetorically
Wednesday	Summary
Friday	Holiday

WEEK SEVEN

Monday	Response
Wednesday	Essays for Summary (pick one essay)
Friday	Composing and Revising a Rhetorical Reading Essay

WEEK EIGHT

Monday	Rhetorical Reading Essay Due to Peers
Wednesday	Rhetorical Reading Essay Due
Friday	Revision and the Writing Process

WEEK NINE

Monday   Placing Points before Particulars
Wednesday   Informative and Surprising Essay
Friday   Examples

WEEK TEN

Monday   Composing and Revising
Wednesday   Informative and Surprising Essay Due to Peers
Friday   Informative and Surprising Essay Due to Peers II

WEEK ELEVEN

Monday   Informative and Surprising Essay Due
Wednesday   Classical Arguments
Friday   Composing

WEEK TWELVE

Monday   Claims, Reasons, and Evidence
Wednesday   Making Sources Useful
Friday   Holiday

WEEK THIRTEEN

Monday   Citing Sources Effectively
Wednesday   Examples
Friday   Review of Composing

WEEK FOURTEEN

Monday   Addressing Objections and Counterarguments
Wednesday   Examples
Friday   Classical Argument Essay Due to Peers

WEEK FIFTEEN

Monday   Classical Argument Essay Due to Peers II
Wednesday   Classical Argument Essay Due
Friday   Final Review

FINAL EXAM

Some options include: presenting students with a short piece of writing that they must summarize, using criteria introduced in Rhetorical Reading unit; or ask students to write a paragraph that has a point and a series of particulars, using skills from Thesis Support unit.

■ SUMMER AND ACCELERATED SCHEDULES

Instructors who are assigned introductory writing courses on an accelerated schedule will have to make some critical decisions about the number of papers they want (or are required) to assign, and the topics or genres of those assignments. Although accelerated courses are often scheduled for the same number of meeting hours as regular semester courses, instructors will not be able to cover an identical amount of material or number of writing assignments; in fact, attempting to do so can result in frustration from the students and less learning overall. The pace of the accelerated term can be overwhelming, and among the ways we can mitigate some of the pressure is to have students write fewer papers than in a regular term but make them longer, or have them write more, but shorter, papers. In either case, consider choosing a single topic that students will address through each writing assignment; thus, we save significant time that otherwise may be devoted to topic selection and direct that time to invention, prewriting, and drafting geared to the genre or essential features of the assignment itself. Those whose departments demand the same number of papers for summer school as for a regular term have little choice but to require shorter ones or to include timed in-class writing. Those with more control over the syllabus may opt for one paper or less per week, for example, or several revisions of only one or two essays.

However, the longer class meeting of the typical summer or accelerated session (two or more hours) also presents some advantages. Instructors can give students more opportunities to do substantial work on drafts in class, and raise questions in process, both to the instructor and peers. Additionally, instructors can observe and conference with students while they write, lending immediacy to the writing and response process. Rather than meeting every other day, accelerated courses usually meet daily, thus lending continuity between classes

Developed by Linda Julian (although slightly modified for this supplement), the following syllabus is for an accelerated or summer session introductory writing course. Given the built-in limitations of the schedule, the instructor has organized this six-week term strategically, anticipating the writing assignments that will provide students with a strong foundation in basic academic rhetorical moves and genres. While such a class cannot be comprehensive as the full term course, what it can do is prepare students to expand and continue practicing these moves in future courses. Like other examples in this chapter, the model given here is skeletal. Instructors will find that fleshing out the syllabus depends on knowing the level of students they will be teaching.

Like some of the other syllabi here, this one assumes the use of a reader. Teachers who wish to emphasize paragraphs, research skills, integrating the computer into composition, or developing the whole essay as a process may adapt other models to accommodate the shorter term.

✓ *Emphasizing Language*

WEEK ONE

Goals	Explain how students may use the *Prentice Hall Reference Guide* to help them work more independently
	Talk about how vocabulary interacts with audience and purpose
	Talk about narration and description as methods for developing paragraphs and essays
Review	Comma splices, run-on sentences, and fragments
Assignments	Read Chapters 1, 2, 6, and 8
	Write a narrative, descriptive paragraph or short essay including sensory detail appealing to all of the senses
	Read one narrative essay and one descriptive essay in the reader

WEEK TWO

Goals	Talk about levels of formality in English and figurative language
	In class, have students write an informal letter, about needing money, to a close friend and then the same content in a letter with a more formal tone, perhaps to a grandparent
	Have students practice writing examples of figurative language about a topic that may seem boring or dull on the surface (a description of the classroom, for example). Talk about definition as a method of organizing paragraphs and essays
Review	Parts of speech and problematic usages of the comma
Assignments	Write a paragraph defining a current slang term and identify your intended audience and purpose
	Look up a basic noun in the *Oxford English Dictionary* and explain in a brief essay how that word's meaning has changed over the centuries (choose a word that has been part of English since about the fourteenth century)

WEEK THREE

Goals	Talk about connotation and denotation and gender-neutral language
	Help students brainstorm to come up with an essay topic on something like language in pop music lyrics, language in advertising, or discriminatory language in the last half of the twentieth century
	Explain to students how to find information online and in the library
	Oversee the development of a "working thesis" and research plan for the essay
	Explain how to judge the reliability of sources
Review	Plagiarism and other kinds of dishonesty in writing
Assignments	Write a research plan for your essay on language
	Submit a list of at least six sources you have found for your essay on language

Use this information to help you narrow your topic and write a "working thesis" and preliminary outline

WEEK FOUR

Goals Oversee the development of students' rough drafts of this essay

Organize a peer-evaluation session of this first complete draft

Talk about mixing concrete and abstract language

Talk about clichés and jargon

Explain the differences in online research and library research

Review Paraphrasing, summarizing, and quoting and choosing the appropriate style sheet for documenting the sources of this essay

Assignments Complete the first draft of your language essay

Pretend you are an advertising agent promoting a new product and write copy for two ads (one for a magazine that appeals to college students and one that appeals to business people) and explain in a paragraph or two what kinds of colors, language, and images you want the final ad to have

Find an article or essay that seems to have clichés or jargon (or both) and describe the audience and purpose you think the piece has

Using this article or essay, write a summary of the whole and a paraphrase of one or two paragraphs, and write a paragraph integrating a quotation from the piece of writing

WEEK FIVE

Goals Explain critical thinking and argument

Talk about regional language, euphemisms, and bureaucratic language

Help students identify an argumentative topic related to language

	Help them locate online and library resources for this topic
	Have students bring to class and share a printed argument (perhaps a letter to the editor) and the logical fallacies and other weaknesses they found in it
Review	Uses of the colon and semicolon
Assignments	Identify an argumentative topic about language (one that you are especially interested in)
	Find five or six sources that provide information on your argumentative topic
	Narrow your topic, make a "working thesis," and write a preliminary outline for your argument, doing further research as necessary

Week Six

Goals	Confer with each student (if possible) about his or her draft of the argument essay
	Organize a peer review of these first drafts
	Aid students as they revise the essay
Review	What students have accomplished during the term
Assignments	Revise your argument and submit it to the teacher
	Write a three- or four-paragraph evaluation of what you have learned about careful use of language

Each of these models is offered only as a guideline for various ways of organizing your introductory writing course. Working with the requirements of her department and institution, and taking into account the preparation and needs of her students, each instructor determines appropriate combinations of mechanics, grammar, rhetoric, model texts, and research, and develops course plans accordingly. Each instructor also reflects conscientiously on her plans as they unfold each term and returns to strategies which work well and rethinks those which do not. Thus, as a document that undergoes constant reconsideration and change, the syllabus can be among our best examples of process writing.

SUGGESTED READING

Baecker, Diann L. "Uncovering the Rhetoric of the Syllabus: The Case of the Missing I." *College Teaching* 46.2 (Spring 1998): 58-62.

Dahlin, Amber. "A Student-Written Syllabus for Second-Semester English." *Teaching English in the Two Year College* 21 (Feb. 1994): 27-32.

Devine, Thomas G. "Caveat Emptor: The Writing Process Approach to College Writing." *Journal of Developmental Education* 14 (Fall 1990): 2-4.

Figg, Kristen M. "Handbook Use in College English I: Classroom Practices and Student Responses." *Teaching English in the Two Year College* 19 (Oct. 1992): 185-91.

Fleming, David. "Rhetoric as a Course of Study." *College English* 61.2 (Nov. 1998): 169-91.

Gold, R. M. "How the Freshman Essay Anthology Subverts the Aims of the Traditional Composition Course." *Teaching English in the Two-Year College* 18 (Dec. 1991): 261-65.

Krest, Margie, and Daria O. Carle. "Teaching Scientific Writing: A Model for Integrating Research, Writing, and Critical Thinking." *The American Biology Teacher* 61.3 (March 1999): 223-27.

Kroll, Keith. "A Profile of Community College English Faculty and Curriculum." *Community College Review* 22 (Winter 1994): 37-54.

Lindemann, Erika. "Three Views of English 101." *College English* 57 (March 1995): 287-301.

Martinsen, Amy. "The Tower of Babel and the Teaching of Grammar: Writing Instruction for a New Century." *English Journal* 90.1 (Sept. 2000): 122-26.

Nilson, Linda Burzotta. *Teaching at Its Best: A Research-Based Resource for College Teachers.* [n.p.]: Anker Publishing, 1998.

Quigley, Dan. "The Evolution of an Online Syllabus." *Computers and Composition* 11.2 (1994): 165-72.

Salvatori, Mariolina. "Conversations with Texts: Reading in the Teaching of Composition." *College English* 58 (April 1996): 440-54.

CHAPTER 4
Using a Handbook
in the College Writing Course

Many of us share with our students memories of teachers who used writing handbooks as a bludgeon, as the final authority on the "rules" of writing which, when memorized, would ultimately produce the right kind of essay—or at least that elusive essay we knew the teacher was looking for. "Dot your I's, cross your T's, and leave a window in your E's" was an infamous refrain in one of my high school writing courses; when this phrase (or the mindset it reflects) framed any discussion of grammar, the handbook's possibilities were dramatically limited, equated with nitpicking and a demand for rote memorization. The handbook's role in providing strategies for the sort of engaged, global improvement we should be pursuing and encouraging with our college composition students was all but abandoned.

Because of their past experiences, few of our students are inclined to, or know how to, use the handbook on their own. One of the most important services we can provide for our students is to show them how to make productive use of the handbook. The process will likely begin by getting students to simply open the book and to discover a variety of ways to use it. We must encourage our students to see the handbook not only as a mechanical "how to" text, but as a guide to open numerous possibilities in the writing process. Much handbook use will continue to revolve around understanding rules and conventions of writing, but rules can be seen as a means to effective writing rather than its end. Approaching a writing handbook in this way is important but difficult: it asks students to shift their perceptions of a "rules book" to a text about techniques of and approaches to writing.

Some methods of incorporating the handbook into writing classes can reinforce our students' unpleasant associations. We probably have had experiences with teachers who grade by identifying every mechanical mistake in a paper, who equate following grammatical rules with effective writing and thus make the handbook the focus of the class and the index of evaluation. And, while punitive measures may be effective, at least to the extent that students are faced with the choice to either use the handbook or face significant loss of credit, those measures may continue to reinforce students' existing perceptions about mechanical correctness as the most important feature of "good writing" and the conventions in the handbook as the exclusive set of rules on which student success and failure depend. When students revise their writing in this kind of environment, they are positioned to see revision as an endless, and largely futile, effort to fix every lapse in the rules. Writing teachers regularly find themselves in a tedious and unproductive cycle of conversations with otherwise good students who, in discussions of draft after draft, insist that they have "fixed everything" that was marked "wrong" on previous versions of their papers. Using the handbook productively may help break free of this cycle, as students begin to see communicative possibilities where they had seen only error or the absence of error.

There are, then, more affirmative ways we can think of incorporating the handbook: through modeling positive uses, by incorporating the handbook's references and response strategies into our own procedures, and by coordinating related chapters and sections of the handbook with specific course assignments and tasks.

■ EARLY IN THE COURSE

Although we should avoid using the handbook as the central text for a course, we can consider any number of ways of incorporating parts of the handbook for class discussion and in concert with specific writing assignments. The open organization of the *Prentice Hall Reference Guide* invites instructors to present information as students need it to meet the challenges of particular writing situations. Retaining and modeling an open and affirmative approach to the handbook encourages students to use the book independently as dictated by their own needs as the term unfolds.

Within the first few weeks of a term—as students are drafting their first writing assignment for instance—instructors can spend some time introducing students to the handbook, describing its contents, various methods for locating contents, and discussing a range of ways it may be used. Through a discussion of Harris's brief preface, "Hints for Using This Book," instructors can shift student perception away from seeing the handbook as a fixed set of rules and help them value the book in additional ways. Students can see the handbook as a set of tools, the possible uses of which are largely dependent on the individual student's needs, rather than as an authoritarian flow chart that indiscriminately takes every student along a proscribed course from "bad writing" to "good writing."

Through prewriting assignments we can ask our students to help us predict effective starting points in the handbook. Either before students begin working on their first major writing assignment, or as they get started, students can brainstorm individually or in small groups to make a list of the ways they perceive their strengths and weaknesses as writers. Students "know" what kinds of writers they are, having been informed by innumerable well-intentioned teachers over the years. If we take students' self-assessment as a cue to direct our introductory work in the handbook, we address specific needs shared by the students and empower them as participants who have significant influence over the progress of the course.

Especially useful in an introduction are Harris' two sections, "Question and Correct" and "Compare and Correct," which reflect the open organization of the handbook. Depending on the kind of, and specificity of, knowledge a student has about grammar and usage questions, the book directs her to relevant chapters/sections. We can also return to class after reading students' self-assessments and tie their questions and concerns to a discussion of the apparatus of the handbook. As we begin to challenge students' understanding of the "rules" of writing they may have been taught through elementary and secondary school, we can use the *Prentice Hall Reference Guide* to tackle the distinction between rules and conventions. We can work through Harris's Glossary of Usage and address some commonly held misconceptions, such as the "rule" to never use "I" as a subject in formal writing, or to clarify common mechanical errors, such as the differences between "their," "they're," and "there."

Instructors can also develop activities for the class or for small groups that will demonstrate the various means of locating information in the handbook. Small student groups can take a series of sentences and together identify punctuation and grammar concerns, locate related sections in the handbook, and work together to revise. Students can then present their findings to the class, discuss the process by which they identified errors and located ways to correct them. Alternately, the instructor can work from overheads or PowerPoint slides and involve the entire class. The choice depends on class size and, especially early in the semester, the instructor's need to direct students toward making effective use of time. Either way though, we can avoid prescriptive attitudes by using students' actual writing needs to direct this work. We will see long-term benefits from such small group work, because the more we model productive uses of time for group work early in the semester, the stronger our students will be when they begin reading and reviewing each others' work in later weeks. Regardless of whether the instructors or students present these revision strategies, the goal is for students to see the handbook as a resource for concerns in their own writing.

■ THROUGHOUT THE TERM

Instructors can direct their students to the handbook by incorporating marking strategies and proofreading symbols that are consistent with it. Harris, for instance, includes a "Response Symbols" page before the book's title page. By adopting Harris's symbols, instructors direct students to the handbook where they will locate definitions of the symbols, then to chapters in the handbook that address the specific issues indicated by the symbols. This marking strategy helps instructors address the first challenge in handbook use—how to get students to open the book for the first time—because the handbook becomes a necessary tool for translating marks on the student's paper. Additionally, the marking symbols in the *Prentice Hall Reference Guide* streamline the process of marking technical errors on student papers. Not only does this aid busy teachers, it also frees us to spend less time in identifying mechanical problems and to spend more time in giving our students more substantial comments on their papers' content and arguments.

Once instructors establish a marking system consistent with the handbook, the book becomes a necessary reference to which students will turn throughout the semester. Each student thus learns to negotiate her way through the handbook according to her own needs as they arise and gains a growing repertoire of references in the handbook for use in different writing situations over the term. Instructors may begin to encourage students' handbook use by focusing comments that focus on local issues—the grammar and mechanics of sentences—in early writing assignments; as writing assignments increase in complexity toward more nuanced forms of argument and research projects, the handbook can serve as a quick reference guide to conventions of citation and uses of source material.

Over the term the handbook emerges as a flexible tool that students can use to address their individual concerns and challenges in drafting and revision. We should encourage, or even require, our students to keep error logs. They will see benefits in overcoming recurring errors as they make effective use of the handbook, and the error log is a significant tool that helps them track their progress and realize their successes during the term. Additionally, when instructors record commonly recurring errors shared by all, or most, of their students, they can organize class periods for focusing on specific chapters and sections in the handbook. Instructors make use of the handbook relevant to the concerns of specific classes, and not an overwhelming set of abstract rules used to bludgeon already overwhelmed students.

Depending on the objectives of the course and the writing assignments chosen by the instructor, many sections of the *Prentice Hall Reference Guide* may be incorporated alongside assignments and as complementary texts to a course's central reader/rhetoric.

When they design course syllabi, instructors should set aside a day prior to a paper's due date for the discussion of challenges specific to the genre, style, or research requirements of the paper. Especially when we assign similar essays over the course of a number of semesters, we are better able to predict the kinds of challenges that are associated with a particular assignment. For instance, discussions of verb tense and of ways to avoid tense-shifting can be addressed in the course of writing an autobiographical/significant event paper in which students are often required to work in both past and present tenses. Proofreading and pattern practice exercises in chapter 17 of the *Prentice Hall Reference Guide* are especially useful. Exercises in the chapter help students move from practicing tense consistency, to identifying unconventional usage, and to making appropriate shifts between tenses.

Likewise, instructors who plan to assign a research paper should set aside time to read and discuss sections in the *Prentice Hall Reference Guide* that deal with the research process, from topic formulation to the incorporation of quotation, paraphrase, and summary, to bibliographic conventions. We must carefully explain that any assigned reading—of even the best handbook—will cause students to understand all the features of research writing. It is during research writing that instructors must reinforce definitions of plagiarism and to discuss strategies for avoiding incorrect documentation; yet, we should also teach research and documentation as concepts, with conventions specific to each method (MLA, Chicago, APA, and so on), rather than lists of rules and sanctions. Chapter 55 in the *Prentice Hall Reference Guide*, which includes brief, yet comprehensive, definitions and examples of improper and conventional documentation strategies, is a great place to get started.

We should also spend a significant amount of time on Chapter 56, working with students on strategies for effective quotation, paraphrase, and summary strategies, as well as conventions of in-text citation. Especially useful is section 56e, "Using Signal Words and Phrases to Integrate Sources," which helps students avoid free-standing quotes by providing them with approaches for signaling and attributing source material. Because students are often overwhelmed by the research paper, when we integrate relevant sections from the *Prentice Hall Reference Guide* at appropriate points in the research writing process, we break the process into a set of interrelated tasks which encourage student confidence in managing a complex writing project. Following on a discussion of Harris's chapters, students will test their own choices and bring their challenges to class meetings and peer review sessions.

In my own writing classes, I take some time as students prepare their first papers to address challenges in conventional usage which most students share and which tend to arise regardless of the type of assignment. A discussion of vague pronoun reference, for instance, models use of the handbook as we work through Chapter 19 in the *Prentice Hall Reference Guide*. As my students and I discuss the types of recurring errors I have selected, along with examples of those errors, students recall their own challenges and include them in the discussion. These queries, in turn, allow members of the class to begin to assist each other by working on problems together. For example, although I have never introduced the question in class, every time the subject of common errors is raised, a student will voluntarily describe the frustrations in learning the difference between the meanings and uses of "who" and "whom." Rather than directly answering the student who poses the question, I can turn it back on the class, asking: "If you wanted to find out the difference between who and whom, and when to use which word, where could you go in the handbook?" Students may turn to the *Prentice Hall Reference Guide's* index and find the entry, "Who, whom," which directs them to pages 125-26, or they may turn to the Divider Directory on the book's inside cover and find that pronoun case and reference are addressed in Chapter 19. Working as a class or in small groups, students become familiar with various ways of locating information in the handbook; they also see each other not only as peers who share many of their own challenges and concerns, but also as resources for addressing and overcoming those concerns.

Students take the examples and strategies for correction provided in the handbook as models for use both during their own composition and revision work and while reviewing each other's writing assignments. The handbook serves an important function in process-oriented writing courses, because it provides a point of departure for a recursive composition and revision cycle: instructors introduce students to writing conventions and provide them with specific references in the handbook; students begin to identify problem areas in their own work, and are, in turn, equipped to help other students in class identify those areas during peer reviews; accumulated practice in identification and revision becomes increasingly habitual as students revise existing work and compose future assignments. This recursive system leads to the kinds of "portable" skills that extend beyond the individual writing course to serve students in any writing situation. Instructors in research writing courses, literature courses, and technical writing courses should continue to incorporate relevant chapters of the *Prentice Hall Reference Guide* to review and to build on strategies developed in introductory composition courses.

The following worksheet has been designed as a "get acquainted with your handbook" exercise for your students. The answer key is also provided.

USING THE PRENTICE HALL REFERENCE GUIDE

The title *Prentice Hall Reference Guide* clearly tells you how you should use the book: as a reference. Just like a dictionary, it's a book that's not meant to be read cover-to-cover; however, you should be very familiar with the *Reference Guide* so that you can quickly and efficiently locate material when you need it. With this in mind, it's worth your time to examine the book and spend a few minutes reading "Hints for Using the Book" on page xvi. As you become familiar with the book, focus on its organization, the types of information in the reference book, and how you would locate a specific piece of information. As soon as you feel comfortable with the organization of the book as well as how to locate material in it, step up and challenge yourself: How efficiently can I use my *Reference Guide*?

1. I've been given a writing assignment. Where in my book might I locate help in finding a topic to write about?_____

2. My instructor says that my paper must have a thesis, but I'm not really sure what that means, so I turn to the following sections in my book. _____

3. I'm writing a compare and contrast paper, but I'm not sure how to organize it, so I turn to the following page: _____

4. I know that introductions and conclusions are important, but I'm not sure what goes into them. I can find help with this on the following page: _____

5. I've decided to try drafting my paper on a computer. On which page would I find hints for using the computer to draft? _____

6. My instructor wants me to work with others in the class as a peer response group. On what page/section does the *Reference Guide* present ideas for what we can we do to help each other with our writing? _____

7. I had some editing done to my paper, and when I got it back, I found the following mark in the margin of the first paragraph: fs. What does fs mean, and where in the book does it tell me what I should do?

_____

_____

_____

8. My editor also suggested that I work on sentence variety. Where in the *Reference Guide* do I find guidelines on sentence variety?

_____

_____

9. I like to use transitions to show relationships among my ideas. I think I'm over using "but" and "however" to show contrast. Where can I find alternative transitions? _____

10. My editor told me to avoid shifts from active to passive voice in my paper. Where in the book is passive voice explained? _____
How do I avoid unnecessary shifts between active and passive voice?

_____

11. I wrote the following sentence in my paper: If I was her, I wouldn't listen to him. My editor told me that I had a problem with verb—subjunctive—mood. Where is this explained, and how should I fix the sentence?_____

_____

12. Where in the book do I find help for the following, and which is correct: The problem is actually among Jeff, Michelle and (I or me?)

_____

13. I know I need to use a comma after an introductory dependent clause that begins with the adverb "If"; however, what are eight additional adverbs used in introductory dependent clauses? _____

_____

_____

14. According to the *Reference Guide*, there are three different uses for apostrophes, and they are _____

_____

_____ found in the following sections: _____

15. The people who applied for the position are: Ms. E. Jones, Mr. B. Barnett, and Ms. M. Root. Is the colon used correctly? Y N. Support for my answer is on page _____; section _____

16. On what page and in what section can I find help with homonyms? _____ Circle the correct word. I know that a sharp change in the weather will (affect, effect) me. What (affect, effect) does the weather have on you?

17. Jeff loves to watch The History Channel; however, I prefer to watch The Learning Channel. This sentence is punctuated correctly according to which section in the *Reference Guide?* _____

18. According to the *Reference Guide* plagiarism results _____

_____

_____

which is found on page _____ section _____.

19. APA format is prescribed by the _____

_____.

Three fields it is used in include: _____

_____

_____

20. According to the *Reference Guide*, "proofreading" means_____

_____

_____

_____which

I found on page _____; section_____.

ANSWER KEY

1. Pages 1-2 and pages 32-33 – 1a, 1b, and 4c

2. 1c and 51f

3. Page 26

4. Page 21

5. Page 10

6. 2d – page 12

7. fs, as listed on "Response Symbols" (the second page from the front cover), means fused sentence. To figure out what to do about a fused sentence, see 6b.

8. Begins on page 93 – section 16

9. Page 88-89 – 15d

10. Page 111 – 17d; see 11d per hint on page 111

11. Verb mood page 111-112 – 17e. Fix the problem by changing the "was" to "were."

12. Hint on page 123. Pronoun case 19a; me.

13. Page 170 – 27b; after, although, as, because, since, until, when, while.

14. Page 183-84 – 28 a-c. apostrophes with possessives, apostrophes with contractions, and apostrophes with plurals.

15. N; page 195; 30f.

16. Page 243-46 – 39e; affect; effect

17. Section 29a.

18. when a writer fails to document a source so that the words and ideas of someone else are presented as the writer's own work. Page 292 – 51b.

19. American Psychological Association; psychology, sociology, business, economics, social work, and criminology.

20. reading your final written work slowly and carefully to catch misspellings and typographical errors. Page 233; 39a.

The following are some additional suggestions for incorporating sections of the *Prentice Hall Reference Guide* into our writing courses.

1. Choose to teach a unit on the writing process, grounding it in Chapter 2 of the handbook. Instructors should begin describing and modeling process-oriented writing strategies early in the semester. They may begin by pointing out that this chapter is not made up of fixed rules; instead it exposes students to a set of planning, prewriting, drafting, and revising strategies from which students are encouraged to test and choose the strategies that will work for them. Students can compare the approaches described by Harris by working in small groups, either after reading a short piece of writing, or following a topic chosen by the class. Students in the group employ different prewriting strategies, such as brainstorming, to produce "for" and "against" responses, free writing a paragraph on the topic, and clustering a series of related ideas; they then compare their results within the group and may present their findings to the class. We can use parts of the chapter to develop collaborative prewriting strategies as well. With a more complex topic, small groups use conversation and the "divide and conquer" strategy to make complex ideas more manageable. By introducing students to a variety of planning methods early in the term, we give them a point of reference in the handbook to which they will turn throughout the term, as assignments and the students' individual writing needs develop.

2. Choose to teach a unit on the paragraph. Especially as students begin writing their first papers, Chapter 3 in the *Prentice Hall Reference Guide* helps to ground students in basic conventions of paragraph development and in a set of organizational strategies for linking multiple paragraphs to each other. Students can test versions of an introductory paragraph with other members of the class, and receive feedback on the effectiveness of the hooks they use, and on the unity and coherence of the paragraph. As students plan a significant event paper, for instance, they can test the effectiveness of opening their papers at various points in the story's chronology, or whether to explain the story's significance in the introduction or to develop it later in the essay. Or if students are starting work on an argument project, such as a problem/solution paper, we can ask them to bring two versions of introductory paragraphs: one open form, seeking a solution, and one closed form, stating the solution up front. Through sharing these paragraphs with peers, students will get feedback on the effects of the two opening moves on their audience, and see the significance of each paragraph in their paper as an integral part of the argument.

Teachers can present Harris's examples in section 3e to model different organizational strategies students can use in their paragraphs and to discuss the different purposes of those strategies. Section 3d includes ways students can think about conclusions to help them avoid using stock concluding cues on which they may have depended in their previous writing projects. When students share brief pieces of their writing, or when we present examples of effective paragraph development to the class as a whole, students may be better equipped for critical reading and productive peer review when they encounter longer pieces of writing.

3. Choose to teach a unit on argument, based on Chapter 4 in the *Prentice Hall Reference Guide*. Teachers can use Harris's description of types of appeal in section 4b to introduce students to logical, emotional, and ethical appeals. Students will readily see the benefits of a critical understanding of appeals, because they use and are subjected to appeals all the time; we can see this particularly in students' everyday experiences with mass media, and, especially, advertising. After reading about and discussing the differences between the three basic forms of appeal, students can bring examples of ads that employ those appeals either individually or in concert with each other. Students might consider some advertisements—those for new cars, for instance—which typically combine logos, pathos, and ethos in their presentation. Or, they might compare the appeals in ads for a similar consumer item: for example, ads for high fashion shoes for women with ads for steel-toed work boots. For a brief writing analysis students might also compare editorial pages from different newspapers and magazines. Students can discuss the ways in which each type of appeal is geared toward the values, knowledge, and predisposition of certain audiences, or speculate on the demographic features of an audience—education, social class, gender, ethnicity, and sexuality—judging from the appeals employed. From these in-class exercises, we can develop writing assignments that ask students to analyze a film, a novel, or an essay through the various types of appeal. They can speculate on the ways the text they choose might have used different types or additional types in order to appeal to wider or different audiences.

4. Ground a unit on the research process in Chapter 51. Because many of our students have experiences with research that are limited to reporting from general audience sources (encyclopedias, newspapers, internet sources), a research assignment in their college writing course can be terrifying, especially when in many courses that assignment looms threateningly at the end of the term. Introductory writing instructors, however, have a significant opportunity to make research writing a real rhetorical activity—one that, like other genres attempts to formulate and answer a question—rather than an empty, formal exercise. As we introduce students to steps that assist them through the research writing process, from topic identification, to initial research, to selection and management of research materials, they will gain in confidence to tackle such unfamiliar conventions. We can use Chapter 51 to help our students shift away from instructor-driven topics and toward developing their own topics based on their interests, their majors, or their anticipated professional fields. The chapter also introduces students to strategies for developing an open form approach to the research writing project, making it driven by a question rather than a topic. After a discussion of possible topics and ways of developing relevant and manageable questions from those topics, students will be invested in their projects and less likely to write encyclopedic, datadump papers.

As students move through the research writing process, we can teach Chapters 54 and 55 in the handbook, which cover strategies for selecting relevant material and for managing the material they select. Discussions centered on evaluation of source material (Chapter 54) help students distinguish between academic, reference, trade, and public affairs materials. Students will be able to weigh more effectively source authors' claims to expertise and authority against forms, genres, and purposes of argument associated with various types of publications. They will be aware of the importance of locating current source materials, and they will gain a critical ability to make wise choices about the type and quality of sources that are relevant to the project on which they are working.

Chapter 56 provides students with strategies for summarizing and incorporating source material. We can use this chapter to teach students about the differences between quotations, paraphrases, and summaries, and the ways in which each can be used effectively. Also important, we can use the chapter to model strategies with which students can effectively introduce, modify, and develop source material in their own work. These strategies are developed further in section 56e, "Using Signal Words and Phrases."

5. If we schedule periodic conferences with individual students or with small groups during the semester, we can use part of a conference time, or schedule specific conference periods, to discuss portions of the handbook that are suited to individual students' needs. This is a good opportunity to explore particular grammar or usage questions that are challenging individual students, or to work with small groups of students around common concerns, such as helping non-native English speaking students negotiate their way through Harris's section on ESL Concerns, focusing, for instance, on Chapter 43 ("American Style in Writing") or Chapter 50 ("Idioms").

Obviously, the more we teach college composition, and especially, the more we teach college composition at one institution, the more we can anticipate and plan for particular challenges surrounding the conventions of written English; which challenges will arise early and which will arise later in the term; and the best ways to incorporate the handbook into the class schedule. At any point in our teaching careers, though, we can begin to test ideas and try out new strategies; to be sure, some of those ideas and strategies won't work—or at least won't work as we expect them to—and yet successes, failures, and near misses alike are the building blocks of the repertoire of strategies we bring to teaching the handbook to our future students.

■ USING THE HANDBOOK TO MARK STUDENT WRITING

Because our students come to our writing classes with a wide range of experiences with teachers' strategies for marking their papers, we can use the handbook to derive marking and notation strategies which will be comprehensible to each student through a common reference text. To assist us in this goal, the *Prentice Hall Reference Guide* includes a list of suggested abbreviations on the inside flap. Each abbreviation is defined and is connected to a particular section or chapter in the handbook in which the error or suggestion is further developed and modeled. In concert with the handbook's marking schema for mechanics, we can also use terms consistent with those used in the handbook when we write our comments and refer to other concepts and conventions in student writing. Students can then use the handbook's index and table of contents to locate relevant explanations and examples to guide them through revisions of their work.

As indicated above, in addition to symbols and page references, we should make significant written comments on student papers. Written comments reinforce what we teach: that we see writing, and our students' papers especially, as more than exercises in mechanical correctness. Our comments show students that the content of their papers is valuable as well. Substantive comments are our means of showing students that their ideas and arguments deserve our intellectual attention, and that we see their writing as a valuable means of entering into a conversation with them.

The following paragraphs from student essays show how writing teachers can use symbols and marking strategies from the handbook in conjunction with written comments. When the student is able to see the possibilities for her writing at both local and global levels, she will be more likely to revise her papers and keep the conversation going with the class and the teacher.

When choosing a college to apply for, there are many things that effect your

decision. Definitely money is most times the number one thing people will

look at. How much is tuition? How much is housing? How many books will

I have to pay for? Once these dollar signs keep adding up in ones head they

start to look at different options. It seems now that the Universities and
³⁵
^{8a}
Colleges are more interested in money and recruits. Not what kind of students

they will receive. They're not worried about how the students will succeed.
^{28b} ⁴²
They are interested in getting their money. Its not personable anymore.

School isn't just an institution on learning any more than a business. The

President of the College or the Dean have gradually turned into a CEO or

President of an industry.

— Important points here. I especially like the fact that you
incorporate a perspective other than the student's. You might even
try developing two paragraphs, one dealing with student perceptions
and one dealing with institutional structure, so that you can include
enough detailed examples to convince your audience. As you revise,
please take a look at sections in the handbook dealing with the
mechanical problems I've marked and work on those issues as well.

As the term progresses and we expect students to become more adept
at locating and responding to errors in their own and each other's work, we
can place proofreading symbols and references to specific sections of the
handbook in the paper's margins. When the student comes across a proofreading symbol in the margin of the paper, she must reread a line, a
sentence, or a paragraph in the paper as she identifies the precise point to
which the symbol refers. In the process of locating an error, the student is
revisiting larger parts of the paper with new eyes, directed by the teacher's
marks but also encouraged to take those marks as points of departure to
develop her own plan for revision.

num   In the debate on whether young people between 18 and 22 years of

" "   age should "support their country" by building housing, working as

fs   teacher's aides, and doing basic community service; my opinion is

wordy   strong in being opposed to this.

Although in some cases, uprooting young adults from their comfort

zones to go out to do good, is a rich cultural experience, in all it is

^and   not fair. Many people, ages 18-22, have set dreams, set goals, set

ref   ambitions for their life as a new adult.

The *Prentice Hall Reference Guide* can anchor students throughout the term, providing a stable point of reference as we move from the first marking strategy to the second, and we gradually encourage students to meet our expectations for expertise with mechanics and other conventions of strong writing. The handbook is an important tool in leading our students toward greater confidence in their writing abilities. With each writing assignment, our references to the handbook and our written comments together encourage our students to become increasingly self-directed as they correct and revise their papers.

We can ask students to keep logs in which they record the types of errors they make and the frequency of errors. We discuss common errors in class and in student conferences, and we direct students to exercises in the handbook that will help them strengthen skills and correct errors. When we ask students to reflect on the progress they have made by the end of the course, they have evidence of their engagement with the conventions of written English—evidence that will inspire them to continue developing as writers. As their perceptions about the usefulness of the handbook change, our students will regard it as a tool and an important reference work that they will continue to find useful throughout their college careers.

Suggested Reading

Boyd, Richard. "Mechanical Correctness and Ritual in the Late Nineteenth-Century Composition Classroom." *Rhetoric Review* 11, no. 2 (Spring 1993): 436–55.

Broad, Bob. "Pulling Your Hair Out: Crises of Standardization in Communal Writing Assessment." *Research in the Teaching of English* 35, no. 2 (Nov. 2000), 213-61.

Fredericksen, Elaine. "Letter Writing in the College Classroom." *Teaching English in the Two Year College,* 27, no. 3 (Mar. 2000): 278-84.

Glasser, Marc. "Grammar and the Teaching of Writing: Limits and Possibilities." *Journal of Technical Writing and Communication* 22, no. 4 (Winter 1993): 23–32.

Hayes, Christopher G. "A Brief Writing Assignment for Introducing Nonsexist Pronoun Usage." *Teaching English in the Two Year College* 28, no. 1 (Sept. 2000): 74-77.

Helton, Edwina L., and Jeff Sommers. "Repositioning Revision: A Rhetorical Approach to Grading." *Teaching English in the Two Year College* 28, no. 2 (Dec. 2000): 157-64.

Reynolds, Patricia R. "Evaluating ESL and College Composition Texts for Teaching the Argumentative Rhetorical Form." *Journal of Reading* 36, no. 6 (March 1993): 474–80.

Shuman, R. Baird. "Grammar for Writers: How Much Is Enough?" *The Place of Grammar in Writing Instruction: Past, Present, Future.* Ed. Susan Hunter and Ray Wallace. Portsmouth, NH: Boynton/Cook, 1995.

Whichard, Nancy Wingardner, et al. "Life in the Margin: The Hidden Agenda in Commenting on Student Writing." *Journal of Teaching Writing* 11, no. 1 (Spring–Summer 1992): 51–64.

Williams, James D. *Preparing to Teach Writing.* Belmont, CA: Wadsworth, 1988. "Rule-Governed Approaches to Language and Composition." *Written Communication* 10 (October 1993): 542–68.

CHAPTER 5

Developing Positive Feedback Strategies

Students bring a host of predictable and largely negative ideas about composition to our writing classes. Just as we must make significant efforts to introduce our students to productive, non-punitive uses of course texts, and to reinforce those uses throughout the semester, so too might we find ourselves working against student experiences with instructor feedback that have been largely negative and discouraging. This chapter introduces some strategies we can use to make our feedback affirmative, and to incorporate written comments that are not limited to pointing out errors and other shortcomings, but which also encourage our students to continue developing as writers.

More often than not, when we hand back graded papers, our students are prone to look first, and sometimes exclusively, for the most apparent indicator of their success or failure: the letter grade or numeric score we have given them. Thus, one of the challenges we face each time we return writing assignments is getting students to understand the comments we write on their papers, rather than simply looking at the letter grades we assign them. Our students are likely to see written remarks as either superfluous in the case of high marks, or as simply, unnecessarily, piling on criticism in the case of low marks. For the latter group of students especially, it is important early in the semester—as we hand back the first graded assignment, for instance—to share with students our own experiences with demoralizing feedback from teachers. If students see us as fellow writers, former students ourselves, who have shared some of their experiences, they will be more likely to value our advice about their efforts to write well, and more receptive to our efforts to change the method and tone we use in our responses. These discussions are important exercises in reflection for us as well, for as we look back in our own experiences, we can also explore possibilities of teaching with compassion.

■ CLARIFY THE PURPOSE OF GRADING

We must introduce our students to the purpose and role of grading, and perhaps more importantly, to its limitations. Our students may reflexively read grades on their papers as the instructor's assessment of general traits about the students themselves. In such cases, a C grade is no longer the teacher's assessment of a student's paper; instead, it is seen as a judgment of traits that lie far afield of the work, such as the student's intelligence, personality, politics, gender, or sexuality (or even their appearance!). We must explain, and reinforce throughout the term, that when we grade their writing assignments, we are not, by extension, grading them as well. If we clearly articulate the uses and limitations of grades, and allow students to voice their apprehension, we can mitigate student resentment and disappointment, responses which can lead to a loss of interest in future writing projects.

These discussions are especially important in departments and institutions where national trends in grade inflation are being challenged. We can summarize institution-wide grading standards on the course syllabus, and discuss the practical application of particular skills and traits in the context of a specific writing assignment. If a student has been accustomed to receiving A grades in high school, she may be quite dejected in receiving a B+ on the first college writing assignment. In such a case, the college instructor may come under fire from the student for grading arbitrarily at best, and at worst, incorrectly. Yet, if we point students toward grading conventions that are articulated and supported by the department or institution, we can begin to change student perceptions of the grading process. We can also use grading rubrics that break up various components of a writing assignment to help students distinguish between the quality of their technical success in grammar and mechanics and the quality of their ideas. Such a distinction serves two ends: on the one hand, students won't reflexively link our criticism of their technical execution of an assignment with a dismissal of the value of their ideas and goals; on the other hand, however, students will also realize that good ideas must be supported with the successful application of generic, stylistic, and mechanical conventions if they are to be fully understood and highly rewarded. If we clarify the use and meaning of grades, our students will be better prepared to see the ways in which grades—and more importantly our comments—might encourage rather than punish them.

■ CHANGE INK

When student papers are returned covered in red ink, whatever eagerness and positive attitudes we have encouraged in our students can fall by the wayside in an instant. The most affirmative and encouraging comments are seen as unfairly judgmental and punitive, simply because the red ink is reflexively associated with error. Many teachers have found that simply changing from red ink to pencil or to blue or green ink can have a positive effect on students' attitudes. We can retain authority in our marks and comments, and, at the same time, come off as less threatening to the students. After all, all the authority we bring to our grading doesn't produce positive results unless the students are willing to read and engage with our comments. Through comments in pencil or in a less threatening color of ink, students see us participating—albeit critically at times—in a conversation with them about their ideas.

■ CHANGE TONE

Similarly, we can balance the comments we write on student papers between those that identify errors, shortcomings, and parts that need improvement, and those that identify students' successes in their writing. While we certainly cannot give only positive comments and high marks to papers that need improvement just to make students feel good about themselves and their writing, if students receive only negative feedback, they may become so discouraged that they no longer want to engage with the writing class or put the necessary effort into future assignments. Thus, we can temper how we identify and explain shortcomings in ways that encourage them to continue working.

One of the ways we can change student perceptions about teacher comments is to ask for feedback from students throughout the term. For instance, we can encourage students to write brief reflective statements which they use as cover sheets for their writing assignments. These statements might include autobiographical reflection, answering questions such as, "What challenges did I foresee when I started thinking about the assignment?" and "How did I meet those challenges?" These reflective statements can also tell us a lot about the ways our students perceive themselves as writers, as they describe elements of the paper they see as especially successful; they can engage with the grading process by directing us to elements of the paper on which they would like additional help and direction. They can also tell us about their experiences with various stages of the writing assignment, from planning and prewriting through drafting and peer review. They will help us understand teaching strategies we use that are effective and ones that we might reconsider; they will tell us about the successes and shortcomings in their collaboration with other students.

As we center on assignments and class schedules that reinforce process-oriented writing, we can also develop methods of evaluation that are similarly oriented in a recursive process. In my introductory writing courses, for instance, I give students the opportunity to revise some of their papers from early in the term for better grades. When they submit revisions, their papers must be accompanied by a one-page reflective statement that describes the ways the new paper responds to my comments and to peer reviews. Not only are students required to account for the changes they made, they are better equipped to anticipate how much they will see their grade improved. Because this component of the revision process requires students to compare their new draft with an earlier one, they will not only see, but document, the improvements they have made in the intervening weeks between drafts. Additionally, when students are invited to share in responding to and shaping grading strategies, they are positioned to agree with and be more receptive to our remarks.

As we mark errors and shortcomings in student writing, we should make significant efforts to identify and comment on the strengths of the work as well. We can add comments such as "good development," "nice transition between these two paragraphs," and "compelling image," which help students see their successes in writing as we identify the features on which they need additional work. Even in identifying shortcomings, we can express our comments affirmatively. If a student has made an important point or opened up a valuable line of questioning, and yet has inadequately developed the point, instead of identifying the lacking development we can write "Great point—tell me more," or invite revision through a question: "Can you provide more detail to help me understand this point?" When we write more extensive summative comments at the end of the paper, we can continue to strike a balance between noting shortcomings and encouraging strengths. For instance, we can open our concluding comments with the student's first name and a positive feature of their writing: "Annie—this is a very strong argument. I especially like the examples you use throughout the paper." When we begin our comments on such a positive note, the student will be more open to reading our suggestions for improvement. Like us, students respond well to compliments, and when we balance our comments, students see that we are looking for more than just their errors when we read their papers, that we notice when they succeed as well.

Throughout the term, we can continue to emphasize student strengths and their improvement from assignment to assignment. We can identify the ways their efforts in later papers have overcome challenges we noted in earlier ones. If we have introduced particular recurring errors in grammar or usage to the class, and have directed students to exercises or other means of correction, then we should be sure to acknowledge their development over time. Even when we find ourselves hard pressed to locate specific improvements or other elements to compliment, we can end our comments with a statement like, "I'm looking forward to seeing your next draft. You have some important ideas here that will get even stronger as you revise."

When students see our interest in their work and see us encouraging them to continue developing their ideas, they will be more willing to work hard to meet our expectations.

■ CHANGE PRIORITIES

Resisting the temptation to mark every error we find in a paper all at once is an important part of practicing balance in our comments. Despite our best intentions to be comprehensive, if we mark every error every time, we risk overwhelming students rather then helping them. When our students see a paper covered in negative comments—especially when those comments are in red ink—they are likely to feel overwhelmed and inadequate, and thus are more likely to give up either in revising or in future assignments. Additionally, when we overmark papers, we are not teaching our students to learn to locate and correct their own errors as effectively as we might be with other strategies.

We can become more selective in the ways we mark student papers. Of course the choices we make about implementing strategies are our own, but we can think about making response strategies as relevant as possible to the assignment and to the topics we have addressed in tutorials with the writing handbook. If, for instance, I have focused an introductory grammar lesson on commonly mistaken words (affect/effect, you're/your, there/their/they're) and commonly misused plural words (media, criteria), students can be expected to identify mistakes in their own and each other's writing thereafter. When I mark those errors on the writing assignment immediately following this tutorial, I am restating and reminding students of conventions with which they should now be familiar. Likewise, if I discuss a particular requirement of content or argument when I introduce a writing assignment, and then reinforce that requirement during peer review sessions, students should expect to have shortcomings in this specific area identified.

Our marking criteria should be flexible, and should vary depending on the genre of paper, on the kinds of preparatory work we have done with our students, and the focus we want to place on different types of error at different points in the term. For instance, early in the term, some teachers may focus their marking on the most common mechanical errors (fused sentences, subject-verb disagreement) and direct their comments to major problems in content and style (clear thesis and topic sentence, and providing sufficient detail and evidence, for example). Others may only comment on content and organization first, inspiring students to think clearly about their subjects, and focus increasingly on mechanics as the term progresses. As the term goes on and students gain confidence in their ability to express their ideas in coherent paragraphs that support a clearly stated thesis, teachers have more success with criticizing problems of style, such as diction and wordiness.

Although handwritten comments are the most common means of providing feedback to our students, we can also experiment with alternative commenting strategies. We might develop response forms, mechanical rubrics on which we mark technical errors and provide commentary. One of my colleagues created a one-page form that lists across the top of the page the five features on which she expects proficiency on the first writing assignment: "Focus" (topic framing), "Question" (specificity of argument), "Support" (evidence), "Organization" (sequence/structure of paragraphs), and "Language" (command of diction and mechanics). Each of the categories is broken into five levels of proficiency, and each proficiency level is explained in a few phrases; in the "Organization" category, for instance, medium-proficient work is described, "Does not proceed smoothly. Some effective paragraphs, some only weakly unified. Awkward or missing transitions," while low-proficient work is described as "Arbitrary or no paragraph structure." The instructor can then check appropriate categories after reading a student's paper, providing the student with adequate description, and yet saving the instructor the time of writing roughly identical comments on multiple papers. Among the benefits of this approach, students are informed about the types of errors they make, but are required to locate the specific instances in their writing; additionally, students are less likely to perceive our comments as taking control over their writing. With a form, we spend less time marking recurring grammatical errors and have more time for writing substantial comments and providing directions for revision. The drawback against which teachers must struggle is, of course, the power of such forms to make responses (and, in the students' eyes, writing itself) into mere formal exercises, rather than an engagement with ideas and the means of expressing them.

■ Conferencing with Students

While we work toward developing more positive approaches of responding to student writing, we can periodically check the effectiveness of our approaches through conferencing with our students. Although we may soon realize that teaching an introductory composition course to twenty-two students can seem like teaching twenty-two different writing courses, we are often forced to teach to the average student, and we find it difficult to give extra specialized attention to both weaker and more advanced students. However, when we include time in the class schedule for student conferences throughout the semester, we have opportunities to work with students individually, to both give and receive valuable feedback about the student's writing and about the course in general. The conferences can be just as important for us as for our students then, because the one-on-one time we spend with them can teach us what we are not clarifying in the classroom and specific concerns and needs we should be responding to in our assignments and comments.

Although most of us work in departments that require us to set aside a specified number of hours per week for students to drop in, there are a number of factors that prevent students from taking advantage of these times. Even when we repeatedly encourage our students to use office hours and sketch out the various reasons for using them (clarifying comments on their papers, testing possible topics for upcoming papers, discussing ways of improving their performance in class), students may feel that we really don't want to be interrupted outside of class times. As with students' initial perceptions of marks and comments on papers, so too may they see meetings with instructors as punishment rather than as an offer of assistance we extend to them. Due, I imagine, to experiences in elementary and secondary school, many students believe that they will be stigmatized by us or by their peers if they see us outside of class time. We must consider ways of making students more likely to seek us out when they have questions and challenges in the class or with their work.

One of the ways we can break through student apprehensiveness about meeting with us is to schedule conferences early in the semester. If, as is required by many departments, we assign a diagnostic essay on the first day of class, we can develop a prompt that invites students to describe the reasons why they chose to go to college, to describe the decisions that led them to our institution, to consider the apprehensions they have about their writing, or to speculate on their goals for the term. We can then use responses as a point of departure for brief, one-on-one meetings with students to discuss their desires and concerns and to consider ways in which the course will assist them. We can ask students what they would like to learn, what they consider to be their strengths and weaknesses. During the visit, we might ask the students to explain their experiences with writing in high school and their current feelings about writing. When they see our interest in their past, students will begin to relax, and through these conferences, we show students that we do not see them as simply a group of anonymous faces in the class, but as unique individuals whose needs and goals are important and who can take an active hand in shaping the class as it unfolds. These early conferences will help students see the teacher and the office setting as inviting rather than threatening, and they will feel more comfortable about seeing us throughout the semester.

Following on these introductory meetings, we should continue to schedule times for student conferences throughout the semester. Even if we have worked hard to make meeting with us as inviting and non-threatening as possible and if we have emphasized the importance of students taking responsibility to get help with their own work as problems arise, they may still be reluctant to come see us. We can reinforce the importance of conferencing by setting up additional meeting times in the term. One effective strategy is to hand back graded writing assignments during scheduled conferences. For instance, after we have graded the second paper of the term, we can have students schedule brief meetings with us, during which we hand back their paper, ask them if they have questions about the comments we have written, or if they need additional explanation of the ways in which comments and marks lead to the paper's grade. Depending on the amount of time we have to schedule these meetings, students can also bring their first papers or diagnostic essays to the conference. We can ask them to describe their work and the progress they have made over the course of writing two papers. This conference is also a good time to invite students to discuss their experiences in class: we can ask them to talk about any challenges they are having up to that point of the course: in understanding assignments, in linking models of successful writing to their own work, in understanding the value of process-oriented writing, in the relationship of course texts to their writing, and so on. These conferences can give us valuable feedback about the effectiveness of our teaching, and help us develop additional ways of meeting our students' needs as early as possible in the term.

We can also anticipate the writing assignments that will demand more individual attention than others and build conference times into the unit. For example, while advanced students will welcome open topic writing assignments, other students may feel cast adrift in a sea of possibilities, and they may believe that there is still a "right" topic that they should be able to find. Conferences will benefit both, for the advanced students have an opportunity to share their ideas with an interested respondent, while other students can use this one-on-one-time to talk about their personal interests or their majors, from which the instructor will be able to either help them select or direct them toward topics that will give them the greatest chance for success.

Similarly, research papers raise numerous challenges for students, and it may be effective to have time set aside for conferences once the assignment has been explained and students have had a chance to do some preliminary research and prewriting. In many introductory composition courses, the research paper is the final writing project, and at this point in the term, students often are feeling incredibly overwhelmed by the assignments, projects, and final exams that are looming shortly ahead. As students are preparing their papers we can schedule conference times to clarify research methods relevant to an individual question, to help them manage the complexity of research materials, or to help them incorporate source material into their research writing. Because the academic research project is the most unfamiliar of genres for many of our students, it is especially important to set aside conference time as they are working on their papers. Even though we will have introduced them to forms of and the necessity of avoiding plagiarism in their work, research papers will raise additional challenges to our students. If we encourage students to bring draft paragraphs that use source material to these conferences, we can help them avoid costly mistakes in citation and incorporation of research before they have submitted their work for a grade.

Although conferences may seem unnecessarily time-consuming at first, many teachers find they take less time and are more effective in relating detailed information to students than writing comments on drafts. As we get a sense of students' work during the term, we can also schedule small group conferences with students during which we can address problems common to the group. In fact, these group conferences can help students more than the teacher alone can—peer interaction can help make students more independent and more excited about writing. Often, as they work together, fellow students are able to see and explain problems and solutions in ways which we cannot, because they share a common language and set of experiences that are unfamiliar to us. The small group conference sets an example of effective peer interaction students will recall as they continue to review each other's work throughout the term.

Despite our best efforts in encouraging students to see us before a problem reaches overwhelming proportions, we will still find ourselves at times facing students who only come to see us once they have received a poor grade or a series of poor grades. When they receive low, or unexpectedly low, grades on their papers, students may react defensively and want to meet with us immediately to challenge their grade. In such cases, it is a good idea to have a policy in place that we do not discuss papers on the day they are handed back. We should tell students that we are happy to meet with them to discuss their grades, but only after they have taken the time to go home and read the comments we have made. Our conferences with them will be truly productive once they have taken the time to look up references to the handbook, to review models in course texts, and to consider the comments we have made in relation to the grade they received. In fact, students will come back to the office with informed question about our comments, and even more importantly, they will have had the time to begin formulating a plan for revision on their own.

When students come to us frustrated or discouraged about an assignment or because they are not able to see the progress they have been or could be making during the term, we can help them go through their papers, identifying and reinforcing the positive comments we originally made in the margins of their papers, or locating additional features of their writing that are improving. In asking students to share multiple drafts with us during conferences, we can help them see the ways they are improving over time, and thus identify achievement they may not have seen and encourage further efforts. We can emphasize a particular paragraph which is especially well structured, which successfully uses transition phrases, and which is especially coherent and unified. We can identify particularly evocative description of events and locations, or particularly compelling dialogue. Even though these examples may have come accidentally into the paper, they stand as reminders to students of their successes; as we raise student awareness of these successes, students will continue to practice successful approaches and will be more willing to work on the weaker points in their writing. We can also emphasize the unique work and contributions of individual students. Non-traditional and underprepared students, for instance, may not have highly refined mechanical skills, but we can compliment their choice of topic, or on the ways their experiences help them bring particularly provocative images to their writing. In short, when we talk with students who are putting effort into the class, we should acknowledge their contributions to the course, accentuate their successes, and encourage them to continue developing their skills.

Sometimes students will seek us out not because of specific problems in their writing, but because of general feelings of inadequacy which are developing as they go to class, read course texts, and work on writing assignments. In such cases, we want to help the student articulate how he or she feels about the assignments and workload or about the writing process. We can ask gently probing questions about the ways they approach coursework and try to help the student articulate specific challenges. With specific issues on the table, teachers can help students come up with ways to make the workload more manageable. Often, if the student finds herself in a process-oriented writing course for the first time, she may have difficulty breaking away from old writing habits which impede developing the new time management strategies necessary for success on writing assignments and in our courses. If we ask the student to explain their process of writing and the time they spend on various components of the process, we can help them see the direct correlation between work habits and success on the writing assignments. When we remind the student that the writing process is built from a series of interrelated steps, they will be able to better manage their time and feel more in control over their writing, and, in the long run, better about their performance in the class.

As we point out students' strengths and shortcomings during conferences, we should also encourage them to apply our comments to their work independently. In other words, we should not use the conference as a time to simply provide the student with a list of successes and problems. Instead, once we have initiated and modeled the process during a conference, we should encourage students to look at our comments in relation to their work, and begin to develop their own plans. Consider encouraging the student to apply comments from one particularly strong point in the paper, to another. If, for instance, I identify a transition between two paragraphs that really worked to tie the student's ideas together, I might identify a set of paragraphs with weaker transitions and ask the student to explain what she might do to apply the effective approach to less successful points in the paper. Our gentle questioning and encouragement makes the students feel more in control of their writing, and helps them become more independent thinkers.

Much of the student conference time should be devoted to addressing the student's questions and concerns about the class and writing assignments. During these times, we should focus on listening and asking follow up questions for clarification and development as necessary. As with the assistance we give students in addressing the technical challenges in their work, asking questions that encourage the student's own ability to solve problems can be far more valuable than directing the student through problems or dictating revisions, which can often reinforce student perceptions of there being a right and wrong way to write papers. Indeed, sometimes we will ask the right question that sends students away from the conference with new energy and self-confidence, eager to begin developing their ideas for a new assignment or ready to take another crack at revising a previous assignment.

Unobtrusive note taking during student conferences can also be valuable for both teachers and students. A record of our meetings with individual students helps us track their growth during a term, identify their achievements, and emphasize the importance of working on recurring challenges. As our students surely know, writing takes effort, and when we show our students we believe that what they say is important enough to be written down, they too will value their ideas all the more. Note taking can be especially effective when students are having trouble with organization, or with moving from prewriting to planning. During a conference that focuses on generating ideas, we can write down the students' remarks as they come up in discussion of a topic, then present those remarks back to them and ask them to locate an organizational pattern that will effectively connect their ideas. This approach helps us to model prewriting strategies and the planning that can quickly and logically develop from an initial question or burst of intellectual energy.

Regardless of the strategies we decide to employ during conferences, we should remain positive and encouraging as we help students overcome their difficulties in our classes. We must, however, also use these times to reinforce for our students realistic expectations about their performance in the course. Students may not come to see us about a series of poor grades on their papers or extended absences from class meetings until it is too late for them to be able to get the grade they desire from the course, or even to receive a passing grade at all. In the case of a student who is likely to receive a failing grade, we can encourage her to complete the course and its writing assignments, and yet also be clear about the chances of passing the course. The more the student participates in class meetings and works on writing assignments, the better prepared she will be to retake and succeed in the course in a future semester.

To be sure, there is an important element of self-protection in remaining realistic and honest with our students about their progress in class and the expectations they have about final grades. Student evaluations of instructors are playing an increasingly prominent role in departmental decisions about the retention of part time instructors and about the tenure and promotion of contract faculty. If we use meeting times to help our students grow as critical thinkers and writers as much as we can, and at the same time strive to remain as honest as possible about the ways in which their performance produces specific results in terms of grades, students will appreciate and reward our work appropriately.

Finally, some teachers—part time and graduate student instructors in particular—may not have offices, or they may have shared office spaces in which scheduling blocks of time for student conferences is more challenging. Even with limited access to office space, we can think of other options on campus for student meetings, such as reserving carrels or group study rooms in the library, or finding a classroom that is empty at regular times. Other teachers may have to weigh the time necessary for conferences against overwhelming course or student loads, or in relation to their other teaching, service, or research responsibilities. We should consider ways of encouraging our students to see us individually throughout the term, but this encouragement may be simply extending an invitation to students to see us during office hours.

■ SOME CHALLENGES OF STUDENT CONFERENCES

While the ability to engage our students through periodic discussions of their writing provides us with one of the greatest pleasures of teaching, we can find ourselves in a fraught position when we are faced with students who wish to share their personal lives with us in ways that we believe will break professional boundaries, or in ways with which we are uncomfortable. This section describes some of the potential challenges of dealing with students personally, and suggests some approaches for dealing with those problems professionally and productively.

Many of us have one or more writing assignment that calls for personal reflection or for description of a significant event in the student's life. While we can make efforts to discourage students from writing about especially traumatic events, illegal activities, or plans to harm themselves or others (some of which teachers may be required by law to report to authorities), when we introduce writing assignments that have personal components, we must still prepare ourselves for breaches. As we develop our class schedules and consider ways of linking student conferences to writing assignments, we should also prepare ourselves for students who might see their writing assignments as an invitation to talk with us about their personal lives and personal problems.

Peer response groups can have a significant impact on steering student writers toward appropriate topics and appropriate ways of expressing their personal feelings and events of autobiographical significance. For instance, when we introduce students to the goals and basic features of a significant event paper, we can remind them that, because the writing process includes peer review sessions, they must select topics that they will be able to write about and to share comfortably with other students. Once provided with these cautions, most students will make wise choices about the kinds of material they include in their papers.

Most of the time, students who wish to tell us about their lives during conference sessions or other one-on-one meetings will talk about personal, but relatively innocuous, problems of the heart. Because many of our students find themselves away from home and parental supervision for the first time in their lives, they may be tempted to see their teachers as proxy confidants or authority figures. At times, our students may also appeal to us for leniency in due dates or other class requirements because of problems in their personal lives. In these cases, we can listen attentively to our students, remain supportive, and yet resist the temptation to offer advice or make unnecessary changes in class policies.

Although student conferences are typically uncomplicated, we should still be prepared for the times when more serious issues come up during meetings. Students are more likely to come to their writing teachers for help with family, social, or school related problems because we know them better than most teachers do. In cases where a student comes to us for advice on serious problems, we should continue to resist the temptation to give advice, and instead, help the student find qualified assistance. In case of student crises, some teachers have a quick reference sheet on hand to help students find on and off campus contacts for religious organizations, psychological, psychiatric, and medical help, suicide and rape crisis hotlines, or assistance in case of food emergencies. This kind of quick reference sheet is available at student centers on most campuses. Just as our students may have been apprehensive about coming to see us for conferences or during office hours, they may also be concerned about seeking counseling or psychiatric assistance. Similar, or even greater stigma can be associated with students who are perceived to be or who perceive themselves in need of help with emotional issues. Because of the similarity of student perceptions though, writing teachers may be in an important position to encourage them to seek other help: if they have overcome their apprehension about seeing us, might they not do the same with someone in the campus counseling center? A student may be reluctant to seek help, but she may be more willing to try it if a teacher she respects suggests the option.

As in any facet of our teaching and professional lives, there are challenges that may occur with student conferences. Typically though, the problems students bring to office hours can be handled with a combination of careful planning and by beginning with positive assumptions about students' abilities and willingness to work on their writing. Students will appreciate the time we spend with them and our interest in their writing; they will see the positive effects of the conversation through and about their writing that unfolds over the term; they will also be prepared to more readily discuss challenges with us and with their other teachers in the future.

SUGGESTED READING

Flynn, Thomas, and Mary King, eds. *Dynamics of the Writing Conference: Social and Cognitive Interaction*. Urbana, IL: National Council of Teachers of English, 1993.

Hacker, Tim. "The Effect of Teacher Conferences on Peer Response Discourse." *Teaching English in the Two Year College* 23 (May 1996): 112-26.

Kuriloff, Pesche E. "Reaffirming the Writing Conference: A Tool for Writing Teachers across the Curriculum." *Journal of Teaching Writing* 10, no. 1 (Spring/Summer 1991): 45–57.

Morse, Philip S. "The Writing Teacher as Helping Agent: Communicating Effectively in the Conferencing Process." *Journal of Classroom Interaction* 29.1 (1994): 9-15.

Newkirk, Thomas. "The Writing Conference as Performance." *Research in the Teaching of English* 29 (May 1995): 193-215.

Patthey Chavez, G. Genevieve, and Dana R. Ferris. "Writing and the Weaving of Multi-voiced Texts in College Composition." *Research in the Teaching of English* 31 (Feb. 1997): 51-90.

CHAPTER 6
Effective Use of Peer Review

Since the 1980s, collaborative learning has taken an increasingly prominent place among the strategies instructors employ in teaching introductory writing effectively. We can certainly see the ways in which, during informal class discussions, superficial or offhand comments from peers can carry far more weight with our students than do the thoughtful, affirmative comments we write on their papers. Rather than rejecting or minimizing the value of student input, we must use our students' predisposition to listen to and learn from each other, and encourage collaboration, yet shape it in ways that help them make productive gains in their writing. We can consider approaches to incorporating various methods of peer review into the writing process, from the earliest invention stages to the polishing of final drafts. Informed, carefully planned, modeled, and directed peer review will work in concert with the teacher's written comments and attention to individual students, encouraging beginning college writers to produce their best work and to develop practices they will use throughout their college careers.

■ PLANNING

We should familiarize ourselves with various approaches to incorporating peer evaluation into the writing process, and consider ways of implementing them depending on our needs, the students' needs, and the demands of a particular writing assignment. As the repertoire of strategies we have at hand increases, and as we test and refine the activities we use, the more adept we become at choosing the appropriate form and detail to link student work with the outcomes we desire. Regardless of the techniques we choose, we must be sure to carefully direct students toward specific goals, from clarifying the broad contours of an assignment and checking topic appropriateness in prewriting to polishing the mechanics of a final draft prior to submission for a grade. When students are unaware of the tasks we expect them to perform during peer evaluation sessions, they are more likely to make unproductive use of the time, providing vague responses that do not encourage participation in future sessions.

The *Prentice Hall Reference Guide* provides guidelines you can use in planning peer review activities. For instance, you can use sections 1a and 1d to clarify the purpose and audience of the writing assignment. In developing peer review prompts for students to use at the planning stage of the assignment, we can help assure students that they are moving in useful and appropriate directions before they move too far into the writing process. Students benefit from testing initial choices with an auditor/reader who can provide a concrete example of an audience member who will be reading the paper in later versions. Naturally, student reviewers also share with authors many questions and concerns about the assignment, topic appropriateness, and ideas for development, so early peer review sessions will help students collectively to raise questions for the instructor.

Although student writers certainly benefit from peer review, we should remind the class that the reviewers themselves benefit as well. Each time students participate as audience members for each other's work they gain valuable experience as critical readers, and take ideas—and, of course, cautions—from other writers' approaches to an assignment.

■ MODELING

We should not send our students blindly into peer review situations. We can help them understand the use we expect them to make of peer review sessions and the goals we wish them to reach at the end of each session. Because they may have had little exposure to peer review practices, instructors have to take significant time early in the term to develop some standards for student interaction. Beginning students are likely to simply gloss over each others' papers and offer more praise than informed criticism. They may be concerned about hurting the author's feelings, fear retributive comments on their own papers, or be concerned about their abilities to make useful comments and recommendations on a peer's work. Other students may be tempted—just as we can be—to overzealously mark papers and offer their peers criticism that is not presented as tactfully as possible. In the first peer review session—and as we work on especially new genres and conventions in later assignments—we can walk students through some of the basic techniques of affirmative, yet productive, evaluation. Consider asking a student to volunteer her paper, or bring a draft of the assignment from a previous course (make sure to remove identifying characteristics from past student papers), then model for the class the kinds of responses that will help authors know not only what they are doing well, but also what they could be doing more effectively.

If we do not have a set of questions prepared for the particular writing assignment, we might use the prompts in section 2d of the *Prentice Hall Reference Guide*, which are applicable to most projects, to get started. Typically, our students will not have any difficulty providing positive comments on model papers, but they may be reticent about pointing out shortcomings and suggesting revisions. We can help them gently direct authors by asking leading questions, such as "Have you thought about . . ." "What if you add . . ." or "How would this point work in a different place in the paper?" which suggest new directions for the project and yet remain centered on the author's ability to make decisions about her own work. We should also emphasize Harris's first suggestion in her list of possible questions, that reviewers should open their responses with positive comments.

Although invention, prewriting, and early drafts may be reviewed with less detailed direction from the instructor, when students begin comparing and reviewing drafts of completed papers, we should compose a list of the specific questions we expect students to respond to as they read each others' work.

■ IMPLEMENTATION

We should encourage our students to work with each other from the earliest stages of invention and planning for a writing project and to continue turning to each other as resources throughout the writing process. We can sustain our students' positive energy toward the class and the writing process when they are assured early on in the process that their topics and plans for development will lead to successful final drafts. Yet, we should also avoid using identical activities at the same point of the writing process in each assignment. As with most techniques we use in teaching, we want to ensure that we keep peer review sessions fresh and interesting for students by varying the frequency and complexity of evaluation activities.

Once students have some practice in reading and responding to each others' work, we should begin implementing peer review in the early stages of the writing process, when stakes are relatively low. We might begin by having them comment only on one section of an essay, such as the introduction. With most writing assignments and genres of college writing, we can develop collaborative activities for our students through which they test their choices of topic and organization at early stages of the process. Many teachers assign as the first project of the term a significant event essay, or a paper which calls for similar autobiographical reflection by the student. After we introduce the basic features of the assignment, students take some time between class meetings to consider the event they wish to describe and have a sense of the significance they intend their audience to take away from their reflection on that event. When students arrive in the next class period, we ask them to form small groups of two or three, and take turns telling their stories to each other. Because students are interested in and enjoy hearing about each other's lives, this planning activity always generates significant feedback which the student can apply to developing an organizational pattern for the paper (such as whether to introduce the paper with the story's significance or to expose it in the conclusion, or how to order the events in the story to have the desired effect on the reader), or to including details (such as dialogue or sensory experiences) which the peer group has asked them to describe.

This early-stage peer review strategy can work well on other papers as well. Students can brainstorm together on writing assignments which have a single topic assigned to the entire class, or they can share opening paragraphs to test their introductory hooks and forecasting. In a problem/solution paper, for instance, introductory paragraphs will cover the background of the problem, outline the stakes of finding a solution, and provide some forecasting of the form of the argument. Particularly if we have students write on local issues (see Chapter 8 of this supplement for an overview of this writing assignment), peer reviewers are likely to represent an informed, interested audience for each others' papers. Not only will students be able to help each other provide sufficient background so that an average reader will understand the problem, they can also encourage writers to explain their personal investment in the problem or its solution through sharing common experiences.

Students can use such early group work to clarify the assignment and the teacher's expectations as well. Regardless of assignment, once students have seen the benefit of peer feedback at early stages of planning, they will continue to seek assistance throughout the drafting process, testing their successes in meeting the requests of the peer group and asking for additional advice. In fact, when the process succeeds on writing assignments early in the term, students will continue to turn to their first peer response group later in the term, even if they are placed with other reviewers. In this way, we have an opportunity to build long lasting cohorts of students who will continue to seek each other out for advice and feedback.

Once students are expected to have completed a writing assignment, we should ask them again to share their work with each other before submitting it for a grade. Especially in later stages of drafting, students need to be given specific directions for responding. If we wish to encourage student centrality in shaping peer review prompts, we can ask them to generate ideas about the features important for success on the writing assignment and develop those features into questions written on the board. Once a discussion is underway, we should encourage students to incorporate key terms and concepts from the *Prentice Hall Reference Guide* and from the course's central reader/rhetoric into their prompts. We should also ask them to recall models from the supplemental readings we have assigned, so that students are able to turn to common points of reference to understand and apply prompts.

We may also have developed specific questions for peer review through our previous experiences with teaching a particular genre, or through prior experience with the types of challenges that occur at a particular time in the term. I include below a final peer review questionnaire that I have used with significant event papers. The questionnaire restates the requirements of the assignment and encourages peer reviewers to assist authors in adding details and revising in ways that will maximize their chances for success when the paper is graded.

Author   _____

Reviewer   _____

Significant event paper goals: 1) describe the experience of a formative event, and 2) demonstrate the significance of that event. As you go through your partner's draft, concentrate on the following questions and make constructive notes of your comments on a separate sheet of paper so the author can look back over them later as s/he works on the final draft.

1. Read through the paper quickly for a first impression. Write down one element of the story that caught your attention (a character, dialogue, description of setting, event, etc.); why was it effective? In one sentence, summarize the central/focus event. In one sentence, state the significance of the event. Has the author established a sense of "critical distance" from the event? Does one event form the subject of the paper, and is the event about the author?

2. Read the draft again more carefully. Is the central event clear to you? Is a context built to establish enough background to understand the central event itself? What strategies does the author use to establish context (setting, preliminary events, etc.)? What works well? What improvements would you suggest? Is there additional information that the author must include?

3. Are there enough details to make the author's story of the event interesting? How could the author enhance/improve the story with details (sensory/emotional description, dialogue, suspense, etc.)? Consider sample readings by Toni Morrison and Eric Miles Williamson.

4. Was the significance of the event stated explicitly by the author, or does s/he imply the significance (that is, call upon the reader to figure it out)? Do you need more background or more description of the author's present state of mind to show either how his/her later life has been affected by this event or how it was the critical/transitional event in a series of earlier events? How and where would you expand?

5. Did the introduction grab your attention and make you interested in the upcoming story? Did the story itself keep your attention? Does the conclusion give you some insight into the author's life? Does the ending work with the expectations you got through the story, or are you surprised by an unexpected twist in the ending? Is there anything you could suggest to improve the overall organization of the paper (like chronology, especially)?

6. Is the paper mechanically sound? Misspellings and grammatical problems should be minimal. Note, either on the author's draft or on your comments sheet, errors in spelling, sentence construction (run-ons and fragments), noun/verb agreement, punctuation, correct adjective/adverb use, etc. Note redundancies and unnecessary conversational language. Suggest strategies for improvement.

As I write peer review guidelines, I remind students of the texts we have read in preparation for the assignment. I incorporate key terms from the handbook and other course texts so that students have specific points of reference as they revise. As students begin to understand, and as I eventually state as they work on future papers, the peer review prompts are also cues for reviewers, like authors, to assess their work prior to submission and to revise as much as possible to ensure their own success. An important result of the peer review process, then, is that students are able to see the criteria that will be used for grading, and thus predict with some accuracy their success on the assignment.

Modeling peer response sessions after the workshop setting of creative writing courses creates a less overtly instructor-directed approach to peer evaluation. On workshop days students hand out copies of their papers to students, present the papers orally, and solicit comments from the class. A student presenter can help shape audience comments by either introducing or closing the presentation with a brief statement on the challenges encountered in the writing process or points she believes to be trouble spots in the essay. Members of the student audience will, typically, come up with both commendation and advice for improving the paper, but instructors must resist the temptation to speak or otherwise direct the discussion before allowing students the opportunity to offer their remarks. As in creative writing classes, though, discussions may turn hostile, so we should be prepared to jump in and help turn student comments in constructive directions.

Whether they are generated by the instructor alone, solicited by a student presenter, or developed in collaboration with the class, we should include all or most of the following features in peer review guidelines:

> What ideas are particularly effective and interesting?

> What seems to be the paper's purpose? What is the writer trying to accomplish?

> What seems to be the paper's main point? Where is it located?

> Do you need additional support or background information to understand the paper's topic or thesis?

> Do you have trouble understanding how the writer gets from one idea to the next? Are the transitions smooth?

> Which sentences are particularly effective? Which words, phrases, or sentences do you find especially strong? Which details do you especially like?

> Are there places where the writer needs to be more specific and less abstract?

> Who seems to be the audience for this essay? How do you know? What words or phrases has the writer used which suggest the audience?

> Do you see any grammatical or punctuation problems which weaken the credibility of the paragraph?

> What specific suggestions can you make to this author to help him or her strengthen the introduction?

Before they begin to work with these prompts, during the first few minutes of a peer review session, we should encourage authors to share with reviewers their own concerns, or highlight particular parts of the essay they wish the reviewer to look at carefully.

Even following careful planning and modeling, instructors should move around the room, listening to student discussions and answering questions about the process. Observing early review sessions helps us spot students who need extra assistance in developing effective responses. If time allows, we should have students produce and receive multiple peer responses for each major writing assignment. One of the most effective ways to organize consecutive peer response sessions is to have students first exchange drafts two class periods prior to the due date, then revise according to that day's review between meetings. During the next class period, students exchange new drafts with a different reviewer, who, responding to the same set of prompts from the first session, helps authors test the effectiveness of their choices. Even if we do not have time to devote two class meetings to peer evaluation, the same piece of writing is likely to impress different readers in different ways, so having multiple peer responses will give students practical experience with accommodating audience concerns.

During invention and prewriting stages, and with final drafts of papers, we need to remind students that what is being evaluated in peer review sessions is a piece of writing, not the person who wrote it. We need to remind them that taking and giving negative criticism may be hard, but that critical response is an essential component of the writing process. As we begin planning for peer review, we might consider keeping the same response groups throughout the term, so that three or four students in a group will become increasingly comfortable with giving and receiving productive criticism. However, we should also consider the importance of switching groups regularly, so that students gain confidence from working with less familiar audiences and receiving different perspectives on their writing.

We should also ask students to write brief reflective pieces that describe the kind of feedback they have received on a writing assignment. Responses may be turned in either on the day of the review or as supplements to the final draft. Additionally, reviewers should reflect on their experiences of critiquing another's work. Either way, students will acknowledge the effectiveness or shortcomings of the peer response activities we have assigned and assist us in retaining useful strategies or improving less useful ones. Such occasional reflective writing places peer review in an integral role in the recursive writing process, through which students will become more informed and engaged readers, and thus more critically aware of audience concerns in their own writing. Most importantly perhaps, students gain the awareness that the ultimate reader of their writing is no longer the English teacher, but an informed and engaged peer.

SUGGESTED READING

Barron, Ronald. "What I Wish I Had Known About Peer-Response Groups but Didn't." *English Journal* 80.5 (Sept. 1991): 24-34.

Berliner, David, and Ursula Casanova. "The Case for Peer Tutoring." *Instructor* 99 (April 1990): 16-18.

Broglie, Mary. "Who Says So? Ownership, Authorship, and Privacy in Process Writing Classrooms: Privacy Issues Regarding Peer-Revision Workshops." *English Journal* 86 (Oct. 1997): 19-23.

Chapman, Orville L., and Michael A. Fiore. "Calibrated Peer Review." *Journal of Interactive Instruction Development* 12.3 (Winter 2000): 11-15.

Harris, Helen J. "Slice and Dice: Response Groups as Writing Processors." *English Journal* 81.2 (Feb. 1992): 51-54.

Hughes, J.A. "It Really Works: Encouraging Revision Using Peer Writing Tutors." *English Journal* 80 (Sept. 1991): 41-42.

Leverenz, Carrie Shively. "Peer Response in the Multicultural Classroom: Dissensus—A Dream (Deferred)." *Journal of Advanced Composition* 14.1 (Winter 1994): 167-86.

Liftig, R.A. "Feeling Good About Student Writing: Validation in Peer Evaluation." *English Journal* 79 (Feb. 1990): 62-65.

McKendy, T. F. "Legitimizing Peer Response: A Recycling Project for Placement Essays." *College Composition and Communication* 41 (Feb. 1990): 89-91.

Sengupta, Sima. "Peer Evaluation: 'I Am Not the Teacher.'" *ELT Journal* 52 (Jan. 1998): 19-28.

Topping, Keith J. "Peer Assessment Between Students in Colleges and Universities." *Review of Educational Research* 68.3 (Fall 1998): 249-76.

CHAPTER 7
An Overview of Grading Methods

Most first year writing instructors will spend as much time during the term grading and responding to student writing as they do to planning and teaching the course. If we are to do conscientious work in evaluation and grading, we must plan to put a significant amount of time and effort into the process, learning about and employing practices that best work for us and our students. Developing and executing an informed, affirmative, carefully planned approach to grading can be one of the most effective ways we can help students.

We have probably seen instructors—or have had instructors in our own experiences—who use grades punitively rather than affirmatively, who mark every single mechanical flaw and point out every gap in logic and development. Although common, these practices rarely help students become better writers, increase their confidence on new projects, or encourage them to value writing; in fact, punitive or overzealous marking can reinforce widely held misperceptions about writing: that good writing is a matter of mechanical correctness and that scores on papers assess the student as a person rather than the quality of a particular assignment.

Regardless of the choices we make about grading systems and their implementation over the term, in relation to rewarding revision and student improvement over the semester, and in concert with other features such as attendance and participation, we must state as clearly as possible the standards of the course on the syllabus. In fact, this feature is required to appear on course syllabi in many departments and institutions. We should consider including on syllabi not only percentage weights or the requirements of individual contract writing and portfolio building, but also a brief overview of the criteria associated with letter grades. Most college catalogs will include a statement on grading standards which are clear and meaningful, but flexible enough to allow for a certain amount of interpretation by instructor and department.

An explanation of grading criteria on the syllabus helps to situate students in relation to the meaning of grades from the first day of class. The explanation also provides instructors with a point of departure to discuss with their students the different expectations of college level work, how those expectations play out specifically in the writing classroom and in relation to established outcomes and standards. As one catalogue explains: "The letter grade 'A' is an honor grade indicating superior achievement; 'B' is a grade indicating commendable mastery; 'C' indicates satisfactory mastery; 'D' indicates substandard progress and insufficient evidence of ability to succeed in sequential courses; 'F' indicates inadequate mastery of pertinent skills or repeated absences from class." Most importantly, when we incorporate statements such as these into syllabi or other course materials, we effectively tie specific values to each grade and challenge inaccurate beliefs about grading standards (such as an "A" grade indicating competence alone).

Once grading standards for the course have been determined, instructors should plan in advance the ways in which writing assignments will lead to the final course grade, how we plan to score major writing assignments, encourage revision, and stress the importance of process-oriented writing. We should consider approaches that strike a balance between, on the one hand, keeping students interested in the course and supporting students toward making improvements in their writing, and on the other hand, applying appropriately rigorous standards to their work. Before making decisions about grading individual papers, instructors should keep in mind their expectations concerning the entire body of work their students will produce over the term, and ways to reward students for improvement through holistic grading. Three of the current best grading practices are using weighted grades, portfolios, and contracts, each of which is described below in some detail.

■ WEIGHTED GRADING

Although emergent assessment systems, such as portfolios, are effective approaches to evaluation, traditional weighted grading remains the most common assessment practice. Certainly, student-centered and student-initiated assessment practices are valuable, but, because they are better prepared than their students to make decisions about evaluation, most teachers will establish at the opening of the course the relative value of each writing assignment. Typically, in this case, teachers will apply a certain percentage toward the final course grade to each assignment or set of assignments that make up a writing unit. In order to reinforce the importance of the writing process, however, we should work to strike a balance between rigor in grading policies and providing students with sufficient opportunities for revision. Only rarely, late in the term for instance, should grades be awarded without also giving students opportunities to rewrite their papers for better scores. We should also consider weighing more heavily assignments later in the term to account for and reward development over time.

As in every evaluative approach, the weighted grading system must be grounded in score criteria that are explained early in the semester and clarified as necessary. We must ensure that students do not see the grading system as arbitrary, but instead as logically tied to identifiable traits which have been explained both generally and in relation to specific writing assignments. For many of us, the qualities that merit a particular letter grade are established by department consensus or by a writing program administrator. These standards help to ensure consistency across sections as well as between introductory writing courses and more advanced courses. Whether grading criteria are derived from department or institutional standards, or are left to our own discretion, we should be sure to clearly explain grades on papers, and ensure that those grades lead logically to final grades in the course. The following are some generally acceptable guidelines for developing standards:

A—the A paper not only fulfills the requirements of the writing assignment, but does so in a fresh, original way. Through sophisticated tone, voice, and diction, the paper meets or exceeds the rhetorical conventions for the genre. The paper is well organized, has a sound and novel thesis, includes well chosen and developed examples, and has few mechanical errors.

B—the B paper meets, and in some respects may exceed, the requirements of the writing assignment. It is thoughtfully prepared, well organized, coherent, and effectively practices the conventions of the genre. Examples are relevant and logically incorporated into the argument. Paragraphs are unified with sufficient transitions, tone is consistent, and there are few mechanical errors. The B paper tends to be as ambitious, but not quite as successful as the A paper in achieving those ambitions.

C—C papers demonstrate competence, an understanding of the assignment and the conventions involved in the genre. These papers are likely to be less fluid and readable that those with higher marks; they often need more effective transitions between paragraphs, or more work to make paragraphs coherent. The thesis is likely to be overly broad and the argument is either simplistic or lacks sufficient evidence and detail. The paper's tone is monotonous and shows little investment by the author. Papers are mechanically correct for the most part, but do not exhibit much variety in sentence structure and word choice.

With these papers especially, we must emphasize for students that the C grade does not denote unsatisfactory work. Our comments on C papers are especially important, because affirmative marking can show students the ways we are rewarding them for their accomplishments, and at the same time, encouraging them to continue working toward better grades on revisions or later papers.

D—for most teachers, D papers are those which attempt to follow the assignment, but have major shortcomings in meeting some of the basic requirements for the assignment, in terms of mechanics, conventions, or both. These papers will lack a clear thesis and have little logical plan for organization; similarly, paragraphs will lack unity and coherence. There is little evidence or only vaguely relevant evidence to support the argument. Papers are likely to have many problems in mechanics: run on sentences, fragments, and little care to word choice and spelling.

F—the F paper does not meet the basic requirements of the assignment. It lacks a clear thesis altogether, and has no clear plan for organization. The paper will have enough mechanical errors to impede reading. F papers may also be mechanically correct and coherent, but off topic or conventions required by the assignment.

Of course, the letter grade by itself will still appear arbitrary or meaningless without sufficient narrative comments which help individual students see how we have arrived at a particular evaluation on their papers. As we write comments in the margins of papers, we should strive to strike a balance between comments which, on the one hand, clearly point out flaws in mechanics and argument, and those which, on the other hand, just as clearly point out strengths and begin to direct the student toward productive revisions.

Another way of explaining the evaluation process is to return papers with a grading rubric that lists features appropriate to the genre and is divided into categories defining levels of competence. Each feature can be assigned a score, and together, the features add up to the paper grade. As an alternative to the more detailed rubric, some instructors will assign split grades, which separate scores for content and mechanics. This practice can be very useful, because students are credited for their ideas, and thus rewarded for and encouraged to continue participating in invention and prewriting activities. However, if we want our students to see content and mechanics as interrelated features of effective writing, we may not want to use the split grade as our only assessment model. Not only are conventions an integral part of good writing generally, they are also critical components—which include not only spelling and sentence structure, but also features such as genre, attributing sources, format, and so on—of each writing assignment we give our students. It may ultimately be misleading and counterproductive to suggest that successful use of appropriate conventions may be considered separately from a paper's content.

Yet, we want to avoid discouraging students with low grades, particularly early in the semester, when it is more important that students simply continue to put effort into the course. Rather than splitting grades, especially in the case of low scoring papers, we may require that a paper be of at least C quality before we assign it a letter grade. Students will then have to begin revising papers quite early in the term, and, in many cases, this early practice will allow them to ultimately meet or exceed our expectations by the end of the term. We may also manipulate grading standards, so that the quality of work required for a C grade is gradually increased over the term. In such a system, students who put a good amount of effort into their projects are not discouraged early in the term, and we can easily explain the appropriateness of standards increasing proportionally with expertise gained through the writing assignments. While each of these strategies can work effectively, we must be sure to inform students of the procedures and standards by which their work will be judged, first in writing on the syllabus, then when the first graded assignment is returned, and throughout the term as necessary.

■ PORTFOLIO GRADING

Portfolio assessment is rapidly being adopted as the standard practice for entire writing programs as well as by individual instructors. While it can be more time consuming than traditional weighted grading, the time spent can be very productive both for instructors and students, because the portfolio system is structured dialogically and continually reinforces process-oriented writing strategies. As they build their portfolios, students enter into an ongoing conversation with teachers about their work, and through regular reflective writing and discussion describe their successes and the ways they have met particular challenges over the entire term or one part of it. For much of the term, the instructor's role is not to grade writing assignments, but instead to encourage revision: the instructor continues to write significant commentary on student papers, but final evaluation may either not appear at all, or may be only roughly categorized by remarks such as "excellent" or "needs revision," rather than letter grades. Only later, often at the end of the term, do students turn in a set of writing assignments, which are usually accompanied by a detailed reflective statement on the writing process and student self-assessment, for grading. When used successfully, the portfolio system thus depends on a collaborative exchange between student reflection and instructor response about each writing assignment, a process which facilitates teaching and evaluation practices that are far more individualized than in other systems.

Instructors who decide to use a portfolio system should carefully plan in advance the contents of the portfolio: the number of writing assignments it will contain, the rate of assessment, and whether the portfolio may contain voluntary as well as required elements. Some instructors will ask students to include all of their writing from the term in the portfolio—from prewriting through final drafts of major assignments to journals and other occasional writing—and ask them to select particular pieces that highlight their strengths. In this case, instructors are able to assess their students' work holistically while having a sense of what the student perceives as particular successes in the course. Other instructors will select certain writing assignments as required elements, and then allow students to choose other work to include in a portfolio. This method is particularly useful for instructors who move their students through a number of writing genres and wish to ensure that an appropriate range is included in the writing sample. A more student-directed approach is to require a certain number of writing assignments or number of pages to be included in the portfolio, and to allow students to choose their most representative work. Regardless of the approach we choose in a portfolio system, we must ensure that many types of writing are finally graded. Each of these methods can be effective in achieving one of the most important benefits of portfolio assessment: increasing student investment in the grading system, and thus the writing process, both of which they will take more seriously.

We should also consider the rate of assessment in a portfolio course. One of the downsides of portfolio grading is that our students are likely to become uneasy at the prospect of having to wait until quite late in the term, or even at the end of the term, to receive any grades at all. We can put students at ease by having a midterm assessment, or by staggering assessment into three periods throughout the term. It may still be valuable, however, to require students to work their hardest on drafting and revising their writing projects all the way to the end of the term. In such courses, instructors may have periodic conferences during which they help the student perform a self-assessment that is not grade-driven, but can give the student a strong indication of the grade level at which they are working. We might also use rubrics to assess various features of student writing—especially on major papers—from argument to mechanics, but not use the rubrics to assign grades to the papers. Students will then have specific indications of their strengths and weaknesses throughout the term as they prepare materials for final grading.

Portfolios may be used either as the sole assessment approach in the course or in concert with weighted grading. If, for instance, we wish to give students more conventional (or at least expected) assessment on each paper by assigning letter grades or numeric scores, we should still consider making a portfolio the final, and most heavily weighted, assignment of the term. We can ask students to reflect on their development over the course, select two papers which best demonstrate what they have learned, and write a narrative course and self-assessment which they will use as a cover page. Because students may be unfamiliar with the portfolio system, we should also be sure to schedule conferences with students toward the end of the term to discuss any difficulties they may be facing in building a successful portfolio or to help them select the work that will best demonstrate their progress over the term.

We have to think carefully about how we plan to evaluate portfolios at the end of the term. Because students will be submitting work that has been significantly revised, we may wish to take into account the level of improvement and effort on papers rather than evaluating the quality of the finished work alone. Because the portfolio system stresses ongoing revision, students are likely to expect that their efforts—as well as the final products—are credited. However, the more we choose to value the amount or rate of revision, the more difficult it will be to maintain consistency from student to student in terms of the equation between letter grade and quality of work. Of course, students who are writing sophisticated, original papers throughout the term do not need to revise as often or as much as weaker writers, and they should not be penalized if their work shows lower rate of revision in their portfolios; nor does every student who revises necessarily improve. Thus, we should clarify for ourselves and for our students at the outset what standards we will use, how much we will reward effort and improvement, and how closely we will monitor consistency in grading overall. Because the portfolio system demands a significant amount of attention to individual students, we should remain flexible and value the work of each student within the terms of evaluation we have established.

■ CONTRACT GRADING

As many first year writing instructors work to decenter their classes, they look for approaches to evaluation that reflect and reinforce the significance of each student and his or her particular needs. There are a number of ways of developing student-initiated grading systems through contracts. As in the portfolio system, students collaborate with the instructor and have an important role in shaping the way in which the instructor looks at their papers throughout the term. Not only will contracts encourage students to become more invested in the evaluation process, they also help students learn the responsibility of sticking to commitments once they are made.

Some teachers use contracts with each writing assignment. As students work through initial drafts and assess their ability to meet or exceed the basic features of the assignment, they develop with the teacher a contract that defines in detail the evidence that will correspond to a particular grade level. Certainly, this approach can make for some time consuming book-keeping, in which instructors must keep track of the means of assessing each assignment for each student. One of the ways we can mitigate the demand on our time in contract grading is to learn and introduce new technologies that are able to manage a range of data without much additional effort than in traditional weighted grading practices.

Alternately, we can use a grading rubric that organizes the basic features of the assignment into a few levels of proficiency and then allow students to choose certain features to be weighed more heavily than others. For instance, on the significant event assignment a student may have the opportunity to apply from ten to twenty percent of the grade to the paper's theme and ten to twenty percent to its development. If the student has chosen a theme she believes will not be well received because it is rather obvious, but believes that her unique and deft development should outweigh the choice of theme, she can submit a rubric with the final paper that directs the instructor to apply ten percent to theme and twenty percent to development. Ultimately, each student's paper will receive a grade or percentage score consistent with other students in the class, but each student will have a significant voice in determining the criteria the instructor uses to arrive at that score.

We may also choose to have students develop contracts to determine how they want particular writing assignments weighed at the end of the term. In a course that requires four major writing projects, an essay exam, a reading journal, and occasional writing, the instructor can allow students to choose the percentage of the final grade distributed to each assignment. Or, students may assign each category of writing certain percentage weights toward the final grade. In this approach, instructors should consider establishing an appropriate percentage range for each category.

As with any system of evaluation, both the individual assignment approach and the assignment weight approach to contract grading raise a set of challenges for instructors. Not only do we need extra time to set up individualized grading systems for each student, we are also likely to face some students who, having developed a contract early in the semester or early in the process of a writing assignment, want to change it at a later time. We should not be too dismissive of students who wish to make changes at appropriate times in the term, for, especially in first year writing courses, students may not always know early on where their strengths and weaknesses lie until they have some practice. However, students will also learn from the process of developing contracts that they must abide by the decisions they have made. If we do choose to alter the contracts of individual students, there are stakes we must consider before we make that decision. Whether we teach at a residential university or at an institution with a commuting student body, our students are always communicating with each other, comparing their experiences with other students in class, and with students in other classes; thus, when one student requests and is awarded a contract change, the instructor should be prepared to face similar requests from other students in the class, and for the pressure to award requests in order to maintain consistency across the class. It is best that we decide at the beginning of the term to alter contracts or not, and to explain—in writing if possible—that decision to our students.

■ MODELING COMMENTARY

In addition to using numeric or symbolic marking systems which refer students to sections in the handbook, teachers should supplement mechanical marks with narrative comments in the margins and at the end of a paper. Comments will likely focus on the skills and concepts relevant to the genre and conventions of the particular writing assignment, on identifying problems, and, most importantly, on complimenting students when they have mastered skills, used especially good images and examples, or made improvements between earlier and later writing assignments. Because we spend a significant amount of time marking and evaluating student papers, we want to see those efforts result in improved student writing, either as students revise already-graded work or as they begin new writing projects. However, when I began teaching college composition I soon realized that, except for an assignment's final letter grade, my efforts in marking student papers largely went unnoticed or unheeded. On the one hand, weak writers assumed that marginal comments were simply harping on their shortcomings, which were more easily and painlessly summarized by the letter grade; on the other hand, strong writers would often assume that a high grade indicated that the paper was already sufficiently strong and that comments were simply superfluous commendations.

Although we can consistently encourage students to look carefully at the comments we have written, we should also show them ways in which written commentary is an integral part of the writing process. Because our students may see themselves and their concerns in the introductory composition course as isolated and irreparably separated from our own, we might consider bringing to class examples of our own writing, which have gone through a revision process that is as rigorous and demanding as that which we expect of our students. We can also demonstrate the ways in which our creative and professional writing exists, like theirs, in a recursive conversation. If we participate in dissertation or book writing groups, or if we send scholarship to journals and presses for peer review, we can bring to class examples of peer response to our work and describe for students the value of the feedback we receive. Our colleagues and professional peers want us to produce the best writing we can, and in many cases will provide us with both harsh criticism and strong commendation. These examples can provide our students with examples of analogous experiences with the writing process that will encourage them to see their work as part of an ongoing academic conversation that is not isolated from their other courses or subsequent years in college.

Discussing the importance of engaged, active reading early in the term will introduce students to strategies they will have to use in writing summaries, strong responses, or exploratory research papers. Many students have been taught not to mark their books and other texts, and we should counter that training by helping them see the value in active marking—whether in the texts themselves or on note cards—as means to tracking arguments, noting examples, and highlighting difficulties in our reading. In the past, I have brought to class examples of books I teach or use in my research that I have heavily marked; whether a case study by Sigmund Freud, a critical essay by bell hooks, a novel by Sherman Alexie, or a short story by Franz Kafka, the comments I make help me recall the strengths and weaknesses of an argument, the examples I want to emphasize in a lecture or essay, and the ways I change over time as I revisit not only the text, but my earlier responses to it. We might also show students examples of classical or Renaissance texts which have been covered with marginal comments by many readers over the course of hundreds of years. Regardless of the strategies we use, we model engaged commentary as a way of encouraging students to see their writing as situated within an intellectual, academic conversation—between themselves and the texts they read, between themselves and other writers in the class, and between themselves and their writing instructor. They will thus begin to look forward to reading the comments we write on their papers, because those comments indicate they ways we value their work and want to help them make it as strong as possible.

This emphasis on the value of written comment will have a positive effect on our students in other parts of the writing process as well. If students see their teachers valuing participation in peer review groups and the feedback received from conversations with other experts in academic fields, they will be encouraged to value the feedback they receive from peers and to make their own best efforts as peer reviewers of classmates' work. In fact, if we model our uses of marginal commentary in our books and in our own writing, we encourage students to see themselves as aspiring experts on their topics or in their fields, whose ideas are important enough to be considered in an academic conversation through shared writing.

■ GRADING PAPERS: TWO EXAMPLES

Following are two copies of a student's paper, one overmarked and too harshly graded and the other less heavily marked and more affirmative. This exploration paper was the first paper in a semester-long introductory college writing course. Students were asked to read three brief essays on the liberal education tradition, to explore the ways in which their own expectations and experiences of higher education had been problematized by the readings, and to conclude with a statement on the significance of the exploration. Both copies are marked with numbers and symbols from the *Prentice Hall Reference Guide.* The second example is the kind of grading that seems to be most helpful in terms of inspiring students to care about revising and continuing to learn about writing. It asks the student questions rather than dictating changes, and the tone of the marginal comments is friendly, not sarcastic and insulting to the student.

Overmarked

A Liberal Education

Last summer I was able to visit some friends from

Australia. We discussed the subject of how the education system

works in Australia. I discovered that they take a test as a [11]

sophomore in high school. They are only allowed to take it once.

If they score high enough, they can get into a university. They

are permitted to finish high school and continue their education

at a university. If you don't make a high test score, you can [11b]

either finish high school or drop out and go to a technical school.

After explaining the way school in Australia worked they asked me about our school system. I told them, "You have a chance even through college to go to a university if that's what you decide." I never understood why their schools where so serious because school was all about having a fun experience.

surely not everyone's purpose?

39

As a class, we read three articles by on Adler, Edmundson, and Bloom and their own theories of education, a "liberal educa-tion." They all have different views of how students see higher education. What higher education really means is to have a higher, "liberal education."

redundant—practically meaningless

red

¶

What is a liberal education? Adler, as well as Edmundson, and Bloom agreed that a liberal education consisting of all humanities, mathematics, and sciences. Adler says, "that by a liberal education, you'll develop the power of mind." Adler, also, believes that a good education should consist of the liberal arts, which is "the ability to have intelligence and imagination to accomplish the liberal arts."

deceptive, since these aren't actually Adler's words

27

15

Why is it that students think that by using the term "higher education," it gives them a good excuse to move out and party? On top of that the schools give the students what they want, an easy education that is enjoyable and interesting.

41a

41a

Bloom gives us reasons of why students are not passionate anymore. He blames it on the professors for not being passion-ate and that it is passed on to the student. Bloom says, "Most professors are specialists, concerned only with their own fields, interested in the advancement in a world where all rewards are on the side of professional development."

19b

what's "it?"

ww

unclear — circular reasoning

Bloom believes that the reason the students are not

you're sure the professor is male?

passionate is because the professor~28~'s don't give background

knowledge to what he is discussing. As students, we don't get

topic shift attached to the subject that the professor is teaching. In high

school, I really was not interested in any subjects in school. The

teacher would get up and say, "here's your work sheets. It's due

at the end of class." I never learned anything that way. My

senior year I took a humanities class~6b~, the teacher was so excited

about what she was teaching us. The day before she taught us

about a new subject she would go out and research and tell us

what does this mean? Be specific.

the new things she learned. This made me excited about it~19~, that

I started researching <u>things</u> even though we didn't need to.

Bloom thinks that if students are just in college to get a job

that it is "better to give up on a liberal education and get on with

a specialty in which there is at least a prescribed curriculum and

a prospective career.~15d~" Students should not be in college just to get

vague a job. They should be in college to get a liberal education.

Whatever it may be, the professors, students, or media, we

need to change this approach of "higher education" and a

not an actual quote – clarify

"liberal education." Edmundson said, "an education should not

be like a TV show, but something that challenges you." Edmund-

son is also concerned about the passion of the students. Passion

how is this fact relevant?

now is looked down on, instead of admired. Even the walking

pace of the students have slowed down. Because there is no

more passion the students won't participate in class because they

are scared to be corrected or to be looked down upon by fellow

students. Now even when Edmundson asks a <u>question</u> in class,

red to make someone answer his <u>question</u>, he almost has to put the answer in the <u>question</u>. He blames this attitude upon the media.

this is too broad

Because of the media, we have lost the ability to be passionate students.

is "the orientation" a person?

Even the colleges want students to have a "fun" and exciting education. The UVSC orientation told us that we need a full education and the only way that is done is if we have a fun

and yet he spends much of his essay explaining why?

experience in college. Edmundson does not understand why in the evaluations that the students are asked, "was this an entertaining or enjoyable class for you?" He thought one of the questions on the evaluation should say, "was the class challenging for

clarify example

you?" Not, "was the class fun." Even colleges don't know how important a liberal education is for students.

All of the authors agree, students need a liberal education but there is no more passion left in the students. They all disagree why the student have no passion. They have changed my mind about my education. I will admit that I don't participate in class because I love to listen to new ideas. I am the cause of "no passion in the class rooms" but when I participate in class it is because the teacher is passionate and so excited to teach us about what she or he has learned about the subject. I

write about the impact on you, not "you"

believe a liberal education is very important because it will help <u>you</u> become a good productive thinker. Whose fault is it that we as students have no passion? I think it is the students mostly but I think the professors can also take some of the blame.

Andrea—Some potentially significant work here, but much more work needed, especially in making clear statements and accurately representing words and ideas from class readings.

More Affirmatively Marked

A Liberal Education

Last summer I was able to visit some friends from

Australia. We discussed the subject of how the education system

works in Australia. I discovered that they take a test as a [11]

sophomore in high school. They are only allowed to take it once.

If they score high enough, they can get into a university. They

are permitted to finish high school and continue their education

at a university. If you don't make a high test score, you can [11b]

either finish high school or drop out and go to a technical school.

an important comparison   After explaining the way school in Australia worked they

asked me about our school system. I told them, "You have a

how do you feel about this cultural difference?   chance even through college to go to a university if that's what

you decide." I never understood why their schools where so [39]

serious because school was all about having a fun experience.

As a class, we read three articles ~~on~~ by Adler, Edmundson,

and Bloom and their own theories of education, a "liberal educa-

red—clearly define key terms, then move on to their significance   tion." They all have different views of how students see higher

education. What higher education really means is to have a

higher, "liberal education."

¶   What is a liberal education? Adler, ~~as well as~~ Edmundson,

and Bloom agreed that a liberal education consisting of all

your point is consistent with Adler's meaning, but distinguish between his words and your paraphrase   humanities, mathematics, and sciences. Adler says, "that by a

liberal education, you'll develop the power of mind." Adler, also, [27]

believes that a good education should consist of the liberal arts,

which is "the ability to have intelligence and imagination to

accomplish the liberal arts."

15
Why is it that students think that by using the term

"higher education," it gives them a good excuse to move out and

41a

conv.
development—
try to use a
more
academic tone

party? On top of that the schools give the students what they

want, an easy education that is enjoyable and interesting.

41a

Bloom gives us reasons of why students are not passionate

19b

interesting—
then the
professors
also respond
to a culture
that doesn't
value the
larger
academic
project?

anymore. He blames it on the professors for not being passion-

ate and that it is passed on to the student. Bloom says, "Most

professors are specialists, concerned only with their own fields,

ww

interested in the advancement in a world where all rewards are

on the side of professional development."

Bloom believes that the reason the students are not

28

what kind of
background,
specifically?

passionate is because the professor's don't give background

sxt

knowledge to what he is discussing. As students, we don't get

attached to the subject that the professor is teaching. In high

school, I really was not interested in any subjects in school. The

teacher would get up and say, "here's your work sheets. It's due

vague—
perhaps you
can tie this
back to
Bloom's claim
that the
college
experience
isn't
distinctive?

at the end of class." I never learned anything that way. My

6b

senior year I took a humanities class, the teacher was so excited

about what she was teaching us. The day before she taught us

about a new subject she would go out and research and tell us

19

the new things she learned. This made me excited about it, that

I started researching things even though we didn't need to.

Bloom thinks that if students are just in college to get a job

that it is "better to give up on a liberal education and get on with

a specialty in which there is at least a prescribed curriculum and

15d

a prospective career." Students should not be in college just to

get a job. They should be in college to get a liberal education.

as above, does Edmundson <u>state</u> this word-for-word, or is this your <u>adaptation?</u> Please clarify

Whatever it may be, the professors, students, or media, we need to change this approach of "higher education" and a "liberal education." Edmundson said, "an education should not be like a TV show, but something that challenges you." Edmundson is also concerned about the passion of the students. Passion

I think I understand your image, but clarify its relation to your point

now is looked down on, instead of admired. Even the walking pace of the students have slowed down. Because there is no more passion the students won't participate in class because they are scared to be corrected or to be looked down upon by fellow students. Now even when Edmundson asks a <u>question</u> in class,

red

to make someone answer his <u>question</u>, he almost has to put the

yes, at least in part

answer in the <u>question</u>. He blames this attitude upon the media. Because of the media, we have lost the ability to be passionate students.

awk—how could you rewrite this sentence for clarity?

Even the colleges want students to have a "fun" and exciting education. The UVSC orientation told us that we need a full education and the only way that is done is if we have a fun experience in college. Edmundson does not understand why in the evaluations that the students are asked, "was this an enter-

a clearer summary would help me understand your point

taining or enjoyable class for you?" He thought one of the questions on the evaluation should say, "was the class challenging for you?" Not, "was the class fun." Even colleges don't know how important a liberal education is for students.

All of the authors agree, students need a liberal education but there is no more passion left in the students. They all disagree why the student have no passion. They have changed my mind about my education. I will admit that I don't participate in class because I love to listen to new ideas. I am the

<u>the</u> cause? Perhaps a <u>part</u> of	cause of "no passion in the class rooms" but when I participate in class it is because the teacher is passionate and so excited to teach us about what she or he has learned about the subject. I believe a liberal education is very important because it will help
keep focused on the impact on <u>you</u>, not on "you"	<u>you</u> become a good productive thinker. Whose fault is it that we as students have no passion? I think it is the students mostly but I think the professors can also take some of the blame.

Andrea—perhaps you're right, that there's enough "blame" to go around for the changes in higher education, but do you then lose your problematizing purpose if your conclusion rests on blame? In all, good points to be made here, but in making those points you should clearly distinguish between the exact words of course texts (quotations) and your interpretations or paraphrases. As you work on the next draft, revisit the handbook and devote some attention to mechanics as well.

■ IDENTIFYING PLAGIARISM IN THE INTERNET AGE

One of the most significant challenges we face in the grading process is encountering and developing effective ways of dealing with academic dishonesty in our students' writing. Although we describe the consequences of plagiarism on our course syllabi and we provide our students with various definitions of plagiarism early in the term, we will still encounter some students who choose to cheat when writing their papers. While we hope that these students are only a small minority of the whole, new technologies temptingly ease the way for our students to either lift passages from already published work and incorporate them without proper citation, or to purchase entire papers from online sources. We certainly do our students a disservice if we do not acknowledge the fact that longstanding, dominant notions of ownership of information are constantly being challenged on the internet, and the ways in which those challenges are significantly shifting writing conventions; however, in first year writing courses especially, we must continue to enforce the distinction between students' original work and that of others. We may personally believe that the increasingly nebulous nature of ownership will have positive results, but when our students are developing their expertise with writing conventions—and particularly because they are writing for grades—the value of individual effort must be maintained. If we allow some students to present the work of experts as their own, they not only learn little if anything in the process, but are also likely to earn higher marks than the students who did their own work. In short, if we do not insist that students produce their own work, we actually risk penalizing students whose work is their own.

Certainly, many plagiarism practices predate the emergence of the internet, and time tested strategies used by instructors to identify plagiarized material remain useful. As in the past, knowing our students and their writing is our best defense against having plagiarized work passed off as the student's own. Unusually sophisticated argument or tone is the best indication that the work is not the author's; when we see a student in English 101 who has been consistently writing C-level work suddenly turn in a paper that looks like it was written by a professional in the field, we may want to investigate further. We should also look carefully at submissions that either exceed the requirements or genre of the writing assignment, or are well written but far off topic; if, for instance, an assignment does not call for research, but the paper has a significant research component, we should at least question the student about her choice to do research. Similarly, if our research writing unit focuses on MLA documentation and bibliography conventions, but a student's paper is turned in using APA conventions, we should query the student about her decision to use a different approach.

Considerate, nonthreatening meetings with our students can be quite revealing, and can separate a student who has inadvertently misattributed source material from a student who has willfully plagiarized another's work. During a meeting we might ask a student to show us early work from the writing process, such as previous drafts or marked source material; we can also ask them to summarize their research process or their findings, or to define specialized terms used in the paper. If there is a marked difference between earlier writing assignments or occasional in-class writing and a suspect work, we can ask the student to explain how their skills have developed over the term.

While the cues alerting instructors to plagiarism remain rather consistent, the emergence of the internet and related file sharing programs have vastly expanded and eased access to materials for students who wish to be dishonest. Instructors must familiarize themselves with internet search engines, such as Google, Yahoo, and Alta Vista, which allow users to search among billions of web pages—posted by individual internet users, newspapers, publishers of academic books and journals, and by chat groups or weblogs around the world—for unique phrases and other idiosyncratic expressions or ideas. One of the quickest ways to check for plagiarism is to search the internet either for a brief, relatively unusual phrase from the paper, or by combining a series of keywords and subject terms used throughout the paper. We may also encourage our departments to purchase access to online plagiarism identification products, such as turnitin.com, which may be packaged with the *Prentice Hall Reference Guide*. If instructors have their students turn in writing assignments both on paper and computer disk, these products allow them to download suspect papers to the site for detection.

Of course, we move toward the best solution for plagiarism when we help students understand the stakes of academic dishonesty, not only in terms of the potential harm to their grades, scholarships, or standing in the department or institution, but also for the academic enterprise at large. We should start a discussion about incorporation of source material on an affirmative note, by explaining the ways that research materials, when conventionally incorporated and attributed, enhance a writer's credibility and allow her entry into a given academic conversation. Additionally, we must spend significant time in class, especially as students begin working with outside sources for research projects, to define and clarify appropriate citation and bibliographic methods for our writing assignments. Provide students with references for identifying material that requires documentation and for ways to avoid plagiarism, as in Chapter 55 of the *Prentice Hall Reference Guide*. We should also make every effort to carefully distinguish between intentional intellectual dishonesty and unintentional plagiarism, which is often the result of confusion about the rules of quotation and attribution. Finally, if we develop writing assignments that encourage students to pursue their own interests in unique and original ways, they will be more invested in the course and less inclined to look for short cuts on the internet, in fraternity files, or elsewhere.

SUGGESTED READING

Addison, Joanne, and Rick Van De Weghe. "Portfolio-based Assessment and Professional Development." *English Education* 32.1 (Oct. 1999): 16-33.

Anderson, Larry, et al. "Reader-Response Theory and Instructor's Holistic Evaluating in and out of Their Fields." *Teaching English in the Two Year College* 21.1 (Feb. 1994): 53-62.

Baker, N.W. "The Effect of Portfolio-Based Instruction on Composition Students' Final Examination Scores, Course Grades, and Attitudes toward Writing." *Research in the Teaching of English* 27 (May 1993): 155-74.

Belanoff, Pat, and Marcia Dickson, eds. *Portfolios: Process and Product.* Portsmouth, NH: Boynton/Cook, 1991.

Bloom, Lynn Z. "Why I (Used to) Hate to Give Grades." *College Composition and Communication* 48 (Oct. 1997): 360-71.

Broad, Bob. "Pulling Your Hair Out: Crises of Standardization in Communal Writing Assessment." *Research in the Teaching of English* 35.2 (Nov. 2000): 213-60.

Bullock, Richard. "Spreading the Word ... and Possibly Regretting It: Current Writing about Portfolios." *Journal of Teaching Writing* 12. 1 (1993): 105-13.

Caulk, Nat. "Comparing Teacher and Student Responses to Written Work." *TESOL Quarterly* 28 (Spring 1994): 181-88.

Chandler, Jean. "Positive Control." *College Composition and Communication* 48 (May 1997): 273-74.

Christensen, N.E "Avoidance Pedagogy in Freshman English." *Teaching English in the Two Year College* 18 (May 1991): 133-36.

Christian, Barbara. "Freshman Composition Portfolios in a Small College." *Teaching English in the Two Year College* 20. 4 (Dec. 1993): 289-97.

Connors, Robert, and Andrea A. Lunsford. "Teachers' Rhetorical Comments on Student Papers." *College Composition and Communication* 44. 2 (May 1993): 200-23.

Duke, C. R., and R. R. Sanchez, "Giving Students Control over Writing Assessment." *English Journal* 83 (April 1994): 47-53.

Elbow, Peter. "Ranking, Evaluation, and Liking: Sorting Out Three Forms of Judgment." *College English* 55.2 (Feb. 1993): 187-206.

Haswell, Richard, and Susan Wyche Smith. "Adventuring into Writing Assessment." *College Composition and Communication* 45. 2 (May 1994): 220-36.

Helton, Edwina L., and Jeff Sommers. "Repositioning Revision: A Rhetorical Approach to Grading." *Teaching English in the Two Year College* 28.2 (Dec. 2000): 157-64.

Hillenbrand, Lisa. "Assessment of ESL Students in Mainstream College Composition." *Teaching English in the Two Year College* 21.2 (May 1994): 125-29.

Hodges, Elizabeth. "The Unheard Voices of Our Responses to Students' Writing." *Journal of Teaching Writing* 21.2 (1992): 203-18.

Jones, Brett D. "Computer-Rated Essays in the English Composition Classroom." *Journal of Educational Computing Research* 20,2 (1999) 169-87.

Knudson, Ruth E. "College Students' Writing: An Assessment of Competence." *The Journal of Educational Research* 92.1 (Sept./Oct. 1998): 13-19.

Metzger, Elizabeth, and Lizbeth Bryant. "Portfolio Assessment: Pedagogy, Power, and the Student." *Teaching English in the Two Year College* 20.4 (Dec. 4 1993): 279-88.

Norton, L. S. "Essay Writing: What Really Counts?" *Higher Education* 20 (Dec. 1990): 411-42.

O'Neill, Peggy. "From the Writing Process to the Responding Sequence: Incorporating Self-Assessment and Reflection in the Classroom." *Teaching English in the Two Year College* 26.1 (Sept. 1998): 61-70.

Peckham, Irvin. "Beyond Grades." *Composition Studies Freshman English News* 21.2 (Fall 1993): 16-31.

Purves, Alan C. "Reflections on Research and Assessment in Written Composition." *Research in the Teaching of English* 26.1 (Feb. 1992): 108-22.

Reeves, Thomas C. "Alternative Assessment Approaches for Online Learning Environments in Higher Education." *Journal of Educational Computing Research* 23.1 (2000): 101-11.

Roemer, Marjorie, Lucille M. Schultz, and Russell K. Durst. "Portfolios and the Process of Change." *College Composition and Communication* 42 (1991): 455-69.

Slevin, James F. "Engaging Intellectual Work: The Faculty's Role in Assessment." *College English* 63.3 (Jan. 2001): 288-305.

Smith, Mark Edward. "Using Markings to Respond to Writing." *English Journal.* 86 (Feb. 1997): 79-80.

Smith, Summer. "The Genre of the End Comment: Conventions in Teacher Responses to Student Writing." *College Composition and Communication* 48 (May 1997): 249-68.

Speck, Bruce W. "Grading Students' Classroom Writing: Issues and Strategies." *ASHE ERIC Higher Education Reports* 27.3 (2000): 1-98.

Sperling, Melanie. "Constructing the Perspective of Teacher-as-Grader: A Framework for Studying Response to Student Writing."

Sweeney, Marilyn Ruth. "Relating Revision Skills to Teacher Commentary." *Teaching English in the Two Year College* 27.2 (Dec. 1999): 213-18.

White, E.M. "Language and Reality in Writing Assessment." *College Composition and Communication* 41 (May 1990): 187-200.

——. "The Opening of the Modern Era of Writing Assessment." *College English* 63.3 (Jan. 2001): 306-20.

Valentino, Marilyn J. "Responding When a Life Depends on It: What to Write in the Margins When Students Self-Disclose." *Teaching English in the Two Year College* 23 (Dec. 1996): 274-83.

CHAPTER 8
Assignments and Activities for Introductory Writing

As we prepare for each term, we need to have considered the skills we want to teach students and to have planned in advance a set of writing assignments and class activities that will allow us to teach those skills most effectively. For many of us, goals for introductory writing courses will be articulated in department-wide outcomes statements, but we will typically have a significant amount of flexibility and independence in determining the assignments and procedures that will allow us to best meet those goals. In programs that require students to take a two-course composition sequence, introductory writing instructors should coordinate their assignments and outcomes with research writing instructors to help students transition as smoothly as possible from one course to the next. Whether formally or informally, we should plan to meet regularly with writing program administrators and other colleagues, either in small groups or across the department, and share our expectations, challenges, and ideas for assignments. Like our students, we benefit from meeting with peers, instructors who share many of our experiences and can be great resources for providing new assignments, course texts, and troubleshooting strategies for activities that are not working as we had anticipated.

The skills we expect students to have when leaving the introductory composition courses will include:

> process-oriented writing
> topic selection and focus
> genre-appropriate organization and development
> appropriate tone, voice, and formality
> critical peer and self evaluation
> consideration of audience
> research methods and source evaluation
> method(s) of citation/documentation
> conventional mechanics

We should keep these goals in mind as we select assignments for the term and plan to introduce and reinforce critical reading and writing skills with relevant activities. Chapter 3 in this supplement covers one important part of the planning process, for careful syllabus writing helps us to form realistic expectations for what we can cover as we envision the term broken up into days, weeks, or units, and to communicate those plans effectively to our students. Once we have chosen a set of assignments, we should continue to plan the ways we will use the time devoted to each project, developing planning and peer review activities, and considering the supplementary texts we will use to generate ideas or model the genre. As we begin each major assignment, we should incorporate prewriting activities that will help students see the writing project emerge as a set of interrelated strategies and that reinforce the importance of envisioning the purpose and audience of the paper. This chapter outlines some of the more common writing projects we may consider assigning in our college composition courses, suggests prewriting projects, and provides some strategies for effective planning.

■ ORGANIZING BY THEME AND BY GENRE

Some teachers will organize their courses around a single theme or a set of closely related themes. They consider subjects familiar to their students, choose one in which students are likely to be interested, and organize a series of writing assignments that address the theme through different genres and present discussions of the theme for different audiences and purposes.

In a theme-oriented course, consider focusing on the issue of higher education. Students may come to college taking their experiences and expectations for granted, but we can introduce them not only to the history of higher education, but also to a variety of contemporary debates concerning the purpose and goals of higher education. By examining works by political pundits, parents of college students, employers, and academics, students will see the ways in which discussions are shaped within a particular group, as well as the assumed audiences of and purposes pursued by the groups. We can invite them to participate in these discussions through writing assignments that might include a position paper, a problem/solution essay, a strong reading/response paper, and an exploratory research project. As students become informed participants in discussions about their own experiences, we encourage them to take an active role in shaping their own years in college and to think critically about their preconceived notions and expectations about the purpose of education.

We can also organize the course by rhetorical type, moving students through the genres and argumentative styles that they will continue to practice and develop throughout their college careers. Common shorter assignments in introductory writing courses include definition, explanation of a concept, description of a place, comparison/contrast, and process; major writing assignments include autobiography/significant event, profile, problem/solution, summary/rhetorical analysis, and exploratory research essays. If we focus on clearly explaining these genres and the rhetorical strategies that contribute to successful papers, and yet leave paper topics open to each student's discretion, we challenge students to do serious thinking about appropriate topics to pursue, and at the same time we present them with significant opportunities to explore their own interests. Certainly, instructors should model appropriate topics with carefully chosen readings, and they should assist students in pursuing and shaping well-conceived topic choices; however, if we leave topic choices as open as possible, we begin to prepare students for the increasingly self-directed work they will do as they get further into their majors and as they move from college into professions or graduate study.

Of course, the two methods of organization are not mutually exclusive. A writing class organized around the theme of higher education may include a personal narrative assignment which asks students to reflect on events that led them to college, or on the reasons why they plan to pursue their majors, or to speculate on the ways in which their college experiences will change them. These reflective essays will be strengthened by readings which provide a history of higher education in the United States, or which compare approaches to higher education between different institutional models or between the United States and other nations. As informed participants in discussions and debates around education, students will be better equipped to think critically about their personal goals and expectations.

Whether we choose the theme or genre approach to organize our courses, we must consider the order in which to present writing assignments to best encourage student development and meet our goals for the course. Assignments early in the term should encourage students to see their audience and the purpose of their writing in concrete terms, so we may ask them to write a brief meditation on the problematic notion of higher education that appeals to their fellow students, or a problem/solution paper that focuses on a local campus or community issue. As students become comfortable with local audiences, we should begin working toward more abstract audiences, such as the larger academic community in an exploratory research project. Although their sophistication as writers will grow with increasingly challenging assignments, if we also have students work on occasional low stakes writing, such as regular journal writing, periodically responding to current events, or creating a web log, students will be able to track their own development and have the opportunity to balance formal writing projects and more personal exchanges with the instructor and other students. In the remainder of this chapter, I describe some major projects that teachers generally assign in their introductory writing courses, along with shorter assignments that work in concert with major projects.

■ SIGNIFICANT EVENT PAPER

Many instructors will make a personal narrative the first assignment in their college writing courses, because students are able to draw on their own experiences and emotions for the subject matter of the paper. Although some students may be challenged by the process of selecting an event on which to focus their paper, they will typically find autobiographical writing a more familiar genre than many of the others we expect them to practice during the term. As we help students explore possible topic choices, we should encourage them to consider types of events that are not only memorable, but are also likely to lead them to sustained reflection on the impact of the events on their lives. Such events might be a moment of learning or discovery, a traumatic event, a moment of decision, an uncharacteristic action, overcoming a challenge, and so on.

In preparing students for the significant event paper, we must be sure to caution them away from certain topics as well. Each student should choose an event that he or she will be able to share with the instructor and with other students in the class. Because they may be tempted to choose a recent event, such as their first day at college, moving into student housing, or the like, we should continue to emphasize the necessity of maintaining critical distance from the event so that the writer can provide significant reflection on the its impact from a present, or sufficiently later, perspective.

The significant event paper is a good assignment to begin developing process-driven writing strategies that we can reinforce throughout the term. After we introduce the genre and purpose of the writing project, and discuss one or more examples of effective autobiographical writing, we can have students consider two or three possible events that they can use to complete the following sentence: "Until I experienced _____, I never understood _____." The compressed form of this invention exercise leads students to choose a relatively isolated event that will be manageable as a paper topic. Sharing their versions of the sentence with the class or in small groups, students will get feedback and encouragement toward an event about which an audience is interested in knowing more.

At an early stage in the exploration and planning of the project, we can have students make some preliminary decisions about the characters, sensory descriptions, and dialogue they will include in the story and about the organization of the paper, such as the order of events, the amount of background information needed, and the explanation of significance. Using notes, and perhaps drafts of introductory paragraphs, students break into pairs or groups of three and tell each other their stories orally. Oral story-telling is a very effective prewriting step in the significant event paper, because authors receive immediate feedback, usually in the form of questions ("What happened next?" "Why did you do that?" "Where did the dog come from?") that help them see gaps in their narration and anticipate the needs and interests of an audience. Just as important, authors are motivated at these early stages of the process by a receptive, encouraging audience to continue developing their papers and make them as strong as possible.

In addition to audience and purpose, the significant event paper provides instructors with opportunities to discuss other features of effective writing, including the incorporation of details, organization, and paragraph development. As students begin to draft their papers, and as peer feedback directs them toward focusing on specific moments, characters, or reactions surrounding the event, we should encourage them to incorporate a variety of details to enliven their stories. Through model texts or student examples, students will see the ways specific details, simile and metaphor, sensory descriptions, dialogue, setting, and so on, direct the reader toward a dominant impression that leads, either implicitly or explicitly, to the event's significance.

Using examples of student writing or other course texts we can ask students to consider the effects of various temporal organization patterns: how might a story be framed by a single moment, beginning at the chronological end, flashing back and working through earlier moments, and then returning to the opening scene to explain the impact of the event? What if the story starts at the chronological middle, opening with the story's climax, flashing back, and then flashing forward toward illustrating the growth of or change in the author? We can use planning strategies from Chapter 2 in the *Prentice Hall Reference Guide* and map out organizational patterns on the board or on overhead slides to help students visualize structures that they might apply to their own papers.

As students are working with various chronological structures, we should also work on paragraph development and transition strategies. Once authors have an idea of the organizational pattern they plan to use, they can begin to break the event into logical units which will become the paper's paragraphs. With these units in place, authors then begin to write topic sentences and transitions that will effectively link the paragraphs together. If we have students read Chapter 15 in the *Prentice Hall Reference Guide*, they will be able to make informed decisions about the purposes of each paragraph and the transition phrases and words they can use to cue readers appropriately.

The significant event assignment not only provides students with a familiar point of entry into the course, it is also an important first step in encouraging beginning college writers to consider every topic—including the apparently self-evident material from their own lives—in terms of academic argument. We set the tone for the remainder of the term, and for the students' college careers, by modeling ways of integrating elements of argument into each writing project.

■ PROBLEM/SOLUTION PAPER

The problem solution paper is another effective writing project for early in the term. As with the significant event project, the genre allows us to cover many of the same concepts of planning, prewriting, organization, and paragraph development, but through a more explicitly argumentative form of appeal. We can help students keep their projects manageable and continue to envision specific audiences for their work if we have them choose locally focused topics—for instance, issues on campus, in the local community, or in their home towns. This focus dissuades students from choosing unmanageable or inappropriately broad topics that cannot be sufficiently covered in a relatively brief writing assignment (abortion, the death penalty, gun control, and the like); instead, it encourages them to draw on their personal experience and consider issues with which they already have some familiarity, such as overcrowding in public schools, interaction with roommates in student housing, local transportation issues, and so on.

As with the personal narrative, we can use the problem/solution genre to encourage students to test multiple organizational patterns and to consider the effects their decisions will have on a variety of audiences. When students begin planning and drafting their papers, we can select a topic at random or ask a student to volunteer a topic (for instance, students at non-residential institutions will often want to talk about parking cost and availability), and have the class map possible arguments through open and closed forms. We can ask them to describe the effect of a thesis-driven organizational pattern on a reader who may be hostile to the author's choice of solution; how would a thesis-seeking pattern draw a hostile reader into the paper and lead her gradually toward accepting the logic of the author's conclusion? What are the effects on the audience of a paper that postpones evaluation of possible solutions until later in the argument versus one that opens by privileging one solution?

We can also follow an autobiographical narrative writing project with the problem/solution paper, because it smoothly draws students from personal reflection alone to the need to consider and address multiple perspectives and arguments. As we describe the basic features of the genre, we should require students to explore two or three possible solutions which they must evaluate in order to choose the solution they plan to support in their conclusion. They will have to consider questions of feasibility, cost, long-term versus short-term benefits, and so on, and then make conscious, explicit decisions about their own reasons for supporting one solution over the others they have introduced. As writers select evaluative criteria, they will have to defend their choices, acknowledge the relative validity of other positions and to anticipate and defend against potential counterarguments.

As students begin to describe their problems and provide background, we can incorporate some exercises that emphasize the relationship between description and narration. We can help students locate cues for exploring perspectives other than their own by demonstrating ways in which writers take relatively inert information about the world or their experiences and invest the information with significance in order to pursue a particular thesis. One effective exercise is to have students make a list of features about the classroom (colors, shapes, smells, and lighting, for instance) and consider how the same piece of data may be cast to express contrary values. For example, students may agree that the walls are white, but we can use that information to express both positive ("the fresh, clean white walls") and negative ("the dull, stark white walls") evaluations. Students in a crowded classroom may at first believe that "cramped and stuffy" is a self-evident, irrefutable evaluation, but we can ask them whether it couldn't also be "intimate and personal" depending on the viewer's angle of vision.

Students can then work in pairs or small groups and compare descriptions of common places and experiences, such as a dorm room, a fast food meal, or a sporting event, and get practice in addressing various perspectives and values as they develop the arguments in problem/solution papers. We might either require or encourage them to include a paragraph in their papers that outlines the criteria they have used to evaluate multiple possible solutions in order to arrive at the one they plan to support. This element of the writing project can be a useful opening to a discussion of rhetorical appeals and teaching students to make informed choices about the ones they plan to use in expressing their support for a solution. Consider incorporating sections of Chapter 4 in the *Prentice Hall Reference Guide* with a discussion of appeals and audience consideration.

■ STRONG RESPONSE PAPER

The strong response paper is an effective assignment, either as a genre unto itself in which students learn strategies of close reading, summary, and response, or in preparation for research writing. Typically, the first part of the strong response paper is a summary of a relatively complex chapter or article-length piece of writing. The summary requires students to have a clear understanding of the language, content, and meaning of the target text, and to select and compress relevant information into a brief form. Students must be able to accurately summarize what they have read before moving to the second part of the strong response: entering into an informed, critical conversation with the author and the text's argument or position. They need to distinguish between the two skills and to incorporate appropriate transitions and other cues that mark their movement from one rhetorical form to another. In both parts of the strong response, students will begin to practice quotation and paraphrase skills, learn how to use attributive tags, and apply a documentation style to bibliographic information.

As we teach strong response writing, we have opportunities to introduce the various rhetorical skills that work together to form an effective paper and to assign brief writing assignments covering those skills. Accurate definitions of topics and key words are necessary not only to demonstrating the writer's working knowledge of the piece in the summary portion of the essay, but also to providing potential points of contention in the strong response. Especially when students are required to work with scholarly, professional, or technical writing, they will certainly encounter unfamiliar words which they must define and place in appropriate contexts to facilitate their own and their reader's entry into the work's subject matter and argument. Students quickly realize that common dictionaries either offer meanings for specialized terms that are too broad, or do not include entries for such terms at all. In order to help them define and explain key words from their writing samples, we should introduce students to specialized, discipline-specific dictionaries and encyclopedias; we should also plan to bring to class sample reference materials, such as the *OED* or specialized medical, legal, or linguistics dictionaries, and model their uses. Students can write a paragraph-length definition of a key word, which might include one or more definitions from discipline-specific reference works, an explanation of the difference between specialized use and the common dictionary definition, comparison and contrast with similar and dissimilar terms, and the student's personal definition of the word.

A related exercise is to have students write a shorter piece explaining important concepts in their texts. Although writers will use the skills of definition to get started—indeed, definitions are integral parts of the explanation—they will also have to include more contextual information and estimate the prior knowledge of their audience as they consider the examples that will bring the concept to life. Typically, they must work harder with the concept than with the definition to avoid slipping into an argumentative tone, and to remain relatively neutral and informative. Whether or not we choose to make concept explanation a separate writing project, we should make it a required component of the strong response paper. Consider having students read sections in Chapter 3 of the *Prentice Hall Reference Guide*, which discuss some patterns of effective organization for explaining concepts.

Depending on our goals or the position of the strong response writing assignment in relation to other course projects, we can direct students toward selecting works in specific genres or works which appeal to specific audience groups on which to base their essays. For instance, if we assign the paper as a prelude to an exploratory paper that works with multiple sources, we can encourage students to choose a piece of academic writing that addresses the topic or question they plan to pursue.

■ RESEARCH PROPOSAL/ANNOTATED BIBLIOGRAPHY

The proposal paper can work as a test drive of research writing, because it is a brief assignment that introduces students to many of the tasks of research retrieval and organization without taking the significant class time necessary to produce a full blown research paper. Because these papers are, typically, no longer than two pages, students must be able to manage a number of tasks effectively: they will likely be asked to propose a research question, present a brief summary of their current thinking on the subject, summarize their preliminary research, and anticipate the shape of their argument.

Most of our students have had some experience with closed form, thesis-driven research writing in previous courses. In college writing courses, however, we should familiarize them with thesis-seeking models that pursue more tentative research questions and demand far more engagement from both author and audience. Chapter 51 of the *Prentice Hall Reference Guide* outlines some approaches for using preliminary research effectively to transform a broad topic into a research question. If we want our students to use, or at least consider, both primary and secondary research methods, they will also summarize their plans to use interviews and surveys in concert with textual sources in the proposal.

We might also consider separating the narrative and bibliographic components of the proposal by requiring students to write annotated bibliographies. Especially if we wish to teach the strategies of strong response writing without assigning a separate paper, we can teach the annotated bibliography as a set of miniature strong responses in which students provide a brief summary and brief evaluation of each source in their working bibliography. In open topic assignments, we want to ensure that students choose sources that are interrelated, so we may also have students provide an indication of each source's relevance to the other sources included in the proposal. Chapter 53 of the *Prentice Hall Reference Guide* provides good strategies for selecting and organizing relevant information from sources. As with the strong response writing assignment, instructors have the opportunity to introduce or revisit particular rhetorical skills, such as definition and classification, as students develop their projects and compose their proposals.

We will get the best results from our students if we give them enough time to explore the library and its resources, to locate and read appropriate sources, and to condense the material into the requirements of the genre. As students are preparing their proposals, instructors should consider dedicating a week of class meetings for independent research. The open topic of the assignment raises unique challenges for each student, so during this research week we should either schedule a round of formal conferences or at least offer extended office hours during class times for students to describe their projects and ask us questions relevant to their question or field of research. We can also use these conference times to help students select manageable sources which either match or do not lie too far afield of their abilities. For instance, a student researching the stakes of blood doping among professional athletes may be discouraged by the specialized language of a biochemist's analysis of a particular chemical's effects on blood composition, but may explore other related disciplines or fields to find a number of biochemical reports more comprehensibly summarized by sports medicine specialists, or for general practitioners.

Especially for courses in which either the range of genres we must cover does not allow enough time for students to produce a research paper, or in courses on accelerated class schedules, the research proposal is a great writing assignment to facilitate students' movement from introductory composition to companion research writing courses.

■ EXPLORATORY RESEARCH PAPER

Either in concert with strong response papers and proposal writing, or as a separate writing assignment, we should consider introducing our students to research writing. The exploratory research paper is an especially good place to begin, because it builds on many of the genres we teach in introductory composition and supplements them with a research component. As a first-person narrative of the research process, students will use familiar strategies of autobiographical writing to structure their papers. Additionally, because they are asked to explore a multifaceted concept or debate—one within an academic field or around a current event, for instance—students will use strategies of incorporating and evaluating multiple perspectives learned from the problem/solution writing assignment. Finally, summary and response strategies learned in the rhetorical analysis project provide students with patterns for introducing, describing, and developing each source used in the paper.

Until recently, comprehensive access to scholarship and other research materials was limited to the largest universities with the financial and physical plant resources to purchase and house millions of volumes. Instructors at community colleges, comprehensive four-year institutions, and small universities were quite hampered in their abilities to teach academic research methods and assign scholarly research projects to their students. As research libraries digitize their catalogs, and in some cases their holdings, and as fax and internet technologies become more widespread on campuses and among students, college writing teachers at all institutional levels should take advantage of their increased access to materials, and should consider introducing students to academic research methods as they teach exploratory writing.

With the increased affordable access to telecommunication and internet technologies, schools that formerly could not aspire to having research libraries are now able to purchase access to academic databases that provide scholarly materials spanning the humanities and social sciences, the fine arts, physical and applied sciences, law, and medicine. At institutions that offer limited local holdings, instructors should familiarize themselves with and introduce students to online delivery services and strategies for locating materials, to performing both general and specific searches, and in methods of devising and permuting search terms. As we scan the various search engines that provide access to scholarship, we will see that some cast a very broad net in their searches. For instance, the Academic Search Premier database is capable of locating general and scholarly/peer reviewed materials, and is not discipline-specific. Students who are uncertain of the academic field they wish to explore, or are unsure of the specific field that relates to their topic, will benefit from starting their research with Academic Search Premier, then refining and repeating their searches in appropriate discipline-specific databases.

For example, if a student is interested in issues around AIDS—a topic which is explored through the academic lenses of philosophy, sociology, economics, law, biotechnology, and, of course medicine—but is unsure of the ways she wants to direct research toward a particular field, she can start her search in Academic Search Premier. After scanning article titles and abstracts, and assessing her own abilities to access the specialized language of various disciplines, she may choose to explore the topic through databases that offer scholarly materials in one area of academic inquiry. She may then choose to focus her research in medicine, using the MEDLINE database, or in philosophy, using Project Muse, or in law, using Legal Collection, each of which offers her access to the full texts of scholarly, peer reviewed materials.

Many students will already be familiar with internet search engines, such as Google and Yahoo, when they arrive in our classes, so developing and permuting search terms will be second nature for them. Despite their similar appearance though, we must be sure to explain the distinctions between general internet searches and those searches that are focused on locating sufficiently academic sources. We should describe features commonly found in scholarly work and provide examples for the class; as students work independently on their projects we can provide them with a checklist of features that students can use to evaluate source material, such as the work's publisher, whether the piece uses specialized language, whether it includes notes and bibliography, and whether the work is peer reviewed. Because many of the academic databases are either exclusively scholarly or allow users to limit their searches to scholarly materials, we should encourage students to conduct research in databases that will return the most appropriate results for their topic and the scope and genre of the writing assignment.

As students begin to read and collect research material, we will also have to explain the various formatting styles used by online delivery services. Depending on the search engine and the source, an article may appear either as a PDF file or as an HTML file. In the former case, a facsimile of the article will be displayed as it appeared in print, which allows students to easily cite material and write bibliographic entries. When a student prints PDF files from her home or campus computer, she has a copy that is essentially identical to the article's original print format. In some cases, HTML formatted articles will indicate page breaks in the print format to allow readers to "see" the article as it originally appeared, as in the example below, from the *Bulletin of the History of Medicine*:

> The early history of the Kaposi's Sarcoma Clinic, located in one of the three cities in the United States in which the AIDS epidemic was first manifest, presents an apt subject for examining a local instance of the complex interplay of forces, both social and biological, that shapes disease recognition and definition, the organization of an initial biomedical response, and some of the

factors influencing these simultaneous processes.[2] This paper focuses on one group of health professionals in one city in the first year after the recognition of a cluster of malignancy and rare infections that later was perceived as a syndrome associated with cellular immune deficiency. Part of a larger study of the biomedical and nursing response to AIDS in San Francisco in the epidemic's first three years,[3] it is necessarily a limited and local examination, which considers only some elements of the intricate interactions involved in constructing an explanatory framework for and medical response to a new disease.[4]

Few if any previous AIDS histories have provided a detailed account of medical organization and the process at the local level of constructing a new disease category.[5] Books by Randy Shilts and Carol Pogash, which [**End Page 652**] include substantial descriptions of aspects of San Francisco's medical response, are journalists' accounts intended for a general audience, not serious historical analyses.[6] The subject of this paper is a clinic that predates AIDS units elsewhere and that has been overlooked in previous historical accounts, except for the book by Shilts.[7]

In other cases, however, an article may be HTML-formatted without indications of page breaks. In these cases, we must help students learn appropriate citation and bibliographic methods for documenting online sources. Additionally, because many online delivery services use idiosyncratic bibliographic conventions, we must teach students to avoid simply copying and pasting information from electronic search engines, and instead, to organize source information according to the bibliographic conventions we are using in class. For example, the Project Muse search engine cites the above article thus:

Hughes, Sally Smith
The Kaposi's Sarcoma Clinic at the University of California, San Francisco: An Early Response to the AIDS Epidemic
Bulletin of the History of Medicine-Volume 71, Number 4, Winter 1997, pp. 651-688-Article.

If we are teaching MLA conventions, students must be able to locate necessary information, exclude unnecessary parts, and organize the information according to the MLA style guide, thus:

Hughes, Sally Smith. "The Kaposi's Sarcoma Clinic at the University of California, San Francisco: An Early Response to the AIDS Epidemic." *Bulletin of the History of Medicine* 71.4 (1997): 651-688.

Many online academic search engines offer comprehensive access to bibliographic material, the subject areas of articles, and article abstracts, but only limited access to complete texts. We should encourage students to use hard copy delivery resources in addition to electronic systems. Increased digitization of research libraries has facilitated quick, free or low-cost access to materials across regions and throughout the country. Most college libraries have interlibrary loan and article delivery services that will locate and provide books and hard copies of articles if they are not available electronically. Instructors must be prepared to help students successfully use the various systems offered by their institutions. Students should be able to locate and fill out forms with the information necessary to locate the text, and be aware of delivery times and length of the loan so that they can effectively budget their research time.

While they do not share the challenges of limited resources faced by instructors at smaller schools, instructors at research universities will have to familiarize themselves with the variety of resources available to them and be prepared to help their students negotiate their ways through multiple library facilities and catalog, storage, and retrieval methods that may be unique to each library or academic discipline on campus.

Clearly, new delivery systems for research materials offer students vastly expanded opportunities to explore the ways in which their interests are examined by scholars, and to pursue their own scholarly interests. However, these systems, especially internet-based search engines, also present new challenges to instructors, who must clarify the distinctions between using the internet to access sufficiently scholarly work, and simply conducting internet research. The exploratory essay not only gives the students a chance to get a taste of the kinds of scholarly work they will be required to do throughout their college careers, but also provides instructors with an especially important opportunity to teach students critical skills of source evaluation and material management which will help them succeed in later research projects.

Whatever method of organization we use for our writing classes, we should reflect regularly on our approaches and assignments, noting which are useful and best promote student development and which we should reconsider or reconfigure to make our courses as effective as possible. We should continually be on the lookout for course texts that address contemporary issues and events, and make efforts to know our students and current student culture so that we can make the writing process and writing assignments as relevant as possible to students. The more invested student writers are in their projects and topics, the better we will sustain their interest as they work toward meeting our goals.

Finally, we should continue to stress the importance of process-oriented writing by encouraging students to revise their major writing projects throughout the term. Consider giving students opportunities to revise papers for improved grades; they will be more likely to tackle revisions if they see the potential for material improvement in their course grade as a result of conscientious attention to the weak points in their writing. Regardless of the way we set up the terms and requirements of revision, we should require students to make global changes to their papers, addressing not only the mechanical errors we have pointed out in our comments, but also larger structural issues, conventions of genre, or better meeting requirements of purpose and audience. We should also require students to produce a reflective statement to be used as a cover for the revision, in which they articulate the changes they have made, describe strategies they have used to overcome challenges they faced in earlier drafts, and how they feel they have improved by revisiting the assignment. When used effectively, the revision process will tie together every component of the college writing course: students have to make informed choices about which papers they can most effectively revisit; they will see their writing situated in a recursive process that demands critical thinking, careful review of the writing assignments, and adequate peer evaluation; their cover statement will help them reflect on the value of revision in their writing.

SUGGESTED READING

Bizzell, Patricia. "Contact Zones and English Studies." *College English* 56. 2. (Feb. 1994): 163-69.

Berzenyi, Christyne A. "How to Conduct a Course-Based Computer Chat Room: Enabling a Space for Active Learning." *Teaching English in the Two Year College* 28.2 (Dec. 2000): 165-74.

Black, Rhonda S., Thomas W. Sileo, and Mary Anne Prater. "Learning Journals, Self-Reflection, and University Students' Changing Perceptions." *Action in Teacher Education* 21.4 (Winter 2000): 71-89.

Capossela, T.L. "Students as Sociolinguists: Getting Real Research from Freshmen Writers." *College Composition and Communication* 42 (Feb. 1991): 75-79.

Fick, V.G. "A History-Based Research Paper Course." *Teaching English in the Two-Year College* 17 (Feb. 1990): 34-35.

Friedman, Eric D., Lisa Haefele, and K.M. Keating. "An Electronic Discussion List in an Undergraduate Writing Course." *Computers and Education* 24 (Apr. 1995): 191-201.

Gillis, Candida. "Writing Partners: Expanding the Audiences for Student Writing." *English Journal* 83.3 (March 1994): 64-67.

Gordon, Heather G. "Using a Reading Experience Journal." *Teaching English in the Two Year College* 28.1 (Sept. 2000): 41-43.

Hourigan, M.M. "Poststructural Theory and Writing Assessment: 'Heady, Esoteric Theory' Revisited." *Teaching English in the Two-Year College* 18 (Oct. 1991): 191-95.

Lent, Robin. "'I Can Relate to That ...': Reading and Responding in the Writing Classroom." *College Composition and Communication* 44.2 (May 1993): 232-40.

Moxley, Joseph M. "Reinventing the Wheel or Teaching the Basics: College Writers' Knowledge of Argumentation." *Composition Studies Freshman English News* 21.2 (Fall 1993): 3-15.

Pullman, George L. "Rhetoric and Hermeneutics: Composition, Invention, and Literature." *Journal of Advanced Composition* 14 no. 2 (Fall 1994): 389-412.

Rankin, Walter. "The Cyberjournal: Developing Writing, Researching, and Editing Skills Through E-mail and World Wide Web." *Educational Technology* 37 (July/Aug 1997): 29-31.

Raymond, R.C. "Personal and Public Voices: Bridging the Gap from Composition to Comp 102." *Teaching English in the Two Year College* 17 (Dec. 1990): 273-82.

Roemer, M.G., et al. "Portfolios and the Process of Change." *College Composition and Communication* 42 (Dec. 1991): 455-69.

Sipe, Rebecca Bowers. "Virtually Being There: Creating Authentic Experiences Through Interactive Exchanges." *English Journal* 90.2 (Nov. 2000): 104-11.

Spivey, N.N. "The Shaping of Meaning: Options in Writing the Comparison." *Research in the Teaching of English* 25 (Dec. 1991): 390-418.

Sullivan, Patrick. "Using the Internet to Teach Composition." *Teaching English in the Two Year College* 28.1 (Sept. 2000): 21-31.

Swartzendruber-Putnam, Dawn. "Written Reflection: Creating Better Thinkers, Better Writers." *English Journal* 90.1 (Sept. 2000): 88-93.

Tucker, Lois P. "Liberating Students Through Reader-Response Pedagogy in the Introductory Literature Course." *Teaching English in the Two Year College* 28.2 (Dec. 2000): 199-206.

Wallace, D.L., and J.R. Hayes. "Redefining Revision for Freshmen." *Research in the Teaching of English* 25 (Feb. 1991): 54-66.

Whitaker, Elaine E., and Elaine N. Hill. "Virtual Voices in 'Letters Across Cultures.'" *Computers and Composition* 15.3 (1998): 331-46.

Further Suggestions for Reading

No matter how hectic the pace in our classes, we must—as profession-als—try to keep up with the scholarship in our field. In the last twenty years much useful information about the theory of teaching composition has appeared, information that can enrich our teaching significantly if we can eke out the time to delve into the theoretical underpinnings of what we do. Recent scholarship has also made available a wealth of practical and theoretical books and articles of a more general nature that those appended to chapters.

Adams, P. D. "Basic Writing Reconsidered." *Journal of Basic Writing* 12 (Spring 1993): 22-36.

Arnold, Jane. "Keeping Language Journals in English Composition." *Teaching English in the Two Year College* 26.1 (Sept. 1998): 71-74.

Carrell, P. L., and L. B. Monroe. "Learning Styles and Composition." *Modern Language Journal* 77 (Summer 1993): 148-62.

Cope, Bill, and Mary Kalantzis, eds. *The Powers of Literacy: A Genre Approach to Teaching Writing.* Pittsburgh: UP of Pittsburgh, 1993.

Branch, Kirk. "From the Margins at the Center: Literacy, Authority, and the Great Divide." *College Composition and Communication* 50.2 (Dec. 1998): 206-31.

Duesterberg, Luann M. "Theorizing Race in the Context of Learning to Teach." *Teachers College Record* 100.4 (Summer 1999): 751-75.

Dwyer, Herbert J., and Howard J. Sullivan. "Student Preferences for Teacher and Computer Composition." *The Journal of Educational Research* 86 (Jan/Feb 1993): 137-41.

Feris, Dana R. "Student Reactions to Teacher Response in Multiple-draft Composition Classrooms." *TESOL Quarterly* 29 (Spring 1995): 33-53.

Fischer, Elizabeth A. "Prescriptions for Curing English Teacher Split Person-ality Disorder." *English Journal* 89.4 (Mar 2000): 40-45.

Fox, Thomas. "Repositioning the Profession: Teaching Writing to African American Students." *Journal of Advanced Composition* 12.2 (Fall 1992): 179-93.

Hawhee, Debra. "Composition History and the Harbrace College Hand-book." *College Composition and Communication* 50.3 (Feb. 1999): 504-23.

Heilker, Paul. "Nothing Personal: Twenty-Five Forays into the Personal in (My) Composition Pedagogy." *Writing Instructor* 12. 2 (Winter 1993): 55-65.

Hindman, Jane E. "Reinventing the University: Finding the Place for Basic Writers." *Journal of Basic Writing* 12.2 (Fall 1993): 55-76.

Johns, A.M. "Written Argumentation for Real Audiences: Suggestions for Teacher Research and Classroom Practice." *TESOL Quarterly* 27 (Spring 1993): 75-90.

Jordan, Henley, and Barry M. Maid. "Tutoring in Cyberspace: Student Impact and College/University Collaboration." *Computers and Composition* 12.2 (1995): 211-18.

Keyser, Marcia W., and Laura R. Lucio. "Adding a Library Instruction Unit to an Established Course." *Research Strategies* 16.3 (1998): 221-29.

Lacina-Gifford, Lorna J., and Neelam Kher-Drulabhji. "Preparing to Teach a Class by Internet." *College Teaching* 44 (Summer 1996): 94-95.

Lindemann, Erika. *A Rhetoric for Writing Teachers*. 3rd ed. New York: Oxford, 1995.

Mirskin, Jerry. "Writing as a Process of Valuing." *College Composition and Communication* 46 (Oct. 1995): 387-410.

Murphy, James J., ed. *A Short History of Writing Instruction from Ancient Greece to Twentieth-Century America*. Davis, CA: Hermagoras, 1990.

Nelson, Jennie. "Reading Classrooms as Text: Exploring Student Writers' Interpretive Practices." *College Composition and Communication* 46 (Oct. 1995): 411-29.

Oblinger, Diana, and Sean C. Rush. *The Future Compatible Campus: Planning, Designing, and Implementing Information Technology in the Academy*. Anker Publishing, 1998.

Radencich, Marguerite C., Kathy Echardt, and Rebecca Rasch. "University Course-Based Practitioner Research: Four Studies on Journal Writing Contextualize the Process." *Research in the Teaching of English* 32 (Feb. 1998): 79-112.

Scott, J. Blake. "The Literacy Narrative as Production Pedagogy in the Composition Classroom." *Teaching English in the Two Year College* 24 (May 1997): 108-17.

Shafer, Gregory. "Composition for the Twenty-First Century." *English Journal* 90.1 (Sept. 2000): 29-33.

Spack, Ruth. "The (in)visibility of the Person(al) in Academe." *College English* 59 (Jan. 1997): 9-31.

Troyka, Lynn Quitman. "The Phenomenon of Impact: The CUNY Writing Assessment Test." *Writing Program Administration* 8 (Fall-Winter 1984): 27-36.

Whitaker, E.E. "A Pedagogy to Address Plagiarism." *College Composition and Communication* 44 (December 1993): 509-14.

Wilson, Smokey. "When Computers Come to English Class." *Teaching English in the Two Year College* 27.4 (May 2000): 387-99.

PART TWO:
Collaborative Writing
by Patricia Kelvin and Scott A. Leonard,
Youngstown State University

■ TEACHING COLLABORATIVE WRITING

This is a manual for practitioners, for the hard-working teacher striving to give students an understanding of rhetoric and the writing process. Whether you have been teaching composition for years and are ready to try something new or you are new to the teaching of writing, we hope this manual can refresh and renew your sense of excitement about teaching. The student comments you will read in this chapter are quoted (with the names changed) directly from the "process logs of memos" that we ask each student to keep for their own, as well as our, evaluation. You will also find some collaborative assignments that have worked in our classrooms. Some of the ideas presented here may work for you in your environment while others will not. But they should be a springboard from which you can dive into your own pool of ideas. While we have mentioned some of the best-known scholars working in the field of collaborative learning and writing throughout our text, we have compiled a more extensive bibliographic essay at the end for those who would like to read further on the subject.

Collaborative writing can be an extremely rewarding experience for both teacher and student. When things work well, students gain confidence in their ability to write and to work with a team. The teacher will feel energized working with a class of active, enthusiastic learners. What could be better than a writing pedagogy that encourages students to discuss every dimension of writing from topic selection to word choice? What more can the writing teacher want than a way to encourage students to view effective writing as a process within their conscious control? Collaboratively written papers, like single-authored texts, go through a series of drafts. But, unlike single-authored texts, collaborative papers will actively integrate concepts of audience, tone, planning and purpose into the writing process because at every step students must explain to one another what they think the paper needs and why.

■ WHY TEACH STUDENTS TO WRITE TOGETHER?

Collaborative Learning is Helpful to Students

The basic premise of what John Trimbur, Kenneth Bruffee and others have called **collaborative learning** is that peer influence is a "powerful educative force" (Bruffee 638). It is the conversation of students working together that disseminates information more surely and erects conceptual scaffolding more efficiently. In the context of the group, the internalized conversation of human thought becomes the externalized authority of the collective. The pedagogy that has developed from these assumptions has transformed both classroom architecture and the teacher's role. Those accustomed to a teacher-directed lecture or discussion classroom might wonder whether organizing students in small groups to discuss course content can lead to anything but idle chat. But those who have assigned small group exercises that give students hands-on practice in generating paper topics, or in appropriately punctuating works-cited entries, or in identifying the cohesive devices that published writers employ, know the power of collaborative learning. Providing students with opportunities to talk and work together in small groups allows them to remember and exchange points of view about what they read for class, to develop concepts more extensively than they could on their own, and for weaker students to learn from their stronger peers. Indeed, collaborative learning is excellent pedagogy because it organizes and focuses the natural human impulse to create knowledge through small-group discussion even as it fosters learning by doing. Those instructors who use response groups in their classes already know the value of collaborative learning. Collaborative writing takes the process even further.

Collaborative Writing is Good Pedagogy

Asking students to write together takes advantage of the substantial benefits derivable from collaborative learning. Student groups of two or more authors working on a single document are able to combine their individual strengths, tackle large and complex projects, share information, challenge each other to think longer and harder about the demands of a writing situation, and model for one another the learnable skills of writing. In groups, students can also divide the work of reading, writing, organizing, and editing.

For almost a decade now, we have observed that writing collaboratively impels students to think about the learning process in ways that individuals writing alone might not. Because writing groups must negotiate everything from meeting times to paper organization to word choice, the individuals within those groups must explain what they think will work for a paper and why—a phenomenon that makes every aspect of text production an occasion for discussion, questioning, and information-sharing. In addition, because students must arrange work time in advance, they tend to procrastinate less and work with a specific sense of what they want or need to accomplish at a given time. Thus, most students, having a limited time to work on a project each week, will begin to see their project as a series of tasks, and pace their work rather than do everything they have time for the night before it is due.

Moreover, our students have often told us that they enjoy the experience of writing and researching together. One student remarked that it felt good having "someone to talk to about [a] project—about how to do it and what to say." The collaborative writing classroom frequently buzzes with energetic conversation, joking, and the excitement of discovering just the right words for a complex idea. But even when all is quiet, or when the conversation is not so jovial, students derive many benefits from the experience. For example, our students frequently report experiencing what cognitive psychologists have called *decentering* effects. As one young woman put it, "working with others in this quarter has really opened my eyes to different perspectives on how to write and on life in general." Other students confirm what many researchers have long suggested: Collaboration is good for students because it allows them to pool their resources. "Jim was our researcher," reported Allison in her process log, "while Kim's editing skills really helped us out at the end."

Collaboration is Typical Work After College

Learning and writing together is more than just good pedagogy; it is the ideal preparation for our students' careers after college. Lunsford and Ede (1990), after surveying seven professional organizations, report that approximately half of all writing in the workplace is, broadly defined, collaborative. Newspaper editorial boards, for example, routinely engage in "peer response" critique and in group brainstorming when determining the position their paper will take on a given issue. Such technical fields as computer science, engineering, or pharmaceuticals consider the planning and writing and editing of multi-author documents standard procedure. Small groups of workers in such nontechnical fields as insurance, psychology, and social work also share the work of creating a wide variety of written products. When Patal from public relations, Chen from economics, and Jastrow from product pricing sit down to draft a corporate report, they pool their expertise to accomplish that task. Writing teachers whose pedagogical goals include helping students prepare for careers are better served by incorporating practice in writing together rather than by teaching only as though they subscribed to the Romantic ideal of the inspired poet-prophet, alone in his or her garret, struggling to put sublime visions to paper. After all, even poet-prophets like Wordsworth and Shelley benefited greatly from sharing ideas and manuscript copy with their friends.

Collaboration Affords Several Advantages

Students can undertake more complex projects when they write together than when they work alone. As writing instructors, we like the fact that, even in a ten-week quarter, collaborative writing projects can be considerably larger in scope than traditional single-writer assignments. Not only can group-members divide the workload but they can also tackle several tasks simultaneously. As Jeanine wrote in her process log:

> After leaving your office, we decided how to split up the work. I had a wedding to attend this weekend and Randy had to work the Memorial [Golf] Tournament. Our time was very tight as the end drew near. (So melodramatic!) [*sic*] For a remedy to this problem, Randy and I thought it would be a good idea for three of us to work on the ethics paper while the others worked on the revision to our earlier paper.

Students writing together can emphasize their strengths rather than their individual weaknesses. Unlike many individual projects in which students' deficiencies stand out, group projects allow students to contribute what they are best at while at the same time learning, from their peers, ways to improve areas in which they are weak. As Jenny wrote in her post-paper analysis memo,

> It took a long time to decide how we were going to do this paper because each of us had different ideas, and we really didn't want to let them go. But finally we decided that Glenn was faster in the library and so he would do the research. I would do the writing, [and] Mel would be the technical expert—he got everything into the computer. We actually got a draft done two days early and we all worked on the revision. I surprised myself by coming up with some better ideas for digging up the research and I had to admit that Mel and Glenn improved the way I'd worded the draft.

Collaboration also encourages social interaction and promotes under-standing of and respect for others. We find that collaborative learning and writing provide students with a sense of community so often missing in large general-education classes. Most of our students begin the term as strangers, but often become friends as well as coworkers. Dan and Frank were Air Force officers in training, majoring in engineering. Eliza, the third member of their group, was a Singaporean national in Hotel Management. She wrote,

> I do enjoy being in the group and I thank you . . . for putting me in this group. It amazes all three of us that we did not have any major disagreements with one another. . . . For this meeting I brought some "hot roasted peas"—a Chinese delicacy for them to taste and they really enjoy it. [*sic*] They are good friends and colleagues to work with.

In addition, collaborative assignments promote originality because each group's approach to an assignment will be as unique as the group that generates it. While we did not begin teaching our students to write collaboratively as a way of discouraging recycled papers from other classes or generic "frat file" themes, we have since discovered that having our students work in groups has virtually eliminated plagiarism. We are continually encouraged to find that students working in groups work harder at topic selection because they must arrive at an approach on which everyone is willing to work.

■ CREATING A COLLABORATIVE CLASSROOM

Reshape the Classroom Landscape

Have you ever wanted to re-create a room? Your garden? Yourself? Creating a collaborative classroom gives you that personal and professional opportunity—imagine sowing an annual garden where you once had only perennials. Like the carefully planted linear rows of the traditional formal garden, the traditional classroom features rows of desks that face the front of the room where the instructor directs classroom activities. By contrast, the collaborative classroom is more like a country garden where the aesthetic is not rigidly constrained but is allowed to flower randomly and exuberantly. Desks are no longer always and only arranged in rows but can be clustered around the room to allow student groups space to talk among themselves. The collaborative classroom is an active and noisy place rather than a quiet and passive one. But the alternative to orderly formality is not unproductive chaos; rather, the noise you hear is the sound of knowledge being created.

Teaching in the collaborative classroom, then, works better with desks that can be moved. Ideally, the collaborative classroom will have round tables and moveable chairs, an arrangement that allows students to work together or singly and to have room enough to spread out and share their in-class assignments, research materials, and drafts. (After all, how many resources can be laid out on the typical student desk?) Interactive Web space, such as those found in WebCT or Blackboard, can enhance collaborative classrooms by creating a virtual meeting place outside the classroom. The overall effect of these classroom changes is to direct students' attention away from the teacher and toward themselves and their peers.

Rethink the Role of the Writing Teacher

The traditional model of the teacher posits one who directs, plans, assigns, grades, controls, and judges, and positions the instructor at the center of activity as *the* decision maker, *the* authority, *the* expert. Obviously, most of us excelled in traditional classrooms, even if some did not thrive in such learning environments. But if the goal of our instruction is to equip students with a working knowledge of sound rhetorical principles and compositional strategies in the surest and most efficient way possible, it should not matter to us whether we drive the car or lay the road. The role of the teacher in a collaborative classroom is considerably different from that conceived in the traditional model. In the collaborative model, the teacher provides the theatre and drafts the script, but the students take center stage. Standing in the wings, the teacher of collaborative writing facilitates, encourages, advises, and nurtures students who can learn by doing in a semi-structured environment.

Does the teacher of collaboration simply walk away from her students and leave all learning entirely in their hands? Emphatically no. While some theoretical positions assert the importance of decentering authority in the collaborative classroom, complete decentering is impossible. So long as a teacher's assessments of papers are the most authoritative response they get, and so long as he or she retains the power to assign permanent grades, the instructor has all the power that matters to most students.

Rather than looking to an impending Students' Paradise where all traces of hierarchical teacher-student power relations have been erased, we prefer to think of the teacher in the collaborative classroom as *sharing* power and using her or his authority to motivate students and to construct a learning environment that will encourage students to grow as thinkers and as writers. In our own teaching practice, we generally find ourselves playing one (or more) of three roles: the reassuring listener (counselor); the dispenser of information and clarifier of assignments (teacher); and the mediator of disagreements (referee). The teacher may well have the ultimate institutional authority, but he or she can also work *with* students on invention and organizational strategies in nondirective ways, negotiating evaluative standards that recognize students' own measures of success.

Encourage Students to Take Responsibility for Learning

The most exciting and professionally liberating part of teaching collaborative writing is that we stop managing and directing the flow of information and conversation in our classrooms and start creating a dynamic learning space in which *students* take the responsibility for learning. In the collaborative learning environment, the teacher moves away from the chalkboard or the overhead projector and organizes students into groups that work together on the many aspects of the writing process. Suddenly, students must be responsible to one another. Teacher-centered classrooms place the onus on the instructor to present information that we hope our students will absorb, albeit passively. But in a classroom where students work in small groups requiring them to create solutions to the problems they identify, the burden for learning is instead placed on the learners.

■ TEACHING COLLABORATION: CONCEPTUAL VOCABULARY AND GROUP BEHAVIORS

Remind Students as They Work Together that Collaborative Groups are Groups of People

While it may sound obvious, one must always remember that, like the individuals who compose them, collaborative groups are unique and human. Students differ in degree of motivation, type of learning style, and overall skill level. Accepting these differences and adjusting one's expectations appropriately will decrease the instructor's frustration. Equally obvious and important to remember is the fact that collaborative writing groups are social in nature. Some students (and some writing teachers) worry that joking around, passing campus gossip, or sharing information about friends and family is counterproductive. However, seemingly off-task chat is not only normal to collaborative groups, it is absolutely necessary. People who have developed a friendly working relationship can be candid with one another. It is very hard to tell a stranger that his or her ideas or writing need work. Therefore, the writing teacher should encourage social interaction within groups but prepare them beforehand for the adjustments that individuals will need to make in order to work successfully with others.

We teach our students the following "Ten Commandments" of working together:

i. COMMIT YOURSELF TO THE SUCCESS OF THE GROUP. When it is just you, you can decide whether or not you want to work hard on a project or come to class. But you do not have that luxury when you work with a group. When you miss class or a group meeting, you owe your group the courtesy of a phone call. And you should make up any time lost to the group.

ii. REMEMBER THAT EACH MEMBER OF YOUR GROUP IS AN INDIVIDUAL. Getting to know each other's strengths, capabilities, and personalities will help your group immensely.

iii. RESPECT THE DIVERSITY OF ABILITIES AND BACKGROUNDS IN YOUR GROUP. These differences may be, at times, frustrating, but diversity is actually the greatest benefit of working in a group.

iv. ASSUME A DIFFERENT IDENTITY WHEN YOU WORK IN A GROUP. Your identity as a member of a group differs from that of the solitary scholar. When your groups writes or speaks, it is "we" and "us," not "me" and "I."

v. ALLOW PLENTY OF TIME FOR COLLABORATIVE WORK. It takes longer to work with someone else than it does to work individually—but the product is invariably stronger. Give your group time for spontaneous, informal talk; many times, this is where the best ideas come from.

vi. ACCEPT SOME CONFLICT. More creative solutions are found with some conflict than without it. However, focus your disagreements on ways of approaching a task and arriving at a satisfactory solution and not on individual personalities or abilities.

vii. DISCUSS CONCERNS AND FRUSTRATIONS OPENLY WITH EACH OTHER. It is best to work problems out as they occur rather than to allow them to fester, unattended, until a crisis brings them out. If members' work habits or attendance bother you, tell them so in a nonthreatening way.

viii. MAKE IT A GROUP PROJECT TO FIND A SOLUTION TO GROUP PROBLEMS. If the group cannot find a solution, talk to the instructor immediately.

ix. LISTEN TO EACH OTHER AND ASK CLARIFYING QUESTIONS. Many problems are simply matters of poor communication.

x. COMPROMISE. Face it, you simply will not get your own way all the time.

Teach Group Roles

The traditional top-down management model of group behavior designates one person the leader and all other group members as followers. Typically, the leader solicits information from the followers, decides what the group should do, and organizes the rest of the group to implement the plan. However, the top-down management approach is rarely successful in the classroom because not all self-appointed (or even elected) leaders have true leadership qualities, and not all followers are completely sanguine about their subservient roles. Furthermore, in the collaborative writing classroom, the top-down management model often inhibits members of a student group from making rhetorical and compositional decisions. In a writing course, everyone needs to learn how to organize, to choose an appropriate topic, and to develop a workable approach to a task. Consequently the instructor in the collaborative writing classroom should work hard to assure that responsibility for projects is equally shared. More often than not, when someone "takes charge" a general breakdown in communication and motivation results. For that matter, vote-taking and a "majority rules" approach to decision making can cause disaffected group members to drop out of the process. *Everyone* has to buy into the topic and the process, or it is no longer a group effort.

Appropriate behaviors for successful group work can be learned. They should not be regarded as intrinsic personal qualities, despite conventional practice. Rather, behaviors should be thought of as contributing to the group's success or detracting from it. First, we teach students to identify and practice a wide range of positive and negative roles that a member of a group might play. We stress that these roles are not permanent, but will vary *during* a group meeting as well as from day to day.

Early studies by social scientists (notably Benne and Sheats) have identified three kinds of behaviors associated with group member performance: group-building roles, group-maintenance roles, and group-blocking roles. We have modified their lists of roles to apply to the writing classroom.

Group Building Roles

THE INITIATOR
➤ suggests new or different ideas for discussion
➤ proposes new or different approaches to the group's process (for problem solving or for writing)

THE ELABORATOR
➤ elaborates or builds on suggestions made by others
➤ gives relevant examples

THE TESTER
➤ restates problem
➤ evaluates the group's progress toward completing assignments

➤ looks for holes in the plan
➤ pulls together or reviews the discussion

THE TASK-DESIGNER
➤ raises questions about member preferences for styles of working
➤ suggests the tasks that the group will need to accomplish its goals

THE RESPONDER
➤ evaluates written work with suggestions for revision

Group Maintenance Roles

THE FACILITATOR
➤ makes sure all group members have a chance to speak
➤ supports the contributions of others

THE VIBES-WATCHER
➤ focuses on the group's process
➤ mediates differences of opinion
➤ reconciles points of view
➤ calls for a break if discussion gets too warm

THE TIME-KEEPER
➤ focuses on task completion
➤ maintains the forward progress of the meeting
➤ when necessary, shifts the group's work back to accomplishing its stated goals

Group Blocking Roles

THE AGGRESSOR
➤ deflates status of others in group
➤ disagrees with others aggressively
➤ criticizes others in group

THE BLOCKER

➤ stubbornly disagrees with and rejects others' views
➤ cites unrelated personal experiences
➤ returns to topics already resolved

THE WITHDRAWER

➤ will not participate
➤ daydreams during group meetings
➤ carries on private conversation within group
➤ is a self-appointed taker of notes

THE RECOGNITION SEEKER

➤ tries to show his or her importance through boasting and excessive talking
➤ is overly conscious of his or her status

THE TOPIC JUMPER

➤ continually changes the subject

THE CONTROL FREAK

➤ tries to take over the meeting
➤ tries to assert authority
➤ tries to manipulate the group

THE LOBBYIST

➤ tries to get the group to work on his or her own special interests

THE CLASS CLOWN

➤ wastes the group's time by constantly showing off and telling funny stories
➤ acts with nonchalance or cynicism

THE BOOR

➤ talks endlessly and irrelevantly about his or her own feelings or experiences

THE DEVIL'S ADVOCATE

➤ when he or she is more devil than advocate

Giving students the conceptual vocabulary necessary to identify and discuss both positive and negative group roles is essential for healthy collaboration. We provide the "Ten Commandments" and the Roles List as handouts. For students to try out these behaviors, we conduct the following role-playing exercise early in the term.

We print out several copies of the Roles List, cut them apart, and number enough roles to place at least one builder, one maintainer, and one blocker in groups of three to five. (Say, we have a class of twenty-four. We number building roles from one through eight, maintaining roles from one through eight, and blocking roles from one through eight. We will, of course, repeat some roles.) Students draw a slip of paper with a role on it and look for the others in the class who share the same number (all the one's work together, all the *two's*, etc.).

Telling the students not to reveal their roles, we offer them a humorous prompt for discussion (such as coming up with a nonviolent sport to replace football; developing unusual ways to use the library after hours for fund-raising, and the like). We give them five to ten minutes to talk about the prompt while playing their assigned roles. We then repeat the exercise with new groups, sometimes enlarging the groups to expand the numbers of roles.

Afterwards, we ask the class to discuss what happened. They find not only that they can recognize the behaviors but that they can assume unfamiliar roles. They also learn how disruptive a blocker can be and how little progress takes place when no one assumes a group-building role. While we reiterate the need for everyone to work on group-building behaviors, we suggest that for each meeting, one member take on the facilitator's role, one the vibes-watcher's, and one the time-keeper's. Rotating these tasks from meeting to meeting helps group cohesiveness and minimizes antagonism.

Other Useful Group Behaviors

We have found that groups manage their time better if they set goals for each meeting—preferably at the end of the previous meeting. Our more successful groups usually agree to an agenda in advance of a meeting and then the timekeeper checks that the previously established goals have been met before the group plans its agenda for the next meeting. When groups discover that they have diverged substantially from the agenda, they can take that occasion to review the group's goals and discuss whether adjustments are necessary.

During all group meetings, everyone should take notes. Too frequently, one of the group's female members is directly or indirectly assigned "secretarial" duty. Alternatively, one person offers to take notes in order to control decision making. We require everyone to record the group's activities and decisions. At the end of each meeting, group members compare notes to assure that they all agree on what happens next. To encourage everyone to take responsibility for keeping track of what is going on, what got said, what got done, and when the group will meet next and why, we usually assign a post-paper memo or journal in which students are asked to report what happened at all group meetings. This memo serves as more than a diary; it also provides an ideal occasion for students to reflect upon the writing process, group interaction, and the ways in which their project evolved from topic selection to final draft.

About Conflict

A number of researchers distinguish between procedural, affective, and substantive conflicts (particularly Putnam, 1986, and Burnett, 1993) as important sources of both positive and negative friction among group members. If the collaborative project is to move forward, substantive conflict, which comprises negotiations about the scope of the project, the nature of the problem, possible solutions, and the form and content of the written product, must occur. Frequently, though, students confuse this vital form of conflict with its destructive counterfeits, affective conflict and procedural conflict. Affective conflict occurs not at the level of ideas, but between individuals who are either pitted against one another in a bid for control of the group or who simply rub each other the wrong way. While teaching consensual group behaviors can minimize conflict arising from a naked power grab, it is virtually impossible to mitigate personality conflicts short of reassigning one or more members of a group. Procedural conflict issues from misunderstandings over who is responsible for what or what the group's next move should be. Discussions emanating from procedural conflict can be quite productive if everyone has an equal say. Groups that work to mitigate against affective conflict usually emerge from the process stronger and with a clearer sense of direction.

Substantive conflict originates in a group's discussion of the form and content of its essay. This form of conflict—even if it is quite spirited—can be the most productive of all. Students who argue with one another for or against the inclusion of illustrative examples, the positioning of information within an essay, and which issues to cover or to exclude are not necessarily fighting. Rather, they are learning about how to write effectively by testing ideas out on their peers. Obviously, group-maintenance roles are extremely important in preventing substantive conflict from degenerating into counterproductive interpersonal exchanges. The communications expert needs to insure that everyone has a chance to voice an opinion and the nurturer needs to draw attention to the strengths in everyone's ideas. Writing instructors should actively encourage lively debate among coworkers who know that they are being heard and appreciated for what they bring to the group.

Responding to Peers in the Collaborative Group

The value of the peer response group is well established in composition pedagogy, and some even consider the peer response group as synonymous with the collaborative writing group. However, the work of the collaborative writing group goes beyond responding to the single-authored drafts of fellow students. In the collaborative group, students develop topics and approaches to writing as well as doing the writing itself. Peer response is a continuous action. Collaborative groups integrate the benefits of peer response into a group's writing process. Students cowriting a document must explain specifically to one another what features of a draft require revision and why.

Responding to and Revising Each Other's Work

We have found that the following advice makes a good handout to guide individual responders and collaborating writer/readers:

➤ Feel free to evaluate and make changes to each other's work.

➤ Remember that it is very difficult for people to relinquish ownership over anything they have written. Here are some suggestions for making this process easier:

  ➤ As a writer, try to create an objective attitude toward your work. People are responding to the words on the page, not to *you* as a person.

  ➤ As a reader/responder/reviser, the best rule is *The Golden Rule*: "Treat others as you would like to be treated." A little sensitivity will go a long way in dealing with your peers' writing.

  ➤ If you recommend changes in something someone else has written, be sure to explain to the writer how and why you changed it. If you do not, you risk alienating that person from your team.

Collaborative groups, like individual writers, can lose sight of the way their writing reads to others. When entire groups exchange papers for response, they will develop a greater sense of writing for a "real" audience if they know that others will be responding to their work. Those who are teaching more than one composition class might exchange papers across classes, which usually minimizes the "kid glove" attitudes with which some students appraise the work of their classmates.

Groups can also form a revision collective with members developing specific areas of expertise for a given assignment. For example, the members of each group can divide the *Reference Guide's* response guidelines (pages 13-14) and revision checklists (pages 16-19) so that all questions are addressed. As an added advantage, having beginning responders work through scripted response sheets like these will help them avoid engaging in either unnecessarily harsh critique ("What a dumb idea!") or unhelpful vague praise ("Sounds great to me!"). On responding days, teachers should direct the focus of comments. It is not appropriate for students to pinpoint typos and usage errors in the first draft when they should be addressing such crucial global issues as organization, point of view, and sufficiency of included information. By the second or third draft, students can pay attention to usage, word choice, and transitions. As a means of building your students' repertoire of response techniques, you can—after some preliminary explanation—ask them to build their own lists of issues they should check for at each stage of the drafting process.

■ Assigning Groups

Assigning Groups is Too Important to Trust to Luck

Although group assignment has received little research attention, teacher lore reveals a number of methods by which students are grouped: dividing students alphabetically; pulling names from a hat; counting students off by threes, fours, or fives; requesting student preferences; classifying students by academic major; or assuring a strong and weak writer in each group, to name a few. These more-or-less random methods can be very useful for breaking the ice (see below), however, when assigning groups for major projects we consciously try to put students together in ways that will assure the highest possible level of group success—both academically and interpersonally. In class on the first day of the term, we sample writing abilities by asking students to write us letters in which they discuss:

➤ their reason(s) for being in the class and their expectations from it,

➤ their level of motivation for the class,

➤ their previous experience with writing, and,

➤ their career expectations.

A week later, we ask students to write a more formal memo to us telling us what to know before placing them in groups, paying particular attention to (a) work and academic schedules, work habits and style (e.g., driven vs. laid-back), (b) previous experience with groups and attitudes about groupwork, (c) other relevant personal data (e.g., whether students think themselves shy or likely to dominate a conversation), and (d) any preferences they might have for working or not working with particular students in the class. After students prepare an initial draft of these memos, we require private conferences which give us a chance to discuss their writing and the information in the memos, and also to let us get to know them better.

In addition, during the first two weeks of class, we introduce small group activities and role-playing exercises for students to learn successful collaboration techniques. These in-class activities also provide opportunities for us to observe how students work together—who is quiet, who is assertive, who stays on task, who gets sidetracked, and so forth. Toward the end of the second week, we assign groups of two to five members according to the following priorities:

➤ Student schedules should permit at least two hours other than class time per week in which all can meet. Often this consideration supersedes all others. After all, students must be able to work *together* on shared work. Even if groups were to meet in class only, students could work toward the group's goals by completing individual responsibilities outside class and then merging their work during class time. Sometimes students may choose to "meet" online; however, this strategy also requires a time commitment outside of class time.

➤ Students should be similarly motivated. Hard workers with high grade motivation should not be placed with those who cannot or will not spend adequate time for the class or who are simply passing. Many theorists believe that strong students should be identified and placed with weak students to encourage peer mentoring. While we find the idea philosophically noble, we have repeatedly found that differing motivation levels create the most significant roadblocks on the journey to success. Highly motivated weak students have the potential to do well and learn a great deal on their own whereas unmotivated students of whatever ability level are the source of most student complaints about collaboration.

➤ Students are not placed with those they had asked not to work with—generally a result of their having worked together in a prior class. If possible, students are placed with students they do ask to work with.

➤ Students with special needs (e.g., nonnative speakers, returning older students, shy students, minority students) are placed with those that intuition suggests might be more accepting of them.

In general, we find that large groups (four to six members) work best for in-class discussion-oriented activities whereas small groups (two or three members) work best for multi-draft writing assignments. Because writing with others—especially at first—generates numerous procedural questions, we "roam" the classroom spending time with each group listening and/or participating as needed. We also require each group to attend a private faculty-office conference for each major assignment. Most groups, however, ask for more than one conference.

Determining Group Longevity

In our ten-week quarters, there is barely enough time for students to get to know each other, let alone to build the comfort and trust necessary to create effective working relationships. Thus, barring catastrophes, we prefer to keep student groups together for the length of the term. Some teachers vary group membership so that students can benefit from exposure to a range of work styles and personality types. However, we have found that such logistical considerations as time availability outside of class usually make a general reshuffling of writing groups unworkable. To give our students the benefits of working with a wide variety of others, we "scatter" the members of collaborative writing groups when we work on in-class group non-writing activities.

What to Do about Ungroupable Students

We always emphasize the necessity of collaborative work and outline in our syllabi, and, during the first class meeting, the unique demands it will place on students (e.g., responsibility to others, required work outside of class, the understanding that writing takes longer with a group than writing solo). Even so, we have occasionally found students for whom working in collaborative groups outside of class poses an exceptional burden. We remember, for example, one student who, in addition to a seventeen-quarter hour academic load, spent four to five hours of road work a day training for an Olympic bicycling event. He could spare only one hour, one day a week, to work with his group. Obviously, a student who cannot meet with others outside the classroom will be unable to contribute fully to his or her group. In this particular case—and the principle applies more widely—the student was allowed to undertake individualized, scaled-down versions of the class's writing projects and thus to fulfill the course requirements.

More frequently, we have encountered students who perform so poorly that they pose a significant liability for their groups. We have had students who seemed almost pathologically driven to subvert the group's efforts through habitual tardiness, failure to complete promised tasks, or by being chronically critical or obstinate. Usually we resolve these difficulties by allowing the problematic student to work alone, so the cooperative students are not penalized or forced to carry the entire workload. Altering evaluation strategies is another method for dealing with difficult group members. In some cases, having separate grades for group process and product may be effective in enabling all to receive the evaluation they deserve. One of my colleagues has had students evaluate themselves and their group members, including self-reporting the percentage of work or support they each contributed toward the final project. Final project grades were then adjusted accordingly to reward those who contributed most or penalize those who did not do their fair share.

Developing Group Ground Rules

Urge each group to develop its own drafting process. Some groups are happier if each member drafts a separate section of the document which the group will merge later as a complete draft. Other groups prefer to have each member draft the entire document, with the group picking and choosing the best parts of each. Still other groups prefer to huddle around a single computer and write the entire document together from scratch. Groups whose members have a hefty campus commute appreciate the ability to conduct at least some of their work independently or by telephone, e-mail, or on-line conferencing. We have even had groups who faxed sections of their papers to each other. The *Prentice Hall Reference Guide* offers guidelines for collaborative writing in section 2d.

In any case, student groups should develop their own work styles, determine their internal management rules, and allocate tasks however they see fit. The instructor can monitor these arrangements by asking students to keep a detailed, confidential log of each group meeting—both in and out of class. The quality of these logs varies of course: high-achieving students might write pages; low-achieving students might write but a few paragraphs, generally focusing on tasks rather than ideas or behaviors.

■ AIMING THE GROUPS TOWARD SUCCESS

Success in the Collaborative Writing Classroom

No matter how many drafts a group project undergoes, at some point the text must be evaluated. But what measures of success are appropriate to a collaborative project? In the traditional writing classroom, the answer is straightforward enough. If a text is logically organized, well-articulated, presented from an interesting point of view, and more or less free of mechanical errors, it can be considered a success. In the collaborative writing classroom, the issue of what constitutes a "good paper" is more complicated. Naturally, a final draft of a collaborative project featuring the above hallmarks of a well-written paper is—at least at the discursive level—successful, but in the collaborative classroom one teaches both how to write and how to work well with others. For this reason, we consider both pedagogical emphases during grading. Some groups collaborate very well together, but for a variety of reasons produce a less than perfect product. Other groups produce an excellent product, but do so by subverting the aims of collaboration. Because we believe the goal of the collaborative writing classroom is to teach both collaboration and writing, then success can only be defined as a combination of good collaboration and a well-written document. Thus, while grading, we consider a student text "good" only when produced by a truly collaborative group.

Obviously, our increasingly grade-conscious students want to know what, exactly, an "A" paper is—especially when they learn that "good collaboration" is a class requirement. We include our students in the process of defining an excellent collaborative paper by asking them to create a list of discursive features and group behaviors that distinguish an "A" paper. First the small groups draw up their lists, and then prioritize them. The class discussion that follows can provide an excellent occasion to talk about what makes a piece of writing interesting to a reader and what kinds of group behavior constitute good collaboration. As groups report what they came up with, we write their ideas on the board and by the end of class have a list of criteria that the students agree should apply to the final evaluation of their writing. This exercise is important not only because it allows collaborative groups input into the grading process, but also because students remind one another of the criteria for a good paper and good collaborative techniques as they work together.

Introduce Collaborative Work Sequentially

An informal survey of collaborative assignments in the writing class indicates that they generally fall into four broad categories:

> ➤ BRIEF ASSIGNMENTS, perhaps short textbook problems, that can be completed within the classroom, usually within one or two class periods. For example, the *Prentice Hall Reference Guide*'s exercises in the sections on tone [42c], or distinguishing between primary and secondary evidence [52a] can be performed collaboratively and result in a brief written summary of findings.

> ➤ SHORT ESSAYS OR BRIEF RESEARCH PAPERS of relatively short duration but which require that groups meet outside class.

> As preliminary exercises for extended research papers, collaborative groups can be sent to the library to do exploratory research on their topic. After consulting all information resource systems, students can collaboratively write a report that discusses their topic's major issues.

> ➤ MAJOR PROJECTS, such as multi-part reports, which are long-term assignments of several weeks' duration requiring extensive nonclassroom work for completion. (See below for examples of major collaborative projects.)

> ➤ TERM-LONG PROJECTS, whether quarter or semester, which are the focus of a course. Ideally, term-long projects should be undertaken in the second of a two-term sequence after students have had several opportunities to write with others.

We find that teaching collaboration works best if it is introduced gradually and sequentially over the course of the term. In the beginning, we assign short-term projects that minimize logistical difficulties and give us an opportunity to assess individual and group dynamics. In addition, several short-term assignments, undertaken early in the semester or quarter when the class is focusing on group roles and peer response techniques, gives students a chance to adapt their customary approaches and behavior patterns to the requirements of collaborative group work before embarking on longer assignments. These brief, out-of-class assignments can also serve as group invention exercises, providing students with an occasion to gather and organize information even as they refine their paper topics. At last, after several brief in-class assignments and at least one short out-of-class exercise, students should be sufficiently comfortable with their group members' working styles and the unique requirements of collaborative writing to embark on a major project. In our classrooms, major projects take about three weeks to complete, which allows time for two or three drafts and for at least two in-class peer response sessions. While we think it is important to ease students into collaborative writing, we also think that students should work on several assignments simultaneously. Life is rarely one discrete task after another, and being required to turn in drafts of major projects even as they begin short writing tasks relevant to their next major project teaches them to manage their time and intellectual activity.

Breaking the Ice

It is important for the instructor in the collaborative writing classroom to recognize the essential nature of writing teams. Therefore, it is good practice to allow a little time at the beginning of each class meeting for groups to chat. (At first, you might have to explicitly tell students that they have about five minutes to catch up on group gossip before class gets rolling.) Before groups are assigned—and certainly right after they have been—it will be necessary to orchestrate some ice-breaking exercises that will give individual students a chance to meet one another and to find out that collaborative writing can actually be fun. Here are some ideas for getting the ball rolling:

Warming Up: In-class Collaborative Assignments

➤ Students compile the group's schedule and phone list.

➤ Students interview each other and report back to the group what they have discovered. This can also lead to the enumeration of expertises, equipment, or capabilities that each member brings to the group.

➤ While students understand the concept of audience in a general way, they also find writing for others intimidating. The following collaborative exercise can help students overcome this anxiety and simultaneously explore the concrete characteristics of an audience.

➤ Divide the class into groups of three to five.

➤ Ask your class to envision a group of refugees rescued from the primitive conditions of nomadic life and brought to a modern American city. Even after being shown how to operate the lights and faucets in their apartments, the refugees remained so innocent of the technologies that we take for granted that they washed their clothes by soaking them in the sink and then pounded them with heavy objects—just as they had done by river banks for generations.

> Ask each group to craft a set of instructions that would tell the refugees how to wash and dry their clothes using a modern washer and dryer. Students will have to bear in mind that they cannot take what they would consider "common knowledge" for granted. Even simple commands like "open the lid" or "check the lint filter" will require careful explanation—perhaps even illustration.

In this exercise, the social nature of the interaction forces students to *articulate and practice* what they know about audience needs. By visiting each of the groups as they work, you can gather a few representative comments demonstrating what your students already know about their audience to share with the entire class when it comes time to synthesize what was learned during the activity.

Create an Ongoing Discussion about Writing Projects

Another way that the collaborative writing instructor can point student groups toward success is to require numerous individual writing assignments that ask students to reflect consciously on what they are learning as a result of writing with others. We usually require three kinds of analytical writing from our students in addition to the brief, short, and major assignments described above:

1: THE WORK PLAN—a descriptive essay that specifies the group's paper topic and outlines the way they anticipate addressing it. The work plan takes the form of a collaboratively produced memo addressed to the instructor which spells out how the work will be organized and the labor divided. Work plans should specify which paragraphs and/or sections each group member will write, who will type the drafts, who will make copies (if required for peer response work), who will proofread, and who will be responsible for the paper getting in on time. In addition, the work plan can be used to encourage students to think about group roles—who will act as facilitator, or questioner, or idea person. There are several advantages to this assignment:

> by introducing "first-timers" to collaborative writing through a comparatively short, concrete project, you give them a chance to adapt to each others' working and writing styles with minimal grade pressure;
> by asking group members to assign themselves specific tasks during the drafting process, you encourage them to think in detail about how they will organize their writing in advance; *and*

➤ by getting students to commit to a plan of action, you can evaluate and respond to the "do-ability" of their projects before too much time and energy has been expended on ideas that will not work. While a work plan constrains students to plan their writing in advance, it need not suggest—as traditional outlines sometimes do—an inviolably rigid structure into which all ideas discovered during writing must fit. In fact, for another short, graded writing task that encourages a critical awareness of the writing process, you can ask students to write a follow-up report that analyzes the ways in which producing the final draft differs from the work plan.

2: THE COLLABORATIVE LOG—an ongoing diary of what the group is doing even as they do it. The collaborative log should articulate the group's agenda for each meeting and should report on who came to the meetings, what each person contributed, and evaluate the degree to which the group's agenda was met. To insure that students keep their collaborative logs up, the instructor can collect them for review about halfway through a major project. As an alternative effort to keep abreast of developments within the group, we have occasionally asked that students write progress reports based on their collaborative logs.

3: THE POST-PAPER ANALYSIS—a synthesis and analysis of how and to what degree the group's project changed from the time of the work plan until the day the final draft was handed in for evaluation. The post-paper analysis (one of our students renamed this paper the "postmortem") should also summarize how the student felt about the work his or her group did. Does the writer consider the group's effort to be good collaboration? What grade does the student think the paper deserves and why? Should everyone receive the same grade?

These writing assignments tend to represent all of James Moffet's "modes of discourse" from the basic *recording* and *reporting* of experiences in collaborative writing groups (as formalized by the collaborative logs) to *generalizing* and *theorizing* (as made available in the postpaper analyses and work plans, respectively). The collaborative writing classroom as we have envisioned it requires many different written products, and the assignments have been created to teach the "content" obtaining to the writing classroom while at the same time encouraging students to make *how* they write an object of reflection and analysis. Thus, we can, through one series of short writing assignments, reinforce classroom discussions of readers' needs and Moffet's modes of discourse, gather "insider" information into the workings of collaborative groups, and give students plenty of practice in writing.

Leave Room for Innovation and the Imagination

Recent research on small group dynamics suggests that the quality and number of ideas generated by invention is enhanced by having group members first engage individually in such prewriting activities as mapping, clustering, and focused free-writing before coming together for group brainstorming. During group brainstorming, collaborative groups should select a "scribe" to record all reactions and ideas that surface as the group works on an assignment. Before the group pursues its topic any farther, have its members repeat the individual-first, group-second prewriting process on the new, narrower idea.

If you are lucky enough to be a classroom equipped with tables and moveable chairs, you can supply each group with large sheets of butcher paper so its members can map out invention topics seated around a table. Group mapping also works if your room has multiple chalkboards. Just be sure your groups are supplied with enough chalk to map their ideas at one of the boards. When students map together they can pool their resources for generative topic ideas and organizational strategies.

■ DESIGNING COLLABORATIVE WRITING ASSIGNMENTS THAT WORK

Selecting a Topic

In general, we think that students rather than instructors should select paper topics. Student motivation is stimulated when they are allowed work on subjects that pique their interest. Of course, the teacher can point students in productive directions. We find that supplying students with a general purpose or genre provides them with a lens through which to focus their interests. Thus, instead of handing students a menu of paper topics, we assign papers dealing with specific themes (see below). For example, the paper on public policy asks student groups to gather as much information as possible on any issue that is an object of law. Within the large purpose of reporting all sides of a public policy debate—or the history of a public policy that directly affects them—students have the freedom to select any of a hundred topics ranging from legislation concerning drinking and voting ages to proposals for solving the nation's growing health-care crisis to the debate surrounding gays in the military. The principle of using topic selection to encourage student motivation can also apply within the groups themselves. Thus, you will want to emphasize to your students the importance of choosing a topic that everyone in the group agrees to. *Consensus* rather than *majority rule* is the key to successful collaboration. A student left out of the initial decision may feel no subsequent commitment to the group effort.

Once groups have selected a topic, we ask each group to write a well-developed audience profile. Have the groups articulate exactly whom they would expect to read their work. For example, if the group decides to write a paper on the parking problem on campus, group members should be clear about whom they see as their primary audience. Do they perceive a secondary audience for their writing as well? What can they assume their primary and secondary audiences know and do not know about the parking problem? How much background will they need to include in their paper to be sure that their readers fully understand the issues they raise? What kind of tone is appropriate for the audiences they have identified? Writing a statement of purpose for their writing can be a useful preliminary to tackling a major project: for example, "This paper will persuade the administration to schedule classes in a way that minimizes parking lot overcrowding at eight in the morning." Alternately, the individual members of the group could write separate statements of purpose, comparing and combining them afterwards.

The Teacher's Role in Drafting

As described above, the teacher in the collaborative learning and writing environment moves to the periphery of the learning activity in order to allow students to step up and take responsibility for their educations. This in no way minimizes the importance of the teacher. The instructor must create an environment hospitable to collaborative learning by creating a variety of in-class and out-of-class exercises that will give students hands-on experience with the vast array of principles and skills that conduce to good writing. Though working around the edges of classroom activity, the teacher must be alert to the sometimes subtle signals that a group is struggling, and must then decide when and if to intervene. The teacher must also be able to move from group to group, and be ready to suggest alternatives, answer questions, point students toward useful resources, or simply to share a joke. If much of the collaboration takes place on-line, the teacher may need the ability to "lurk" in some group conversations and activities.

Thus, even punctuation lessons can be an opportunity for student interaction. Instead of defining such abstract notions as what commas are and why participle, infinitive, and absolute phrases need them [27], the teacher can set a task that will require students in groups to read, review, analyze, and use the comma rule information in their *Reference Guides*. Or students can identify such sentence-level units as restrictive and nonessential clauses [27c], coordinate adjectives [27e], and quotations [27g] in their own writing. To encourage them to synthesize and apply the abstract information in the *Reference Guide* to their own, very concrete writing, students also could be asked to create short documents that report how many of which kind of unit they discovered and whether or not a comma should be used in such a case. Thus even learning punctuation rules can be fun when students learn, analyze, and apply their new-found knowledge together. Ask each member of a group to be the "expert" on a particular mark of punctuation: commas, periods, semicolons, colons, quotation marks, and so forth. In proofreading, let each "expert" find the errors and explain to the writer how to correct them. On successive papers, have the students rotate the punctuation assignments, so that each gains expertise in all areas of punctuation. For underprepared students, starting with just commas, say, or periods, is less intimidating than learning and applying all punctuation rules at once. Peer discussion and reinforcement of the rules provides a more effective learning experience than asking individual students to correct teacher-marked errors.

Modify Assessment and Grading

Some instructors assign a single grade to the entire group; others assign grades individually, and others use some combination of the two methods, each student receiving both a group grade and an individual grade. While it is typical practice to assign grades based on the technical quality and discursive maturity of the final text, the success of a collaborative assignment should derive from other bases as well:

➤ the completion of the project

➤ the finding of an appropriate solution or resolution to the problem or case

➤ the group's equitable allocation of work or tasks

➤ nonwritten aspects of the completed project (such as oral presentation, visuals, and the evaluation and presentation of numerical data)

➤ the students' sense of successful completion

➤ the students' having learned something about group processes

Whether an instructor measures these factors in formal assessment or informally for course development, we believe that each represents an important part of what is taught through the collaborative project. We have heard it jokingly suggested that teaching collaborative writing will diminish an instructor's workload by having students work collaboratively. Would that it were true! We have found that even though the collaborative method causes the exchange of twenty-five individual papers and drafts for eight or so collaboratively-produced papers and drafts, the time it takes to evaluate collaboratively produced papers evens the scale. And, of course, instructors must also judge the information they gain from all those smallish writing assignments that help students analyze and synthesize the writing process.

Creating Prompts That Encourage Analysis, Synthesis, and Self-reflection

For the collaborative writing instructor, the most demanding expenditure of creative energy is planning writing assignments that can accomplish many goals simultaneously. As discussed above, the writing instructor must deploy a wide range of writing assignments—and at the right time—in order to teach students how to collaborate effectively and how, when collaborating, to write with precision and power. Despite the difficulty of creating workable prompts, we usually follow a few general principles:

> ➤ Prompts should lay out an activity that encourages conversation, information exchange, and speculation, and that results in a written product.

> ➤ Prompts should ask students either to analyze a content-oriented issue in a sample text or synthesize the group's discussion of the prompt.

> ➤ Prompts should make it the students' responsibility to discover what principles apply to a given problem. It defeats the purpose of collaborative learning if you tell them what they will find if they look closely enough at the situation you have drawn to their attention. Likewise, prompts should ask students to engage in an activity that gives them practice using a particular concept (e.g., the audience analysis and discovering purpose exercise described above).

> ➤ Prompts should solicit self-reflection. Individuals should be urged to respond personally to the situations and issues that your prompts bring into focus.

In addition to this general advice about creating prompts, we further suggest that you avoid leading groups into discussing and writing about volatile, irresolvable subjects. Collaboration works when students can share and develop concepts and ideas. Positions set in stone are rarely amenable to any kind of modification, and an inability to negotiate a position on an issue will likely make negotiation of writing processes impossible as well. Topics like abortion, gun control, religious beliefs, or family values do not work very well as discussion or paper topics because—despite our students' natural attraction to them—they are not conducive to the development of congenial relations among group members nor to the development of balanced papers.

■ DIAGNOSING PROBLEMS IN THE COLLABORATIVE GROUP

Collaborative learning, collaborative writing, and collaborative projects are extraordinarily useful, but not unproblematic, tools for the teacher of writing. As teachers new to collaborative writing soon learn, despite their best efforts, sometimes collaborative projects simply do not work. While the benefits of collaboration in the writing classroom are manifold, it is important to be aware of what we call "collaborative breakdown." Because the dynamics of each class can vary widely, **monitor each group's progress.** Among the clues to incipient breakdown are:

> ➤ Individual student anxiety as interim or final deadlines approach;
> ➤ A group's inability to decide what to do or how to do it;
> ➤ Students asking to change groups or have an assignment modified; and
> ➤ A work load that seems inequitably distributed.

To increase the likelihood that the instructor will learn of any problems in time to intervene, part of every collaborative project should include individual assessments by the students. These can take the form of conferences, journals, or the memos and/or progress reports we referred to above. Equally important, the instructor should schedule group work on regular class days so that he or she can sit in on each group to evaluate how well they are functioning.

Watching for the Five Fields of Dissonance

In our studies of student collaborative work, we have identified five major causes of trouble: 1) logistical difficulties; 2) personality conflict; 3) differing cognitive abilities; 4) differences in epistemological development; and 5) differences in social background. While these vexing spirits can rarely be cast out by the instructor, being able to identify them may permit a teacher to modify an assignment or better evaluate its success.

THE LOGISTICS OF COLLABORATION. Perhaps there are a fortunate few instructors who have no students who are working at least one job to make ends meet and gain work experience while they are in school. But many of us expect that at least half our students will have one or two part-time jobs in addition to their full-time class load. In some cases, students have family responsibilities, too. In one of our early collaborative writing classes, Chuck reported, "Tom, Michelle, and I all work different hours, and getting together to write out drafts of our paper was impossible." Competing demands on our students' time may make it impossible or extremely difficult for them to work outside the classroom as a group and, as we have already mentioned, the instructor should make every effort to minimize scheduling conflicts. Providing interactive Web-based tools can help students work around differing schedules and time constraints.

DIFFERENCES IN COGNITIVE ABILITY. Another area of difficulty that can work against successful collaboration is differing cognitive maturity. Cognitive development specialists tell us that the composing process comprises a tremendous variety of mental operations, ranging from understanding the assignment, to remembering relevant facts, to imagining and seeking to meet the needs of an audience, to organizing data in such a way that it may be presented in a clear and logical manner (e.g., Flower and Hayes, 1984), but it also includes the basics of literacy—reading and writing. Thus, when we speak of the cognitive maturity of a writer or a group of writers we are referring to the facility with which that writer or that group can usefully conceptualize and execute the requirements of a writing task. And of course, not all students are created with equal abilities. Some students will be able to conceptualize problems and propose solutions posed by and directed toward a writing task more adequately than their facility with the language will allow them to demonstrate on paper. Conversely, there are writers who are extremely facile with the language, but whose thinking is nevertheless superficial.

In the context of collaborative work, a form of cognitive dissonance occurs when students with varying levels of cognitive maturity tackle a problem together—a situation which holds both pedagogical promise and peril. The promise is that students, regardless of maturity, can learn problem-solving techniques and efficient strategies for reading, writing, and organizing more effectively from one another than from a textbook or a teacher (Daiute, 1986). The peril lies in the fact that cognitive dissonance frequently leads to frustration and impatience, and even to the formation of factions or the dissolution of the group itself. The more cognitively mature student may become impatient with her less advanced group members and usurp control of the project.

EPISTEMOLOGICAL DEVELOPMENT IN CONFLICT. In his study of Harvard students, William G. Perry (1970) proposed a nine-stage scale of epistemological development along which the individual moved from **dualism**—an authoritarian, black-or-white view of the world, to **multiplicity**—the recognition of other points of view; and finally a commitment in **relativism**—taking a personal stand while also accepting other points of view. Epistemological dissonance occurs when different members of a group are at different stages along Perry's continuum. The problem for classroom collaboration is not only that students may be operating at different epistemic levels, but also that students cannot comprehend the "ways of knowing" of their co-members. The dualist, regardless of the sophistication of his or her writing abilities, cannot understand how the group can develop alternative solutions to a problem. A student at the multiplistic stage may be able to recognize views other than his or her own, but be unable to evaluate their relative strengths. Achieving consensus can be difficult when a member of a group does not know how to compare and choose among alternative solutions that may appear to have equal merit. Such a student may bow to the loudest voice or, unsure of his or her own position, say simply "do what you guys want to do." Even a student who may have attained the upper reaches of Perry's scale (and we do not believe that "a commitment in relativism" is the likely endpoint for most individuals) may not tolerate the dogmatism or apparent "wishy-washyness" of the less epistemologically advanced student and may react either by withdrawing from the group or by attempting to dominate it.

PERSONAL DISSONANCE. Most instructors know when they have a personality problem in class. A student's aberrant behavior or argumentative stance manifests itself early in the term. In a work setting, such an individual would be weeded out—or at least pruned—early in his or her employment history, but rarely is a student so disruptive that he or she is ejected from class. Yet even a small disruptive element is antithetical to group process, and a perverse streak may totally sabotage a group's work. Other personality problems are the aggressive student whose personality force dominates the other students and the shy or quiet student who is unable to present his or her views or is unable to take on the parts of the assignment that he or she is best suited for. Related to this phenomenon is the dissonance that can arise from students who have differing levels of motivation. Students who need high GPAs in order to qualify for scholarships in their majors will not appreciate being grouped with students who are taking your class credit/no-credit. Some students want to put forth the least amount of work possible while others take great pride in each task. Even without considering grades, students do not always come to class with the same priorities and degree of commitment. The instructor cannot change a student's personality or supply motivation, but she can teach students about the ways in which personality and motivation factors can affect group interaction. The teacher can also consider these factors when assigning groups—when logical considerations do not completely dictate groupings.

SOCIAL DISSONANCE. This little-discussed area of interpersonal friction can be defined as the clashing work behaviors that derive from differing socioeconomic backgrounds and which influence task representation, work ethic, and degree of imagination or risk-taking. Rather than viewing the matter in stereotypical terms—"working class attitudes," "women's ways of knowing," etc.—we see this area of dissonance as deriving from differing "dialects of behavior." Although what we have called the "dialect of behavior" shares much conceptually with a "discourse community," we believe that the behavioral dialect encompasses more than shared discourse. It was only after teaching at three very different institutions that we became aware of the considerable differences in response that could be engendered by the same assignments. For example, in responding to an ethics case regarding a corrupt politician, students in Arcata, California and Columbus, Ohio saw it as only the behavior problem of one individual. Students in Youngstown, Ohio, on the other hand, assumed mob connections and a general corruption in politics. In Arcata, environmental concern among students is taken for granted; in Columbus, it is much less widespread. As another example, in the Youngstown area, positions of authority and responsibility are accorded considerable deference. Thus, on second reference in a newspaper, a lawyer is identified as "Attorney Smith." Professors with doctorates are always "Dr." In both Columbus and Arcata, "Dr." is usually reserved for physicians and dentists, and attorneys are not accorded special status.

Behavioral dialect may also account for the degree of comfort a student experiences with hierarchical or non-hierarchical structures; the degree to which a student resists responsibility for her or his education; and the expectation the student has for the location of authority—all of which have implications for the decentered, non-hierarchical, shared-authority collaborative classroom. Such social factors can cause collaborative breakdown when members of a group do not share the same behavioral dialect or when a shared behavioral dialect does not permit satisfactory completion of an assignment. Interestingly, factors attributable to behavioral dialect often supersede attitudes or behaviors predicted from class, ethnic, or gender theory.

Mediating Conflict

While there are many potential sources of collaborative breakdown in the writing classroom, those considering teaching collaborative writing for the first time should know that complete breakdown is the exception and not the rule. Most groups instinctively compensate for tensions and imbalances—if for no other reason than they want to pass the class. But most frequently, collaborative groups demonstrate that human beings are thoroughly social animals with considerable reserves of tolerance, understanding, and humor to smooth their ways to successful completion of a shared task—whatever the perceived reward. This table distills responses that experience has shown can help teachers of collaborative writing nurture students' innate social strengths:

FIELD OF DISSONANCE	INSTRUCTOR RESPONSE
LOGISTICAL	• Acknowledge students' scheduling difficulties by showing flexibility on due dates and course expectations. • Allow in-class group work time. • Set up on-line conferencing sites • Arrange groups with consideration for schedules.
PERSONAL	• Solicit students' self-appraisals and preferences. • Provide alternative models for behavior in groups (suggest such roles as "idea person," "elaborator," and "group scribe") to minimize reliance on traditional leader-follower paradigm. • Be willing to give a disruptive personality an individual assignment rather than insisting on group participation.
COGNITIVE	• Recognize that all students are not created with equal abilities nor does their cognitive development proceed at the same pace. • Graduate the complexity of assignments over the course of the term to permit what development can take place to take place. • Group students at different cognitive levels only when motivation appears equal. • Accept that students' intellectual contributions may not be equal.
EPISTEMIC	• Recognize that students at the lower end of the development scale cannot perceive the views of those in positions above them. • Because students at the lower end of the epistemic scale may be incapable of responding to open-ended assignments or assignments in which a group is expected to develop its own approach, be prepared to provide explicit directions.
SOCIAL	• Develop awareness of and adjust to local knowledge. • Provide in-class opportunities for encountering and discussing other perspectives, other norms.

■ ASSIGNMENTS THAT WORK

Some Field-tested Prompts To Get You Started

Ultimately, the only way to learn how to teach writing in a collaborative classroom is to devise the best syllabus you can and give it a whirl. All of the advice presented in these pages derives from years of trial and error, and while we have had some spectacular failures along the way, we do not think that those classes where failures occurred learned less about writing that those we conducted according to the more traditional model. Collaborative writing, like democracy, may be the worst way to teach writing—except for all other ways of teaching it. What follows are several assignments that have proven winners in many collaborative writing classes. We hope that, like us, you will be amazed at how creative students can be when they are fully engaged in the learning and writing process.

Research Paper 1: Thinking Green

Everyone is talking about our deteriorating environment—deforestation, strip mining, acid rain, overfishing, over-fertilization, the difficulties of disposing of toxic and nuclear wastes. But what are the facts? What do you really know about any environmental issue? Where does your information come from? How reliable is it? This assignment lets you gain some expertise in at least one area of environmental concern and draw your own conclusions.

What information you will need: Once you have decided on a topic, you will need to dig up information on at least three issues: 1) the physics of the problem—how the environmental impact occurs; 2) the biology of the problem—what happens to the plants and animals affected by the problem, and 3) the socioeconomics of the problem—the human activities and needs that occasion the environmental impact. (Some papers will also have to consider the "chemistry of the problem"—what chemical compounds are released as a result of the environmental impact and what chemical reactions result from this release.)

How you actually organize the paper will, as always, be dependent on the logic that best explains your chosen topic. However, generally speaking, the reader can understand the biology of a problem better than he or she already understands why the affected organisms are in harm's way in the first place. It may be, though, that you find it more sensible to explain the socioeconomics of the problem you are studying even as you relate how that problem occurs. In any case, you will need to work out a provisional strategy and present it in your work plan.

Editorial

As stated in the syllabus, you will work collaboratively with several other students to develop and write a persuasive essay on a subject upon which you all agree. To get to this point, you will need to do some legwork.

STEP 1: Write brief papers (approximately 350–500 words) in which each of you explains the significance of the issue you have chosen.

STEP 2: Each member of the group will write a paper explaining the facts of the issue.

STEP 3: Divide the group. One half will write a pro paper and the other half, a con paper.

STEP 4: Finally your group will reach consensus on the issue and write a persuasive essay advocating the position you have agreed on. You will use secondary sources to build your case. (If students struggle to come to consensus on a position, they may try to develop a Rogerian argument instead.)

GRADING: Significance: 3 points, Facts: 5 points, Pro/Con: 7 points, Final Essay: 10 points—for a total of 25 points.

As you have learned from the editorials that you have read and those shared in class, educated opinions are the basis of strong persuasion, and facts are the basis for educated opinions. Persuading others to follow the course of action you advocate—whether voting for a candidate, contributing to the United Way, or wearing seat belts—requires that you not only provide sound reasoning but that you consider the audience you are trying to persuade and the purpose you have in persuading them.

While it may be said that "everyone is entitled to his or her opinion," everyone is not entitled to have that opinion listened to. There are good opinions and bad ones; part of your job in this assignment is to determine which opinions are valid and which are not.

In general, opinions whose credibility relies on higher authority (the government, the Constitution, the Bible, etc.) are not arguable and only rarely can they be used to bring about change in the hands of the editorial writer. Thus, any argument you wish to advance that uses the Bible or other religious work as authority will probably be inappropriate in this class. Rather, your job is to seek out the facts that explain and issue—taking great care in the source of those facts—sort through those facts, write opinions that support each side of an issue (for example, on using or not using motorcycle helmets) and then write an editorial, or public policy statement, on that issue—a fact-based persuasive essay.

Pick a subject all of you are content with. Obviously, any topic on which you cannot be objective is out: no gun control, abortion, prayer in the schools, or anything else which causes members of the group to raise their voices. Instead, select a subject which is interesting, which is under contention, and for which information is readily available.

A good editorial runs about 500 to 750 words, almost never more. However, an explanation of the facts and a discussion of opinion may, in fact, run a lot longer. One of the jobs of the editorial is to distill those facts to educate the reader.

While your facts and opinion essay must be documented, the final editorial should not be.

Research Paper 2: How Public Policy Is Created

It is easy to criticize government officials: to say they are crooks, they don't keep promises, they aren't principled, or they just do not use common sense. But these easy criticisms fail to consider the difficulty of creating laws that are simultaneously intelligent, fair, and politically possible. The question remains: What influences shape public policy? What information is considered? What pressures do special-interest groups exert? How do such abstract and occasionally relative moral values like right and wrong figure in the making of public policy? The ultimate goal of this assignment, then, is to pick a public policy issue, to figure out what is being said about it and by whom, and to explain to your readers how power, fact, opinion, and belief have influenced (or are influencing) law and behavior.

What information you will need: Choose an area of public policy that interests you, read all you can about it, and write a report that explains what you found out. The possibilities are almost endless—health care, gay marriage, America's role in Iraq (or anywhere else), standardized testing in public schools, campaign finance reform, "sin taxes" on items, such as alcohol or cigarettes, stem cell research, drug testing of athletes—*you* name it! But watch it! This is *not* a persuasive paper; you will not be arguing one point of view or another. Instead, you will be presenting *all* the points of view on a given issue in a way that fairly represents them.

Stuck for ideas? Read through the front sections of the *Washington Post* or the *New York Times* or *Los Angeles Times* for the last couple of weeks and see what public policy issues they are discussing. Your group should find something you think is crucial.

Organizing your research: You will probably find it most logical to begin by discussing the problem that the public policy you are investigating has been proposed to solve. What is its history? What is its social impact? Who is affected? What would the proposed policy do to change the status quo? What is the hoped-for result? It would be all right to give more weight to the legislative history of your issue than its social effects, but you must discuss some of both.

■ MORE ABOUT COLLABORATION

While collaborative writing has become an important focus of composition studies in the past ten years, the idea of an individual's copyright to "intellectual property" is relatively new. The history of writing extends back five thousand years, but the notion that a solitary individual can create "original" written work and then possess that work as property has only existed for a little over two hundred years (cf. Ede and Lunsford, 1–6). Prior to the seventeenth century, books frequently compiled the written work of others and only infrequently cited the original writers. Prior to the seventeenth century, written ideas, like talk, belonged to everyone in a linguistic community. Indeed, before mass literacy and the widespread availability of inexpensive printed materials, written ideas were only available to most through oral transmission. These communal notions about intellectual property gradually changed as it became increasingly possible for individual writers to achieve fame and fortune through their pens. Yet, even as novelists, poets, and playwrights became increasingly more concerned with the ownership of their words, the industrial revolution created its own species of corporately owned language (Ede and Lunsford, 5). Throughout the nineteenth century and into our own time, written discourse in science, business, and industry has become a corporate product. Most scientific reports rely on the work and ideas of teams of researchers. Corporations frequently distribute information to shareholders and the public that acknowledges no one but the company.

Today our students are bewildered by the range of views on intellectual property. While software companies and the music and movie industries wage international war on copyright "pirates," those same companies ask their employees to imagine their individual efforts as contributions to a large team. One might well create a new software program for Microsoft, but one should not expect authorship credit. Preparing for their careers, students pass through an academic establishment that is deeply concerned that students *do their own work*. Plagiarism and cheating are represented as moral bankruptcy while the sharing of information is discouraged. Graduate students in the sciences might well find themselves conducting experiments and writing reports for senior scientists for which they receive no name credit in institutions where they could be expelled for passing off the words of others as their own. English majors could easily find themselves taught to value the individual genius and unique creative power of Virginia Woolf in classes entitled "Woolf and the Bloomsbury Circle."

It is in this conflicted context that recent research on collaborative writing has been conducted. Beginning as early as 1963, Derek J. de Solla Price noted the increase in the number of scientific articles written by large teams. From the mid-sixties until the early seventies, Price (1963), Hagstrum

(1964), Clarke (1964), Price and Beaver (1966), Zuckerman (1967), Weinberg (1970), and Crane (1972) identified the research and reporting practices of those working in the sciences and social sciences. In 1973, Kenneth Bruffee introduced the fledgling discipline of composition studies to "practical models of collaborative learning." Response to Bruffee's early work was slow in emerging, however. In the 1970s, composition studies were largely preoccupied with the claims of "expressivist" and "writing-as-process" schools of thought—both of which emphasized the importance of the *individual's* voice, ideas, and composing processes. It was not until the early 1980s, when Richard Gebhardt (1980) and John Clifford (1981) each published essays discussing the ways in which collaboration affects writing pedagogy, that a large number of researchers began to examine collaborative learning and writing from the compositionist's point of view.

Since the early 1980s, research on collaborative writing has divided itself into three main strands: 1) studies and analysis of collaboration in "nonacademic settings"; 2) defining and describing models of collaboration; and 3) the interpersonal dynamics of collaborative groups. Beginning with Faigley and Miller's "What We Learn Writing on the Job" (1982), it is clear that research into the collaborative activities of those working outside the academy has become the most important research site. Odell and Goswami's *Writing in Nonacademic Settings* (1985) is perhaps the most logical starting place for those interested in off-campus collaborative activity. Introduced in Odell and Goswami's collection are several oft-cited essays on collaborative writing research, including Paul Anderson's "What Survey Research Tells Us about Writing at Work" and Paradis, Dobrin, and Miller's "Writing at EXXON ITD: Notes on the Writing Environment of an R&D Organization." Yet, despite the historical importance of Odell and Goswami's collection, the "seminal" text on collaborative writing is Ede and Lunsford's superbly researched *Single Texts/Plural Authors* (1990), which presents a history of notions of authorship, statistical information on what kinds of writing really are done in the world outside the academy, and a rationale for a collaborative pedagogy. Other important texts on nonacademic collaboration are Lay and Karis's *Collaborative Writing in Industry: Investigations in Theory and Practice* (1990) and Burnett and Duin's *Collaboration in Technical and Professional Communication: A Research Perspective* (1995).

The second important area in collaborative research is composed of those studies which consider the various kinds of collaboration. While many of those investigating what collaboration is and how it works do their work in nonacademic settings, the emphasis on models of collaboration can derive from any research base. Killingsworth and Jones's and Couture and Rhymer's 1989 studies, for example, pay particular attention to defining what workplace collaboration is and when it occurs, while Beard, Rhymer, and

Williams focus their 1989 essay on how properly to assess collaborative writing groups. Several essays describing nonacademic models for collaboration, including those by Debs and Selzer, can be found in Fearing and Sparrow's collection *Technical Writing: Theory and Practice* (1989). One can also find important essays discussing conceptual frameworks for understanding collaboration in Forman's *New Visions of Collaborative Writing* (1992). Other useful texts discussing models of small groups are Hare's somewhat dated *Handbook of Small Group Research* (1976), Swap's *Group Decision Making* (1984), and Hirokawa and Poole's *Communication and Group Decision-Making* (1986). Those particularly interested in how collaborative models drawn from industry have been translated into collaborative writing pedagogy should consult Phillips's *Teaching How to Work in Groups* (1990).

The last major area in collaborative writing research investigates the "sociology" of small groups. In addition to the aforementioned collection by Forman, one will find a good overview of relevant small-group dynamics in Blyler and Thralls's *Professional Communication: The Social Perspective* (1993). Included in this volume is Burnett's "Conflict in Collaborative Decision-Making," which those new to teaching collaborative writing should find valuable as a summary of research into how conflict can either mediate or enhance the quality of collaborative efforts. Our own "Fields of Dissonance in the Collaborative Writing Classroom" builds on Burnett's work by presenting an even more complex picture of the small group working dynamic. In addition to small group "conflict," gender studies perspectives have also been brought to bear on research into collaboration. Lunsford and Ede's "Rhetoric in a New Key" (1990), for example, distinguishes between a predominantly male "hierarchical mode of discourse" and the predominantly female "dialogic mode." Lay's "The Androgynous Collaborator: The Impact of Gender Studies on Collaboration" (1992) also asserts the importance of gender in determining interpersonal dynamics in groups, suggesting that attention must be paid to gender stereotyping when students evaluate their collaborative groups. Raign and Sims's 1993 "Gender, Persuasion Techniques, and Collaboration" amplifies the issues raised in Lunsford and Ede and also in Lay. In addition to these important articles, Nadler, Nadler, and Todd-Mancillas's *Advances in Gender and Communication Research* (1987) provides a good starting point for those interested in exploring communications theory, gender, and language.

Still other researchers have urged the importance of incorporating self-monitoring strategies into collaborative work—most notably, Forman and Katsky's article discussing the importance of groups remaining aware of both writing and group processes (1986). To build a solid general background in how small groups work we suggest reading around in Morse and Phelps's *Interpersonal Communication: A Relational Perspective* (1980), Klauss and Bass's *Interpersonal Communication in Organizations* (1982), Rolloff and Miller's *Interpersonal Processes: New Directions in Communication Research* (1989), Ross's *Small Groups in Organizational Settings* (1989), Napier and Gershenfeld's *Groups: Theory and Experience* (fifth edition, 1993), and Frey's *Group Communication in Context* (1994).

WEB RESOURCES FOR PART II (TEACHING COLLABORATIVE WRITING)

Web Resources can be found at www.prenhall.com/harris under Instructor's Resources.

WORKS CITED

Beard, John D., Jone Rymer, and David L. Williams. "An Assessment System for Collaborative-Writing Groups: Theory and Empirical Evaluation." *Journal of Business and Technical Communication* 3 (1989): 29–51.

Bruffee, Kenneth. "Collaborative Learning: Some Practical Models." *College English* 35 (1973): 634–42.

———. "Collaborative Learning and the 'Conversation of Mankind.' " *College English* 46 (1984): 635–52.

Burnett, Rebecca E. "Conflict in Collaborative Decision-Making." *Professional Communication: The Social Perspective.* Eds., Nancy R. Blyler and Charlotte Thralls. Newbury Park, CA: SAGE, 1993. 144–62.

Burnett, Rebecca E. and Ann Hill Duin. *Collaboration in Technical and Professional Communication: A Research Perspective.* Hillsdale, NJ: Erlbaum, forthcoming 1995.

Clarke, Beverly. "Multiple Authorship Trends in Scientific Papers." *Science* 143 (1964): 822–24.

Clifford, John. "Composing in Stages: The Effects of a Collaborative Pedagogy." *Research in the Teaching of Writing* 14 (1981): 37–53.

Couture, Barbara and Jone Rymer. "Interactive Writing on the Job: Definitions and Implications of 'Collaboration.' " *Writing in the Business Professions.* Ed. Mura Kogan. Urbana, IL: National Council of the Teachers of English, 1989.

Crane, Diane. *Invisible Colleges: Diffusion of Knowledge in Scientific Communities.* Chicago: University of Chicago Press, 1972.

Daiute, Collette. "Do 1 and 1 Make 2?: Patterns of Influence by Collaborative Authors." *Written Communication* 3 (1986): 382–408.

De Solla Price, Derek J. *Little Science, Big Science.* New York: Columbia University Press, 1963.

De Solla Price, Derek J. and Donald Beaver. "Collaboration in an Invisible College." *American Psychologist* 21 (1964): 241–63.

Ede, Lisa and Andrea A. Lunsford. *Single Texts/Plural Authors: Perspectives on Collaborative Writing.* Carbondale, IL: Southern Illinois University Press, 1990.

Faigley, Lester and Thomas Miller. "What We Learn from Writing on the Job." *College English* 44 (1982): 557–69.

Fearing, Bertie E. and W. Keats Sparrow. *Technical Writing: Theory and Practice.* New York: Modern Language Association, 1989.

Flower, Linda and John R. Hayes. "Images, Plans, and Prose: The Representation of Meaning in Writing." *Written Communication* 1 (1986): 120–60.

Forman, Janis. *New Visions of Collaborative Writing.* Portsmouth, NH: Boynton/Cook, 1992.

Forman, Janis and Patricia Katsky. "The Group Report: A Problem in Small Group or Writing Processes?" *The Journal of Business Communication* 23 (1986): 23–35.

Frey, Lawrence R. *Group Communication in Context: Studies of Natural Groups.* Hillsdale, NJ: Erlbaum, 1994.

Gebhardt, Richard. "Teamwork and Feedback: Broadening the Base of Collaborative Writing." *College English* 42 (1980): 69–74.

Hagstrum, Warren O. "Traditional and Modern Forms of Scientific Teamwork." *Administrative Science Quarterly* 9 (1964): 241–63.

Hare, A. Paul. *Handbook of Small Group Research.* New York: Free Press, 1976.

Hirokawa, Randy Y. and Marshall S. Poole. *Communication and Group Decision-Making.* Beverly Hills: SAGE, 1986.

Killingsworth, M. Jimmie and Betsy G. Jones. "Division of Labor or Integrated Teams: A Crux in the Management of Technical Communication?" *Technical Communication* 36 (1989): 210–21.

Klauss, R. and B.M. Bass. *Interpersonal Communication in Organizations.* New York: Academic, 1987.

Lay, Mary M. "The Androgynous Collaborator: The Impact of Gender Studies on Collaboration." New Visions of Collaborative Writing. Ed. Janis Foreman. Portsmouth, NH: Boynton/Cook, 1992. 82–104.

Lay, Mary M. and William M. Karis. *Collaborative Writing in Industry: Investigations in Theory and Practice.* New York: Baywood, 1990.

Lunsford, Andrea A. and Lisa Ede. "Rhetoric in a New Key: Women and Collaboration." *Rhetoric Review* 8 (1990): 234–41.

Moffett, James. *Teaching The Universe Of Discourse.* Boston: Houghton Mifflin, 1983.

Morse, B.W. and L.A. Phelps. *Interpersonal Communication: A Relational Perspective.* Minneapolis: Burgess, 1980.

Nadler, Lawrence B., Marjorie K. Nadler, and William R. Todd-Mancillas. *Advances in Gender and Communication Research.* Lanham: University Press of America, 1987.

Napier, Rodney W. and Matti K. Gershenfeld. *Groups: Theory and Experience.* Boston: Houghton Mifflin, 1993.

Odell, Lee and Dixie Goswami. *Writing in Nonacademic Settings.* New York: Guilford, 1985.

Perry, William G. *Forms of Intellectual and Ethical Development in The College Years.* New York: Holt, 1970.

Phillips, Gerald M. *Teaching How to Work in Groups.* Norwood: Ablex, 1990.

Putnam, Linda L. "Conflict in Group Decision-Making." *Communication and Group Decision-Making.* Eds., Randy Y. Hirokawa and Marshall S. Poole. Beverly Hills: SAGE, 1986. 175–96.

Raign, Kathryn Rosser. "Gender, Persuasion Techniques, and Collaboration." *Technical Communication Quarterly* 2 (1993): 89–104.

Rolloff, M.E. and G.R. Miller. *Interpersonal Processes: New Directions in Communication Research.* Beverly Hills: SAGE, 1989.

Ross, Raymond S. *Small Groups in Organizational Settings.* Englewood Cliffs, NJ: Prentice Hall, 1989.

Swap, George and Associates. *Group Decision Making.* Beverly Hills: SAGE, 1984.

Thralls, Charlotte and Nancy Roundy Blyler. *Professional Communication: The Social Perspective.* Newbury Park: SAGE, 1993.

Trimbur, John. "Consensus and Difference in Collaborative Writing." *College English* 51 (1989): 602–16.

Weinberg, Alvin M. "Scientific Teams and Scientific Laboratories." *Dædelus* 99 (1970): 1056–75.

Zuckerman, Harriet. "Nobel Laureates in Science: Patterns of Productivity, Collaboration, and Authorship." *American Sociological Review* 32 (1967): 391–403.

PART THREE:
ESL Writers in the Composition Class
by Cynthia Myers, *Iowa State University*

■ INTRODUCTION

When I was in my second semester of teaching freshman composition as a graduate student, I had an articulate and motivated Colombian student in my class. I enjoyed having Julio in class and optimistically hoped that my course could help him mature as a writer. One day after class, he approached me with a paper I had corrected and kindly asked me to explain a few of the mistakes he had made: He wanted to thoroughly understand which situations required the present perfect and which required the past perfect. I launched into an explanation, but as I talked, I suddenly realized that I had only a vague notion of the answer. I knew it had something to do with time frame, but why exactly couldn't Julio say "I have lived in Kansas since six months ago"? It was not something I had ever really considered, nor was it a grammar question that had come up in my teaching of high school English to native speakers.

I began to notice how many grammar errors I had corrected on Julio's paper: the page was covered with green ink. I also began to suspect that my corrections were probably not going to help him avoid making the mistakes another time. I noticed how few substantive comments I had made to help him with revising his material and reorganizing his ideas. I began to feel embarrassed, and then apologetic, and finally inadequate. How could I help him improve his writing without becoming mired in long and confusing grammar explanations? How could I help him improve his grammar when I had such an incomplete understanding of the language myself?

I tell the story because I believe my feelings of incompetence at that time have probably been felt by many teachers suddenly faced with nonnative English speakers whose questions and whose presence in a class with native speakers are disquieting. As teachers of writing, we want to help all students, but without specialized training we may be uncertain how to proceed. Will we embarrass a quiet Japanese student if we ask him to share an especially poetic description with the rest of the class? Is it useful to mark the many errors that appear on an Indonesian student's first draft? Should we tell a Puerto Rican student that her lateness to class is disruptive since we know that her Latin American sense of time is different from our own? Should we avoid calling on a Chinese student whose spoken English is difficult to understand? And, in addition to the many questions we may have about individual nonnative speakers, how do we handle classroom dynamics to encourage the native speaking students to include nonnative speakers when they choose collaborative or peer review groups? How can we foster an atmosphere in which all students feel empowered?

My role as coordinator of a program of cross-cultural freshman English classes at a large state university has given me some insights into the challenges faced by composition teachers who work with classes made up of half nonnative and half native speakers, particularly when the teachers have little experience in teaching ESL (English as a second language). It has also given me a new appreciation for the stimulating diversity of a composition class with students from varied backgrounds and also for the benefits to the U.S. students in a class with international classmates.

Of course, not all non-native speakers are international students. Some are migrants or recent immigrants who have been educated in U.S. schools. At times these students communicate well orally, but find that ESL errors manifest themselves in their writing. Migrant and immigrant students also bring varying levels of fluency in this native language and varying levels of education to the college classroom.

Whether non-native English speakers comprise half a class or are scattered more sparsely throughout sections of freshman English, the insights and experiences of international students can enrich any class. Students learn to collaborate with students from different backgrounds, gaining skills that will make them more cosmopolitan citizens of the world. Goals of a writing course may include encouraging students to draw material from multiple perspectives, growing beyond a narrow view of the world, and thinking critically, goals which can be facilitated when differing views are represented. Regardless of their cultural background, students can learn to tolerate ambiguity and avoid automatic judgments, and having a culturally mixed class can broaden the perspectives of both U.S. and international students. Students can also learn that culture is much more than an assemblage of curious customs, that it is at the very root of our personalities, ideas, and beliefs.

Though ESL students may be initially apprehensive about taking a composition course, they have much to gain from the experience. In many universities, freshmen enroll primarily in large lecture classes; a composition class may be one of the few in which professors know their names, or in which they have a chance to get acquainted with their classmates. For those ESL students who are international students, they often spend much of their time associating with a support group of other students from their own cultures; though they may wish to make American friends, international students often do not find opportunities to get well-acquainted with U.S. students. The intimate setting of a composition class can be an ideal opportunity for an international student to make U.S. friends. Additionally, the more chances an international student has to practice listening, speaking, and writing, the more likely she will be to improve her abilities to communicate in English. This practice occurs with more intensity and frequency in the writing classroom than in many content area classes.

The first section of this chapter examines cultural issues that make studying in the United States a challenging situation for many international students and suggests ways in which a composition teacher can integrate international students into the classroom. It also discusses some of the general concerns in cross-cultural education and provides insights into the differing perspectives of international students. The second section describes some of the difficulties new international students may have in speaking and listening. It discusses classroom activities that have proved useful in helping ESL students improve their listening comprehension and speaking abilities. The third section looks more specifically at writing pedagogy for the ESL student, covering such issues as understanding differences in rhetorical expectations of native and nonnative students, handling errors in ESL student's writing, and adapting pedagogical techniques like peer review and collaborative writing to a class including nonnative students.

■ CULTURAL ISSUES

New international students face big adjustments when coming to the U.S. to study. Not only is the language a challenge, but even well-meaning Americans can cause distress for newly arrived students. Mui, from Malaysia, wrote this in her journal:

> When I first came, I was very frightened because I did not understand the American way of doing things. I can clearly remember my first time on the campus. It was a afternoon, but the campus was as quiet as midnight because the university was closed for winter break. I was walking alone with a campus map in my right hand and worrying that I would not be able to find all my classes. An American guy approached me as I walked along the sidewalk. As he got closer, he said "Hi." I looked around and there was nobody else except the two of us. "He must be saying hi to me," I thought. I was so scared! I whispered in my heart, "My goodness, I hope he won't attack a helpless girl like me. He must be a crazy

person." I walked faster with my head down and ignored him. My heart was beating and I could hardly breathe. I just couldn't believe it when he passed me by without any assault! Later, as I was here a longer time, I realized that saying "hi" or smiling to strangers was to be friendly to them. I hoped that the guy wouldn't misinterpret that foreigners were cold and unfriendly.

Reading her journal, we cannot help but sympathize with Mui's terror. If this situation caused her to panic, one might imagine that other, more complex situations could be very confusing. New international students sometimes have great difficulty knowing what is appropriate or expected in a given situation. For example, a new student in one of my ESL classes confided to me that he had been unable to sleep for a week because his American roommate would enter their dorm room at two or three in the morning talking loudly to friends, would turn on the light and the stereo, and would often not go to bed until dawn. To the international student, his roommate's behavior was incomprehensibly rude, yet my student was uncertain whether or not this unkindness was inappropriate for an American. He had no idea whether or not he should complain, either to the roommate or to someone else. And in the meantime, he was attempting to attend class and study through a blur of exhaustion.

These two situations were resolved favorably: Mui noticed the differences in greeting customs and began to feel comfortable with them; my tired student spoke to his RA and eventually arranged to move into another room. But other situations may continue to provoke uneasiness, discomfort, or confusion. The anthropologist Edward Hall (1959) explains that ". . . culture is more than mere custom that can be shed or changed like a suit of clothes" (46), and ". . . culture controls behavior in deep and persisting ways, many of which are outside of awareness and therefore beyond conscious control of the individual" (48).

Some students may never feel entirely comfortable with the relaxed, "anything goes" atmosphere in an American classroom: It violates all they have been taught about the teacher's proper authority and the respect owed by a student. Though they may manage to understand and function in a U.S. classroom, they may never feel completely "at home" in a class where students interrupt the teacher or pack up their books to leave while the teacher is still talking. Another student may grow to understand that American friends are not intending to be rude when they say "Let's get together sometime?" but never call, yet it may continue to seem impolite.

We need to recognize rather than trivialize the differences in deeply-rooted cultural values. As Hall (1959) points out, the most useful aspect of learning about cultural differences is gaining a deeper understanding of one's own culture. "The best reason for exposing oneself to foreign ways is to generate a sense of vitality and awareness—an interest in life which can come only when one lives through the shock of contrast and difference" (53). If teachers understand the complex challenges facing their international students, they can work to make the composition classroom a place where some cultural issues can be explored. At the very least, they can provide a supportive atmosphere where U.S. and international classmates can learn together.

It is also well worth remembering that international students are an amazingly diverse group of people. They come from backgrounds very different from one another, have widely varying goals and attitudes about studying in the United States, and certainly have different skills. My comments are not meant to minimize these differences, nor am I intending to "lump" all international students into one large, easily-explainable group. However, certain difficulties reappear among students from many backgrounds, and several issues about cross-cultural communication are worth exploring. The following suggestions may help to clarify areas confusion, misinterpretation and difficulty experienced by many international students.

Nonverbal Communication

Anyone who has done reading on cultural diversity is aware that students from other cultures and the "average American" may interpret matters of personal space and body language very differently. My consciousness was raised about this issue during my first semester as a teaching assistant. A Nigerian student in my class frequently came for office hours to get extra advice about his writing. I enjoyed talking with him and got to know him well from our frequent conversations. We would begin the conference with me behind my desk and him on the chair to the right of the desk where all my students sat when they came in to talk to me. As we talked about his writing, he would invariably gather up his papers and move his chair so that we were sitting side by side. Though I didn't feel threatened by him, I found myself feeling uncomfortable sitting with our shoulders touching, and I would unconsciously edge my chair farther away. As we talked, my student would scoot his chair closer; I would move farther. I finally realized what was happening when I found that I was leaning into the wall at the left side of my desk: inch by inch, he had pursued me there. He felt comfortable at a closer distance than I did—a phenomenon I had read about but never experienced before.

Hall (1959) provides insights into this phenomenon for his U.S. readers:

> In Latin America the interaction distance is much less than it is in the United States. Indeed, people cannot talk comfortably with one

another unless they are very close to the distance that evokes either sexual or hostile feelings in the North American. The result is that when they move close, we withdraw and back away. As a consequence, they think we are distant or cold, withdrawn and unfriendly. We, on the other hand, are constantly accusing them of breathing down our necks, crowding us, and spraying our faces. (p. 209)

Students from other cultural backgrounds may also have differing conventions for who may touch whom and in what circumstances. A Japanese student may feel that her space has been invaded if an American student puts his feet on the back of her chair. Asian students often express surprise at U.S. couples publicly hugging or kissing, yet may find the taboo against same-sex touching odd. One assumes, until one has reason to know otherwise, that all people operate under the same unspoken rules for nonverbal appropriateness, and it may come as a disquieting shock to realize that one's own internalized rules are not held by others. "Since most people don't think about personal distance as something that is culturally patterned, foreign spatial cues are almost inevitably misinterpreted" (Hall & Hall, 1990, p. 12).

Eye gaze varies across cultures, too, with some cultures encouraging direct eye contact and others considering direct eye contact too forward or insulting. Once during a discussion of this topic, a student told me that he would never stare at a woman's eyes. He felt that she would certainly interpret this as him indicating sexual interest in her. When I asked what place was the appropriate spot for his eyes, he responded seriously, "Her chest." It is often pointed out that Vietnamese students show respect by directing their eyes downward, not by making direct eye contact. Conversely, students from the Middle East may feel that Americans do not keep eye contact long enough.

Teachers tend to be focused on the verbal channel of expression, and may not have a conscious awareness of nonverbal communication (Morain, 1978). They should educate themselves about some of the differences in nonverbal communication, especially if international students comprise a good portion of their students. Differences in gesture, eye contact, touch and movement are interestingly discussed by many writers. Particularly accessible are collections by Valdes (1986) and Byrd (1986) as well as the classics by Hall. ESL texts can also be interesting resources for a teacher interested in cross-cultural differences. Genzel & Cummings (1994) and Levine, Baxter, & McNulty (1987) are good resources.

Trying to define one's own cultural expectations for nonverbal communication can be an interesting topic of class discussion if several nationalities are represented. A teacher can have students discuss questions like these:

➤ How do you enter a classroom if you are late and arriving after the class has begun?

➤ How do you greet a friend of the opposite sex after not seeing him/her for several months? Of the same sex? How do you greet a friend when you see him/her for the second time in the same day?

➤ What body language would you use when you meet your parents at the end of the school year?

➤ In what circumstances, if any, would you expect to be able to smell a friend? Would you find it offensive, normal, embarrassing?

➤ In what circumstances would you walk hand in hand or arm in arm with a friend?

➤ What gestures are considered rude in your culture? Why?

Although issues such as these do not go to the root of cultural differences, they can raise students' awareness and make them more sensitive not only of their classmates but also their own cultural assumptions.

Time Codes

Most North Americans have heard of the Spanish term "mañana" and realize that the expression says something about the relative cultural importance of being on time or doing things "right now." U.S. residents assume that this stereotype simply means that Latin Americans "put off for tomorrow what they should do today," yet the underlying cultural values are much more complex. Levine and Wolfe (1985) interviewed Brazilian students to better understand their sense of time, and noted that the Brazilian students felt less regret about being late and were less likely to be bothered that someone else was late than students from North America. As a matter of fact, the Brazilian students believed that a consistently late person was probably more successful than one who was on time.

Hall & Hall (1989) describe the distinction between "monochromatic" and "polychromatic" time. People who are monochromatic focus on one thing at a time, while in polychromatic cultures, people are comfortable with doing many things at once. The U.S. is a monochromatic culture: time is seen as linear, and it is scheduled, compartmentalized and talked about as if it were tangible. It can be "spent," "saved," "wasted," and "lost" (13). In polychromatic cultures, keeping to a schedule is less important than interacting with people, and students with a polychromatic sense of time may have trouble understanding why it is important to their teachers for them to come promptly to class or an appointment. Students would opt to be late for an appointment rather than rudely end a conversation they are having with a friend.

Being aware that a student is not intentionally trying to be rude may help a teacher interpret this behavior correctly. Though they may occasionally be late for class, Latin American or African students may also stay after class to chat and will likely not be among the group packing up their backpacks to head out the door before the class is over. And of course, many students who would not worry about the clock in their home countries will make an effort to be on time when they are in the United States.

An American student wrote about her growing understanding of a Puerto Rican classmate's different sense of time:

> I talked to Ana one day during class and she mentioned that she was uncomfortable with the way people here said, "Hi, how are you!" without waiting for a response. She said it was rather shallow. It didn't dawn on me that I said those words often until I heard myself saying them to Ana herself two days later. I was in a *big* hurry to get to one of my classes and I saw Ana on one of the paths. I was practically running when I saw her, and because I was happy to see Ana, I said 'Hi, how are ya!' as I kept on going. As soon as the words came out of my mouth, I knew I had said something really stupid. I stopped to talk to her for awhile and I left feeling a little happier. Even though I was in a hurry, I still made it on time.

This kind of insight into another person's perspective is exactly what we can hope for in a class where students are working together with others from different cultures.

Sensitive Cultural Issues

One of the instructors in our program recently raised an interesting question: "What if an ESL student writes a paper setting forth cultural values that the teacher simply cannot accept?" (Falck-Yi, personal communication). This teacher was imagining a situation in which a student made a claim that men were superior to women, or that an oldest child was evil if he did not care for aging parents, or that one's government must be obeyed blindly.

It is certainly true that students from other cultures will have, and will express, values that are not shared by many U.S. teachers. However, this also occurs in writing classes for U.S. students: the teacher with a liberal perspective will feel uncomfortable about a student's praise of Rush Limbaugh; many writing teachers have disagreed with student papers containing racist comments. Given that the situation is not uncommon, most teachers will attempt to approach such writing with sensitivity. A teacher can ask the student questions to help him more clearly define his ideas, a teacher can suggest alternative viewpoints or point out inconsistencies in his arguments, but in the end, a teacher must respect the student's right as an individual to hold differing beliefs.

At times, teachers may find they have unexpectedly strayed into "taboo" areas. Several years ago, I thought I would try a creative descriptive assignment in an ESL class. I brought several varieties of apples to class, gave one to each class member, and asked them to describe the apples in detail. I suggested they look carefully at the outside of the apple, but also that they take several bites to describe the taste and texture. The class included two students from Malaysia, one from Indonesia, one from Saudi Arabia and one from Egypt, and I noticed several minutes into the activity that none of them were eating their apples. Suddenly, it struck me: we were in the month of Ramadan when Muslims fast during daylight hours! I was momentarily afraid that I had offended them, but they graciously took the opportunity to explain their religious beliefs to the rest of the class. My mistake provided an opportunity for learning.

Some culturally sensitive topics are worth exploring in the classroom. Teachers may find that with some international students, they not only need to explain techniques for avoiding sexist language (Section 40 in the *Prentice Hall Reference Guide*), but also may need to explain the rationale behind the concept. In addition, with current concerns about sexual harassment, students from different cultures may need to be sensitized to the fact that their "normal" manner of approaching people of the opposite sex can be misinterpreted. A student from Honduras recently told one of the teachers in our program that when he saw college women sunning themselves on public lawns, he assumed he would be welcome to go up next to them, sit down, and begin a conversation. When his American classmate said that the sunbathing woman might think he was harassing her, the student was puzzled. "Why is it worse to go up and talk to someone," he asked, "than it is to stare at them without speaking the way the U.S. men do?" To the Honduran student, the impersonal staring of the American men was more insulting than the approach he perceived as direct and friendly.

Tyler (1994) describes a situation in which an male tutor from India was working with an American female undergraduate in a volunteer situation. The female student complained that the tutor had made sexual advances during the tutoring session because his leg had brushed against hers several times and he had not apologized. Tyler notes that it was clear that the touch had been unintentional, and that the Indian tutor had not recognized that this casual contact required an apology.

Teachers should be aware that students from some cultures may not feel at all comfortable criticizing their government or their parents, will balk at topics that offend their religious sensibilities, and may have differing attitudes about relations between the sexes. Teachers should attempt to understand their students' viewpoints and appreciate the diversity they bring to the classroom. At the same time, giving the international students more complex insights into U.S. culture can also be a useful goal.

Another issue that may come up with some nonnative speakers, particularly those who are immigrant or migrant students, is a sense of resistance to language development. Some may see the acquisition of a new language as a threat to their native culture and even to their family relationships. Learning language changes us; it changes our understanding of the world. For some, that change is undesirable, and they may subvert efforts to become fluent in standard English. Richard Rodriguez and other writers have shared this sense of conflict in their autobiographical pieces. This conflict is not limited to learning a second language, either. Other writers, such as bell hooks and Amy Tan, have described the conflict between using the language of home and the language of the institution and how these changes in their language affected their relationships and even their sense of identity. Reading about and discussing these conflicts can help student pinpoint the source of dissonance they may feel in learning academic English. Students can find space to write about these issues in narrative, descriptive, compare and contrast, or argumentative essays.

■ LISTENING AND SPEAKING SKILLS FOR ESL STUDENTS

Although the focus of a composition course is writing, an international student needs to be able to comprehend and speak in order to participate fully in the class. U.S. students can be sensitized to the difficulties facing the international students, and a teacher can encourage communication between native and nonnative speakers.

Listening

Especially for newly-arrived students, coping with the average American's idiomatic, connected speech can be challenging. Many students from East Asian countries have learned a sort of "textbook" English, focusing on translation, memorizing model texts, and rigorously studying formal English grammar. Some have never taken a class in which they had to speak; some have never communicated with a native speaker; many have learned from British English models. Imagine the surprise a Korean student feels when she hears her American partner on the first day of class say something that sounds like "Whaddayawanna do?" She can, without difficulty, read the words "What do you want to do?" but her classmate's pronunciation is unexpectedly confusing.

Of course most native speakers realize that English is not always spoken the way that it is written, that words like *thought, throughout,* and *rough* share common spelling but have different pronunciations. However, many native speakers don't realize that the natural speech patterns for Americans are not easily predictable from written text. Words within phrases are linked, as in the previous example, and vowels in unstressed syllables may be reduced (not pronounced clearly) or omitted entirely. For instance, the phrase *back and forth* will be spoken *back 'n forth* and *wants to go* is said *wants t' go.* Native speakers probably write *should of* rather than *should have* because, as it is spoken, the word sounds more like *of* than *have.*

Sound changes also occur—are said to be assimilated—when certain consonants occur together. For example, *could you* becomes *couldja* where the *d* and *y* combine into a sound like *dj,* or "What was your name?" becomes "What *wazshur* name?" Finally, stress patterns in English sentences can affect meaning in a way quite unusual in other languages. "He's leaving on *Friday,*" "*He's* leaving on Friday" and "He's *leaving* on Friday" are appropriate in slightly different contexts. Similarly, "I went to the white *house*" is not the same as "I went to the *White* House!" It's no wonder that new inter-national students sometimes appear puzzled! (See pronunciation texts like Gilbert, 1994 for detailed explanations of these phenomena.)

Academic idioms can make understanding classroom spoken English even more difficult for a new student. Academic discourse is rife with idiomatic expressions: "Will you *pass back* the *handout*"; "There's a *pop quiz* today"; "I'll *post the scores* at *midterm*"; "You can take a *make-up test.*" The vocabulary of the writing classroom may be just as opaque for a new international student. *First draft, peer editing, brainstorming,* and *prewriting* may not only be unfamiliar terms, but may not link into an already existing schema in the international student's mind.

Even more troublesome for international students are the many idioms and slang expressions that native speakers use unconsciously in their informal speech. "That was over my head"; "It's on the tip of my tongue," and "I'm between a rock and a hard place" are not immediately transparent to a nonnative speaker. Sports idioms like "way out in left field," "pinch hitter," or "couldn't make it to first base" are used frequently in everyday language, but are meaningless to a student who is unfamiliar with baseball. And slang expressions from "grunge" to "nerd" also can confuse the second language learner.

Many nonnative students are eager to learn new idioms, but they may not always have an effective strategy for acquiring them. I recall one diligent student who was studying a small paperback book as I walked into class. When I asked Ming what he was reading, he told me he was learning American slang from his book, which provided translations into Chinese. I expressed enthusiasm for his efforts, and asked him to give me an example. He looked down, and read his most recently learned idiom: "Paint the town red." I explained that that particular idiom was rather outdated, and commiserated about the difficulty of keeping up-to-date on slang. I confided that I frequently had to ask my teenage children to explain popular expressions. Ming decided to ask some of his American friends for current alternatives before he began to say "Paint the town red."

The complexities of comprehending spoken English may seem overwhelming, but encouraging the nonnative speakers to use their native classmates as "slang informants" is useful for both the U.S. and international students. The nonnative students should be encouraged to bring their questions about idiomatic expressions; it is an enlightening experience for the native speakers to attempt to define terms that they use without thinking, and identifying idioms can raise their awareness. For example, international students frequently ask "When I thank people, why do they say 'sure' or 'you bet' instead of 'you're welcome'?" or "What exactly should I say when an American says 'What's happening'?" A student recently asked me, "What's the difference between 'Oh boy' and 'Oh man'? Why don't you say 'Oh girl' or 'Oh woman'?" Struggling with questions like these makes a native speaker more sensitive to his or her own language. If the nonnative students seem to feel uncomfortable asking their classmates for help with idioms, students can use their journals for recording expressions and terms they don't understand. This allows a teacher to give feedback privately.

Often, students who are not following class discussion or who do not understand something their teachers have said may not indicate that they are having trouble; the problems only become evident when the teacher collects a homework assignment. Students may be reluctant to show that they do not understand because they consider asking questions insulting, since it would communicate that the teacher had not explained well enough. Other students may simply be too shy or fearful to tell the teacher that they don't understand. Putting instructions in writing can be a helpful way of backing up oral comments. Additionally, encouraging students to come for individual help in an office conference can be a nonthreatening way for them to ask questions.

Native speaking students may need some guidance to respond to their ESL classmates in a helpful way. Levine, Baxter & McNulty (1987) quote a nonnative speaker who was frustrated talking with an American, "When I say . . . 'Please repeat,' he often repeats everything he said before, only louder, and faster. Why doesn't he speak more slowly when he repeats? Why does he repeat so many sentences? Usually, after he repeats, I still don't understand" (65). If several nonnative students in a class appear to be having difficulty with listening, the teacher may wish to address the issue directly. One can request that the native speakers speak slowly (not more loudly) and be willing to stop to explain expressions their classmates don't know. Additionally, rather than repeating the exact words that were initially misunderstood, a native speaker can try paraphrasing, using different expressions to communicate the same idea. The teacher can model this technique if it seems that students are having trouble communicating. Also, if the teacher occasionally stops to explain an idiom to the nonnative students, the U.S. students in the class may wish to add their perspectives or suggest alternative idioms, and will become sensitized to the difficulties of the nonnative speaker in understanding these expressions.

Speaking

While nonnative students' listening problems may not be obvious, especially if they seem to be paying attention, their speaking abilities are often more apparent. A student may know what she wants to say, but not be able to articulate her ideas; another may speak quickly, but with impenetrable pronunciation.

Speaking fluency will improve with practice, and I encourage my students to take advantage of every opportunity to talk they can find. However, even students who wish to practice interacting may feel inhibited raising their hands in class and may never feel comfortable enough to interrupt a classmate. One should recognize that nonnative students may have differing expectations regarding what goes on in a classroom. Students may feel that the best and proper way to learn is to sit silently and diligently take notes on the professor's lecture. They may be surprised to be expected to participate in class discussion, or they may attempt to participate but not find a way to "get a word in edgewise." Research into communication patterns reveals differences even between New Yorkers and Californians in their sense of the length of silent pauses between speakers or their tendency to interrupt one another (Tannen, 1984). If speakers from the U.S. differ, one can assume that speakers from various parts of the world will have very different unconscious expectations about how to get the attention of a classmate or how to take a turn in the conversation.

In a class with mixed nationalities, a teacher may find, at least initially, that the native speakers are dominating class discussions. However, a teacher can provide positive reinforcement when a nonnative student does respond to a question, can call on the nonnative speakers to encourage their participation, and should model supportive behaviors like repeating a difficult to understand comment so that the whole class can understand or providing an appropriate phrase or word if a student is struggling to find one.

Using Small Group Activities

Even though reticent students may never eagerly participate in a whole-class discussion, such students often open up in the safer context of a small group or pair. For this reason, using small groups for discussion of a reading, for examining sample student writing, or for a revision exercise can encourage the international students to participate. Other small group activities can include collaboratively gathering information, problem-solving, and annotating or evaluating readings (Reid, 1993).

Small group work may be a new experience for international students, but if the groups are structured carefully, they can be an effective way of encouraging discussion from quiet students. Assigning groups allows the instructor to mix international and U.S. students and avoids a situation in which the U.S. students choose their friends, leaving the international students to feel like the last ones picked for the seventh grade soccer game. On the other hand, a native speaker may feel excluded if several students from the same language background carry on a discussion in their language rather than in English, and ground rules about using English in class are sometimes useful.

Just as with native speakers, gender balance can also affect group dynamics; for example, a Muslim woman may feel more uncomfortable than a U.S. woman if asked to work with a group of male classmates. Ideally, the teacher of a culturally-mixed language class should avoid stereotyping her students (the Muslim woman might be just as outspoken and confident as her American classmate), but should remain sensitive to the cultural and gender makeup of student groups.

Of course native speakers can dominate the discussion of small groups, or they may take over a collaborative project without consulting the international students. It is often useful to specifically discuss some of the benefits and problems in cross-cultural communication before students are placed into groups. Additionally, one can set ground rules for discussions which include the participation of every member to encourage native speakers to solicit the ideas of the nonnative students. Or, if students regularly discuss class readings in small groups, rotating the "chair" or "reporter" who summarizes the group's work will necessitate that all the students have a turn. Also, including readings nonnative students can connect to, such as pieces dealing with language or cultural difference, can ensure nonnative students have expertise to add to the conversation. Structuring the group exercises, too, can guarantee that each student gets a voice: for example, if the assignment requires recording responses and ideas from every group member and incorporating those ideas into a summary, then each student's opinions will, by the nature of the assignment, be solicited.

Group activities certainly allow students to use and develop listening and speaking skills in the writing classroom. (Schlumberger & Clymer, 1989) Additionally, teachers should not hesitate to encourage nonnative students' participation in whole class activities and in group oral presentations. More specific comments on using peer review and collaborative writing will follow in the next section.

■ WRITING SKILLS FOR ESL STUDENTS

New teachers should remember that international students vary widely in their writing abilities. A teacher should not automatically assume that the nonnative speakers students will be the ones with the most pressing problems. On the contrary, teachers often say that the international students are among the best writers in their classes, willing to take on serious issues and work hard at improving their writing. Certainly, the nonnative speakers are often highly-motivated students, and they may be more focused on their academic goals than some of their native speaking classmates.

In our multicultural society, a student with a non-English name and appearance may well be as "American" as the blonde Jane Smith sitting beside her. Second generation immigrants can have interesting cultural perspectives, but their writing skills may be indistinguishable from other U.S. students. A permanent resident, immigrant student who learned English in a U.S. junior high school may be fluent in spoken English, yet may retain nonnative-like problems in grammar or expression. Leki (1992) describes one such Vietnamese student who did not want to take an ESL class for "foreigners" because she clearly wished to be considered an American; however, the student struggled in the regular composition class because of her English abilities. ESL students who have been educated in the U.S. may not be considered for placement into ESL courses despite lingering difficulties with standard English. At some U.S. universities, the distinction between first language basic writers and ESL writers has become blurred with the effects of bilingual education as well as the fact that students have immigrated at different ages (Santos, 1992). Certainly, too, students' educational backgrounds in their first languages will affect their abilities in the new language.

Given that there is no "typical" nonnative speaker in a composition class, how can a teacher meet the diverse needs of ESL students in helping them gain greater writing skills? Teachers can be reassured that many of the techniques used to teach writing to native speakers work equally well with ESL students. However, understanding culturally-based writing differences and gaining insights into ESL students' expectations will help teachers evaluate their students' needs more accurately.

Assumptions About Writing and Learning to Write

Since composition classes are such an expected feature of U.S. college and university curricula, it may come as a surprise that many students who come from different educational backgrounds have not had instruction in writing in their own language (Leki, 1992). In some cultures, writing instruction may embody very different values. I have already mentioned that students may feel uncomfortable with the casual atmosphere in U.S. classrooms and may be surprised that they are supposed to participate in class discussions. Other aspects of the U.S. composition class may also be unexpected.

If they come from university systems in which students can freely choose whether or not to attend lectures during the semester, students may feel that the frequent, daily homework assignments given in typical freshman level-classes are unnecessary busywork. One South American student commented that these classes were like high school classes, with the teacher always checking up on the student and attendance expected. He was accustomed to more freedom at the university level. On the other hand, some students adapt to these expectations and indicate that they appreciate the frequent practice and feedback. I often mention at the beginning of a course that a writing class is very different from most others: instead of absorbing a body of knowledge, students are developing skills. For this reason homework, frequent reading and writing, as well as regular attendance are essential in giving students practice in the skills they are learning.

Other differences may not be as obvious but may deeply affect a student's ability to write compositions. Students may have come from traditions in which the appearance of a piece of writing is judged as an important feature, and thus may be very uncomfortable handing in drafts that have cross-overs, arrows, or marginally-added phrases. I have frequently had to reassure students that I could read any but the most indecipherable handwriting and that I would not grade them on the neatness of their rough drafts. In fact, the concept of writing more than one draft may be surprising to them, and the rationale for asking them to do so should be carefully explained. Additionally, some students may have come from educational systems in which they were expected to do exactly as the teacher says. The respect and honor that they give to their teachers may be flattering, but a composition teacher can find it frustrating to find his own ideas and suggestions incorporated, whole cloth, into a student's papers. He may find that a student resists taking a strong personal stance in an argument or that, having taken a stance, the student does not feel a need to support or defend it. Teachers will probably resist students' requests for writing models to copy; they may not understand students' reluctance to critique an essay. These differences can make a mismatch between the teacher's and the ESL students' expectations in a class.

Rhetorical Features

A student once mentioned that the Chinese have a saying to describe the way that writing should work: "Open the door and see the mountain." She explained that the Chinese writer would paint a picture for the reader, building detail by detail, until finally, the mountain was revealed. If, on the other hand, one considers "the mountain" to be the main purpose of a piece of English writing, then we might imagine that the appropriate approach when writing in English is to first tell the reader she is going to see a mountain before she ever opens the door! In other words, the approach a writer takes to a piece of discourse—the choices a writer makes about what a reader needs or wants, what evidence to include, and how to organize—is influenced by the conventions of her culture.

A number of researchers have found interesting differences in writing conventions deemed appropriate in different populations. In a series of studies, Purves (1986) found differences between national groups in aspects such as how personal or impersonal writing was supposed to be, whether writing should be abstract or concrete, and how a writer should provide text coherence. People of the same culture tend to agree on what is appropriate proof for an assertion: English readers expect facts and statistics and are not convinced by extensive use of analogy, metaphor, intuition and the authority of the ancients. "Yet conventions of argumentation in other cultures may require precisely that recourse to analogy, intuition, beauty, or shared communal wisdom" (Leki, 1992, p. 92). Hinds (1987) makes the distinction between "reader-responsible" and "writer-responsible" writing. The Japanese expect the reader to make inferences and may feel insulted if a writer is too explicit, while English readers may see the Japanese approach as circular and vague. I have had Latin American college students balk at my requests for personal examples: to them, a personal example seemed immature or babyish; they preferred theoretical generalizations.

In her introductory essay in the Annotated Instructor's Edition to the handbook, Reid summarizes Robert Kaplan's (1966) exploratory study of nonnative students' organizational patterns. Though these patterns are certainly simplistic, Reid points out that the field of contrastive rhetoric can offer insights into some of the difficulties that the nonnative writer faces in understanding the best way to organize a piece of writing in a specific context. As a matter of fact, I have occasionally drawn Kaplan's diagrams on the board, and asked ESL students to comment about whether or not these simplified patterns seem to represent patterns with which they are familiar. Showing the straightforward expectations of an English-speaking audience as an arrow often brings nods of understanding.

Matalene (1985), who spent a semester teaching in Taiyuan, China, explains that some of her Western expectations baffled her students. She wanted originality, directness, and self-expression; her students valued indirectness, memorization, and references to Chinese classics. Not only was the definition of good writing different, but so was the very function of rhetoric. She concludes that for teachers who work with students from varied backgrounds, "our responsibility is surely to try to understand and appreciate, to admit the relativity of our own rhetoric, and to realize that logics different from our own are not necessarily illogical" (806).

The current theory about contrastive rhetoric does not hold the "deterministic view that speakers of other languages think differently" (Grabe and Kaplan, 1989, p. 264). Instead, literacy skills are learned, are transmitted through the system of education, and are culturally shaped; differences reflect preferred conventions. One should realize that, "as conventions, those that the United States espouses are no better or worse than those espoused in other cultures" (Purves, 1986, p. 50).

As writing teachers, we can be so influenced by our notions of appropriateness in writing, that we sometimes forget that we, too, are looking at writing through a cultural lens. Thus, rather than asserting that the U.S. approach is the "right" or "best" or "only" way of organizing or arguing, I usually present such material as a series of options. I may say that a native speaker of English will expect that a piece of writing be more, rather than less, direct; will prefer concrete, personal examples to an abstract statement of truth; will want explication rather than implications. When phrased in terms of the reader's expectations, learning these conventions becomes like learning customs. Understanding this, too, helps a teacher evaluate students' papers more fairly.

Plagiarism

Given the very different traditions of ESL students, one might expect differing conventions for citing or copying source material. There is a clear contrast between our emphasis on individuality and finding an "authentic voice" in writing and an emphasis on the commonality of knowledge and a reverence for the wisdom of the elders, and this difference may account for differences in views of plagiarism (Leki, 1992). Matalene (1985) emphasizes that basic literacy in Chinese requires amazing feats of memorization of the thousands of characters in the language. Combine that with the importance of learning texts from classical Chinese writing, memorization of set phrases and proverbs, and one can see that for a Chinese student, learning to write means memorizing, copying, and following well-proven patterns, something very different from the U.S. writing teacher's expectation of originality, authenticity, and creativity.

To students from many cultures, it is a novel idea that a writer owns his words, as if they were property, so students may be surprised at the anger and shock provoked in his teacher when he copies a source without citing it. Additionally, some students have learned to write by memorizing models on specific topics: they are able to churn out an error-free paper by writing the text they have memorized word for word. Students may feel that since the original author conveyed her message so clearly and beautifully, they would be foolish to put that message in their own clumsy prose.

Writing teachers can be sensitive to the fact that plagiarism is not considered as a serious transgression in all cultures. At the same time, one needs to clearly explain the expectations of a U.S. audience, for students certainly will be writing papers for other courses, may be working on scientific reports in graduate work at U.S. universities, and may write in many contexts in which they cannot copy verbatim. As with rhetorical features, I explain the underlying attitudes about plagiarism in the U.S. to my students, emphasizing the importance of learning to quote and paraphrase accurately as an expected skill in U.S. university classes.

These being skills that are also difficult for native speakers, many composition teachers will choose to spend class time practicing summary, paraphrase, and quotation (see Chapter 56 in the *Prentice Hall Reference Guide*). One should realize that these techniques are especially challenging for nonnative speakers, and a teacher will find the time well-spent to help students practice and to explain the importance and usefulness of the skills.

Students' Goals

A more troubling issue is that international students often have very different goals for learning to write than do native speakers. Many international students intend to get an education and return to their own countries. Holding these students to the same writing standards that one would expect from U.S. students seems counterproductive (Land and Whitley, 1989). We can also question the goal of having nonnative students use English for self-discovery, since native-language writing would surely be more appropriate for such a venture, and since some students may not see this as a natural purpose for writing (Leki, 1992; Matalene, 1985). If teachers are not aware of these important, and essentially political, issues, they may make unfair and unrealistic assumptions about their ESL students. Leki (1992) covers this problematic issue effectively.

■ HELPING ESL STUDENTS IN THE COMPOSITION CLASSROOM

The needs of ESL students are, as I have indicated, complex and varied, and teachers may wish to keep some of these issues in mind as they plan a syllabus, select a text, consider assignment topics, and respond to their ESL students' writing. For example, if a number of ESL students can be typically expected in a class, a teacher may wish to choose a cross-cultural reader that includes selections written from international perspectives. (See, for example, Holeton, 1995, Verberg, 1994, or Hirschberg, 1992). These readers can provide a springboard for stimulating class discussions, and they allow students from varied backgrounds to read about attitudes and perspectives different from their own.

Some other currently-available multicultural readers naturally focus on the diversity of the U.S. population, and although they can be an excellent choice for a class with immigrant and minority students, texts focusing on U.S. minorities may have a very "American" bias. Though they are inclusive of the U.S. population, they may not address issues that international ESL students find compelling. On the other hand, some teachers have chosen not to use a multicultural reader and have found that standard readers can be fascinating for ESL students who are trying to understand U.S. culture. Regardless of whether teachers choose a multicultural reader or one with standard U.S. readings, they should also consider their ESL students when choosing which readings to assign. Fiction written in dialect can be impenetrable for ESL students, and lengthy essays take much more reading time for an ESL student. A teacher may wish to consider providing some background for readings that assume a knowledge of U.S. history and culture and plan to give extra help orienting students to long or difficult readings.

Responding to ESL Writing

Recognizing that ESL students have varied needs and goals, and that they may well have different notions about what makes a piece of writing effective, teachers can be reassured that strategies for responding to ESL writing are really little different from those for responding to native speakers. Most research discourages teachers from focusing on errors early in the writing process, assuming that an early focus on error will not allow a student to think about more substantiative matters. Providing opportunities for students to get feedback as they work on a piece of writing is also quite important. Research has shown that students tend not to pay attention to the comments written on penultimate drafts of their papers, and that these comments can be confusing, contradictory, and unclear (Zamel, 1985). Rather than seeing oneself as an evaluator, stepping in at the last minute to grade the final copies of students papers, a teacher should become involved early in the process. Encouraging students to come in for conferences, providing short miniconsultations during class with individual students, helping students work through the revision process are all useful methods of providing feedback. When one does provide feedback on a draft, focusing on content and organization before looking at errors is likely to be most productive.

Strategies for Dealing with ESL Errors

In order to help ESL students reduce their mistakes in grammar and mechanics, a teacher new to ESL teaching may wish to learn something about current theories of language learning. The following summary provides some abbreviated background.

Popularized in the 1950s and influenced by structural linguistics and behavioral psychology, the audio-lingual approach held that language was learned by conditioning (Brown, 1994). Teachers had students memorize pattern drills and dialogues so that they could learn without making mistakes: errors were considered bad, since they would compete for the correct forms, and language teachers paid much attention to students' mistakes. Though widely used for a time, this approach to language teaching was based on several misconceptions. Brown notes that "language was not really acquired through a process of habit formation and overlearning, that errors were not necessarily to be avoided at all costs . . ." (71).

New views of language learning have necessitated changes in pedagogy. Now we know that language learning occurs as the patterns of the new language are internalized through meaningful communication in a variety of contexts. And pedagogical approaches have changed to provide these rich communicative contexts. Errors are considered a natural part of language learning, not something to be rigorously avoided: they occur for complex reasons, as a learner generalizes about incompletely learned patterns in the new language or guesses about the existence of forms in the new language which occur in the first (Leki, 1992).

Of course these changes in language teaching also affect the teaching of second language writing. Teachers influenced by ESL writing research now spend less effort in correcting errors or in attempting to keep students from making them. Leki (1992) points to two factors that have influenced this turn away from a focus on errors: some research shows that faculty from other disciplines have greater tolerance for ESL students' errors than do English teachers; and, second, correcting those errors has little effect on students' abilities to avoid making mistakes. If students will not be penalized in other courses for occasional nonnative lapses, then what is the purpose of English teachers demanding native-like fluency? And why invest tremendous time and energy correcting errors if this activity has negligible results? For example, in a controlled research study, Robb, Ross, & Shortreed (1986) examined the effect of four types of feedback on written error. Regardless of whether teachers elaborately corrected all student errors, marked the type of error with a coding system, or simply indicated the location of the error, the groups did not show statistically measurable differences. Since error correction can be incredibly time consuming, most ESL teachers do not attempt to correct all the mistakes a student makes, and may wish to consider a certain number of errors as a kind of foreign accent in writing (Harris & Silva, 1993).

However, students may have different expectations about what kind of teacher feedback will help them improve. Leki (1991) points out that an ESL student's past success with learning English by memorizing grammar rules and focusing on errors may conflict with a writing teacher's wish to emphasize content. Her survey found that ESL students were very interested in their teachers pointing out errors and they claimed to look carefully at their teachers' corrections. However, she notes other studies which indicate that teachers' corrections have little effect on improving student writing. So, though ESL students may expect their teachers to mark all their errors, the usefulness of doing so is in doubt.

It is sometimes easy to lose perspective about the importance of different conventions when faced with ESL students' papers. I once listened to a group of experienced and well-meaning composition teachers who were debating how to handle the "spelling errors" that came from a student using British rather than American English. ("Colour," "practise," and "judgement" are examples.) I was surprised that such a topic would be an issue, first because there were so many more substantive issues to discuss about the students' writing, and second, that the Americans felt the British spellings were "errors"! A teacher can certainly encourage students to follow expected academic conventions—including formatting, punctuation, and spelling—but she would be wise to adopt a flexible attitude about these conventions when evaluating ESL writing.

The fact does remain, however, that ESL students may make more serious errors that are distracting and frequent. In his examination of research studies comparing native and nonnative student writers, Silva (1993) notes that ESL students make a larger number of errors than native speakers in many categories, including vocabulary and semantic choice, control of syntax, and problems with verbs, prepositions, articles, and nouns.

Given that composition teachers want to help students reduce the seriousness and frequency of errors, what strategies can they use? First, teachers should avoid the impulse to make all the corrections for the students, and certainly they need not mark every error. It is sometimes possible to find a pattern that can be pointed out to a student or to focus on a particular type of error that seems distracting in a particular paper. For example, a control of verb tense shifts will be important in a paper that begins with generalized truths ("The relationship of parent and child is important"), moves to personalized statements indicating duration of time ("I have always loved my parents . . ."), and then shifts to an example from the past ("But when I was thirteen . . ."). Showing a student how the tense helps set the time frame of the sentence or paragraph could be productive if she is writing a paper where verb shifts are required. Also, focusing on one particular error may prevent a student from feeling overwhelmed by the many possible mistakes he has made. If I see that a student is having trouble with a particular structure, I may have the student proofread his next draft for that one structure only. The student can feel a sense of accomplishment, then, for spotting nearly all the subject-verb agreement errors, or all the sentence fragments, and this makes editing more manageable.

If teachers plan to choose one kind of error for the focus of comments, they can consciously choose a rationale to decide which kind of error to emphasize. Leki (1992) suggests several strategies. One approach is to focus on errors that are also made by native speakers such as subject-verb agreement or sentence boundary errors, since they may be the kind of errors that trigger assumptions about a person's educational background. Another approach is to look at more global errors, those that interfere with the reader's understanding, and to ignore the local errors which merely distract.

Yet another method is to focus on systematic, rule-governed grammatical features rather than those which are idiosyncratic. Leki gives the example of *assignments*, which takes a plural ending, and *homework*, which does not (1992, p. 131) as an idiosyncratic example that can't be learned by applying rules. On the other hand, students can learn the system for verb formation to avoid making mistakes like **He can **goes***. They simply need to apply a predictable formula: following a modal verb (*can, could, shall, should*, etc.), the next verb takes the "bare infinitive" form (the infinitive without the word *to*, the most simple form of the verb). However, students will be much less likely to find errors in verbal complements:

I hope *to go* and I dislike *going* are right, but

*I hope *going* and *I dislike *to go* are wrong.

(Here, the rule is much less clear: verbs like *hope*, *want* and *decide* are followed by the infinitive, while verbs like *dislike, avoid, enjoy*, or *suggest* are followed by the gerund form. The problem is in deciding which kind of complement is required by the main verb.)

Though grammarians have invented complicated methods of deciding which category of verbs require infinitives and which require gerunds, the explanations are often so complex that students find them impenetrable. (See Celce-Murcia & Larsen-Freeman, 1983, for a summary.) These forms, like prepositions or phrasal verbs, nearly require memorization, since either the governing rules are not particularly systematic or the "system" is not transparent to the average ESL student. In order to correct errors of this sort, students can rely on lists of verbs (like those in the Handbook p. 808) and attempt to memorize those they use most frequently. But when choosing the type of error to have students focus on, it may be more productive for a teacher to suggest that students proofread for other kinds of errors—those which are more obviously rule-governed—and teachers may wish to focus on these more systematic issues in their comments.

A comprehensive ESL grammar series like *Grammar Dimensions*, (Larsen-Freeman, 1994) or a small ESL handbook like *Grammar Troublespots* (Raimes, 1992) can provide more background in ESL grammar for a teacher who needs extra help.

Teaching Suggestions

Many of the assignments and class activities that work for native speakers are also useful for nonnative students. A nongraded journal, popular in many composition classes, can improve the fluency of nonnative speakers.

Providing students with frequent opportunities to revise, or using portfolio grading can be a useful way to help ESL students improve, taking the focus away from producing error-free early drafts. Avoiding this early focus on error is also important so that students can concentrate on more substantial matters of content and organization.

Other common practices are less effective for international students. For example, graded in-class writings are particularly difficult for international students. Under time pressure, they may not be able to write fluently, and certainly will produce many more grammatical errors than they would if they were allowed time to revise. Though for fluency practice, frequent writing is useful, an emphasis on graded in-class writing can be counter-productive, particularly if international students are held to rigid correctness standards. On the other hand, in-class essay exams are common methods of assessment in college. Some composition teachers include timed-writing as a means of helping their students improve the ability to understand an essay exam prompt, and to organize and write answers to the kind of exam questions they might be asked on tests in other courses. If the focus is on interpreting the prompt, on organizing, and on finding a few clear details of support, then timed, in-class work can be useful.

It is also productive to guide students through the prewriting process, helping them find new ways of selecting topics, narrowing them, gathering and developing ideas (see Chapter 1 in the *Prentice Hall Reference Guide*). If students choose their own topics for their papers, new ESL students may need guidance. Not having the background in writing the kind of personal or persuasive essays that are expected, they may have little idea of the kind of topic which would be appropriate. Showing them typical student papers or referring them to the handbook samples is a first start in helping them see a range of appropriate topics. Students may choose topics which seem extremely broad or vague for a composition class. Keeping in mind that a student is learning new expectations about appropriate conventions for U.S. compositions, a teacher can guide a student to narrow a broad topic or to find a personal angle in the same way that he gives that advice to U.S. students.

If an instructor assigns some of the writing topics for the course, care should be taken to choose topics which will allow international students to write from their own backgrounds and from their own perspectives. Most general topics work effectively: if a readings unit focuses on topics like family relationships, growing up, political change, education, language, an international student can write with a personal angle. Teachers in our program have also had success with some more culturally-based topics. Students have explored different versions of familiar folk tales like

Cinderella, or examined the values expressed in movies like *The Joy Luck Club*. Additional topics have included childhood games, common superstitions, coming-of-age celebrations, and the cultural implications of the architectural design of homes.

If there are a number of international students in a class, focusing an assignment on familiar proverbs can be one way of opening students' minds to cultural differences. Several teachers in our program have had students bring "old sayings" from their culture and translate them into English. Small discussion groups compare their proverbs, looking for similarities and differences. For instance, the English "to lock the barn after the horse gets out" is much like the Chinese "to dig a well after one is thirsty." But the Chinese expression "You can still lock the door after the sheep have left" means that a person can learn from her mistakes, a rather different interpretation than the English idiom.

Students are often fascinated to learn sayings from their classmates' cultures, and the discussion opens students to understanding the power of figurative language. Some teachers have had their students write about what cultural values are represented by the proverbs of their culture. Have we adopted Franklin's "the early bird gets the worm" because we are a competitive culture? When you hear the Japanese saying, "The nail that sticks up will be hammered down," do you sympathize with the nail or the hammer, and does this say something about your cultural orientation? (For a similar assignment, see Reid, 1993, p. 170.)

Finally, directly examining the idea of cultural stereotypes can be enlightening for native and nonnative students alike, particularly after students are comfortable enough with each other to discuss such a potentially threatening topic. Our world view is "so shaped by our culture that reality is thought to be objectively perceived through our own cultural pattern, and a differing perception is seen as either false or 'strange' and is thus oversimplified" (Brown, 1994, p. 166). Stereotypes assume that general characteristics distinguishing a group are held by all members of that group: they can be accurate as far as a description of a "typical" group member but become inaccurate because they do not account for individual differences. Stereotypes can have positive effects in that they allow us to systematize our knowledge and make comparisons between the familiar and unfamiliar (Brown, 1994). However, they become destructive if we assume that every member of a group will fit neatly into the oversimplified and inflexible picture we have.

For example, one student wrote:

> As an individual from the Middle East, my image of the USA was
> not a very good one. I imagined the USA as a society full of

crimes, drugs and all type of social problems. I never imagined that I can leave my car opened and come back to find it. I never imagined that people would be friendly. All of that was the result of the stereotype of the USA in the Middle East. Yet that is not the only stereotyping problem I have seen. The Middle Eastern image in the USA is not much better. A large portion of the population here thinks that Middle Easterners are nothing but a group of rich crazy people with four wives.

One often finds in discussions of stereotypes that U.S. students can be unaware of the stereotypes that others hold of them. A Canadian teacher in our program said that, in general, U.S. residents are seen as "rich, loud, and insensitive." U.S. students may respond to such a comment with astonishment. The following quotations from international students about the stereotypes they hold of American society can be useful starting points for discussion. Originally from Fieg and Blair (1975), they were cited by Kohls (1981):

> FROM COLOMBIA: "The tendency in the U.S. to think that life is only work hits you in the face . . ."
>
> FROM ETHIOPIA: "The American seems very explicit: he wants a 'Yes' or 'No'—if someone tries to speak figuratively, the American is confused."
>
> FROM IRAN: "To place an aged or senile parent in a nursing home is appalling for our people; taking care of one's parents is the children's duty. Only primitive tribes send their old and infirm off to die alone."
>
> FROM KENYA: "Americans appear to us rather distant . . . . it's like building a wall. Unless you ask an American a question, he will not even look at you . . . individualism is very high."
>
> FROM INDIA: "Americans seem to be in a perpetual hurry. Just watch the way they walk down the street. They never allow themselves the leisure to enjoy life; there are too many things to do." (pp. 7–8)

The topic of stereotyping can be an effective one for a writing class and is often included in texts with readings on multicultural issues. Students can describe typical stereotypes of people from their own culture, explain where the stereotypes originated, and analyze how accurate or inaccurate they are. Becoming aware of the inaccuracy in stereotyping others is one of the great benefits that freshmen can gain in a composition class where these issues have been explored. (See Dunnett, Dubin, and Lezberg, 1986, p. 150 for a different assignment dealing with stereotyping.)

If teachers do choose to guide students in choosing writing topics, they should be careful to avoid topics that require knowledge of U.S. culture, or at the very least provide background for the nonnative students. One student complained that it was impossible to write on the topics her teacher had assigned: high school dating and drugs in American high schools. She had never dated, since girls in her culture did not go out unchaperoned, and she had no knowledge beyond what she read in the papers about drugs in U.S. high schools. Another teacher suggested that a good topic for her half-international class was the meaning of Columbus's discovery of the Americas, yet none of her Asian students had an understanding of Columbus or the effect of his explorations on the New World. Instead, they had learned about the Chinese cultural revolution or the formation of Bangladesh. Imagine the difficulty U.S. students would have in giving a personal slant to these historical topics! On the other hand, the topic of Columbus might be an excellent one for Latin American students. A teacher simply needs to be sensitive to the ESL students in a class and approach topic suggestion with a certain flexibility.

Finally, a teacher should also respect the international students' wishes about sharing personal material or writing about cultural issues from the perspective of their nationalities. A Russian student in our program complained that all of his teachers wanted him to write about the effects of the fall of the communist government on Russian society. He said he was tired of the topic and that he did not find it interesting or compelling: he never wanted to be asked about it again! Other students may have lived through traumatic times and not wish to share these deeply personal memories with anyone. And others may wish to be assimilated into U.S. society and do not want to draw attention to their differences.

Using Peer Review and Collaborative Writing

Several researchers provide cautions about using peer editing and collaborative projects with ESL students. Bosley (1993) notes that the manner in which collaborative projects are structured may "represent a Western cultural bias" (51). She points out cultural assumptions about the importance of individualism, of recognizing individual achievement, and of formulating assignments as problem-solving exercises. Similarly, the typical structure of peer review sessions in the U.S. classroom may not be comfortable for students from collectivist cultures like Japan and China. (Carson & Nelson, 1994) In the United States, writing groups often function for the benefit of the individual student: students listen to classmates' comments in order to improve their own piece of writing. But students from collectivist cultures are more accustomed to group activities which function for the benefit of the group. They may be reluctant to criticize classmates and may be "concerned primarily with group harmony at the expense of providing their peers with needed feedback on their compositions" (Carson & Nelson, 1994, p. 17). Other problems may relate to different communication styles leading to conflict among collaborators and differing understanding of what makes writing good (Allaei & Connor, 1990).

Keeping these concerns in mind, however, most teachers who have worked with international students do find a number of benefits in using peer review and collaborative writing. Authentic readers provide a greater motivation for students to revise, students receive feedback from multiple perspectives, they better understand how to meet the needs of their readers, and they may discover that other students are also struggling with putting their ideas into writing (Mittan, 1989). Peer review enables students to see how other students write and to see the different approaches their classmates take to the assignment.

Several suggestions can make peer review groups go more smoothly. Especially for the nonnative students, it is important to explain clearly what they are going to be doing and what the expected outcome will be. If students have done other group activities—discussing readings, for instance—they will be more comfortable with the small group setting. Useful ideas include having students read and discuss articles on differences in cross-cultural communication, and modeling the peer review behavior with a sample piece of writing in front of the class before the peer review sessions begin (Allaei & Connor, 1990; Mittan, 1989; Reid, 1993). Teachers can also have students discuss student drafts from past semesters, photocopied so that students can use them in groups. (I have found my students quite generous in giving me written permission to use their papers anonymously.) This allows students to practice the skills of small group review before they take the emotional plunge of having their own work examined.

When students do bring in their own work, I always have them respond to specific questions, starting positively by identifying something that works well in the writing. Reid (1993) points out that "the goal of peer response/review is not so much to judge . . . as to cooperate in a communicative process, helping others in the classroom community to balance individual purposes with the expectations of the readers" (209). Thus, I never ask my students "What grade would you give this paper?" or "Is this a good or bad paper?" Instead, I have students focus on their responses as readers, by answering questions like these: "Can you easily sum up the writer's main purpose in writing?"; "Was there any place that you wanted more information from the writer?"; and "Were there places where you had trouble following the argument of the writer?" Allowing plenty of time for peer review is important, and having students focus on spoken comments during the class period will avoid a silent classroom where students spend the hour writing their responses. Grimm (1986) suggests having students take their notes home to draft written comments for their classmates, and this idea seems especially useful for international students who will take longer to formulate their responses in writing. When peer review is effective, students gain a greater facility in identifying the aspects of their classmates' writing that give them difficulty as readers, and they will be able to transfer that knowledge to their own writing (Allaei & Connor, 1990).

Collaborative projects, too, can be effective in a class with international students. Assignments in which groups or pairs of students work together can draw on the basic understanding and interests of several students. One teacher in our program had his students work in groups to write final projects in which they did original research. One group went to the local mall and tested their hypothesis that the native speakers would be approached more quickly and more positively by the store clerks. Another group drew from their collective knowledge to write a guidebook for new international students who had just come to study at the university: the native speakers were able to contribute their greater knowledge of standard campus procedures and American customs, while the nonnative speakers could provide insights to the problems faced by new nonnative students.

Again, as with peer review groups, specific instruction will be helpful for collaborators. Burnett (1993a, 1993b) notes that co-authors who are willing to criticize one another's rhetorical choices and voice their disagreement in constructive ways produced higher quality documents than those students who simply nodded agreement to whatever their collaborators suggested. She suggests modeling this "substantive conflict" (1993a, p. 134) by providing students with specific information about successful collaborative behaviors and modeling particular "verbal moves" (1993b, p. 73) that a student can use for purposes such as prompting, challenging, or contributing information. Though Burnett's research focuses on native speaker collaboration, this suggestion is even more important for a class with nonnative students who may lack the verbal repertoire for voicing disagreement. Also, showing students that they can provide feedback to their collaborators in a spirit of friendly disagreement may help students understand that it is possible to disagree without causing "loss of face." Burnett also suggests having the teacher model constructive criticism by working in front of the class with a student or colleague to illustrate how writers can improve their collaborations.

In short, the methods used to teach peer review and collaboration to native speakers can be adapted quite readily for a class with ESL students. Both techniques have the added benefits of getting quiet students more involved in the classroom, providing opportunities for speaking and listening practice for ESL students, and building understanding and group solidarity between the U.S. students and their international classmates. Additionally, of course, the most valuable benefit is that these techniques help students improve their writing skills.

■ CONCLUSION

A teacher of writing can welcome ESL students, knowing not only that the class can be a tremendous help to the students but also that the students may offer much to the class. The stimulating discussions that can occur in the small group setting of the composition class, the opportunity to share their cultural backgrounds and to learn about others' views, and the chance to more clearly understand U.S. academic expectations all benefit the ESL student tremendously. Additionally, in contributing their unique perspectives, ESL students add to the education of the U.S. students in the class. One U.S. student wrote this in his evaluation of a cross-cultural composition class:

> My feelings have definitely changed about people from other cultures since I've joined this class. Before this semester I carried with me many misconceptions. The main reason was because before now I had not had the opportunity to talk to people. This class has shown me that people from other parts of the world share my same frustrations, concerns, joy and happiness. I have learned to enjoy working with my classmates and working to become more open-minded.

In discussing the benefits of cross-cultural classes, Patthey-Chavez and Gergen write, "the presence of different voices and visions of the world can be transformed into an instructional resource" (76). Whether a teacher has many ESL students or just a few, this resource can be a source of opportunity and inspiration.

REFERENCES

Allaei, S. K. & U. M. Connor. "Exploring the Dynamics of Cross-cultural Collaboration in Writing Classrooms." *The Writing Instructor* (Fall 1990): 19–28.

Brown, H. D. *Principles of Language Learning and Teaching*, 3rd ed. Englewood Cliffs, NJ: Prentice Hall, 1994.

Bosley, D.S. "Cross-cultural Collaboration: Whose Culture Is It, Anyway?" *Technical Communication Quarterly* 2.1 (1993): 51–62.

Burkhalter, Nancy, and Samuel W. Pisciotta. "Language and Identity: A Reading-to-Write Unit for Advanced ESL Students." *Teaching English in the Two Year College* 27.2 (Dec. 1999): 208–08.

Burnett, R.E. "Decision Making During the Collaborative Planning of Co-authors." In A. Penrose & B.M. Sitko, eds. *Hearing Ourselves Think: Cognitive Research in the College Writing Classroom.* New York: Oxford UP, 1993: 125–146.

Carroll, Pamela S., Frances Blake, and Rose Ann Camalo. "When Acceptance Isn't Enough: Helping ESL Students Become Successful Writers." *English Journal* 85 (Dec. 1996): 25–33.

Carson, J. & G. Nelson. "Writing Groups: Cross Cultural Issues." *Journal of Second Language Writing* 3.1 (1994): 17–30.

Dong, Yu Ren. "The Need to Understand ESL Students' Native Language Writing." *Teaching English in the Two Year College* 26.3 (Mar. 1999): 277–85.

Ferris, Dana, and John Hedgcock. *Teaching ESL Composition: Purpose, Process, and Practice.* Mahwah, NJ: Lawrence Eribaum Associates, 1998.

Genzel, R. & M. G. Cummings. *Culturally Speaking: A Conversation and Culture Text,* 2nd. ed. Boston: Heinle and Heinle, 1994.

Gilbert, J. *Clear Speech,* 2nd ed. Cambridge: Cambridge UP, 1994.

Hall, E. T., and M. Hall. *Understanding Cultural Differences: Keys to Success in West Germany, France, and the United States.* Yarmouth, ME: Intercultural Press, 1990.

Harris, M. and T. Silva. "Tutoring ESL Students: Issues and Options." *College Composition and Communication* 44.4 (1993): 525–537.

Heath, Shirley Brice. "Re-creating Literature in the ESL Classroom." *TESOL Quarterly* 30 (Winter 1996): 7776–79.

Hirshberg, S. *One World, Many Cultures.* New York: Macmillan, 1992.

Holeton, R. *Encountering Cultures,* 2nd ed. Englewood Cliffs, NJ: Prentice-Hall, 1995.

Kasper, Loretta F. "ESL Writing and the Principle of Nonjudgmental Awareness: Rationale and Implementation." *Teaching English in the Two Year College* 25 (Feb. 1998): 58–66.

———. "Writing to Read: Enhancing ESL Students' Reading Proficiency Through Written Response to Text." *Teaching English in the Two Year College* 23 (Feb. 1996): 25–33.

Larsen-Freeman, D.(ed.). Grammar Dimensions (four-book series). Boston: Heinle & Heinle, 1994.

Leki, I. "The Preferences of ESL Students for Error Correction in College-Level Writing Classes. *Foreign Language Annals* 24.3 (1994): 203–11.

———. *Understanding ESL Writers: A Guide for Teachers.* Portsmouth, NH: Boynton/Cook, 1992.

Matsuda, Paul Kei. "Composition Studies and ESL Writing: A Disciplinary Division of Labor." *College Composition and Communication* 50.4 (June 1999): 699–721.

Patthey-Chavez, G. & C. Gergen. "Culture as an Instructional Resource in the Multi-ethnic Composition Classroom." *Journal of Basic Writing*, 11.1 (1992): 75–96.

Raimes, A. *Grammar Troublespots: An Editing Guide for Students* (2nd ed.). New York: St. Martin's, 1992.

Reid, J. M. *Teaching ESL Writing.* Englewood Cliffs, NJ: Regents/Prentice Hall, 1993.

Santos, T. "Ideology in Composition." *Journal of Second Language Writing* 1.1 (1992): 1–15.

Silva, T. "Toward an Understanding of the Distinct Nature of L2 Writing: The ESL Research and Its Implications." *TESOL Quarterly* 27. 4 (1993): 657–76.

Tyler, A. "Sexual Harassment and the ITA Curriculum." *The Journal of Graduate Teaching Assistant Development* 2.1 (1994) 31–41.

Verberg, C. J. *Ourselves Among Others: Cross-cultural Readings for Writers* (3rd ed.). New York: St. Martin's, 1994.

PART FOUR

Reading and Writing About Literature: A Primer for Students

by Edgar V. Roberts, *Lehman College of the City University of New York*

Foreword

The following primer, which is modified and adapted from the ninth edition of *Writing About Literature* and the fifth edition of *Literature: An Introduction to Reading and Writing*, is written to students, and is designed for their use. It contains a condensed overview of the nature of literature, the ways of reading and reacting to a primary text (which here is "The Necklace," the famous story by Guy de Maupassant), and the methods of moving from early and unshaped responses to finished drafts of essays.

It would be most desirable to duplicate the entire primer for distribution to classes, but barring that, students should at least receive copies of the story and the sample essays to facilitate study and classroom discussion.

It is my hope that the overview provided here will stimulate students to carry out deeper and more methodical explorations of literary works. Literary understanding and appreciation should be acquired as early as possible, and students should never end their quests for the enjoyment, understanding, and power that literature provides.

—Edgar V. Roberts

Reading and Writing About Literature

■ **WHAT IS LITERATURE, AND WHY DO WE STUDY IT?**

We use the word **literature**, in a broad sense, to mean compositions that tell stories, dramatize situations, express emotions, and analyze and advocate ideas. Before the invention of writing thousands of years ago, literary works were necessarily spoken or sung, and were retained only as long as living people continued to repeat them. In some societies, the oral tradition of literature still exists, with many poems and stories designed exclusively for spoken delivery. Even in our modern age of writing and printing, much literature is still heard aloud rather than read silently. Parents delight their children with stories and poems; poets and story writers read their works directly before live audiences; plays and scripts are interpreted on stages and before moving-picture cameras for the benefit of a vast public.

No matter how we assimilate literature, we gain much from it. In truth, readers often cannot explain why they enjoy reading, for goals and ideals are not easily articulated. There are, however, areas of general agreement about the value of systematic and extensive reading.

Literature helps us grow, both personally and intellectually. It provides an objective base for knowledge and understanding. It links us with the cultural, philosophic, and religious world of which we are a part. It enables us to recognize human dreams and struggles in different places and times that we otherwise would never know existed. It helps us develop mature sensibility and compassion for the condition of *all* living things—human, animal, and vegetable. It gives us the knowledge and perception to appreciate the beauty of order and arrangement—gifts that are also bestowed by a well-structured song or a beautifully painted canvas. It provides the comparative basis from which to see worthiness in the aims of all people, and it therefore helps us see beauty in the world around us. It exercises our emotions through interest, concern, sympathy, tension, excitement, regret, fear, laughter, and hope. It encourages us to assist creative and talented people who need recognition and support. Through our cumulative experience in reading, literature shapes our goals and values by clarifying our own identities—both positively, through acceptance of the admirable in human beings, and negatively, through rejection of the sinister. It enables us to develop perspectives on events occurring locally and globally, and thereby it gives us understanding and control. It is one of the shaping influences of life. It makes us human.

Types of Literature: The Genres

Literature may be classified into four categories or *genres*: (1) prose fiction, (2) poetry, (3) drama, and (4) nonfiction prose. Usually the first three are classed as **imaginative literature**.

The genres of imaginative literature have much in common, but they also have distinguishing characteristics. **Prose fiction**, or **narrative fiction**, includes **myths, parables, romances, novels,** and **short stories**. Originally, *fiction* meant anything made up, crafted, or shaped, but today the word refers to prose stories based in the imaginations of authors. The essence of fiction is **narration**, the relating or recounting of a sequence of events or actions. Fictional works usually focus on one or a few major characters who change and grow (in their ability to make decisions, awareness and insight, attitude toward others, sensitivity, and moral capacity) as a result of how they deal with other characters and how they attempt to solve their problems. Although fiction, like all imaginative literature, may introduce true historical details, it is not real history. Its main purpose is to interest, stimulate, instruct, and divert, not to create a precise historical record.

Poetry expresses a monologue or a conversation grounded in the most deeply felt experiences of human beings. It exists in many formal and informal shapes, from the brief **haiku** to the extensive **epic**. More economical than prose fiction in its use of words, poetry relies heavily on **imagery, figurative language,** and **sound**.

Drama is literature designed to be performed by actors for the benefit and delight of an audience. Like fiction, drama may focus on a single character or a small number of characters; and it enacts fictional events as if they were happening in the present. The audience therefore becomes a direct witness to the events as they occur, from start to finish. Although most modern plays use prose dialogue, on the principle that the language of drama should resemble the language of ordinary persons as much as possible, many plays from the past, such as those of ancient Greece and Renaissance England, are in poetic form.

Nonfiction prose consists of news reports, feature articles, essays, editorials, textbooks, historical and biographical works, and the like, all of which describe or interpret facts and present judgments and opinions. In nonfiction prose the goal is to present truths and sound conclusions about the factual world of history, science, and current events. Imaginative literature, although also grounded in facts, is less concerned with the factual record than with the revelation of truths about life and human nature.

For the purpose of exploring techniques for reading, responding, and writing about literature, the following discussion will focus on the genre of fiction.

■ ELEMENTS OF FICTION

Works of fiction share a number of common elements. For reference here, the more significant ones are **character**, **plot**, **structure**, and **idea** or **theme**.

Character

Stories, like plays, are about characters—characters who are *not* real people but who are nevertheless *like* real people. A **character** may be defined as a reasonable facsimile of a human being, with all the good and bad traits of being human. Most stories are concerned with characters who are facing a major problem which may involve interactions with other characters, with difficult situations, or with an idea or general circumstances that force action. The characters may win, lose, or tie. They may learn and be the better for the experience or may miss the point and be unchanged.

It is a truism that modern fiction has accompanied the development of a psychological interest in human beings. Psychology itself has grown out of the philosophical and religious idea that people are not evil by nature, but rather that they have many inborn capacities—some for good and others for bad. People are not free of problems, and they make many mistakes in their lives, but they nevertheless are important and interesting, and are therefore worth writing about, whether male or female; young or old; white, black, tan, or yellow; rich or poor; worker or industrialist; traveler or resident; aviator, performer, mother, daughter, homemaker, prince, general, bartender, or checkout clerk.

The range of fictional characters is vast: A married couple struggling to repay an enormous debt, a woman meditating about her daughter's growth, a young man learning about sin and forgiveness, a young woman struggling to overcome the bitter memory of early sexual abuse, a man regretting that he cannot admit a lie, a woman surrounded by her insensitive and self-seeking brothers, a man preserving love in the face of overwhelming difficulties, a woman learning to cope with her son's handicap—all these, and more, may be found in fiction just as they may also be found in all levels and conditions of life. Because as human beings all of us share the same capacities for concern, involvement, sympathy, happiness, sorrow, exhilaration, and disappointment, we are able to find endless interest in such characters and their ways of responding to their circumstances.

Plot

Fictional characters, who are drawn from life, go through a series of life-like **actions** or **incidents**, which make up the story. In a well-done story, all the actions or incidents, speeches, thoughts, and observations are linked together to make up an entirety, sometimes called an **organic unity**. The essence of this unity is the development and resolution of a **conflict**—or conflicts—in which the **protagonist**, or central character, is engaged. The interactions of causes and effects as they develop **sequentially** or **chrono-logically** make up the story's **plot**. That is, a story's actions follow one another in time as the protagonist meets and tries to overcome opposing forces. Sometimes plot has been compared to a story's map, scheme, or blueprint.

Often the protagonist's struggle is directed against another character—an **antagonist**. Just as often, however, the struggle may occur between the protagonist and opposing groups, forces, ideas, and choices—all of which make up a collective antagonist. The conflict may be carried out wherever human beings spend their lives, such as a kitchen, a bedroom, a restaurant, a town square, a farm, an estate, a workshop, or a battlefield. The conflict may also take place internally, within the mind of the protagonist.

Structure

Structure refers to the way a story is assembled. Chronologically, all stories are similar because they move from beginning to end in accord with the time needed for *causes* to produce *effects*. But authors choose many different ways to put their stories together. Some stories are told in straight-forward sequential order, and a description of the plot of such stories is identical to a description of the structure. Other stories, however, may get pieced together through out-of-sequence and widely separated episodes, speeches, second-hand reports, remembrances, dreams, nightmares, periods of delirium, fragments of letters, overheard conversations, and the like. In such stories, the plot and the structure diverge widely. Therefore, in dealing with the structure of stories, we emphasize not chronological order but the actual *arrangement* and *development* of the stories as they unfold, part by part. Usually we study an entire story, but we may also direct our attention toward a smaller aspect of arrangement such as an episode or passage of dialogue.

Idea or Theme

The word **idea** refers to the result or results of general and abstract thinking. In literary study the consideration of ideas relates to meaning, interpretation, explanation, and significance. Fiction necessarily embodies issues and ideas. Even stories written for entertainment alone are based in an idea or position. Thus, writers of comic works are committed to the idea that human difficulties can be treated with humor. More serious works may force characters to make difficult moral choices—the thought being that in a losing situation the only winners are those who maintain honor and self-respect. Mystery and suspense stories rest on the belief that problems have solutions, even if they may not at first seem apparent. Writers may deal with the triumphs and defeats of life, the admirable and the despicable, the humorous and the pathetic, but whatever their goal, they are always expressing ideas about human experience. We may therefore raise questions such as these as we look for ideas in fiction: *What does this mean? Why does the author include it? What idea or ideas does it show? Why is it significant?*

Fictional ideas may also be considered as major **themes** which tie individual works together. Often an author makes the theme obvious, as in the Aesop fable in which a man uses an ax to kill a fly on his son's forehead. The theme of this fable might loosely be expressed in a sentence like "the cure should not be worse than the disease." A major theme in Maupassant's "The Necklace" (see p. 227) is that people may be destroyed or saved by unlucky and unforeseeable events. The accidental loss of the borrowed necklace is just such an event, for this misfortune ruins the lives of both Mathilde and her husband.

The process of determining and describing the themes or ideas in stories is never complete; there is always another theme that we may discuss. Thus in "The Necklace," one might note the additional themes that adversity brings out worth, that telling the truth is better than concealing it, that envy often produces ill fortune, and that good fortune is never recognized until it is lost. Indeed, one of the ways in which we may judge stories is to determine the degree to which they embody a number of valid and important ideas.

■ THE FICTION WRITER'S TOOLS

Narration

Writers have a number of modes of presentation, or "tools," which they may use in writing their stories. The principal tool (and the heart of fiction) is **narration**, the reporting of actions in sequential order. The object of narration is to *render* the story, to make it clear and to bring it alive to the reader's imagination through the movement of sentences through time. The writer of narrative may include all the events leading up to and following major actions, for a narration moves in a continuous line, from word to word, scene to scene, action to action, and speech to speech. As a result of this chronological movement, the reader's comprehension must necessarily also be chronological.

Style

The medium of fiction and of all literature is language, and the manipulation of language—the **style**—is a primary skill of the writer. A mark of a good style is *active verbs*, and nouns that are **specific** and **concrete**. Even with the most active and graphic diction possible, writers can never render their incidents and scenes exactly, but they may be judged on how vividly they tell their stories.

Point of View

One of the most important ways in which writers knit their stories together, and also an important way in which they try to interest and engage readers, is the careful control of **point of view**. Point of view is the **voice** of the story, the speaker who does the narrating. It is the way the reality of a story is made to seem authentic. It may be regarded as the story's *focus*, the *angle of vision* from which things are not only seen and reported but also judged.

Basically, there are two kinds of points of view, but there are many variations, sometimes obvious and sometimes subtle. In the first, the **first-person point of view**, a fictitious observer tells us what he or she saw, heard, concluded, and thought. This viewpoint is characterized by the use of the *I* pronoun as the speaker refers to his or her position as an observer or commentator. The **speaker**, or **narrator**—terms that are interchangeable—may sometimes seem to be the author speaking directly using an **authorial voice**, but more often the speaker is an independent character—a **persona** with characteristics that separate her or him from the author.

In common with all narrators, the first-person narrator establishes a clearly defined relationship to the story's events. Some narrators are deeply engaged in the action; others are only minor participants or observers; still others have had nothing to do with the action but are transmitting the reports of other, more knowledgeable, witnesses. Sometimes the narrator uses the *we* pronoun if he or she is represented as part of a group that has witnessed the action or participated in it. Often, too, the narrator might use we when referring to ideas and interpretations shared with the reader or listener—the idea being to draw readers into the story as much as possible.

The second major point of view is the **third person** (*she, he, it, they, her, him, them,* etc.). The third-person point of view may be (1) **limited**, with the focus being on one particular character and what he or she does, says, hears, thinks, and otherwise experiences, (2) **omniscient**, with the possibility that the activities and thoughts of all the characters are open and fully known by the speaker, and (3) **dramatic**, or **objective**, in which the story is confined *only* to the reporting of actions and speeches, with no commentary and no revelation of the thoughts of any of the characters unless the characters themselves reveal their thoughts dramatically.

Understanding point of view usually requires subtlety of perception—indeed, it may be one of the most difficult of all concepts in the study of fiction. In fuller perspective, therefore, we may think of it as the *total position* from which things are viewed, understood, and communicated. The position might be simply physical: *Where was the speaker located when the events occurred, or Does the speaker give us a close or distant view of the events?* The position might also be personal or philosophical, as in the commentary by the narrator in Maupassant's "The Necklace."

Point of view is one of the major ways by which authors make fiction vital. By controlling point of view, an author helps us make reasonable inferences about the story's actions. Authors use point of view to raise some of the same questions in their fiction that perplex us in life. We need to evaluate what fictional narrators as well as real people tell us, for what they say is affected by their limitations, attitudes, opinions, and degree of candidness. For readers, the perception of a fictional point of view can be as complex as life itself, and it may be as difficult—in fiction as in life—to evaluate our sources of information.

Description

Together with narration, a vital aspect of fiction is **description**, which is intended to cause readers to imagine or re-create the scenes and actions of the story. Description can be both physical (places and persons) and psychological (an emotion or set of emotions). Excessive description sometimes interrupts or postpones a story's actions, so that many writers include only as much as is necessary to keep the action moving along.

Mood and **atmosphere** are important aspects of descriptive writing, and to the degree that descriptions are evocative, they may reach the level of **metaphor** and **symbolism**. These characteristics of fiction are a property of all literature, and you will also encounter them whenever you read poems and plays.

Dialogue

Another major tool of the writer of fiction is **dialogue**. By definition, dialogue is the conversation of two people, but more than two characters may also participate. It is of course the major medium of the playwright, and it is one of the means by which the fiction writer makes a story vivid and dramatic. Straight narration and description can do no more than make a secondhand assertion ("hearsay") that a character's thoughts and responses exist, but dialogue makes everything firsthand and real.

Dialogue is hence a means of *showing* rather than *reporting*. If characters feel pain or declare love, their own words may be taken as the expression of what is on their minds. Some dialogue may be terse and minimal; other dialogue may be expanded, depending on the situation, the personalities of the characters, and the author's intent. Dialogue may concern any topic, including personal feelings, reactions to the past, future plans, changing ideas, sudden realizations, and political, social, philosophic, or religious ideas.

The language of dialogue indicates the intelligence, articulateness, educational levels, or emotional states of the speakers. Hence the author might use *grammatical mistakes, faulty pronunciation,* or *slang* to show a character of limited or disadvantaged background or a character who is trying to be seen in that light. *Dialect* shows the region from which the speaker comes, just as an *accent* indicates a place of national origin. *Jargon* and *cliché* suggest self-inflation or intellectual limitations—usually reasons for laughter. The use of *private, intimate expressions* might show people who are close to each other emotionally. Speech that is interrupted by *voiced pauses* (e.g., "er," "ah," "um," "you know"), or speech characterized by *inappropriate words* might show a character who is unsure or not in control. There are many possibilities in dialogue, but no matter what qualities you find, writers include dialogue to enable you to know their characters better.

Tone and Irony

In every story we may consider **tone**, that is, the ways in which authors convey attitudes toward readers and also toward the story material. **Irony**, one of the major components of tone, refers to language and situations that seem to reverse normal expectations. *Word choice* is the characteristic of **verbal irony**, in which what is meant is usually the opposite of what is said, as when we *mean* that people are doing badly even though we *say* that they are doing well. Broader forms of irony are *situational* and *dramatic*: **Situational irony** refers to circumstances in which bad things happen to good people, or in which rewards are not earned because forces beyond human comprehension seem to be in total control. In **dramatic irony** characters have only a nonexistent, partial, incorrect, or misguided understanding of what is happening to them, while both readers and other characters understand the situation more fully. Readers hence become concerned about the characters and hope that they will develop understanding quickly enough to avoid the problems bedeviling them and the pitfalls endangering them.

Symbolism and Allegory

In literature, even apparently ordinary things may acquire **symbolic** value; that is, everyday objects may be understood to have meanings that are beyond themselves, bigger than themselves. In fiction, many functional and essential incidents, objects, speeches, and characters may also be construed as symbols. Some symbols are widely recognized and therefore are considered as **cultural** or **universal**. Water, flowers, jewels, the sun, certain stars, the flag, altars, and minarets are examples of cultural symbols. Other symbols are **contextual**; that is, they take on symbolic meaning only in their individual works, as when in Maupassant's "The Necklace" Mathilde and her husband move into an attic flat to save money that they need to repay their enormous debt. These new quarters may be taken to symbolize the hardship experienced by the poor.

When a complete story, in addition to maintaining its own narrative integrity, can be applied point-by-point to a parallel set of situations, it is an **allegory**. Many stories are not complete allegories, however, even though they may contain sections having allegorical parallels. Thus, the Loisels' long servitude in Maupassant's "The Necklace" is similar to the lives and activities of many people who perform tasks for mistaken or meaningless reasons. "The Necklace" is therefore allegorical even though it is not an allegory.

Commentary

Writers may also include **commentary**, **analysis**, or **interpretation**, in the expectation that readers need insight into the characters and actions. When fiction was new, authors often expressed such commentary directly. Henry Fielding (1707–1754) divided his novels into "books," and included a chapter of personal and philosophic commentary at the beginning of each of these. In the next century, George Eliot (1819–1880) included many extensive passages of commentary in her novels.

Later writers have kept commentary at a minimum, preferring instead to concentrate on direct action and dialogue, and allowing readers to draw their own conclusions about meaning. In first-person narrations, however, you may expect the narrators to make their own personal comments. Such observations may be accepted at face value, but you should recognize that anything the speakers say is also a mode of character disclosure and therefore is just as much a part of the story as the narrative incidents.

The Elements Together

These, then, are the major tools of writers of fiction. For analytical purposes, one or another of them may be considered separately so that the artistic achievement of a particular author may be recognized. It is also important to realize that authors may use all the tools simultaneously. The story may be told by a character who is a witness, and thus it has a **first-person point of view**. The major **character**, the **protagonist**, goes through a series of **actions** as a result of a carefully arranged **plot**. Because of this plot, together with the author's chosen method of **narration**, the story will follow a certain kind of arrangement, or **structure**, such as a straightforward **sequence** or a disjointed series of **episodes**. One thing that the action may demonstrate is the **theme** or **central idea**. The writer's **style** may be manifested in **ironic** expressions. The description of the character's actions may reveal **irony of situation**, while at the same time this situation is made vivid through **dialogue** in which the character is a participant. Because the plight of the character is like the plight of many persons in the world, it is an **allegory**, and the character herself or himself may be considered as a **symbol**.

Throughout each story we read, no matter what characteristics we are considering, it is most important to realize that a work of fiction is an entirety, a unity. Any reading of a story should be undertaken not to break things down into parts, but to understand and assimilate the work *as a whole*. The separate analysis of various topics, to which this book is committed, is thus a *means* to that end, *not* the end itself. The study of fiction, like the study of all literature, is designed to foster our growth and to increase our understanding of the human condition.

■ READING A STORY AND RESPONDING TO IT ACTIVELY

Regrettably, our first readings of works do not provide us with full understanding. After we have finished reading a work, we may find it embarrassingly difficult to answer pointed questions or to say anything intelligent about it at all. But more active and thoughtful readings give us the understanding to develop well-considered answers. Obviously, we need to follow the work and to understand its details, but just as important we need to respond to the words, get at the ideas, and understand the implications of what is happening. We rely on our own fund of knowledge and experience to verify the accuracy and truth of situations and incidents, and we try to articulate our own emotional responses to the characters and their problems.

To illustrate such active responding, the following story, "The Necklace" (1884), by the French writer Guy de Maupassant (1850–1893), is printed with marginal annotations like those that any reader might make during original and follow-up readings. Many observations, particularly at the beginning, are *assimilative*; that is, they do little more than record details about the action. But as the story progresses, the comments begin to reflect conclusions about the story's meaning. Toward the end, the comments are full rather than minimal; they result not only from first responses but also from considered thought. Here, then, is Maupassant's "The Necklace."

Guy de Maupassant, an apostle of Gustave Flaubert, was one of the major nineteenth-century French naturalists. He was a meticulous writer, devoting great attention to reality and to economy of detail. His stories are focused on the difficulties and ironies of existence not only among the Parisian middle class, as in "The Necklace," but also among both peasants and higher society. Two of his better-known novels are *A Life* (1883) and *A Good Friend* (1885). Among his other famous stories are "The Rendezvous" and "The Umbrella." "The Necklace" is notable for its concluding ironic twist, and for this reason it is perhaps the best known of his stories.

Guy de Maupassant (1850–1893)

The Necklace   1884

Translated by Edgar V. Roberts

She was one of those pretty and charming women, born, as if by an error of destiny, into a family of clerks and copyists. She had no dowry, no prospects, no way of getting known, courted, loved, married by a rich and distinguished man. She finally settled for a marriage with a minor clerk in the Ministry of Education.

She was a simple person, without the money to dress well, but she was as unhappy as if she had gone through bankruptcy, for women have neither rank nor race. In place of high birth or important family connections, they can rely only on their beauty, their grace, and their charm. Their inborn finesse, their elegant taste, their engaging personalities, which are their only power, make working-class women the equals of the grandest ladies.

She suffered constantly, feeling herself destined for all delicacies and luxuries. She suffered because of her grim apartment with its drab walls, threadbare furniture, ugly curtains. All such things, which most other women in her situation would not even have noticed, tortured her and filled her with despair. The sight of the young country girl who did her simple housework awakened in her only a sense of desolation and lost hopes. She daydreamed of large, silent anterooms, decorated with oriental tapestries and lighted by high bronze floor lamps, with two elegant valets in short culottes dozing in large armchairs under the effects of forced-air heaters. She imagined large drawing rooms draped in the most expensive silks, with fine end tables on which were placed knickknacks of inestimable value. She dreamed of the perfume of dainty private rooms, which were designed only for intimate tête-à-têtes with the closest friends, who because of their achievements and fame would make her the envy of all other women.

> "She" is pretty but poor. Apparently there is no other life for her than marriage. Without connections, she has no entry into high society, and marries an insignificant clerk.

> She is unhappy.

> A view of women that excludes the possibility of a career. In 1884, women had little else than their personalities to get ahead.

> She suffers because of her cheap belongings, wanting expensive things. She dreams of wealth and of how other women would envy her if she had all these fine things. But these luxuries are unrealistic and unattainable for her.

When she sat down to dinner at her round little table covered with a cloth that had not been washed for three days, in front of her husband who opened the kettle while declaring ecstatically, "Ah, good old boiled beef! I don't know anything better," she dreamed of expensive banquets with shining placesettings, and wall hangings portraying ancient heroes and exotic birds in an enchanted forest. She imagined a gourmet-prepared main course carried on the most exquisite trays and served on the most beautiful dishes, with whispered gallantries which she would hear with a sphinx-like smile as she dined on the pink meat of a trout or the delicate wing of a quail.

Her husband's taste is for plain things, while she dreams of expensive gourmet food. He has adjusted to his status. She has not.

5   She had no decent dresses, no jewels, nothing. And she loved nothing but these; she believed herself born only for these. She burned with the desire to please, to be envied, to be attractive and sought after.

She lives for her unrealistic dreams, and these increase her frustration.

She had a rich friend, a comrade from convent days, whom she did not want to see anymore because she suffered so much when she returned home. She would weep for the entire day afterward with sorrow, regret, despair, and misery.

She even thinks of giving up a rich friend because she is so depressed after visiting her.

Well, one evening, her husband came home glowing and carrying a large envelope.

A new section in the story.

"Here," he said, "this is something for you."

She quickly tore open the envelope and took out a card engraved with these words:

> *The* CHANCELLOR OF EDUCATION *and*
> MRS. GEORGE RAMPONNEAU
> *request that*
> MR. AND MRS. LOISEL
> *do them the honor of coming to dinner*
> *at the Ministry of Education*
> *on the evening of January 8.*

An invitation to dinner at the Ministry of Education. A big plum.

10   Instead of being delighted, as her husband had hoped, she threw the invitation spitefully on the table, muttering:

"What do you expect me to do with this?"

"But honey, I thought you'd be glad. You never get to go out, and this is a special occasion! I had a lot of trouble getting the invitation. Everyone wants one. The demand is high and not many clerks get invited. Everyone important will be there."

She looked at him angrily and stated impatiently: "What do you want me to wear to go there?"

15 He had not thought of that. He stammered: "But your theater dress. That seems nice to me . . ."

He stopped, amazed and bewildered, as his wife began to cry. Large tears fell slowly from the corners of her eyes to her mouth. He said falteringly: "What's wrong? What's the matter?"

But with a strong effort she had recovered, and she answered calmly as she wiped her damp cheeks:

20 "Nothing, except that I have nothing to wear and therefore can't go to the party. Give your invitation to someone else at the office whose wife will have nicer clothes than mine."

Distressed, he responded:

"Well, all right, Mathilde. How much would a new dress cost, something you could use at other times, but not anything fancy?"

She thought for a few moments, adding things up and thinking also of an amount that she could ask without getting an immediate refusal and a frightened outcry from the frugal clerk.

Finally she responded tentatively:

25 "I don't know exactly, but it seems to me that I could get by on four hundred francs."

He blanched slightly at this, because he had set aside just that amount to buy a shotgun for Sunday lark-hunts the next summer with a few friends in the Plain of Nanterre.

However, he said:

"All right, you've got four hundred francs, but make it a pretty dress."

As the day of the party drew near, Mrs. Loisel seemed sad, uneasy, anxious, even though her gown was all ready. One evening her husband said to her:

It only upsets her.

She declares that she hasn't anything to wear.

He tries to persuade her that her theater dress might do for the occasion.

Her name is Mathilde. He volunteers to pay for a new dress.

She is manipulating him.

The dress will cost him his next summer's vacation. (He doesn't seem to have included her in his plans.)

A new section, the third in the story. The day of the party is near.

209

30   "What's the matter? You've been acting funny for several days."

She answered:

"It's awful, but I don't have any jewels to wear, not a single gem, nothing to dress up my outfit. I'll look like a beggar. I'd almost rather not go to the party."

Now she complains that she doesn't have any nice jewelry. She is manipulating him again.

He responded:

"You can wear a corsage of cut flowers. This year it's all the rage. For only ten francs you can get two or three gorgeous roses."

35   She was not convinced.

"No . . . there's nothing more humiliating than looking shabby in the company of rich women."

She has a good point, but there seems to be no way out.

But her husband exclaimed:

"God, but you're silly! Go to your friend Mrs. Forrestier, and ask her to lend you some jewelry. You know her well enough to do that."

He proposes a solution: borrow jewelry from Mrs. Forrestier, who is apparently the rich friend mentioned earlier.

She uttered a cry of joy:

40   "That's right. I hadn't thought of that."

The next day she went to her friend's house and described her problem.

Mrs. Forrestier went to her mirrored wardrobe, took out a large jewel box, opened it, and said to Mrs. Loisel: "Choose, my dear."

She saw bracelets, then a pearl necklace, then a Venetian cross of finely worked gold and gems. She tried on the jewelry in front of a mirror, and hesitated, unable to make up her mind about each one. She kept asking:

Mathilde will have her choice of jewels.

45   "Do you have anything else?"

"Certainly. Look to your heart's content. I don't know what you'd like best."

Suddenly she found a superb diamond necklace in a black satin box, and her heart throbbed with desire for it. Her hands shook as she picked it up. She fastened it around her neck, watched it gleam at her throat, and looked at herself ecstatically.

A "superb" diamond necklace.

Then she asked, haltingly and anxiously:

"Could you lend me this, nothing but this?"

50   "Why yes, certainly."

This is what she wants, just this.

She jumped up, hugged her friend joyfully, then hurried away with her treasure.

She leaves with the "treasure."

The day of the party came. Mrs. Loisel was a success. She was prettier than anyone else, stylish, graceful, smiling and wild with joy. All the men saw her, asked her name, sought to be introduced. All the important administrators stood in line to waltz with her. The Chancellor himself eyed her.

She danced joyfully, passionately, intoxicated with pleasure, thinking of nothing but the moment, in the triumph of her beauty, in the glory of her success, on cloud nine with happiness made up of all the admiration, of all the aroused desire, of this victory so complete and so sweet to the heart of any woman.

She did not leave until four o'clock in the morning. Her husband, since midnight, had been sleeping in a little empty room with three other men whose wives had also been enjoying themselves.

55 He threw, over her shoulders, the shawl that he had brought for the trip home—a modest everyday wrap, the poverty of which contrasted sharply with the elegance of her evening gown. She felt it and hurried away to avoid being noticed by the other women who luxuriated in rich furs.

Loisel tried to hold her back:

"Wait a minute. You'll catch cold outdoors. I'll call a cab."

But she paid no attention and hurried down the stairs. When they reached the street they found no carriages. They began to look for one, shouting at cabmen passing by at a distance.

They walked toward the Seine, desperate, shivering. Finally, on a quay, they found one of those old night-going buggies that are seen in Paris only after dark, as if they were ashamed of their wretched appearance in daylight.

60 It took them to their door, on the Street of Martyrs, and they sadly climbed the stairs to their flat. For her, it was finished. As for him, he could think only that he had to begin work at the Ministry of Education at ten o'clock.

She took the shawl off her shoulders, in front of the mirror, to see herself once more in her glory. But

---

Marginal notes:

A new section.
The Party. Mathilde is a huge success.

Another judgment about women. Does the author mean that only women want to be admired? Don't men want admiration, too?

Loisel, with other husbands, is bored, while the wives are having a ball.

Ashamed of her shabby wrap, she rushes away to avoid being seen.

A come down after the nice evening. They take a wretched-looking buggy home.

"Street of Martyrs." Is this name significant?

Loisel is down-to-earth.

suddenly she cried out. The necklace was no longer around her neck!

She has lost the necklace!

Her husband, already half undressed, asked: "What's wrong?"

She turned toward him frantically:

65 "I . . . I . . . I no longer have Mrs. Forrestier's necklace."

He stood up, bewildered:

"What? . . . How? . . . It's not possible!"

And they looked in the folds of the gown, in the folds of the shawl, in the pockets, everywhere. They found nothing.

They can't find it.

He asked:

70 "You're sure you still had it when you left the party?"

"Yes. I checked it in the vestibule of the Ministry."

"But if you'd lost it in the street, we would've heard it fall. It must be in the cab."

"Yes, probably. Did you notice the number?"

"No. Did you see it?"

75 "No."

Overwhelmed, they looked at each other. Finally, Loisel got dressed again:

"I'm going out to retrace all our steps," he said, "to see if I can find the necklace that way."

And he went out. She stayed in her evening dress, without the energy to get ready for bed, stretched out in a chair, drained of strength and thought.

He goes out to search for the necklace.

Her husband came back at about seven o'clock. He had found nothing.

But is unsuccessful.

80 He went to Police Headquarters and to the newspapers to announce a reward. He went to the small cab companies, and finally he followed up even the slightest hopeful lead.

He really tries. He's doing his best.

She waited the entire day, in the same enervated state, in the face of this frightful disaster.

Loisel came back in the evening, his face pale and haggard. He had found nothing.

"You'll have to write to your friend," he said, "that you broke a clasp on her necklace and that you're having it fixed. That'll give us time to look around."

She wrote as he dictated.

Loisel's plan to explain delaying the return. He takes charge, is resourceful.

85   By the end of the week they had lost all hope. And Loisel, looking five years older, declared: "We'll have to see about replacing the jewels."

    The next day they took the case which had contained the necklace and went to the jeweler whose name was inside. He looked at his books: "I wasn't the one, Madam, who sold the necklace. I only made the case."

90   Then they went from jeweler to jeweler, searching for a necklace like the other one, racking their memories, both of them sick with worry and anguish.

    In a shop in the Palais-Royal, they found a necklace of diamonds that seemed to them exactly like the one they were looking for. It was priced at forty thousand francs. They could buy it for thirty-six thousand.

    They got the jeweler to promise not to sell it for three days. And they made an agreement that he would buy it back for thirty-four thousand francs if the original was recovered before the end of February.

    Loisel had saved eighteen thousand francs that his father had left him. He would have to borrow the rest.

    He borrowed, asking a thousand francs from one, five hundred from another, five louis° here, three louis there. He wrote promissory notes, undertook ruinous obligations, did business with finance companies and the whole tribe of loan sharks. He compromised himself for the remainder of his days, risked his signature without knowing whether he would be able to honor it, and, terrified by anguish over the future, by the black misery that was about to descend on him, by the prospect of all kinds of physical deprivations and moral tortures, he went to get the new necklace, and put down thirty-six thousand francs on the jeweler's counter.

95   Mrs. Loisel took the necklace back to Mrs. Forrestier, who said with an offended tone: "You should have brought it back sooner; I might have needed it."

    She did not open the case, as her friend feared she might. If she had noticed the substitution, what would

---

° *louis*: a gold coin worth twenty francs.

Margin notes

Things are hopeless.

They hunt for a replacement.

A new diamond necklace will cost 36,000 francs, a monumental amount.

They make a deal with the jeweler. (Is Maupassant hinting that things might work out for them?)

It will take all of Loisel's inheritance plus another 18,000 francs that must be borrowed at enormous rates of interest.

Mrs. Forrestier complains about the delay.

Is this enough justification for not telling the truth? It seems to be for the Loisels.

she have thought? What would she have said? Would she not have taken her for a thief?

Mrs. Loisel soon discovered the horrible life of the needy. She did her share, however, completely, heroically. That horrifying debt had to be paid. She would pay. They dismissed the maid; they changed their address; they rented an attic flat.

A new section, the fifth.

She learned to do the heavy housework, dirty kitchen jobs. She washed the dishes, wearing away her manicured fingernails on greasy pots and encrusted baking dishes. She handwashed dirty linen, shirts, and dish towels that she hung out on the line to dry. Each morning, she took the garbage down to the street, and she carried up water, stopping at each floor to catch her breath. And, dressed in cheap house dresses, she went to the fruit dealer, the grocer, the butchers, with her basket under her arms, haggling, insulting, defending her measly cash penny by penny.

They suffer to repay their debts. Loisel works late at night. Mathilde accepts a cheap attic flat, and does all the heavy housework herself to save on domestic help.

She pinches pennies, and haggles with the local tradesmen.

100   They had to make installment payments every month, and, to buy more time, to refinance loans.

They struggle to meet payments.

The husband worked evenings to make fair copies of tradesmen's accounts, and late into the night he made copies at five cents a page.

Mr. Loisel moonlights to make extra money.

And this life lasted ten years.

For ten years they struggle, but they endure.

At the end of ten years, they had paid back everything—everything—including the extra charges imposed by loan sharks and the accumulation of compound interest.

The last section. They have finally paid back the entire debt.

Mrs. Loisel looked old now. She had become the strong, hard, and rude woman of poor households. Her hair unkempt, with uneven skirts and rough, red hands, she spoke loudly, washed floors with large buckets of water. But sometimes, when her husband was at work, she sat down near the window, and she dreamed of that evening so long ago, of that party, where she had been so beautiful and so admired.

Mrs. Loisel (how come the narrator does not say "Mathilde"?) is roughened and aged by the work. But she has behaved "heroically" (¶ 98), and has shown her mettle.

105   What would life have been like if she had not lost that necklace? Who knows? Who knows? Life is so peculiar, so uncertain. How little a thing it takes to destroy you or to save you!

A moral? Our lives are shaped by small, uncertain things; we hang by a thread.

Well, one Sunday, when she had gone for a stroll along the Champs-Elysées to relax from the cares of the week, she suddenly noticed a woman walking with a child. It was Mrs. Forrestier, still youthful, still beautiful, still attractive.

Mrs. Loisel felt moved. Would she speak to her? Yes, certainly. And now that she had paid, she could tell all. Why not?

She walked closer.

"Hello, Jeanne."

110   The other gave no sign of recognition and was astonished to be addressed so familiarly by this working-class woman. She stammered:

"But . . . Madam! . . . I don't know. . . . You must have made a mistake."

"No. I'm Mathilde Loisel."

Her friend cried out:

"Oh! . . . My poor Mathilde, you've changed so much."

115   "Yes. I've had some tough times since I saw you last; in fact hardships . . . and all because of you! . . ."

"Of me . . . how so?"

"You remember the diamond necklace that you lent me to go to the party at the Ministry of Education?"

"Yes. What then?"

"Well, I lost it."

120   "How, since you gave it back to me?"

"I returned another exactly like it. And for ten years we've been paying for it. You understand this wasn't easy for us, who have nothing. . . . Finally it's over, and I'm damned glad."

Mrs. Forrestier stopped her.

"You say that you bought a diamond necklace to replace mine?"

"Yes, you didn't notice it, eh? It was exactly like yours."

125   And she smiled with proud and childish joy.

Mrs. Forrestier, deeply moved, took both her hands.

"Oh, my poor Mathilde! But mine was only costume jewelry. At most, it was worth only five hundred francs! . . ."

Sidebar notes:

A scene on the Champs-Elysées. She sees Jeanne Forrestier, after ten years.

They seem to have lost contact with each other totally during the last ten years. Would this have happened in real life?

Jeanne notes Mathilde's changed appearance.

Mathilde tells Jeanne everything.

SURPRISE! The lost necklace was **not** real diamonds, and the Loisels slaved for no reason at all. But hard work and sacrifice probably brought out better qualities in Mathilde than she otherwise might have shown. Is this the moral of the story?

■ READING AND RESPONDING IN A JOURNAL

The comments included alongside the story demonstrate the active reading-responding process you should apply to everything you read. Use the margins in your text to record your comments and questions, but, in addition, plan to keep a *journal* for lengthier responses. Your journal, which may consist of a notebook, note cards, separate sheets of paper, or a computer file, will be immensely useful to you as you move from your initial impressions toward more carefully considered thought.

In keeping your journal, your objective should be to learn assigned works inside and out and then to say perceptive things about them. To achieve this goal, you need to read the work more than once. You will need a good note-taking system so that as you read, you can develop a "memory bank" of your own knowledge about a work. You can draw from this fund of ideas when you begin to write. As an aid in developing your own procedures for reading and "depositing" your ideas, you may wish to begin with the following "Guidelines for Reading" [pages 360–62]. Of course, you will want to modify these suggestions and to add to them, as you become a more experienced, disciplined reader.

Using the Names of Authors When Writing About Literature

For both men and women writers, you should typically include the author's *full name* in the *first sentence* of your essay. Here are few model first sentences:

> Guy de Maupassant's "The Necklace" is a story that concludes with a surprise.

> "The Necklace," by Guy de Maupassant, is a story that concludes with a surprise.

For all later references, use only the author's last name (such as *Maupassant* for this story). However, for the "giants" of literature, you should use the last names exclusively. In referring to writers like Shakespeare and Milton, for example, there is no need to include *William* or *John*.

In spite of today's informal standards, do not use an author's first name, as in "*Guy* skillfully creates suspense and surprise in 'The Necklace.'" Also, do not use a familiar title before the names of dead authors, such as "*Mr.* Maupassant's 'The Necklace' is a suspenseful and pathetic story." Use the last name alone.

As with all conventions, of course, there are exceptions. If you are referring to a childhood work of a writer, the first name is appropriate, but shift to the last name when referring to the writer's mature works. If your writer has a professional or a noble title, such as "*Judge* O'Connor," "*Governor* Cross," "*Lord* Byron" or "*Lady* Winchelsea," it is not improper to use the title. Even then, however, the titles are commonly omitted for males, so that most references to Lord Byron and Lord Tennyson should be simply to "Byron" and "Tennyson."

Referring to living authors is somewhat problematic. Some journals and newspapers, like the *New York Times*, use the respectful titles *Mr.* and *Ms.* in their reviews. However, scholarly journals, which are likely to remain on library shelves for many decades, follow the general principle of beginning with the entire name and then using only the last name for subsequent references.

RESPONDING TO LITERATURE: LIKES AND DISLIKES

People read for many reasons. In the course of daily affairs, they read signs, labels, price tags, recipes, or directions for assembling a piece of furniture or a toy. They read newspapers to learn about national, international, and local events. They might read magazines to learn about important issues, celebrities, political figures, and biographical details about significant persons. Sometimes they might read to pass the time, or to take their minds off pressing problems or situations. Also, people regularly read out of necessity—in school and in their work. They study for examinations in chemistry, biology, psychology, and political science. They go over noun paradigms and verb forms in a foreign language. They read to acquire knowledge in many areas, and they read to learn new skills, new information, and new ways to do their jobs better.

But, aside from incidental, leisurely, and obligatory reading, many people turn to imaginative literature, which they read because they like it and find it interesting. Even if they don't like everything they read equally, they nevertheless enjoy reading and usually pick out authors and types of literature that they like.

It is therefore worth considering those qualities of imaginative literature that at the primary level produce responses of pleasure (and also of displeasure). You either like or dislike a story, poem, or play. If you say no more than this, however, you have not said much. Analyzing and explaining your likes and dislikes requires you to describe the reasons for your responses. The goal should be to form your responses as judgments, which are usually *informed* and *informative*, rather than as simple reactions, which may be *uninformed* and *unexplained*.

Sometimes a reader's first responses are that a story or poem is either "okay" or "boring." These reactions usually mask an incomplete and superficial first reading. They are neither informative nor informed. As you study most works, however, you will be drawn into them and become *interested* and *involved*. To be interested in a poem, play, or story is to be taken into it emotionally; to be involved suggests that your emotions become almost wrapped up in the characters, problems, outcomes, ideas, and expressions of opinion and emotion. Both "interest" and "involvement" describe genuine responses to reading. Once you get interested and involved, your reading ceases to be a task or an assignment and grows into a pleasure.

Use Your Journal To Record Your Responses

No one can tell you what you should or should not like, for liking is your own concern. While your reading is still fresh, therefore, you should use your journal to record your responses to a work in addition to your observations about it. Be frank in your judgment. Write down what you like or dislike, and explain the reasons for your responses, even if these are brief and incomplete. If, after later thought and fuller understanding, you change or modify your impressions, write down these changes too. Here is a journal entry that explains a favorable response to Maupassant's "The Necklace":

> I like "The Necklace" because of the surprise ending. It isn't that I like Mathilde's bad luck, but I like the way Maupassant hides the most important fact in the story until the end. Mathilde does all that work and sacrifice for no reason at all, and the surprise ending makes this point strongly.

This paragraph could be developed as part of an essay. It is a clear statement of liking, followed by references to likable things in the story. This response pattern, which can be simply phrased as "I like [dislike] this work because . . . ," is a useful way to begin journal entries because it always requires an explanation of responses. If at first you cannot explain the causes of your responses, at least make a brief list of the things you like or dislike. If you write nothing, you will probably forget your reactions. Recovering them later, either for discussion or writing, will be difficult.

GUIDELINES FOR READING

1. OBSERVATIONS FOR BASIC UNDERSTANDING

A. EXPLAIN WORDS, SITUATIONS, AND CONCEPTS. Write down words that are new or not immediately clear. If you find a passage that you do not quickly understand, decide whether the problem arises from unknown words. Use your dictionary, and record the relevant meanings in your journal, but be sure that these meanings clarify your understanding. Make note of special difficulties so that you may ask you instructor about them.

B. DETERMINE WHAT IS HAPPENING. For a story or play, where do the actions take place. What do they show? Who is involved? Who is the major figure? Why is he or she major? What relationships do the characters have with one another? What concerns do the characters have? What do they do? Who says what to whom? How do the speeches advance the action and reveal the characters? For a poem, what is the situation? Who is talking, and to whom? What does the speaker say about the situation? Why does the poem end as it does and where it does?

2. NOTES ON FIRST IMPRESSIONS

A. MAKE A RECORD OF YOUR REACTIONS AND RESPONSES, which you may derive from your marginal notations. What did you think was memorable, noteworthy, funny, or otherwise striking? Did you worry, get scared, laugh, smile feel a thrill, learn a great deal, feel proud, find a lot to think about? In your journal, record these responses and explain them more fully.

B. DESCRIBE INTERESTING CHARACTERIZATIONS, EVENTS, TECHNIQUES, AND IDEAS. If you like a character or an idea, explain what you like, and do the same for characters and ideas you don't like. Is there anything else in the work that you especially like or dislike. Are parts easy or difficulty to understand? Why? Are there any surprises? What was your reaction to them? Be sure to use your own words when writing your explanations.

3. DEVELOPMENT OF IDEAS AND ENLARGEMENT OF RESPONSES

A. TRACE DEVELOPING PATTERNS. Make an outline or a scheme: What conflicts appear? Do these conflicts exist between people, groups, or ideas? How does the author resolve them? Is one force, idea, or side the winner? Why? How do you respond to the winner or to the loser?

B. WRITE EXPANDED NOTES ABOUT CHARACTERS, SITUA-TIONS, AND ACTIONS. What explanations need to be made about the characters? What actions, scenes, and situations invite interpretation? What assumptions do the characters and speakers reveal about life and humanity generally; about themselves, the people around them, their families, and their friends; and about work, the economy, religion, politics, philosophy and the state of the world and the universe? What manners or customs do they exhibit? What sort of language do they use? What literary conventions and devices have you noticed, and what do these contribute to the action and ideas of the story?

C. WRITE A PARAGRAPH OR SEVERAL PARAGRAPHS DESCRIB-ING YOUR REACTIONS AND THOUGHTS. If you have an assignment, your paragraphs may be useful later because you might transfer them directly as early drafts. Even if you are making only a general preparation, however, always write down your thoughts.

D. MEMORIZE INTERESTING, WELL-WRITTEN, AND IMPOR-TANT PASSAGES. Use note cards to write them out in full, and keep them in your pocket or purse. When walking to class, riding public transportation, or otherwise not occupying your time, learn them by heart.

E. ALWAYS WRITE DOWN QUESTIONS THAT ARISE AS YOU READ. You may raise these in class, and they may also aid your own study.

State Reasons For Your Favorable Responses

Usually you can equate your interest in a work with liking it. You can be more specific about favorable responses by citing one or more of the following:

- ➤ You like and admire the characters and what they do and stand for. You get involved with them. When they are in danger you are concerned; when they succeed, you are happy; when they speak, you like what they say.

- ➤ After you have read the last word in a story or play, you are sorry to part with these characters and wish that there were more to read about them and their activities.

- ➤ Even if you do not particularly like a character or the characters, you are nevertheless interested in the reasons for and outcomes of their actions.

- ➤ You get so interested and involved in the actions or ideas in the work that you do not want to put the work down until you have finished it.

- ➤ You like to follow the pattern of action or the development of the author's thoughts, so that you respond with appreciation upon finishing the work.

- ➤ You find that reading enables you to relax or to take your mind off a problem or a pressing responsibility.

- ➤ You learn something new—something you had never before known or thought about human beings and their ways of handling their problems.

- ➤ You learn about customs and ways of life in different places and times.

- ➤ You gain new insights into aspects of life that you thought you already understood.

- ➤ You feel happy or thrilled because of reading the work.

- ➤ You are amused, and you laugh often as you read.

- ➤ You like the author's ways of describing scenes, actions, ideas, and feelings.

- ➤ You find that many of the expressions are remarkable and beautiful, and are therefore worth remembering.

State Reasons For Your Unfavorable Responses

Although so far we have dismissed *okay* and *boring* and have stressed *interest, involvement,* and *liking*, it is important to know that disliking all or part of a work is normal and acceptable. You do not need to hide this response. Here, for example, are two short journal responses expressing dislike for Maupassant's "The Necklace":

1. I do not like "The Necklace" because Mathilde seems spoiled, and I don't think she is worth reading about.
2. "The Necklace" is not an adventure story, and I like reading only adventure stories.

These are both legitimate responses because they are based on a clear standard of judgment. The first response stems from a distaste for one of the main character's unlikable traits, and the second from a preference for rapidly moving stories that evoke interest in the dangers that main characters face and overcome.

Here is a paragraph-length journal entry that might be developed from the first response. Notice that the reasons for dislike are explained. They would need only slightly more development for use in an essay:

I dislike "The Necklace" because Mathilde seems spoiled, and I don't think she is worth reading about. She is a phony. She nags her husband because he is not rich. She never tells the truth. I dislike her for hurrying away from the party because she is afraid of being seen in her shabby coat. She is foolish and dishonest for not telling Jeanne Forrestier about losing the necklace. It's true that she works hard to pay the debt, but she also puts her husband through ten years of hardship. If Mathilde had faced facts, she might have had a better life. I do not like her and cannot like the story because of her.

As long as you include reasons for your dislike, as in the list and in the paragraph, you can use them again in considering the story more fully, when you will surely also expand thoughts, include new details, pick new topics for development as paragraphs, and otherwise modify your journal entry. You might even change your mind. However, even if you do not, it is better to record your original responses and reasons honestly than to force yourself to say you like a story that you do not like.

Try to Put Dislikes into a Larger Context

Although it is important to be honest about disliking a work, it is more important to broaden your perspective and expand your taste. For example, a dislike based on the preference for only mystery or adventure stories, if generally applied, would cause a person to dislike most works of literature. This attitude seems unnecessarily self-limiting.

If negative responses are put in a larger context, it is possible to expand the capacity to like and appreciate good literature. For instance, some readers might be preoccupied with their own concerns and therefore be uninterested in remote or "irrelevant" literary figures. However, if by reading about literary characters they can gain insight into general problems of life, and therefore their own concerns, they can find something to like in just about any work. Other readers might like sports and therefore not read anything but the daily sports pages. What probably interests them about sports is competition, however, so if they can follow the *competition* or *conflict* in a literary work, they will have discovered something to like in that work.

As an example, let us consider again the dislike based on a preference for adventure stories, and see whether this preference can be widened. Here are some reasons for liking adventures:

1. Adventure has fast action.
2. It has danger and tension, and therefore interest.
3. It has daring, active, and successful characters.
4. It has obstacles that the characters work hard to overcome.

No one could claim that the first three points apply to "The Necklace," but the fourth point is promising. Mathilde, the major character, works hard to overcome an obstacle: She pitches in to help her husband pay the large debt. If you like adventures because the characters try to gain worthy goals, then you can also like "The Necklace" for the same reason. The principle here is clear: If a reason for liking a favorite work or type of work can be found in another work, then there is reason to like that new work.

The following paragraph shows a possible application of this "bridging" process of extending preferences. (The sample essay is also developed along these lines.)

I usually like only adventure stories, and therefore I disliked "The Necklace" at first because it is not adventure. But one of my reasons for liking adventure is that the characters work hard to overcome difficult obstacles, like finding buried treasure or exploring new places. Mathilde, Maupassant's main character in "The Necklace," also works hard to overcome an obstacle—helping to pay back the money and interest for the borrowed 18,000 francs used as part of the payment for the replacement necklace. I like adventure characters because they stick to things and win out. I see the same toughness in Mathilde. Her problems get more interesting as the story moves on after a slow beginning. I came to like the story.

The principle of "bridging" from like to like is worth restating and emphasizing: *If a reason for liking a favorite work or type of work can be found in another work, then there is reason to like that new work.* A person who adapts to new reading in this open-minded way can redefine dislikes, no matter how slowly, and may consequently expand the ability to like and appreciate many kinds of literature.

An equally open-minded way to develop understanding and widen taste is to put dislikes in the following light: An author's creation of an *unlikable* character, situation, attitude, or expression may be deliberate. Your dislike might then result from the author's *intentions.* A first task of study, therefore, is to understand and explain the intention or plan. As you put the plan into your own words, you may find that you can like a work with unlikable things in it. Here is paragraph that traces this pattern of thinking, based again on "The Necklace":

> Maupassant apparently wants the reader to dislike Mathilde, and I do. At first, he shows her being unrealistic and spoiled. She lies to everyone and nags her husband. Her rushing away from the party so that no one can see her shabby coat is a form of lying. But I like the story itself because Maupassant makes another kind of point. He does not hide her bad qualities, but makes it clear that she herself is the cause of her trouble. If people like Mathilde never face the truth, they will get into bad situations. This is a good point, and I like the way Maupassant makes it. The entire story is therefore worth liking even though I still do not like Mathilde.

Both of these "bridging" analyses are consistent with the original negative reactions. In the first paragraph, the writer applies one of his principles of liking to include "The Necklace." In the second, the writer considers her initial dislike in the context of the work, and discovers a basis for liking the story as a whole while still disliking the main character.

The main concern in both responses is to keep an open mind despite initial dislike and then to see whether the unfavorable response can be more fully and broadly considered.

However, if you decide that your dislike overbalances any reasons you can find for liking, then you should explain your dislike. As long as you relate your response to the work accurately and measure it by a clear standard of judgment, your dislike of even a commonly liked work is not unacceptable. The important issue is not so much that you like or dislike a particular work *but that you develop your own abilities to analyze and express your ideas.*

■ WRITING ESSAYS ON LITERARY TOPICS

Writing is the sharpened, focused expression of thought and study. It begins with the search for something to say—an idea. Not all ideas are equal; some are better than others, and getting good ideas is an ability that you will develop the more you think and write. As you discover ideas and write them down, you will also improve your perceptions and increase your critical faculties.

In addition, because literature itself contains the subject material, though not in a systematic way, of philosophy, religion, psychology, sociology, and politics, learning to analyze literature and to write about it will also improve your capacity to deal with these and other disciplines.

Writing Does Not Come Easily: Don't Worry—Just Do It

At the outset, it is important to realize that writing is a process that begins in uncertainty and hesitation, and that becomes certain and confident only as a result of diligent thought and considerable care. When you read a complete, polished, well-formed piece of writing, you might believe at first that the writer wrote this perfect version in only one draft and never needed to make any changes and improvements in it at all. Nothing could be further from the truth.

If you could see the early drafts of writing you admire, you would be surprised and startled—and also encouraged—to see that good writers are also human and that what they first write is often uncertain, vague, tangential, tentative, incomplete, and messy. Usually, they do not like these first drafts, but nevertheless they work with their efforts and build upon them: They discard some details, add others, chop paragraphs in half, reassemble the parts elsewhere, throw out much (and then maybe recover some of it), revise or completely rewrite sentences, change words, correct misspellings, and add new material to tie all the parts together and make them flow smoothly.

Three Major Stages of Thinking and Writing

For good and not-so-good writers alike, the writing task follows three basic stages. (1) The first stage—*discovering ideas*—shares many of the qualities of ordinary conversation. Usually, conversation is random and disorganized. It shifts from topic to topic, often without any apparent cause, and it is repetitive. In discovering ideas for writing, your process is much the same, for you jump from idea to idea, and do not necessarily identify the connections or bridges between them. (2) By the second step, however—*creating an early, rough draft of a critical paper*—your thought should be less like ordinary conversation and more like classroom discussion. Such discussions generally stick to a point, but they are also free and spontaneous, and digressions often occur. (3) At the third stage—*preparing a finished essay*—your thinking must be sharply focused, and your writing must be organized, definite, concise, and connected.

If you find that trying to write an essay gets you into difficulties like false starts, dead ends, total cessation of thought, digressions, despair, hopelessness, and other such frustrations, remember that *it is important just to start.* Just simply write anything at all—no matter how unacceptable your first efforts may seem—and force yourself to come to grips with the materials. Beginning to write does not commit you to your first ideas. They are not untouchable and holy just because they are on paper or on your computer screen. You may throw them out in favor of new ideas. You may also cross out words or move sections around, as you wish. However, if you keep your first thoughts buried in your mind, you will have nothing to work with. It is essential to accept the uncertainties in the writing process and make them work *for* you rather than *against* you.

DISCOVERING IDEAS

You cannot know your own ideas fully until you write them down. Thus, the first thing to do in the writing process is to dig deeply into your mind and drag out all your responses and ideas about the story. Write anything and everything that occurs to you. Don't be embarrassed if things do not look great at first, but keep working toward improvement. If you have questions you can't answer, write them down and plan to answer them later. In your attempts to discover ideas, use the following prewriting techniques.

Brainstorming or Freewriting Gets Your Mind Going

Brainstorming or **freewriting** is an informal way to describe your own written but private no-holds-barred conversation with yourself. It is your first step in writing. When you begin freewriting, you do not know what is going to happen, so you let your mind play over all the possibilities that you generate as you consider the work, or a particular element of the work, or your own early responses to it. In effect, you are talking to yourself and writing down all your thoughts, whether they fall into patterns or seem disjointed, beside the point, or even foolish. At this time, do not try to organize or criticize your thoughts. Later you can decide which ideas to keep and which to throw out. For now, *the goal is to get all your ideas on paper or on the computer screen.* As you are developing your essay later on, you may, *at any time*, return to the brainstorming or freewriting process to initiate and develop new ideas.

Focus on Specific Topics

1. DEVELOP SUBJECTS YOU CREATE WHEN TAKING NOTES AND BRAINSTORMING. Although the goal of brainstorming is to be totally free about the topics, you should recognize that you are trying to think creatively. You will therefore need to start directing your mind into specific channels. Once you start focusing on definite topics, your thinking, as we have noted, is analogous to classroom discussion. Let us assume that in freewriting, you produce a topic that you find especially interesting. You might then start to focus on this topic and to write as much as you can about it. The following examples from early thoughts about Maupassant's "The Necklace" show how a writer may zero in on such a topic—in this case, "honor"—once the word comes up in freewriting:

> Mathilde could have gone to her friend and told her she had lost the necklace. But she didn't. Was she overcome with shame? Would she have felt a loss of honor by confessing the loss of the necklace?

> What is honor? Doing what you think you should even if you don't want to, or if it's hard? Or is it pride? Was Mathilde too proud or too honorable to tell her friend? Does having honor mean going a harder way, when either way would probably be okay? Do you have to suffer to be honorable? Does pride or honor produce a choice for suffering?

Mathilde wants others to envy her, to find her attractive. Later she tells Loisel that she would feel humiliated at the party with rich women unless she wore jewelry. Maybe she is more concerned about being admired than about the necklace. Having a high self-esteem has something to do with honor, but more with pride.

Duty. Is it the same as honor? Is it Mathilde's duty to work so hard? Certainly her pride causes her to do her duty and behave honorably, and therefore pride is a step towards honor.

Honor is a major part of life, I think. It seems bigger than any one life or person. Honor is just an idea or a feeling—can an idea of honor be larger than a life, take over someone's life? Should it?

These paragraphs do not represent finished writing, but they do demonstrate how a writer may attempt to define a term and determine the degree to which it applies to a major character or circumstance. Although the last paragraph departs from the story, this digression is perfectly acceptable because in the freewriting stage, writers treat ideas as they arise. If the ideas amount to something, they may be used in the developing essay; but if they don't, they can be thrown away. The important principle in brainstorming is to record *all* ideas, with no initial concern about how they might seem to a reader. The results of freewriting are for the eyes of the writer only. (A student once began a freewriting exercise by indicating his desire for a large bowl of ice cream. Although the wish had nothing to do with the topic, it did cause the student to begin writing and to express more germane ideas. Needless to say, the original wish did not get into the final essay.)

2. BUILD ON YOUR ORIGINAL NOTES. An essential way to focus your mind is to mine your journal notes for relevant topics. For example, let us assume that you have made an original note on "The Necklace" about the importance of the attic flat where Mathilde and her husband live after they paid for the replacement necklace. With this note as a start, you can develop a number of ideas, as in the following:

The attic flat is important. Before, in her apartment, Mathilde was dreamy and impractical. She was delicate, but after losing the necklace, no way. She becomes a worker when in the flat. She can do a lot more now.

M. gives up her servant, climbs stairs carrying buckets of water, washes greasy pots, throws water around to clean floors, does all the wash by hand.

While she gets stronger, she also gets loud and frumpy—argues with shopkeepers to get the lowest prices. She stops caring for herself. A reversal here, from incapable and well groomed to coarse but capable. All this change happens in the attic flat.

Notice that no more than a brief original note can help you discover thoughts that you did not originally have. This act of stretching your mind leads you to put elements of the story together in ways that create support for ideas that you may use to build good essays. Even in an assertion as basic as "The attic flat is important," the process itself, which is a form of concentrated thought, leads you creatively forward.

    3. RAISE AND ANSWER YOUR OWN QUESTIONS. A major way to discover ideas about a work is to raise and answer questions as you read. The "Guidelines for Reading" will help you formulate questions (pages 238–39), but you may also raise specific questions like these (assuming that you are considering a story):

> ➤ What explanations are needed for the characters? Which actions, scenes, and situations invite interpretation? Why?

> ➤ What assumptions do the characters and speakers reveal about life and humanity generally; about themselves, the people around them, their families, and their friends; and about work, the economy, religion, politics, and the state of the world?

> ➤ What are their manners or customs?

> ➤ What kinds of words do they use: formal or informal words, slang or profanity?

> ➤ What literary conventions and devices have you discovered, and how do these add to the work? (When an author addresses readers directly, for example, that is a **convention**; when a comparison is used, that is a **device**, which might be either a **metaphor** or a **simile**.)

Of course you may raise other questions as you reread the piece, or you may be left with one or two major questions that you decide to pursue.

    4. USE THE PLUS-MINUS, PRO-CON, OR EITHER-OR METHOD TO PUT IDEAS TOGETHER. A common method of discovering ideas is to develop a set of contrasts: plus-minus, pro-con, either-or. Let us suppose a plus-minus method of considering the character of Mathilde in "The Necklace": Should she be "admired" (plus) or "condemned" (minus)?

PLUS: ADMIRED	MINUS: CONDEMNED?
After she cries when they get the invitation, she recovers with a "strong effort"—maybe she doesn't want her husband to feel bad.	She only wants to be envied and admired for being attractive (end of first part), not for more important qualities.
She really scores a great victory at the dance. She does have the power to charm and captivate.	She wastes her time daydreaming about things she can't have, and whines because she is unhappy.
Once she loses the necklace, she and her husband become impoverished. But she does "her share . . . completely, heroically" (paragraph 98) to make up for the loss.	She manipulates her husband into giving her a lot of money for a party dress, but they live poorly.
Even when she is poor, she still dreams about that marvelous, shining moment. She gets worse than she deserves.	She assumes that her friend would think she was a thief if she knew she was returning a different necklace. Shouldn't she have had more confidence in the friend?
At the end, she confesses the loss to her friend.	She gets loud and coarse, and haggles about pennies, thus undergoing a total cheapening of her character.

Once you put contrasting ideas side by side, as in this example, you will get new ideas. Filling the columns almost demands that you list as many contrasting positions as you can and that you think about how material in the work supports each position. It is in this way that true, genuine thinking takes place.

Your notes will therefore be useful regardless of how you finally organize your essay. You may develop either column in a full essay, or you might use the notes to support the idea that Mathilde is too complex to be either wholly admired or wholly condemned. You might even introduce an entirely new idea, such as that Mathilde should be pitied rather than condemned or admired. In short, arranging materials in the plus-minus pattern is a powerful way to discover ideas that can lead to ways of development that you might not otherwise find.

   5. TRACE DEVELOPING PATTERNS. You can also discover ideas by making a list or scheme for the story or main idea. What conflicts appear? Do these conflicts exist between people, groups, or ideas? How does the author resolve them? Is one force, idea, or side the winner? Why? How do you respond to the winner or to the loser?

   Using this method, you might make a list similar to this one:

> Beginning: M. is a fish out of water. She dreams of wealth, but her life is drab and her husband is ordinary.
>
> Fantasies—make her even more dissatisfied—punishes herself by thinking of a wealthy life.
>
> Her character relates to the places in the story: the Street of the Martyrs, the dinner party scene, the attic flat. Also the places she dreams of—she fills them with the most expensive things she can imagine.
>
> They get the dinner invitation—she pouts and whines. Her husband feels discomfort, but she doesn't really harm him. She manipulates him into buying her an expensive party dress, though.
>
> Her dream world hurts her real life when her desire for wealth causes her to borrow the necklace. Losing the necklace is just plain bad luck.
>
> The attic flat brings out her potential coarseness. But she also develops a spirit of sacrifice and cooperation. She loses, but she's really a winner.

   These observations all focus on Mathilde's character, but you may wish to trace other patterns you find in the story. If you start planning an essay about another pattern, be sure to account for all the actions and scenes that relate to your topic. Otherwise, you may miss a piece of evidence that can lead you to new conclusions.

   6. LET YOUR WRITING HELP YOU DEVELOP YOUR THINKING. No matter what method of discovering ideas you use, it is important to realize that *unwritten thought is incomplete thought.* Make a practice of writing notes about your reactions and any questions that occur to you. Very likely they will lead you to the most startling discoveries that you finally make about a work.

DRAFTING YOUR ESSAY

As you use the brainstorming and focusing techniques for discovering ideas, you are also beginning to draft your essay. You will need to revise your ideas as connections among them become more clear, and as you reexamine the work for support for the ideas you are developing, but you already have many of the raw materials you need for developing your topic.

Create a Central Idea

By definition, an essay is *a fully developed and organized set of paragraphs that develop and enlarge a central idea.* All parts of an essay should contribute to the reader's understanding of the idea. To achieve unity and completeness, each paragraph refers to the central idea and demonstrates how selected details from the work relate to it and support it. The central idea will help you control and shape your essay, and it will provide guidance for your reader.

A successful essay about literature is a brief but thorough (not exhaustive) examination of a literary work in light of a particular element, such as **character**, **point of view**, or **symbolism**. Typical central ideas might be (1) that a character is strong and tenacious, or (2) that the point of view makes the action seem "distant and objective," or (3) that a major symbol governs the actions and thoughts of the major characters. In essays on these topics, all points must be tied to such central ideas. Thus, it is a fact that Mathilde Loisel in "The Necklace" endures ten years of slavish work and sacrifice. This fact is not relevant to an essay on her character, however, unless you connect it by showing how it demonstrates one of her major traits—in this case, her growing strength and perseverance.

Look through all of your ideas for one or two that catch your eye for development. If you have used more than one prewriting technique, the chances are that you have already discovered at least a few ideas that are more thought-provoking, or important, than the others.

Once you choose an idea that you think you can work with, write it as a complete sentence. A *complete sentence* is important: A simple phrase, such as "setting and character," does not focus thought the way a sentence does. A sentence moves the topic toward new exploration and discovery because it combines a topic with an outcome, such as "The setting of 'The Necklace' reflects Mathilde's character." You may choose to be even more specific: "Mathilde's strengths and weaknesses are reflected in the real and imaginary places in 'The Necklace.' "

With a single, central idea for your essay, you have a standard for accepting, rejecting, rearranging, and changing the ideas you have been developing. You may now draft a few paragraphs to see whether your idea seems valid, or you may decide that it would be more helpful to make an outline or a list before you attempt to support your ideas in a rough draft. In either case, you should use your notes for evidence to connect to your central idea. If you need more ideas, use any of the brainstorming-prewriting techniques to discover them. If you need to bolster your argument by including more details that are relevant, jot them down as you reread the work.

Using the central idea that *the changes in the story's settings reflect Mathilde's character* might produce a paragraph like the following, which stresses her negative qualities:

> The original apartment in the Street of Martyrs and the dream world of wealthy places both show negative sides of Mathilde's character. The real-life apartment, though livable, is shabby. The furnishings all bring out her discontent. The shabbiness makes her think only of luxuriousness, and her one servant girl causes her to dream of having many servants. The luxury of her dream life heightens her unhappiness with what she actually has.

Even in such a discovery draft, however, where the purpose is to write initial thoughts about the central idea, many details from the story are used in support. In the final draft, this kind of support will be absolutely essential.

Create a Thesis Sentence

With your central idea to guide you, you can now decide which of the earlier observations and ideas can be developed further. Your goal is to establish a number of major topics to support the central idea and to express them in a **thesis sentence**—an organizing sentence that plans or forecasts the major topics you will treat in your essay. Suppose you choose three ideas from your discovery stage of development. If you put the central idea at the left and the list of topics at the right, you have the shape of the thesis sentence. Note that the first two topics have been taken from the discovery paragraph.

CENTRAL IDEA	TOPICS
The setting of "The Necklace" reflects Mathilde's character.	1. Real-life apartment 2. Dream surroundings 3. Attic flat

This arrangement leads to the following thesis statement:

> Mathilde's character growth is related to her first apartment, her dream-life mansion rooms, and her attic flat.

You can revise the thesis statement at any stage of the writing process if you find that you do not have enough evidence from the work to support it. Perhaps a new topic may occur to you, and you can include it, appropriately, as a part of your thesis sentence.

As we have seen, the central idea is the glue of the essay. The thesis sentence *lists the parts to be fastened together*—that is, the topics in which the central idea is to be demonstrated and argued. To alert your readers to your essay's structure, the thesis sentence is often placed at the end of the introductory paragraph, just before the body of the essay begins.

WRITING A FIRST DRAFT

To write a first draft, you support the points of your thesis sentence with your notes and discovery materials. You may alter, reject, and rearrange ideas and details as you wish, as long as you change your thesis sentence to account for the changes (a major reason why most writers write their introductions last). The thesis sentence just shown contains three topics (it could be two, or four, or more), to be used in forming the body of the essay.

BEGIN EACH PARAGRAPH WITH A TOPIC SENTENCE. Just as the organization of the entire essay is based on the thesis, the form of each paragraph is based on its **topic sentence**. A topic sentence is an assertion about how a topic from the predicate of the thesis statement supports the central idea. The first topic in our example is the relationship of Mathilde's character to her first apartment, and the resulting paragraph should emphasize this relationship. If you choose the coarsening of her character during the ten-year travail, you can then form a topic sentence by connecting the trait with the location, as follows:

> The attic flat reflects the coarsening of Mathilde's character.

Beginning with this sentence, the paragraph can show how Mathilde's rough, heavy housework has a direct effect on her behavior, appearance, and general outlook.

USE ONLY ONE TOPIC—NO MORE—IN EACH PARAGRAPH. Usually you should treat each separate topic in a single paragraph. However, if a topic seems especially difficult, long, and heavily detailed, you may divide it into two or more subtopics, each receiving a separate paragraph of its own. Should you make this division, your topic then is really a section, and each paragraph in the section should have its own topic sentence.

WRITE SO THAT YOUR PARAGRAPHS DEVELOP OUT OF YOUR TOPIC SENTENCES. Once you choose your thesis sentence, you can use it to focus your observations and conclusions. Let us see how our topic about the attic flat may be developed as a paragraph:

> <u>The attic flat reflects the coarsening of Mathilde's character.</u> Maupassant emphasizes the burdens she endures to save money, such as mopping floors, cleaning greasy and encrusted pots and pans, taking out the garbage, and hand-washing clothes and dishes. This work makes her rough and coarse, an effect that is heightened by her giving up care of her hair and hands, wearing the cheapest dresses possible, and becoming loud and penny-pinching in haggling with the local shopkeepers. If at the beginning she is delicate and attractive, at the end she is unpleasant and coarse.

Notice that details from the story are introduced to provide support for the topic sentence. All the subjects—the hard work, the lack of personal care, the wearing of cheap dresses, and the haggling with the shopkeepers—are introduced not to retell the story but rather to exemplify the claim the writer is making about Mathilde's character.

Develop an Outline

So far we have been developing an **outline**—that is, a skeletal plan of organization for your essay. Some writers never use formal outlines at all, preferring to make informal lists of ideas, whereas others rely on them constantly. Still other writers insist that they cannot make an outline until they have finished their essays. Regardless of your preference, *your finished essay should have a tight structure.* Therefore, you should create a guiding outline to develop or to shape your essay.

The outline we have been developing here is the **analytical sentence outline**. This type is easier to create than it sounds. It consists of (1) an *introduction*, including the central idea and the thesis sentence, together with (2) *topic sentences* that are to be used in each paragraph of the body, followed by (3) a *conclusion*.

WRITING BY HAND, TYPEWRITER, OR WORD PROCESSOR

It is important for you to realize that writing is an inseparable part of thinking and that unwritten thought is an incomplete thought.

Because thinking and writing are so interdependent, it is essential to get ideas into a visible form so that you may develop them further. For many students, it is psychologically necessary to carry out this process by writing down ideas by hand or typewriter. If you are one of these students, make your written or typed responses on only one side of your paper or note cards. Doing this will enable you to spread your materials out and get an actual physical overview of them when you begin writing. Everything will be open to you; none of your ideas will be hidden on the back of the paper.

Today, word processing is thoroughly established as an indispensable tool for writers. The word processor can help you develop ideas, for it enables you to eliminate unworkable thoughts and replace them with others. You can move sentences and paragraphs tentatively into new contexts, test out how they look, and move them somewhere else if you choose.

In addition, with the rapid printers available today, you can print drafts even in the initial and tentative stages of writing. Using your printed draft, you can make additional notes, marginal corrections, and suggestions for further development. With the marked-up draft for guidance, you can go back to your work processor and fill in your changes and improvements, repeating this procedure as often as you can. This facility makes the machine an additional incentive for improvement, right up to your final draft.

Word processing also helps you in the final preparation of your essays. Studies have shown that errors and awkward sentences are frequently found at the bottoms of pages prepared by hand or with a conventional typewriter. The reason is that writers hesitate to make improvements when they get near the end of a page because they shun the dreariness of starting the page over. Word processors eliminate this difficulty completely. Changes can be made anywhere in the draft, at any time, without damage to the appearance of the final draft.

Regardless of your writing method, it is important to realize that *unwritten thought is incomplete thought.* Even with the word processor's

box continued on next page➤

screen, you cannot lay everything out at once. You can see only a small part of what you are writing. Therefore, somewhere in your writing process, prepare a complete draft of what you have written. A clean, readable draft permits you to gather everything together and to make even more improvements through the act of revision.

When applied to the subject we have been developing, such an outline looks like this:

TITLE: How Setting in "The Necklace" Is Related to the Character of Mathilde

1. **INTRODUCTION**
   a. *Central idea*: Maupassant uses his setting to show Mathilde's character.
   b. *Thesis statement*: Her character growth is related to her first apartment, her daydreams about elegant rooms in a mansion, and her attic flat.
2. **BODY:** *Topic sentences* a, b, and c (and d, e, and f, if necessary)
   a. Details about her first apartment explain her dissatisfaction and depression.
   b. Her daydreams about mansion rooms are like the apartment because they too make her unhappy.
   c. The attic flat reflects the coarsening of her character.
3. **CONCLUSION**
   Topic sentence. All details in the story, particularly the setting, are focused on the character of Mathilde.

The *conclusion* may be a summary of the body; it may evaluate the main idea; it may briefly suggest further points of discussion; or it may be a reflection on the details of the body.

Use the Outline in Developing Your Essay

The three sample essays that follow in this section are organized according to the principles of the analytical sentence outline. To emphasize the shaping effect of these outlines, all central ideas, thesis sentences, and topic sentences are underlined. In your own writing, you may underline or italicize these "skeletal" sentences as a check on your organization. Unless your instructor requires such markings, however, remove them in your final drafts.

FIRST SAMPLE ESSAY, FIRST DRAFT

The following sample essay is a first draft of the topic we have been developing. It follows the outline presented here, and includes details from the story in support of the various topics. It is by no means, however, as good a piece of writing as it can be. The draft omits a topic, some additional details, and some new insights that are included in the second draft (pages 270–71). It therefore reveals the need to make improvements through additional brainstorming and discovery-prewriting techniques.

How Setting in "The Necklace" Is Related to the Character of Mathilde

[1]   In "The Necklace" Guy de Maupassant does not give much detail about the setting. He does not even describe the necklace itself, which is the central object in his plot, but he says only that it is "superb" (paragraph 47). <u>Rather, he uses the setting to reflect the character of the central figure, Mathilde Loisel.</u>* All Maupassant's details are presented to bring out her traits. <u>Her character development is related to her first apartment, her daydreams about mansion rooms, and her attic flat.</u>†

[2]   <u>Details about her first apartment explain her dissatisfaction and depression</u>. The walls are "drab," the furniture "threadbare," and the curtains "ugly" (paragraph 3). There is only a simple country girl to do the housework. The tablecloth is not changed daily, and the best dinner dish is boiled beef. Mathilde has no evening clothes, only a theater dress that she does not like. These details show her dissatisfaction with life with her low-salaried husband.

[3]   <u>Her dream-life images of wealth are like the apartment because they too make her unhappy</u>. In her daydreams about life in a mansion, the rooms are large, filled with expensive furniture and bric-a-brac, and draped in silk. She imagines private rooms for intimate talks, and big dinners with delicacies like trout and quail. With dreams of such a rich home, she feels even more despair about her modest apartment on the Street of Martyrs in Paris.

[4]   <u>The attic flat reflects the coarsening of Mathilde's character</u>. Maupassant emphasizes the burdens she endures to save money, such as mopping floors, cleaning greasy and encrusted pots and pans, taking out the garbage, and hand-washing clothes and dishes. This work makes her rough and coarse, an effect that is heightened by her giving up care of her hair and hands, wearing the cheapest dresses possible, and becoming loud and penny-pinching in haggling with the local shopkeepers. If at the beginning she is delicate and attractive, at the end she is unpleasant and coarse.

---

*Central Idea
†Thesis sentence.

[5]   In summary, Maupassant focuses everything in the story, including the setting, on the character of Mathilde. Anything extra is not needed, and he does not include it. Thus he says little about the big party scene except the necessary detail that Mathilde was a great "success" (paragraph 52). It is this detail that brings out some of her early attractiveness and charm (despite her more usual unhappiness). Thus, in "The Necklace," Maupassant uses setting as a means to his end—the story of Mathilde and her needless sacrifice.

■ DEVELOP AND STRENGTHEN YOUR ESSAY THROUGH REVISION

After finishing a first draft like this one, you may wonder what more you can do. You have read the work several times, discovered ideas to write about through brainstorming techniques, made an outline of your ideas, and written a full draft. How can you do better?

The best way to begin is to observe that *a major mistake writers make when writing about literature is to do no more than retell a story or reword an idea.* Retelling a story shows only that you have read it, not that you have thought about it. Writing a good essay requires you to arrange your thoughts into a pattern that can be followed by a perceptive reader.

Use Your Own Order of References

There are many ways to escape the trap of summarizing stories and to set up your own pattern of development. One way is to stress *your own* order when referring to parts of a work. Do not treat details as they happen, but rearrange them to suit your own thematic plans. Rarely, if ever, should you begin by talking about a work's opening; it is better to talk first about the conclusion or middle. As you examine your first draft, if you find that you have followed the chronological order of the work instead of stressing your own order, you may use one of the prewriting techniques to figure out new ways to connect your materials. The principle is that you should introduce references to the work to support the points you wish to make, and only these points.

Use Literary Material as Evidence in Your Argument

Whenever you write, your position is like that of a detective using clues as evidence for building a case, or of a lawyer using evidence as support for an *argument.* Your goal should be to convince your readers of your own knowledge and the reasonableness of your conclusions.

It is vital to use evidence convincingly so that your readers can follow your ideas. Let us look briefly at two drafts of a new example to see how writing may be improved by the pointed use of details. These are from drafts of a longer essay on the character of Mathilde.

A comparison of these paragraphs shows that the first has more words than the second (158 to 120), but that it is more appropriate for a rough

1	2
The major extenuating detail about Mathilde is that she seems to be isolated, locked away from other people. She and her husband do not speak to each other much, except about external things. He speaks about his liking for boiled beef, and she states that she cannot accept the big invitation because she has no nice dresses. Once she gets the dress, she complains because she has no jewelry. Even when borrowing the necklace from Jeanne Forrestier, she does not say much. When she and her husband discover that the necklace is lost, they simply go over the details, and Loisel dictates a letter of explanation, which she writes in her own hand. Even when she meets Jeanne on the Champs-Elysées, she does not say a great deal about her life but only goes through enough details about the loss and replacement of the necklace to make Jeanne exclaim about the needlessness of the ten-year sacrifice.	The major flaw of Mathilde's character is that she is withdrawn and uncommunicative, apparently unwilling or unable to form an intimate relationship. For example, she and her husband do not speak to each other much, except about external things such as his taste for boiled beef and her lack of a party dress and jewelry. With such an uncommunicative marriage, one might suppose that she would be more open with her close friend, Jeanne Forrestier, but Mathilde does not say much even to her. This flaw hurts her greatly, because if she were more open she might have explained the loss and avoided the horrible sacrifice. This lack of openness, along with her self-indulgent dreaminess, is her biggest defect.

than a final draft because the writer does little more than retell the story. The paragraph is cluttered with details that do not support any conclusions. If you examine it for what you might learn about Maupassant's actual use of Mathilde's solitary traits in "The Necklace," you will find that it gives you but little help. The writer needs to consider why these details should be shared, and to revise the paragraph according to the central idea.

On the other hand, the details in the right-hand paragraph all support the declared topic. Phrases such as "for example," "with such," and "this lack" show that the writer of paragraph 2 has assumed that the audience knows the story and now wants help in interpretation. Paragraph 2 therefore guides readers by *connecting the details to the topic*. It uses these details *as evidence*, not as a retelling of actions. By contrast, paragraph 1 recounts a number of relevant actions but does not *connect* them to the topic. More details, of course, could have been added to the second paragraph, but they are unnecessary because the paragraph demonstrates the point with the details used. There are many qualities that make good writing good, but one of the most important is shown in a comparison of the two paragraphs: *In good writing, no details are included unless they are used as supporting evidence in a pattern of thought.*

Keep to Your Point

Whenever you write an essay about literature—or, for that matter, any essay about any subject—you must pay great attention to organization and to the correct use of references to the work assigned. As you write, you should constantly try to keep your material unified, for should you go off on a tangent you are no longer controlling but are being controlled. It is too easy to start with your point but then wander off and just retell the story. Once again, resist the tendency to be a narrator. Instead, be an interpreter, an explainer.

CHECK THE DEVELOPMENT AND ORGANIZATION OF YOUR IDEAS

It bears repeating over and over again that the first requirement of a good essay is to introduce a point or main idea and then stick to it. Another major step toward excellence is to make your central idea expand and grow. The word *growth* is a metaphor describing the creation of new insights, the disclosure of ideas that were not at first noticeable, and the expression of original, new, and fresh interpretations.

Try to Be Original

In everything you ever write, it is important that you try to be original. You might initially claim that you cannot be original when you are writing about someone else's work. "The author has said everything," might go your argument, "and therefore I can do little more than follow the story." This claim presupposes that you have no choice in selecting material and no opportunity to make individual thoughts and original contributions.

But you do have choices and opportunities to be original. One obvious area of originality is *the development and formulation of your central idea.* For example, a natural first response to "The Necklace" is "The story is about a woman who loses a borrowed necklace and endures hardship to help pay for it." Because this response refers only to events in the story and not to any idea, an area of thought might be introduced if the hardship is called "needless." Just the use of this word alone demands that you explain the differences between *needed* and *unneeded* hardships, and your application of these differences to the heroine's plight would produce an original essay. Even better and more original insights could result if the topic of the budding essay were to connect the dreamy, withdrawn traits of the main character to her misfortunes and also to general misfortunes. A resulting central idea might be "People themselves create their own difficulties." Such an idea would require you to define not only the personal but also the representative nature of Mathilde's experiences, an avenue of exploration that could produce much in the way of a fresh, original essay about "The Necklace."

You can also develop your ability to treat your subject freshly and originally if you plan the body of the essay *to build up to what you think is your most important and incisive idea.* As examples of such planning, the following brief outline suggests how a central idea may be widened and expanded:

SUBJECT: MATHILDE AS A GROWING CHARACTER

1. Mathilde has normal daydreams about a better life.
2. She takes a risk and then loses, in trying to make her daydreams seem real.
3. She develops by facing her mistake and working hard to correct it.

The list shows how a subject may be enlarged if you treat your exemplifying topic in an increasing order of importance. In this case, the order moves from Mathilde's habit of daydreaming to the development of her character strength. The pattern shows how you can meet two primary standards of excellence in writing—organization and growth.

Clearly, you should always try to develop your central idea. Constantly adhere to your topic, and constantly develop it. Nurture it and make it grow. Admittedly, in a short essay you will be able to move only a short distance with an idea, but you *should never be satisfied to leave the idea exactly where you found it.* To the degree that you can learn to develop your ideas, you will receive recognition for increasingly original writing.

WRITE WITH YOUR READERS IN MIND

Whenever you write, you must decide how much detail to discuss. Usually you base this decision on your judgment of your readers. For example, if you assume that they have not read the work you are writing about, you will need to include a short summary as background. Otherwise, they may not understand your argument.

Consider, too, whether your readers have any special interests or concerns. If they are particularly interested in politics, sociology, religion, or psychology, for example, you may need to select and develop your materials accordingly.

Your instructor will let you know who your audience is. Usually, it will be your instructor or your fellow students. They will be familiar with the work and will not expect you to retell a story or summarize an argument. Rather, they will look to you as an *explainer* or *interpreter*. Thus, you may omit details from the work that do not exemplify and support your central idea, even if the details are important parts of the work. What you write should always be based on your developing idea together with your assessment of your readers.

USE EXACT, COMPREHENSIVE, AND FORCEFUL LANGUAGE

In addition to being original, organized, and well developed, the best writing is expressed in *exact, comprehensive,* and *forceful* language. At any stage of the composition process, you should try to correct your earliest sentences and paragraphs, which usually need to be rethought, reworded, and rearranged.

TRY TO MAKE YOUR SENTENCES MEANINGFUL. First of all, ask yourself whether your sentences really *mean* what you intend or whether you can make them more exact and therefore stronger. For example, consider these two sentences from essays about "The Necklace":

It seems as though the main character's dreams of luxury cause her to respond as she does in the story.

This incident, although it may seem trivial or unimportant, has substantial significance in the creation of the story; by this I mean the incident that occurred is essentially what the story is all about.

These sentences are inexact and vague, and therefore unhelpful; neither of them goes anywhere. The first sentence is satisfactory up to the verb "cause," but then it falls apart because the writer has lost sight of the meaning. It is best to describe *what* that response is, rather than to be satisfied with nothing more than that there *is* a response. To make the sentence more exact, we may make the following revision:

Mathilde's dreams of luxury make it impossible for her to accept her own possessions, and therefore she goes beyond her means in order to attend the party.

With this revision, the writer could consider the meaning of the story's early passages and could contrast the ideas there with those in the latter part. Without the revision, it is not clear where the writer might go.

The second sentence is vague because again the writer has lost sight of the topic. If we adopt the principle of trying to be exact, however, we may bring the dead sentence to life:

> The accidental loss of the necklace, which is trivial though costly, supports the narrator's claim that major turns in life are produced not by earthshaking events, but rather by minor ones.

TRY TO MAKE YOUR SENTENCES COMPLETE AND COMPREHENSIVE. Second, in addition to being exact, it is vital to make sentences—all sentences, but particularly thesis and topic sentences—complete and comprehensive. As an example, consider the following sentence from an essay about "The Necklace":

> The idea in "The Necklace" is that Mathilde and her husband work hard to pay for the lost necklace.

Although this sentence promises to describe an idea, it does not do so. Instead, it merely describes the major action of the story. Therefore, it needs to benefit from additional rethinking and rephrasing to make it more comprehensive, as in the these two revisions:

> In "The Necklace" Maupassant shows that hard work and responsibility are basic and necessary in life.
>
> Maupassant's surprise ending of "The Necklace" symbolizes the need for always being truthful.

Both new sentences are connected to the action described by the original phrasing, "Mathilde and her husband work hard to pay for the lost necklace," although they point toward differing treatments. The first sentence concerns the virtue shown by the Loisels in their sacrifice. Because the second sentence includes the word *symbolizes*, an essay stemming from it would stress the Loisels' mistake in not confessing the loss. In dealing with the symbolic meaning of their failure, an essay developed along the lines of the sentence would focus on the negative aspects of their characters, and an essay developed from the first sentence would stress their positive aspects. Either of the revised sentences, therefore, is more comprehensive than the original sentence and thus would help a writer get on the track toward an accurate and thoughtful essay.

Of course it is never easy to create fine sentences, but as a mode of improvement, you might create some self-testing mechanisms:

➤ **FOR TREATING STORY MATERIALS.** Always relate the materials to an idea or a point. Do not say simply that "Mathilde works constantly for ten years to help pay off the debt." Instead, blend the material into a point, like this: "Mathilde's ten-year effort shows the *horror of indebtedness*," or "Mathilde's ten-year effort *demonstrates the emergence of her strength of character*."

➤ **FOR RESPONSES AND IMPRESSIONS.** Do not say simply, "The story's ending left me with a definite impression," but *state* what the impression is: "The story's ending surprised me and also made me sympathetic to the major character."

➤ **FOR IDEAS.** Try to make the idea clear and direct. Do not say "Mathilde is living in a poor household," but rather get at an idea like this one: "The story of Mathilde shows that living in poverty reduces the quality of life."

➤ **FOR CRITICAL COMMENTARY.** Do not be satisfied with a statement such as "I found 'The Necklace' interesting," but try to describe what was interesting and *why* it was interesting: "I found 'The Necklace' interesting because it shows how chance and bad luck may either make or destroy people's lives."

Good writing begins with attempts, like these, to rephrase sentences to make them really say something. If you always name and pin down descriptions, responses, and judgments, no matter how difficult the task seems, your sentences can be strong because you will be making them exact.

SAMPLE ESSAY—IMPROVED DRAFT

If you refer again to the first draft of the essay about Maupassant's use of setting to illustrate Mathilde's character (page 262), you might notice that several parts of the draft need extensive reworking and revising. For example, paragraph 2 contains a series of short, unconnected comments, and the last sentence of that paragraph implies that Mathilde's dissatisfaction relates mainly to her husband rather than to her general circumstances. Paragraph 4 focuses too much on Mathilde's coarseness and not enough on her sacrifice and cooperation. The draft also ignores the fact that the story ends in another location, the Champs Elysées, where Maupassant continues to demonstrate the nature of Mathilde's character. Finally, there is not enough support in this draft for the contention (in paragraph 5) that *everything* in the story is related to the character of Mathilde.

To discover how these issues may be more fully considered, the following revision of the earlier draft creates more introductory detail, includes an additional paragraph, and reshapes each of the paragraphs to stress the relationship of central idea to topic. Within the limits of a short assignment, the essay illustrates all the principles of organization and unity that we have been discussing here.

Maupassant's Use of Setting in "The Necklace" to Show the Character of Mathilde

---

[1]   In "The Necklace" Guy de Maupassant uses setting to reflect the strengths and weaknesses of the main character, Mathilde Loisel.* As a result, his setting is not particularly vivid or detailed. He does not even provide a description of the ill-fated necklace—the central object in the story—but states no more than that it is "superb" (paragraph 47). In fact, he includes descriptions of setting only if they illuminate qualities of Mathilde's character. Her changing character may be related to the first apartment, her daydreams about mansion rooms, the attic flat of the Loisels, and the public street.†

[2]   Details about the modest apartment of the Loisels on the Street of Martyrs indicate Mathilde's peevish lack of adjustment to life. Though everything is serviceable, she is unhappy with the "drab" walls, "threadbare" furniture, and "ugly" curtains (paragraph 3). She has domestic help, but wants more servants than the simple country girl who does the household chores in the apartment. Her embarrassment and dissatisfaction are shown by details of her irregularly cleaned tablecloth and the plain and inelegant boiled beef that her husband adores. Even her best theater dress, which is appropriate for apartment life but which is inappropriate for more wealthy surroundings, makes her unhappy. All these details of the apartment establish that Mathilde's dominant character trait at the story's beginning is maladjustment. She therefore seems unpleasant and unsympathetic.

[3]   Like the real-life apartment, the impossibly expensive setting of her daydreams about living in a mansion strengthens her unhappiness and her avoidance of reality. All the rooms of her fantasies are large and expensive, draped in silk and filled with nothing but the best furniture and bric-a-brac. Maupassant gives us the following description of her dream world:

> She imagined a gourmet-prepared main course carried on the most exquisite trays and served on the most beautiful dishes, with whispered gallantries which she would hear with a sphinxlike smile as she dined on the pink meat of a trout or the delicate wing of a quail. (paragraph 4)

With impossible dreams like this one, her despair is complete. Ironically, this despair, together with her inability to live with reality, brings about her undoing. It makes her agree to borrow the necklace (which is just as unreal as her

---

*Central Idea
†Thesis sentence

[4] daydreams of wealth), and losing the necklace drives her into the reality of giving up her apartment and moving into the attic flat.

Also ironically, the attic flat is related to the coarsening of her character while at the same time it brings out her best qualities of cooperativeness and honesty. Maupassant emphasizes the drudgery of the work Mathilde endures to maintain the flat, such as walking up many stairs, washing floors with large buckets of water, cleaning greasy and encrusted pots and pans, taking out the garbage, handwashing clothes, and haggling loudly with local tradespeople. All this reflects her coarsening and loss of sensibility, also shown by her giving up hair and hand care, and wearing the cheapest dresses. The work she performs, however, makes her heroic (paragraph 98). As she cooperates to help her husband pay back the loans, her dreams of a mansion fade and all she has left is the memory of her triumphant appearance at the Minister of Education's party. Thus the attic flat brings out her physical change for the worse at the same time that it also brings out her psychological and moral change for the better.

[5] Her walk on the Champs-Elysées illustrates another combination of traits— self-indulgence and frankness. The Champs-Elysées is the most fashionable street in Paris, and her walk to it is similar to her earlier indulgences in her daydreams of upper-class wealth. But it is on this street where she meets Jeanne, and it is Mathilde's frankness in confessing the loss and replacement to Jeanne that makes Mathilde, finally, completely honest. While the walk thus serves as the occasion for the story's concluding surprise and irony, Mathilde's being on the Champs-Elysées is totally in character, in keeping with her earlier reveries about luxury.

[6] Other details in the story also have a similar bearing on Mathilde's character. For example, the story presents little detail about the party scene beyond the statement that Mathilde is a great "success" (paragraph 52)—a judgment that shows her ability to shine if given the chance. After she and Loisel accept the fact that the necklace cannot be found, Maupassant includes details about the Parisian streets, about the visits to loan sharks, and about the jewelry shops in order to bring out Mathilde's sense of honesty and pride as she "heroically" prepares to live her new life of poverty. Thus, in "The Necklace," Maupassant uses setting to highlight Mathilde's maladjustment, her needless misfortune, her loss of youth and beauty, and finally her growth as a responsible human being.

Several improvements to the first draft may be seen here. The language of paragraph 2 has been revised to show more clearly the inappropriateness of Mathilde's dissatisfaction. In paragraph 3, the irony of the story is brought out, and the writer has connected the details to the central idea in a richer pattern of ideas, showing the effects of Mathilde's despair. Paragraph 5— new in this revision—includes additional details about how Mathilde's walk on the Champs-Elysées is related to her character. In paragraph 6, the fact that Mathilde is able "to shine" at the dinner party is interpreted according to the central idea. Finally, the conclusion is now much more specific, summarizing the change in Mathilde's character rather than saying simply that the setting reveals her "needless misfortune." In short, the second draft reflects the complexity of "The Necklace" better than the first draft. Because the writer has revised the first-draft ideas about the story, the final essay is tightly structured, insightful, and forceful.

SUMMARY

To sum up, follow these guidelines whenever you write about a story or any kind of literature:

> Never just retell the story. Use story materials only to support your central idea or argument.

> Throughout your essay, keep reminding your reader of your central idea.

> Within each paragraph, make sure that you stress your topic idea.

> Develop your topic. Make it bigger than it was when you began.

> Always make your statements exact, comprehensive, and forceful.

> Never just retell the story.

> **Never just retell the story.**

> *Never just retell the story.*

■ WRITING ABOUT RESPONSES: LIKES AND DISLIKES

Now that we have looked briefly at the processes of writing, with two drafts of the same essay for illustration, we are ready to apply the principles of development to another topic for writing—this one about likes and dislikes (already mentioned, pages 241–49). In writing about your responses, rely on your initial informed reactions. It is not easy to reconstruct your first responses after a lapse of time, so you will need your journal observations to guide you in prewriting. Develop your essay by stressing those characters, incidents, and ideas that interest (or do not interest) you.

As with many essays, you will be challenged to connect details from the work to your central idea. That is, once you have begun by stating that you like (or dislike) the story, you might forget to highlight this response as you enumerate details. Therefore you need to stress your involvement in the work as you bring out evidence from it. You can show your attitudes by indicating approval (or disapproval), by commenting favorably (or unfavorably) on the details, by indicating things that seem new (or shopworn) and particularly instructive (or wrong), and by giving assent to (or dissent from) ideas or expressions of feeling.

Organize Your Essay About Likes and Dislikes

INTRODUCTION. Briefly describe the conditions that influence your response. Your central idea should be why you like or dislike the work. Your thesis sentence should include the major causes of your response, which are to be developed in the body.

BODY. The most common approach is to consider specific details that you like or dislike. The list on page 240 may help you articulate your responses. For example, you admired a particular character, or you got so interested in a story that you could not put it down, or you liked a particular passage in a poem or play, or you felt thrilled as you finished reading the work. Also, you may wish to develop a major idea, a fresh insight, or a particular outcome, as in the sample paragraph on page 237, which shows a surprise ending as the cause of a favorable response.

A second approach is to explain any changes in your responses about the work (i.e., negative to positive and vice versa). This approach requires that you isolate the causes of the change, but it does not require you to retell the story from beginning to end.

1. One way to deal with such a change—the "bridge" method of transferring preference from one type of work to another—is shown in the sample essay below.

2. Another way is to explain a change in terms of a new awareness or understanding that you did not have on a first reading. Thus, for example, your first response to "The Necklace" might be unfavorable or neutral because the story may at first seem to move rather slowly. But further consideration might lead you to discover new insights that change your mind, such as the needs to overcome personal pride and to stop minor resentments from growing and festering. Your essay would then explain how these new insights have caused you to like the story.

CONCLUSION. Here you might summarize the reasons for your major response. You might also face any issues brought up by a change or modification of your first reactions. For example, if you have always held certain assumptions about your taste but like the work despite these assumptions, you may wish to talk about your own change or development. This topic is personal, but in an essay about your personal responses, discovery about yourself is legitimate and worthy.

Sample Essay

Some Reasons for Liking Maupassant's "The Necklace"

[1]   To me, the most likable kind of reading is adventure. There are many
reasons for my preference, but an important one is that characters in adventure
stories work hard to overcome obstacles. Because Guy de Maupassant's "The
Necklace" is not adventure, I did not like it at first. But in one respect the story
is <u>like</u> adventure: The major character, Mathilde, works hard with her husband,
Loisel, for ten years to overcome a difficult obstacle. <u>Thus, because Mathilde does
what adventure characters also do, the story is likable.</u>* <u>Mathilde's appeal results
from her hard work, strong character, and sad fate, and also from the way our
view of her changes.</u>†

[2]   <u>Mathilde's hard work makes her seem good.</u> Once she and her husband are
faced with the huge debt of 18,000 francs, she works like a slave to help pay it
back. She gives up her servant and moves to a cheaper place. She does the
household drudgery, wears cheap clothes, and bargains with shopkeepers. Just
like the characters in adventure stories who do hard and unpleasant things, she
does what she has to, and this makes her admirable.

[3]   <u>Her strong character shows her endurance, a likable trait.</u> At first she is
nagging and fussy, and she always dreams about wealth and tells lies, but she
changes and gets better. She recognizes her blame in losing the necklace, and she
has the toughness to help her husband redeem the debt. She sacrifices "heroically" (paragraph 98) by giving up her comfortable way of life, even though in
the process she also loses her youth and beauty. Her jobs are not the exotic and
glamorous ones of adventure stories, but her force of character makes her as
likable as an adventure heroine.

[4]   <u>Her sad fate also makes her likable.</u> In adventure stories the characters
often suffer as they do their jobs. Mathilde also suffers, but in a different way,
because her suffering is permanent while the hardships of adventure characters
are temporary. This fact makes her especially pitiable because all her sacrifices
are not necessary. This unfairness invites the reader to take her side.

[5]   <u>The most important quality promoting admiration is the way in which
Maupassant shifts our view of Mathilde.</u> As she goes deeper into her hard life,
Maupassant stresses her work and not the innermost thoughts he reveals at the
beginning. In other words, the view into her character at the start, when she
dreams about wealth, invites dislike; but the focus at the end is on her achievements, with never a complaint—even though she still has golden memories, as the
narrator tells us:

> But sometimes, when her husband was at work, she sat down near the
> window, and she dreamed of that evening so long ago, of that party,
> where she had been so beautiful and so admired. (paragraph 104)

A major quality of Maupassant's changed emphasis is that Mathilde's fond memories do not lead to anything unfortunate. His shift in focus, from Mathilde's
dissatisfaction to her sharing of responsibility and sacrifice, encourages the
reader to like her.

---

* Central Idea
† thesis sentence

[6] "The Necklace" is not an adventure story, but Mathilde has some of the good qualities of adventure characters. Also, the surprise revelation that the lost necklace was false is an unforgettable twist, and this makes her more deserving than she seems at first. Maupassant has arranged the story so that the reader finally admires Mathilde. <u>"The Necklace" is a skillful and likable story.</u>

Commentary on the Essay

This essay demonstrates how a reader may develop appreciation by transferring a preference for one type of work to a work that does not belong to the type. In the essay, the "bridge" is an already established taste for adventure stories, and the grounds for liking "The Necklace" are that Mathilde, the main character, shares the admirable qualities of adventure heroes and heroines.

In paragraph 1, the introduction, the grounds for transferring preferences are established. Paragraph 2 deals with Mathilde's capacity to work hard, and paragraph 3 considers the equally admirable quality of endurance. The fourth paragraph describes how Mathilde's condition evokes sympathy and pity. These paragraphs hence explain the story's appeal by asserting that the main character is similar to admirable characters from works of adventure.

The fifth paragraph shows that Maupassant, as the story unfolds, alters the reader's perceptions of Mathilde from bad to good. For this reason, paragraph 5 marks a new direction from paragraphs 2, 3, and 4: It moves away from the topic material itself—Mathilde's character—to Maupassant's *technique* in handling the topic material.

Paragraph 6, the conclusion, restates the comparison and also introduces the surprise ending as an additional reason for liking "The Necklace." With the body and conclusion together, therefore, the essay establishes five separate reasons for approval. Three of these, derived directly from the main character, constitute the major grounds for liking the story, and two are related to Maupassant's techniques as an author.

Throughout the essay, the central idea is brought out in words and expressions such as "likable," "Mathilde's appeal," "strong character," "she does what she has to," "pitiable," and "take her side." Many of these expressions were first made in the writer's journal; and, mixed as they are with details from the story, they make for continuity. It is this thematic development, together with details from the story as supporting evidence, that shows how an essay on the responses of liking and disliking may be both informed and informative.

WEB RESOURCES

Web Resources can be found at **www.prenhall.com/harris** under Instructor's Resources.

PART FIVE

Business and Public Writing
by Linda Julian, *Furman University*

Teaching Writing Skills to Eager Learners

Even the most reluctant students of writing—those whose eyes have glazed over during important discussions of purpose, audience, organization, revision, and precise grammar—sharpen their pencils and look with renewed interest at the syllabus when teachers discuss business writing skills. These skills, usually the same ones students have unenthusiastically grappled with in writing essays, suddenly appeal because they are bathed in the golden glow of the marketplace. Students know that to get jobs and keep them, they must master the basic skills of writing for the workplace. Those writing skills which have previously been only marginally palatable take on the allure of "real life" when they are taught using documents from the world of business. In the related area of writing for the public at large, they are eager to learn how to use their writing skills to advantage in the public forum to voice opinions effectively about issues that matter to their own lives.

Many students have had part-time and summer jobs and know firsthand that employers expect competent writers on the job and often reward skillful writers with promotions and higher salaries. Students who have had little or no work experience are curious about the world of work and eagerly apply themselves to learning writing skills that may give them a head start in an increasingly competitive job market. Therefore, teachers who have been constantly battling apathy about writing suddenly discover that they have eager learners who will work diligently to craft a job application letter, a letter of demand for a replacement stereo speaker, or a proposal for a more equitable vacation plan.

On the other hand, students often have misconceptions about business writing that teachers should anticipate and deal with at the outset. Students sometimes think that workplace writing comes with a specialized vocabulary that smacks of governmentese and business lingo. Thus, they will labor to make simple and clear ideas sound "businesslike," usually by adding clichés and mixing phrases from the nineteenth-century ("Pursuant to," "beg to acknowledge," "per your request," for example) with inflated diction ("first and foremost," "in view of the fact that," "make an evaluation of the processes currently being used," for example). This inflated diction often results from overuse of the passive voice, linking verbs, circumlocution, and tautology. We need to make clear from the beginning that business writing—like all good writing—relies on using language appropriate to the audience and purpose. Students may be surprised to learn that workplace writing is not the most formal kind of writing and therefore usually contains contractions and simple, direct words put together effectively. It also relies on dynamic verbs.

Students may also be surprised to learn that the brevity of many letters and other business documents and the speed with which some are produced do not mean that these documents are easy to write or that the writer should take the task lightly. On the contrary, students should realize that often the brief letters are the most challenging. They should also see that every letter is a public relations statement about the writer, a first impression that can easily go wrong if the writer is careless and unconcerned about the impression created in business documents. In fact, a student who can write an excellent business letter is well on the way to excellence in all kinds of writing.

One major difference between business writing and other kinds of writing is the emphasis on efficiency and timeliness in workplace writing. Students probably have never stopped to consider the most important principle governing most business writing: Time is money. A discussion of this point may make a striking beginning for a unit on business writing. Students generally do not equate the writing they do with saving or wasting money, but teachers can show them that when messages are unclear and have to be questioned in follow-up letters and calls, busy workers are wasting time and effort that could be better spent in making money. They need to know that a letter costs about $20 for a company to write and mail. This substantial expense may have to be doubled or tripled when follow-up communications are required by inadequate messages.

They also need to know that business sometimes is lost on the basis of a poor first impression made by a sloppy or poorly written document. Students can readily see that a letter is like an introduction to a stranger: appearance and substance and tact either make the person want to get to know the newcomer—or not.

Finally, a major misconception that we need to correct is students' impression that secretaries will "fix" their writing once the students have jobs. As teachers, we need only ask students how secure they feel about their grammar and mechanics and general writing skills and then to imagine where and how a secretary, who may not have a college degree and the level of competence they have, could have acquired the necessary skills to make their higher-ups look good on paper. They must understand that in this age of word processing, more and more executives do their own typing and editing at the computer, relying little on secretaries for editorial help.

General Characteristics of Workplace Writing

As in other kinds of writing, the most important decisions a business writer must make are the purpose of the document and the audience for it. Many business documents fail to achieve their goal because the writer tosses off a letter or report too quickly to plan the strategy appropriate to the audience and purpose (see the *Prentice Hall Reference Guide*, Chapter 1).

Audience and purpose dictate major decisions about business documents: the choice of format, the organizational plan, the amount of background information necessary, the assumptions the writer can make about the reader, the level of language, the tone, and even the kinds of sentences appropriate for the task. Often students begin writing without knowing what they want to achieve with the piece of writing. For this reason, teachers may need to spend time having students analyze the purpose and audience for various types of business documents. In addition, many teachers require students to write a note, either on a cover sheet or in the upper-right hand corner of each assignment, identifying the intended audience and purpose. To emphasize the importance of audience and purpose, teachers may also want to have students write planning documents for each assignment, at least for the first few. Such a planning document might include answers to the following questions:

> ➤ Who is my audience?
> ➤ What do I know about my audience?
> ➤ What level of language will be appropriate for this reader?
> ➤ How much background information will I have to give this audience?
> ➤ On first glance, will the reader be receptive, neutral, or negative toward my message?
> ➤ What action do I want the reader to take?
> ➤ What strategies can I use to get the reader to take this action?
> ➤ What impression do I want this document to make on my reader?

In the business world, where time is money, students can also see that economical use of language is important. The most effective business documents avoid unnecessary passive voice, overuse of linking verbs, expletive constructions, tautological phrasing, and circumlocution. Students should also focus on the need for sentences that average fifteen to seventeen words so that documents may be read quickly, without the reader's having to reread in order to comprehend long, convoluted sentences. Also to engineer easy reading in business documents, teachers should point out the need for cumulative sentences as the dominant pattern rather than periodic sentences, which require readers to work harder at decoding the message.

Paragraphs, too, may be somewhat shorter in many business documents than they are in some kinds of essays. Students can see that shortening paragraphs and using a topic sentence at the top of each paragraph aids in quick, efficient reading.

On the other hand, we must help students see that using the fewest number of words possible is not necessarily the best goal for a document. Economy does not mean brutally stripped-down language. Rather we need to emphasize that economy means using the fewest number of words to convey the tone and strategy of the message we are trying to send. Bluntness rarely wins friends and influences people—at least not in a positive way.

Another point we need to make to our students is that many business documents are not read in their entirety. Some longer documents, especially proposals and reports, rely on headings and clear paragraph structure to enable overworked businesspeople to skim documents, reading only the parts they have immediate interest in.

Asked to identify the major differences between business writing and essay writing, students rarely think of these stylistic matters beyond making documents "sound" like business documents by using "business" language, but students quickly point out the differences in format. However, they underestimate how important adherence to conventional format is in workplace writing. As teachers, we can help them understand that although format is not the be-all and end-all of good business writing, deviating from acceptable formats is risky:

Why Care About Format?

➤ Business readers expect documents to look a certain way and may be distracted if they do not. Writers want to avoid doing anything that may distract a reader from processing the message.

➤ Writers who do not follow conventional formats may communicate that they do not think such things important, a message not likely to please a prospective employer or customer.

➤ Writers who do not follow conventional formats may suggest that they have not bothered to learn what the conventions of business are, a message that might not inspire confidence in the writer or his or her products or services.

See Chapter 64 of the *Prentice Hall Reference Guide* for specific suggestions about how to format business documents.

■ MAJOR KINDS OF WORKPLACE WRITING

All students know that workplace writing includes letters and memos, but many do not know that letters communicate between two companies or a company and individuals and use addresses that are outside the company and that memos communicate within a company. They usually do not know about the many kinds of reports, proposals, and public relations documents that require research, planning, revision, editing, and proofing just as more familiar kinds of documents do.

Furthermore, students have become so accustomed to using e-mail for friendly messages to friends and family that they generally lack real understanding of the ways e-mail functions in the world of work and the problems it can cause if not used carefully (see the *Prentice Hall Reference Guide*, Chapter 42a).

A good way to begin a unit on workplace writing is to teach students how to write routine letters asking for information and then to have them write to companies or visit local companies requesting samples of some of the following kinds of documents:

Kinds of Business Documents

➣ Letter expressing favorable information
➣ Letter expressing neutral information
➣ Letter expressing negative information
➣ Letter ordering a product or service
➣ Letter acknowledging an order
➣ A job application package-cover letter and resume
➣ A letter of recommendation
➣ A letter of congratulations
➣ A letter report
➣ A letter proposal
➣ A memo expressing favorable information
➣ A memo expressing neutral information
➣ A memo expressing negative information
➣ A memo explaining how to do something
➣ A memo analyzing how something works
➣ A feasibility report

➤ An informational report

➤ A proposal for changing a procedure or service

➤ A persuasive report

➤ A company brochure

➤ A news release

➤ An annual report

Students making such requests should ask the company to delete the names of the writer and addressee on letters and memos to protect the privacy of the employees who wrote them.

Discussion about the kinds of skills involved in writing these varied documents should prove fruitful. Students need to see that knowing such organizational plans as comparison and contrast, narration, cause and effect, process analysis, and argument is critical. They will also recognize that in the samples, the problems with grammar and format are distracting and potentially destructive to the success of the message.

■ STRATEGIES FOR LETTERS AND MEMOS

Writing effective letters and memos requires that the writer have a strategy for the document before beginning to write. In addition to thinking about the audience and emphasizing the reader by using second-person pronouns more than first-person pronouns, the writer also needs to decide where in the message to put the most important information. In deciding on placement, the writer must consider whether the message is likely to be received favorably, neutrally, or unfavorably.

Favorable letters and memos open with the important information and then follow up with the details. For example, a memo saying that an employee's trip has been approved would begin with that information. People enjoy receiving positive information and will usually continue reading the letter or memo to find out the details once they have been given the good news.

Neutral messages, often routine documents like orders, responses to inquiries, or acknowledgments of orders or shipments, should be handled in much the same way. Writers should, however, make an effort to be as positive and empathetic to the reader as possible, especially in the opening and closing sentences.

Unfavorable news, sometimes called a "bad news message," requires a different approach—a much less direct beginning. Readers who read bad news in the first line of a letter or memo may not read the reasons for the bad news or notice the helpful alternatives, which an unskilled writer may have put after the bad news in the document. An effective bad news letter usually reverses this process, beginning with a positive tone and giving the reasons for the unfavorable news—and only then giving the bad news. The advantage of this arrangement is that the reader's disappointment or anger is more likely to be softened if he or she can see the reasoning explained in stages from the beginning. This kind of letter or memo can be even more effective when the writer can help the reader by suggesting other ways the reader might achieve the goal or solve the problem. (See the next page for an example of a "Bad News" letter.)

■ EMPLOYMENT DOCUMENTS

Students' keen interest in getting summer jobs as well as entry-level jobs at graduation motivates them to pay close attention to instruction about employment documents. Such interest is a boon to writing teachers, because it gives them the opportunity to emphasize points about writing in general that students may not have heeded in other units. Those students who have paid little attention to talk about audience, purpose, and revision suddenly sit up a little straighter and make eye contact with the teacher.

Most students have at least heard of a resume, though most do not know how to write an acceptable one. Few seem to understand that a job application package has two parts: the resume and the job application letter, also known as a cover letter. They also need to know about additional kinds of letters that are involved in getting a job, such as thank you letters following interviews, inquiries about the status of an application, and letters accepting or rejecting a job.

One of the most difficult lessons to teach about employment documents is that they must be perfect and conventional. One of the best ways to make this point is to invite a human resources director or other executive to the class to discuss the number of resumes that are rejected simply because of sloppy appearance or a misspelling. Students need to hear that their resumes may not be read at all if the layout conveys a lack of attention to convention.

They need to know that for a college student, even a graduating senior, resumes are expected to be no longer than one page. Longer resumes risk not being read. Only employees who have been out of school for several years and, thus, have job experience should have multiple-page resumes.

Preparing to Write the Resume

Before they even begin drafting a resume or looking at sample resumes, students should be encouraged to spend time doing a thorough self-analysis. In particular they should list their previous or current jobs, activities, academic qualifications, and skills (especially experience with computers, foreign languages, money management, and travel). School activities can reveal leadership, experience with financial management, and organizational skills.

Some students are discouraged about beginning a resume because they think they do not have anything to put on one. That empty-resume feeling, however, is rarely the case. Students need help in seeing that their four years' work with a sorority or a service group has taught them much about planning, public relations, budgeting, and accountability. On the other hand, students must learn that employers are on the lookout for padded resumes, those that contain inflated—or even dishonest—descriptions of routine jobs or activities.

Writing the Resume

Once students have done some brainstorming about their own achievements, they are ready to think about how a resume ought to look. At this point, teachers may find it useful to have the class critique both effective and ineffective resumes. Career Placement personnel at the school may be able to come to class to discuss the most recent trends in resume writing.

The most common kind of arrangement for resumes of graduating or continuing students is the reverse-chronological resume. Under its three or four main headings—Education, Employment Experience, Activities and Honors, and Personal—activities are cited from most recent to oldest. Because the educational block is generally the most important for students, it comes first. Often it will include a subheading for school- related activities. This section normally does not refer to high school activities or graduation unless they were extraordinary (attending high school abroad, for example), though students who are not graduating from college may wish to list their high school and graduation date.

As with employment history, this educational history needs to be accurate in terms of exact dates. If gaps of a year or more appear, these need to be explained in the cover letter. Many job placement experts suggest that in the educational block, students should give their GPA (but only if it is above 3.0 on a 4.0 scale), note what percentage of their college expenses they have earned themselves, and list special courses outside the major that show additional expertise that might attract an employer's eye—for example, particular computer programs, foreign language proficiency, journalism courses, etc.

As part of this block, often under a heading like Educational Activities and Awards, students should list their memberships and achievements. The most difficult part of this section is that many students have difficulty in making parallel the elements of such a list. They need to be reminded to clarify (in parenthesis) unclear, abbreviated, or Greek titles of organizations and to explain briefly what certain responsibilities might mean if an office has an unusual title. Although this section is commonly placed under the larger Education notation (which should be in larger type), it may also be a separate section after the Employment Experience section.

Similarly, in the Employment Experience section, students should succinctly describe the duties of a position they held, particularly if the job title is not descriptive. All jobs which involve managing money or being responsible for it should be listed. Students should list only the most recent jobs if their employment history goes back to their teens and includes numerous jobs. As in the education block, entries ought to be parallel in structure and specificity (see the discussion in section 64b of the *Prentice Hall Reference Guide*).

If the writer chooses to include a personal section, which many employers like to see, it may mention such items as hobbies and willingness to relocate. Employers like to know that candidates have interests other than career goals.

Job-seekers who have been out of school for a while or who are in specialized or creative fields may prefer to do an Emphatic Resume, one which highlights special talents and achievements first, following these with Education and Activities sections.

Job placement experts disagree about two elements on resumes, and they seem evenly split in their vote. Some favor the use of a Job Objective at the beginning of the resume, but others argue that such an objective is a waste of space that could be better used for more specific details about the applicant. Those who do not favor their use argue that it is the cover letter that tailors the job application package to the job, not the resume. Recently employment experts have pointed out that resumes submitted electronically need to include the Job Objective, to distinguish applicants for this job from those who are applying for other positions within the company.

Similarly, experts are divided about whether or not applicants should list reference on the resume or simply state that they are available. Those who favor listing references on the resume argue that doing so saves the company a step and may, in a time of urgency in hiring, expedite consideration of those resumes that have them listed. Those who argue against listing them say that references may change and that the list takes space better used to show the qualifications of the applicant.

Whether or not references appear on the resume, students need to be reminded that listing someone as a reference is rude unless permission to do so has been arranged beforehand. Also students need to be told that family, friends, and ministers are neither useful nor appropriate references. They should list two or three professors, one outside the major if possible, and one or two former employers. Reference lists should give professional titles and full names, professional addresses, and telephone numbers. These days, many employers prefer to check references by telephone, partly because doing so saves time and partly because it minimizes the fear of lawsuits that could result from unfavorable recommendations.

In addition, students need to be reminded that their name, not the word resume, should go top and center. The resume is a sales document for a person, and that person's name should be the first thing a reader sees.

Formatting the Resume

The resume, like the cover letter, should appear on business weight stationery, not photocopy paper. The paper should be white or off-white, and the printer cartridge should be fresh and dark.

A margin of an inch and a half effectively frames the resume and keeps it from seeming too crowded on the page. The font should be 10 or 12 pitch, not smaller. Students need to work at spacing until they can uniformly space between major sections. They may need to cut or tighten up some descriptions or entries.

■ COVER LETTERS

Job application letters have one major purpose: to win a job interview for the writer. These letters, which usually accompany resumes, should be no longer than a page and should avoid overusing first-person pronouns such as *I* and *me*, even though the letter is about the writer. Such pronouns should be positioned within sentences and paragraphs rather than at the beginning, where they receive more emphasis.

In general, cover letters have three parts. The first paragraph should explain how the writer learned about the job. The applicant should say that the letter is in response to an ad in a particular newspaper or magazine, giving the date of the ad and the title of the position as it was listed in the ad. Or, if the applicant found out about the job through a contact, he or she should mention the person who made the job information available.

If the letter is a blanket letter, a job solicitation letter, that the applicant is sending to many firms in a particular geographic area or a specialization, the opening should make clear that the writer knows what kinds of positions are typically open so that he or she avoids a vague and negative opening like "I would like to apply for any entry-level job with your company" or "Please consider me for any new positions in management." Such statements usually result in the application's immediate rejection.

The second paragraph should highlight qualifications, though it should not simply list what is on the attached resume. This paragraph also provides an opportunity for the writer to explain potentially negative impressions such as gaps in dates on the resume, low grades, a major in a field different from the area in which the applicant is pursuing a job, the lack of extracurricular activities, or reasons why employment was brief or terminated at a particular company.

The third paragraph, which, like the first, should be only four or five lines long, should request an interview. Career experts are divided on whether the applicant should offer to call the employer to set up the interview or whether the applicant should simply express willingness to have an interview at the employer's convenience, leaving it to the employer to make the initial contact (Chapter 64 in the *Prentice Hall Reference Guide* provides sample cover letters and advice for writing cover letters).

■ OTHER EMPLOYMENT LETTERS

Students should be aware that looking for jobs may require letters beyond job application letters. Among the kinds of letters they may need to write are letters requesting recommendations, letters requesting applications, letters thanking a prospective employer for an interview, letters inquiring about the status of an application, letters accepting or declining a job, and letters responding to a rejection letter from a company.

Job-seekers should telephone or write former teachers, current teachers, or former employers and request permission to list them as references on applications or resumes. Such a letter of request should be brief. If requesting that a letter be sent to a potential employer, the writer should give complete information to the person writing the recommendation: to whom it should be sent (complete name, title, and address) and the deadline for receipt of the recommendation. If some time has passed since the writer worked for or was the student of the person being asked for the recommendation, he or she should remind the person writing the recommendation about the past job or courses when they knew one another. As a courtesy, the writer should say that he or she will let the reader know about the outcome of the application.

Letters requesting applications should specify the exact position for which the application is being requested and ask about the deadline for returning it. Similarly, letters soliciting information about possible openings should make clear the exact kind of job the writer seeks.

Once job-seekers have had an interview, they should write promptly to thank the appropriate personnel for the interview. This brief letter reinforces the job candidate's interest in the job at the same time that it acknowledges the time and energy expended on the interview. It should mention some comments that were made in the interview or allude to something the candidate learned about as a result of the interview. Such a letter should be sent to the primary interviewer, though it should be sent also to anyone who spent a considerable amount of time with the job-seeker. (The next page shows an example of this type of letter.)

In some cases a person who has had an interview with a company may not hear immediately about the status of the application. If the applicant has several offers but has not heard about the status of the application at his or her top choice, the applicant should write a letter of inquiry. Such a follow-up letter gives the applicant a chance to share any additional information that might strengthen the application, and it gives the applicant an opportunity to express continued interest in the company.

A letter accepting a job should begin with the positive information of the acceptance, ask whatever practical questions may have arisen since the interview, and express enthusiasm about the opportunity. The writer should begin by thanking the firm for the confidence in him or her expressed in the offer. Like other "bad news" letters, a letter turning down a job should briefly give the reasons for declining the offer before it makes the statement of rejection.

When the applicant is turned down by a company—usually in a rejection letter—the applicant should respond. Occasionally, such responses, especially those that show appreciation for the interview process and continued interest in the company, may keep the applicant's file alive for future consideration.

Most students do not understand that companies expend much money and time in the process of hiring. Hiring is expensive. Applicants should always express their appreciation for interviews and for job offers, even those they decline.

■ PROPOSALS AND REPORTS

Two of the most common kinds of workplace documents are proposals and reports. These documents occur in many kinds of formats and serve many kinds of purposes in the workplace, everything from documenting travel expenses to studying the feasibility of installing a new air-conditioning system in a factory. Both kinds of documents may be extremely brief or extremely long, and they may be either formal or informal, depending on the purpose and audience.

Most students will have had only the most cursory acquaintance with many of these kinds of documents, though teachers can remind students that many of the documents students handle routinely are versions of these workplace documents. For example, students are familiar with agendas and minutes for meetings, and often they have sent school administrators requests for funding or arguments for changes in policies or facilities.

Students usually need to be told that some overlapping occurs with the terms *proposal* and *report*. Proposals are always persuasive: They always argue for some kind of change. Many documents that are called reports are, in fact, proposals. For example, feasibility reports always analyze the need for and potential success of change, but when they go so far as to argue for particular change based on the findings, they become proposals.

Reports may be informative or persuasive. Many routine business documents are informative reports: summaries of articles or speeches, travel reports, inspection reports, instructions, budget reports, procedural reports, and research reports, to name only a few.

Reports and proposals are often classified as *formal* or *informal*. These terms have nothing to do with length, and the terms *formal* and *informal* do not refer to the relative difficulty of the material, the tone, or the level of language. Both informal and formal proposals and reports may take the form of letters or memoranda. The major distinction is that a formal report usually is bound and usually contains subordinate documents of various kinds.

■ FORMAL REPORTS

Formal reports may be as brief as five to ten pages or as long as several hundred pages. The defining characteristics of formal reports are the numerous supplementary parts, many of which students will never have seen.

Parts of Formal Reports in the Order of Appearance in the Report

TITLE PAGE—A page that gives the title of the report, the name of the company requesting the report, the date, the name of the writer of the report, and the company represented by the writer of the report.

LETTER OR MEMO OF TRANSMITTAL—A communication that accompanies the final report and is addressed to the person designated to receive the report. A letter is used when the report goes to someone outside the writer's firm; a memo is used when the report goes to someone within the firm. **Table of Contents—A listing of the page on which each part of the report appears.**

LIST OF FIGURES—A list by title of graphs, charts, and other visual aids and the pages on which they are found.

ABSTRACT OR EXECUTIVE SUMMARY—A one-page summary of the main findings of the report. Abstracts are more technical and are meant for specialized readers; executive summaries are intended for more general managers.

BODY—The text of the report, which may be single- or double-spaced.

CONCLUSIONS—The findings of the report, often summarized in a numbered list. In informative reports, this is the last part of the report before the appendices and bibliography. RECOMMENDATIONS—In persuasive reports, this is a list, usually numbered, of actions that should be taken based on the conclusions drawn in the study.

APPENDIX—Usually titled and lettered consecutively (Appendix A, Appendix B, etc.), appendices are used for information that may be of interest to the reader but which would interrupt the focus if it were in the body of the report.

BIBLIOGRAPHY—A listing of sources used in the report. These may be classified under such headings as *Primary Sources* and *Secondary Sources*, or they may be combined in a list alphabetized by last name of the author. Bibliographies in workplace writing may use any of the major style sheets, but most often they use either the MLA style or the APA style for documentation.

Unlike informal reports, these kinds of reports are often bound like books or have other kinds of special binding. Many companies generate formal reports internally for their own use, but many others hire consultants to analyze conditions or to study the feasibility of projects.

■ INFORMAL REPORTS AND PROPOSALS

Like formal reports, informal reports may be brief or lengthy. Although they do not include the many parts of a formal report, they may include such parts as conclusions, recommendations, appendices, and a bibliography.

If the informal report or proposal is being sent within the company, it usually has a memorandum heading. If it is being sent outside the company, it may take the form of a letter, or it may have a letter as a cover document.

An informal proposal, like a formal one, has four special parts in the body. The introduction gives the background information necessary for the reader to understand the proposal. The second section is the proposal itself. The third section is the budget, and the fourth section is conclusions, which ties the parts of the document together and discusses negative and positive results of proceeding with the plan as it is discussed in the document.

HEADINGS IN REPORTS

Both formal and informal reports and proposals use headings for separate sections. The major reason for using headings is to make it possible for the reader to easily find the parts he or she wants or needs to read. Rarely is a report or proposal read in its entirety. A busy executive, for example, may read only the executive summary, the budget part of the body, and the conclusions and recommendations.

Students need to understand, however, that headings do not replace transition. Headings are required in addition to all of the kinds of transitional devices good writers use in any kind of writing—repetition of key words, use of transitional words and phrases, use of pronouns, and use of parallelism. In a formal report, the headings may correspond to entries in the table of contents.

The placement and size of headings suggest the relative importance of the information introduced by them. Writers have five levels of headings from which to choose. These levels are similar to the levels in a traditional outline that uses Roman numerals, capital letters, Arabic numerals, small letters, and so on. Here are the kinds of headings, and information about their relative placement:

FIRST DEGREE HEADING
This level can be used for the title of the report and for major sections in a long report. It is all capitals and centered.

<u>Second-Degree Heading</u> This level is used for major sections in a short report and major subdivisions in a long one. Only the first letters in words are capitalized, and the heading is underlined.

<u>Third-Degree Heading</u> This kind of heading looks like a second-degree heading, but it begins at the left margin.

<u>Fourth-degree heading</u>. This heading is on the same line as the sentence it precedes. Only the first word is capitalized, and the heading begins at the left margin.

<u>Fifth-degree headings</u> are part of the sentence that they introduce. They begin at the left margin, and only the first word is capitalized.

Most students will have had little if any experience in using headings, and as a result, they will have some predictable problems. As with outlining, they need to be taught that if a section of a report cannot be divided into at least two sections, it cannot be divided: that is, any heading must always have at least one other at its level. Similarly, as writers work to achieve structural parallelism in topic outlines, they must also make subordinate headings in a given section parallel with one another. In addition, students need to be reminded that headings are not mixtures of sentences and phrases. Most headings in workplace writing are phrases (see section 63d in the *Prentice Hall Reference Guide* for more information about headings).

Just as students generally dislike outlining, they also resist working to write precise, effective headings. This part of report writing is best left until students have done enough research and writing to have become interested in the project.

In addition to learning about headings, students may also be learning about visual aids, often referred to as graphics, in reports and proposals. Although visuals are used in most lengthy reports and proposals, they also figure prominently in other kinds of workplace writing, especially oral presentations (see sections 63 b and c in the *Prentice Hall Reference Guide* for more information about incorporating visuals into a report).

■ PUBLIC WRITING

Part of our responsibility as teachers is helping students understand how to express themselves on issues important to their own lives. They may want to write their mayor or senator. They may need to rally neighbors to protest reduced services by the city. They may want to argue their positions in a letter to the editor, or they may need to write a news article or press release to publicize a fundraising event for a sorority or fraternity or for a children's group. In addition, students are increasingly posting book reviews and other articles on the Internet.

In all of these cases, students must learn how to write for an audience that they do not know and they must learn to establish credibility as a public spokesperson.

We must teaching students to analyze what they have in common with prospective readers, what experiences they bring to the debate that lend credibility to their argument, what reputable sources they can cite to shore up their views, and what facts they have found that will strengthen their position (see Harris's Chapter 64 in the *Prentice Hall Reference Guide*).

As in any good argument, students writing to share views in a debate should concede that the opponents may be right on certain points, because doing so shows that the writer has thought carefully about the issue from many points of view. The writer should maintain a positive tone, refraining from name-calling and insults to those who think differently.

Dear Editor:

The recent debate over the cost of enforcing "No Littering" laws has led to confusion among some citizens of this community, and as a resident of Mobile for the last twenty years, I would like to share some thoughts about this important issue.

Surely the projected cost of $73,000 for two full-time officers to oversee the prosecution of those who trash our streets, parks, and other green areas is a small price to pay for the many benefits our community will reap if we can penalize those who litter.

Not only will the fines imposed on those caught off-set a third of this cost, according to the recent report of consultants hired by the city, but the added revenue from taxes paid by new businesses will more than pay for the rest.

The 2001 reports by two area Chambers of Commerce as well as a recently released ten-year study by the state's Economic Development Commission document that last year alone, our part of the state lost eighteen businesses that explored opening here because of the "trashy appearance of the major roads leading into the city," according to the state analysis of economic development.

Littering is a selfish, wasteful act that must not be ignored by our community. We can easily afford to pay for the proposed employees. Indeed, we can't afford <u>not</u> to.

Miguel Sanchez
115 Edgemont Road

Writing a news release is an important skill for our students to learn, whether they eventually need to do so as part of a job or as a result of non-profit activities in the community. A news release should look professional. Its heading should list the name, address, and telephone number as well as an e-mail address of the contact person responsible for verifying information or giving further details. The heading also should include the release date for the information.

The body of the news release should answer the journalistic questions of *who, what, where, when, why,* and *how* in a brief, clear statement that begins with the most important information to be publicized.

Students should know that many organizations and businesses attempt to use news releases to promote an individual or publicize a product or service rather than pay for advertising. Releases that are padded with promotional details that obscure the news value are likely to be discarded without a careful reading.

Here is a news release announcing a festival that will raise money for local non-profit arts groups.

FOR IMMEDIATE RELEASE

CONTACT: Edwin Conners
            12 Stonegate Terrace
            Charleston, S.C.
            843-928-4768

SPRING FLING TO AID ARTS GROUPS

A Spring Fling April 9–10 in downtown Charleston will raise money to benefit six local non-profit groups.

Festival-goers will be able to sample specialties of 18 local restaurants, hear six jazz and chamber music groups, enjoy four folk dance groups, and take in a wide array of arts and crafts from a three-state area. Games and rides will be available for children ages 3–10.

On both days Meeting Street will be closed to traffic from 10 a.m. to 11 p.m. in the two blocks around the Visitors' Center to accommodate stages, display areas, and temporary food court.

Admission to the festival is free, but musical events will cost five dollars, food tickets will cost two dollars for each sample, and games and rides will cost one dollar.

Visitors may browse through the arts and crafts areas at no charge. Ten percent of the sales of arts and crafts items will be donated to the proceeds of the festival.

Benefiting from the festival's proceeds will be the Carolina Youth Chorale, the Young Artists of the Low Country, the Charleston Children's Theater, the Symphony's Candy Concerts, the Lowenthal Ballet Troupe, and the Goosecreek Youth Orchestra.

* * *

■ ACTIVITIES FOR TEACHING WORKPLACE AND PUBLIC WRITING

In addition to suggestions in other sections of this supplement, teachers may wish to try some of these activities to interest students in the complexities of workplace writing and to further their understanding of public writing.

Letter-Writing Activities

1. Students enjoy role-playing, and teachers can increase students' enthusiasm for writing by assigning roles in small groups and having them

solve problems by writing letters. For example, one student in a group might be a disgruntled parent writing to a teacher to complain about a class policy; another student might be the teacher, who must write both to the parent and to inform his or her principal; the student who takes the role of the principal may need to write to the school board about the continued harassment of teachers by parents, etc. Many such scenarios give effective opportunities for students to practice letter-writing. These scenarios also provide students with good practice in ascertaining audience and purpose.

2. The teacher might divide the class into groups and have each group represent an organization on the campus, writing a persuasive letter asking for an increased budget to the student activities board which funds such groups.

3. Students can assume roles having to do with employment scenarios. They can practice writing all of the kinds of employment documents they may encounter in trying to find out about jobs, apply for a job, thank someone for an interview, check on the status of their application, etc.

4. Students particularly enjoy writing real letters of complaint to companies and organizations from whom they had had poor service or products and sharing the companies' responses with the class. The responses provide great texts for class discussion of strategy and tone.

5. Students often ask for teacher to write them letters of recommendation, but rarely have had the chance to write one themselves. Students can develop a letter of recommendation for themselves or can recommend a friend, classmate, family member, or colleague for a job, award, scholarship, or other recognition.

Report-Writing Activities

1. To teach students about precision in language, have groups of them draft questionnaires all on the same subject, but a subject they could actually poll the student body at large about. Comparing the ways each group went about the questioning and the differences in tone and precision will teach students a lot about efficiency in language.

2. Ask students to sample a small group of peers (twenty or so) about an issue and to analyze their findings. They might to this sampling with a written questionnaire or with an interview.

3. Ask students to request sample formal and informal reports from local companies. Then have them analyze the parts of each report and offer suggestions for improving it.

4. For an original experience with a formal report, ask students to come up with an issue at the school or in the community that they would like to investigate. For this they might use a questionnaire for students,

interviews with several key people, primary documents at the school, and secondary reading. With a topic as simple as "The Reasons Students Transfer from State" or "The Campus Security Force: Overcharging for Parking Violations?," students have the opportunity to write everything from a letter of transmittal to conclusions and recommendations. You may wish to require a number of visual aids and an appendix or two. This assignment could also be a method for teaming students with students from other classes, including classes outside of your department.

5. Ask students to design a Public Relations campaign to inform all constituencies of the university that tuition will rise by six percent the following year. They can practice writing letters, proposals, reports, and other kinds of documents.

Activities in Public Writing

1. Have students write a letter to the Dean or President of the university arguing that a policy or requirement should be changed.

2. Have students write a review of a recent book for posting on the Internet.

3. Ask students to use Internet resources to get the address of their U.S. Senator (and name, if they do not know who their senator is) and to write a letter of support or opposition to a current issue.

4. Ask students to write a letter to the editor (or respond to a letter to the editor) in the school or community newspaper.

5. Have students write a news release announcing an upcoming event on campus.

WEB RESOURCES

Web Resources can be found at www.prenhall.com/harris under Instructor's Resources.

SUGGESTED READING

Adler-Kassner, Linda, Robert Crooks, and Ann Watters. *Writing the Community: Concepts And Models for Service-Learning in Composition.* Washington, DC: American Association for Higher Education, 1998.

Bailey, Edward P., Jr. *The Plain English Approach to Business Writing.* New York: Oxford UP, 1990.

Blackburn, Elizabeth, and Kelly Belanger. "You-Attitude and Positive Emphasis: Testing Received Wisdom in Business Communication." *The Bulletin of the Association for Business Communication* 56.2 (June 1993): 1–9.

Blase, Dean Woodring. "A New Sort of Writing: E-Mail in the English Classroom." *English Journal* 90.2 (Nov. 2000): 47–51.

Boone, Louis E., David L. Kurtz, and Judy R. Block. Contemporary Business Communication. Englewood Cliffs, NJ: Prentice Hall, 1994.

Brusaw, Charles T., Gerald J. Alfred, and Walter E. Oliu. *The Business Writer's Handbook.* 6th ed. New York: St. Martin's, 2000.

Collins, Paul S. *Community Writing: Researching Social Issues Through Composition.* Mahwah, NJ: Lawrence Eribaum Associates, 2001.

Conlin, Joseph. "The Write Stuff." *Sales and Marketing Management* (Jan. 1998): 71–75.

Coogan, David. "E-Mail Tutoring: A New Way to Do New Work." *Computers And Composition* 12.2 (1995): 171–81.

Elliot, Norbert, Margaret Kilduff, and Robert Lynch. "The Assessment of Technical Writing: A Case Study." *Journal of Technical Writing and Communication* 24.2 (Winter 1994): 19–37.

Faidman, Anne. "Mail." *The American Scholar* 69.1 (Winter 2000): 7–11.

Fredericksen, Elaine. "Letter Writing in the College Classroom." *Teaching English In the Two Year College* 27.3 (Mar 2000): 278–84.

Greenly, Robert. "How to Write a Resume." *Technical Communication* 40 (Feb. 1993): 42–48.

Guffey, Mary Ellen. *Business Communication: Process and Product.* 3rd ed. Belmont, CA: Wadsworth, 1999.

Henry, Julie. "E-mail Style is :-(for Writing." *The Times Educational Supplement* 4392 (Sept. 1, 2000): 5.

Hoffman, Marvin. "On Teaching Technical Writing: Creative Language in the Real World." English Journal 81.2 (Feb. 1992.): 58–64.

Hyde, Paul. "E-mail: Is It a Blessing or Curse?" *The Masthead* 52.2 (Summer 2000): 20.

Jablonski, Jeffrey. "Teaching the Complexity of Business Proposals." *Business Communications Quarterly* 62.3 (Sept. 1999): 108–12.

Jackson, Tom. The Perfect Resume. New York: Doubleday, 1990.

Kowalski, Kathiann M. "Dear Editor . . . (How to Write Letters to the Editors of Newspapers)." *Cobblestone* 22.2 (Feb. 2001): 20.

Krajewski, Lorraine, and Gwendolyn Smith. "From Letter Writing to Report Writing: Bridging the Gap." *Business Communication Quarterly* 60.4 (Dec. 1997): 88–91.

Krause, Tim. "Preparing an Online Resume." *Business Communication Quarterly* 60.1 (March 1997): 59–61.

Lauer, Janice M. "Persuasive Writing on Public Issues." *Composition in Context: Essays in Honor of Donald C. Stewart.* Ed. W. Ross Winterowd and Vincent Gillespie. Carbondale, IL: Southern Illinois UP, 1994: 62–72.

McCune, Jenny C. "Get the Message." *Management Review* 86 (Jan. 1997): 10–11.

Moran, Charles. "Notes Toward a Rhetoric of E-mail." *Computers and Composition* 12.1 (1995): 15–21.

Munro, John, and David Howes. "The Effect of Cognitive Style on Learning to Write a Letter of Complaint." *The British Journal of Educational Psychology* 68.2 (June 1998): 243–54.

Patterson, Valerie. "Resume Talk from Recruiters." *Journal of Career Planning & Employment* 56.2 (Jan. 1996): 33–39.

Pirto, John. "University Student Attitudes Toward E-mail as Opposed to Written Documents." *Computers in the Schools* 14.3–4 (1998): 25–32.

Rabb, Margaret Y, and Richard Scoville. "Tips for Great Reports." *PC World* 10.4 (April 1992): 224–31.

Shafer, Gregory. "Using Letters for Process and Change in the Basic Writing Class." *Teaching English in the Two Year College* 27.3 (Mar 2000): 285–92.

Subramanian, Ram, Robert G. Insley, and Rodney D. Blackwell. "Performance and Readability: A Comparison of the Annual Reports of Profitable and Unprofitable Corporations." *Journal of Business Communication* 30.2 (1993): 49–61.

Troyka, Lynn Quitman. *Majoring in the Rest of Your Life: College and Career Secrets for Students.* Englewood Cliffs, NJ: Prentice Hall, 1999.

Vassallo, Philip. "U-mail, I-mail—More Effective Business E-Mail." *Etc.* 55.2 (Summer 1998): 195–203.

PART SIX:
Integrating Computers
into the Writing Classroom
By Linda Julian, *Furman University*

■ TECHNOLOGY IN THE NEW MILLENNIUM: TOOLS FOR READING AND RESEARCH

Twenty years ago most college students did not own or have much access to computers. Only in the early 1990s did computers become affordable enough for the public to embrace this technology, and not until the mid 1990s did the Internet become accessible to the public at large. In the beginning the Internet was almost exclusively the domain of scientists, university professors, and the military.

Today most college students, as well as those from kindergarten through high school, either own a computer or have access to one in the classroom, school library, or public library. In fact, many young children know more about computer resources and using computers than their teachers do. Public school teachers and college instructors who once thought computer technology was a passing fancy have had to realize that they can no longer be Luddites but must embrace the new possibilities of the computer age if they are to educate their students as productive citizens of the twenty-first century.

While colleges and universities have had to grapple less with issues of fair allocation of computers and the scarcity of them than public schools, still colleges vary greatly in the number of computers available to their students and the kinds of resources offered by these computers. Some colleges have computer labs for students, some have computerized classrooms, some have computers only in the library, and some require entering students to bring computers to campus, even wiring dormitory rooms to connect students to a campus network as well as the Internet.

However, no matter what kind of computer resources are offered, all teachers of writing must understand how to use these resources best to help students improve their skills in writing and research so that they will not be left behind their peers in entering the workforce or going into graduate programs. If we do not help all students use computer technology as a tool for their learning and work, we teachers are, to a great degree, abdicating our responsibilities to them.

Those teachers who have begun to use computers in teaching composition have done so to greater and lesser degrees. Some have put their entire course online, everything from the syllabus and assignments to chat rooms and other resources for their students. Others are wading in slowly, using word processing programs to help their students come up with ideas, outline essays, write drafts, and revise them. Some, in fact, limit their use of computers in the classroom to showing students how to do research online.

Muriel Harris's *Prentice Hall Reference Guide*, 6th ed., offers much help in using computers for teachers and students alike. In addition, Harris's emphasis on the process of writing (see Chapters 2–4) easily enables teachers to adapt some of the stages of writing to computer instruction, even if they choose to limit the use of computers. A glossary of basic computer terminology is included at the end of this chapter of the supplement. Finally, Prentice Hall and its partners offer many online resources for both the teacher and student. (See the online resources listed under Instructor's Resources on the web at www.prenhall.com/harris.)

■ ADVANTAGES AND DISADVANTAGES OF TEACHING WITH COMPUTERS

Although teachers who do not want to learn about computers, who hate new technology, and who do not see real value in embracing technology can cite many reasons to support their decisions, those who see the advantages can make stronger arguments.

Disadvantages

Among the disadvantages to teaching with computers mentioned by some teachers are these:

➤ Students with poor keyboarding skills may be frustrated by their inability to write quickly enough to keep up with in-class work.

➤ Valuable time may be spent teaching word-processing and research skills that could be better spent working on students' writing.

➤ Class time may be wasted if the technology is not functioning properly.

➤ Student do not back-up their work may find all their efforts lost.

➤ Student who lack access to or experience with technology are disadvantaged in classrooms that emphasize computer use.

➤ Some students will be tempted to surf the Net or play computer games rather then concentrate on instruction.

➤ The classroom might become machine-oriented rather than people-oriented.

➤ A computer cannot have a conference with a writer or teach writing.

➤ Teachers may need special training

➤ A computer classroom is not a quiet place, and some students may not be able to focus on their writing with noise.

➤ Tools, such as spell or grammar check, may prevent students from proofreading carefully.

➤ Students might become too dependent on the computer and expect it to do the thinking for them.

➤ Students may not learn how to do library research and may rely on unreliable, but easily accessible web sources for research.

➤ In on-line courses instructors spend may need to do far more individualized instruction, which is time consuming.

➤ Plagiarism is harder to detect, and it is easier for students to access "paper mill" essays.

Many of these reasons for not using computers are only minor concerns at best today, when most students know more technology than many of their teachers. Some are not true. For example, computers *can* be used to make assignments and to have conferences with students. The teacher who fears having to spend time teaching computer skills misunderstands the times: students generally know basic word-processing skills.

Advantages

The advantages seem more significant than the disadvantages of using computers to teach writing:

➤ Students will look forward to writing because they enjoy technology.

➤ Many students find composing on computer easier than composing by hand.

➤ Students will develop skills necessary for them to become more independent learners.

➤ The students can more easily identify and move through the stages of writing, and this ease will underscore Harris's philosophy that students must see writing as a process, not a product.

➤ Using the computer might improve reading comprehension for some students.

➤ Students will find revision less laborious, especially when they want to move chunks of their essays.

➤ Students can utilize various software programs designed to help them brainstorm, organize, or revise their work.

➤ Many word processing programs provide templates for various types of documents students will be asked to produce.

➤ Students will learn skills that will help them in the job market. In fact, not being able to word process and use the Internet may disadvantage students seeking jobs.

➤ Students will learn writing and research skills that will empower them in their other courses.

➤ Learning to use a computer and increasing their knowledge of word-processing and research skills may build self-esteem in some students.

➤ Students may develop a greater sense of pride in their own work, because it appears neat and even professional to them. Many employers and instructors have come to expect this professional appearance in all documents.

➤ The appearance of writing on a computer screen may make students think writing is more important than they had realized before.

➤ Students will likely learn to work in a more individualized way— a real plus since teachers want students to see that they have their own styles and methods, unlike those of other students.

➤ Students may be able to see their own errors in spelling, grammar, and transitions, among other problems, if they read it on-screen and then on a neat printout.

➤ Students can use online spelling and grammar checks (though we must explain that these are not infallible).

➤ Students can easily assist each other in proofreading and writing.

➤ Doing peer review and other interactive assignments on the computer may lead to valuable interaction among students.

➤ Students can do peer-work using the computer.

➤ The computer provides a neat and easy way for students to do journal entries.

➤ Teachers can collect disks or have students e-mail their papers as attachments. This method can also be used for peer-response.

➤ E-mail can mean contact with the teacher or classmates twenty-four hours a day, seven days a week, so students will likely feel more connected to the teacher and classmates. Sometimes the teacher's answering a question by e-mail will make the student feel an even closer relationship to the teacher as well as providing a kind of security that help is only an e-mail away.

> Technology enables students to give more professional and effective presentations by using presentational software.

> Technology allows teachers to develop more creative and motivating assignments, including designing Web pages and developing electronic portfolios.

> Teachers can supplement classroom discussion with threaded discussions and chat rooms; they can supplement print materials with web links.

> Learning to use technology can make teachers more marketable and more effective.

■ USING COMPUTERS TO TEACH WRITING SKILLS

Many teachers use word processors to help students brainstorm about topics and the ways to develop them. Some use computers to help students outline their essays and write drafts. And whether or not they formally use computers in the classroom to help students revise their essays, most teachers see that the ease of revision using the computer encourages students to continue their revision through several drafts. Even receiving the final paper has become much easier for many teachers: they ask students to submit essays via e-mail or as attachments to e-mail.

PREWRITING WITH COMPUTERS

Many of our students complain that they do not know anything to write about, but some brainstorming and other prewriting exercises using the computer can help them see that they, in fact, know much more than they realize and that they have things to say that will interest readers.

Teachers may also find that invention exercises using only a word-processing program work well. Having students use the outlining feature to break down topics to give them a narrowed enough focus for a thesis can work. Also effective is having the students turn off their monitors while they do free-writing as brainstorming. Although some may be uncomfortable at first not seeing what they are writing, most will come to feel comfortable and see the value in letting ideas flow freely without constant self-censoring. Once students have topics narrowed, pairing students to ask questions about the topic and its development through e-mail can stimulate the invention of further ideas.

Word-processing programs and e-mail may be used to great advantage to help in early drafting stages. One technique is to divide the class into groups of three and ask them to huddle around one computer, with one of them as typist. You might have them take an overly general thesis, which you could submit to all machines at once, and try narrowing it collaboratively and drafting an introduction together.

You could use this kind of collaborative assignment to reinforce skills related to any part of the essay. For example, if you are stressing transitional paragraphs, you might send them an essay lacking these and have them collaboratively write them. Or, you might ask each group to do communal brainstorming, coming up with several workable theses they have pulled out of a too-general statement. On the paragraph level, one can have small groups write certain types of paragraphs (definition or compare and contrast, for example).

In these collaborative assignments, you should probably include a strong writer, and average writer, and a weak writer. They can all learn from each other in important ways. The weak writers, who may feel inadequate or perhaps even hopeless as writers, can develop some confidence in the discussions as they see that the process is not as mysterious as they had thought. The average writer can develop more confidence by helping to guide the weaker writer, and this writer can gain confidence from the stronger writer by recognizing that he or she is on the right track and not so far from the mark after all. Even the strong writer can learn: he or she can see, from listening to the other two, that what he or she has thought of as stupidity or lack of interest on the part of some classmates, really is frustration, struggle, and true lack of understanding the writing process. Having realized this, the strong writer is likely to be more patient and more helpful to those students he or she has previously pegged as lazy, dumb, or uninterested.

If the teacher doesn't want to use much class time for collaborative writing, he or she can still make use of e-mail to help the students help themselves. The teacher can give students some ground rules for peer evaluation and ask them to work in groups of a certain size to e-mail their paragraphs or essays to one another (mailing as attachments makes them easier to read) and to e-mail responses to the teacher-generated questions to the students in their groups. They should also mail a copy of their responses to the teacher. From these copies, the teacher can detect which students are progressing in understanding the process, which are still struggling with the current subject-matter, and which are not taking seriously the peer responses. Collaboration can be made even easier if your campus subscribes to interactive Web-based classroom tools, such as WebCT or Blackboard.

Going online can help students in a variety of ways. Narrowing topics may involve research, and the use of the computer to do research is a great benefit. (See Using Computers for Research, below.) It can help them further with problems of grammar and mechanics if they access one of the many on-line resources such as **http://owl.english.purdue.edu/**. This is one of the foremost writing help-centers online. (See Chapter 3 in this supplement.) Also, online sources can help greatly with document design. See the discussion below as well as that in Chapter 5 in the *Prentice Hall Reference Guide*.

DRAFTING AND REVISING USING THE COMPUTER

Looking at the size and shape of paragraphs can show students the lack of transition or supporting details. Students often do not see these problems in handwritten drafts. Composing with a word processor can make it easy for students to highlight their thesis and topic sentences and stay on track rather than going off on tangents. Writing with the computer can also make it easier for students to move from one part of the paper to another, writing parts out of order. Although they can move around in handwritten drafts, many dislike the messiness and disorder, even in drafts. Some students take more pride in their work when they see it neatly typed on the screen. Having typed drafts also makes it easier for peers to share each other's essays than trying to read often-illegible handwriting. In addition, having typed drafts makes it easier for many students to spot their own errors in grammar and punctuation.

Some students are so inured to handwritten drafts that, initially at least, they may feel that their creativity and train of thought are hampered by this strange process. And occasionally teachers find real Luddites in their classes, students who are so anti-technology that they don't even want to try it. In these cases, we want to encourage students to increase their computer skills, but not at the cost of absolutely paralyzing their ability to write. With these students, we may perhaps want to insist that they do *some* part of the writing process on the computer—perhaps brainstorming or outlining—to help them build the confidence they need to expand their computer skills.

Once we have helped students try invention exercises or other brainstorming activities (see Harris, Chapter 2), we want to help them learn to take advantage of the ease and benefits of drafting on the computer.

When in the drafting process a student should concentrate on editing and spelling is a point of contention among many teachers. Some teachers teach students to proofread for grammar, spelling, and punctuation each time they write a revision. Other teachers want students to concentrate in early drafts on the organizational problems, transitions, and fleshing out ideas, saving the "surface" editing for the final revision or two. Whichever position a teacher subscribes to, the *Prentice Hall Reference Guide* offers much help with all stages of revision and editing (see Chapter 2e and f). Harris offers checklists for various kinds of revision, both macrocosmic (the paragraphs and whole essay) and microcosmic (sentence level problems).

Students will, of course, rely on the spellcheckers and grammar checkers, but teachers must point out the problems with totally relying on these tools. Spellcheckers have much smaller dictionaries that those in the average desk dictionary, so they often will not have words the students need to spell. Similarly, grammar checkers, while they may help with some errors, often do not identify other errors; and sometimes they give wrong or incomplete advice. Looking at these tools will not lead the students too far astray, but students need to be made well aware of their shortcomings and limitations. Students can be taught to use the "Find" command to seek out their individual writing problems, such as confusing "there" and "their" or using wordy phrases.

As students move from one draft to another, they should be encouraged to keep hard copies of each draft as well as copies on their disks, perhaps using a different computer folder for each revision. They should also keep a revision log, keeping up with the kinds of changes they made in each draft. Such records may help them understand better their own composing process. Keeping a computer list of errors the teacher points out on each final draft can show them particular types of errors they need to concentrate on in the proofing and editing process.

Sometimes students need to be reminded that over many drafts their focus may change so much that the original working title they gave the essay at first no longer accurately conveys its final substance well. Therefore, they may need to revise even the title of the essay.

Those students who have not had much experience with revision may have difficulty with revising, because they do not want to give up what they have already done: these particular words in the first draft seem much more meaningful to them than they will once students have learned how to use the process of revision to help them express their ideas in the most effective ways.

Finishing the Final Draft and Designing the Document

Once students have written their final drafts, they may find the computer a great help in enabling them to highlight the thesis, topic sentences, transitions, and perhaps even examples or other supporting details. Sometimes the reality of what they underline does not match what they think they have written. Once they have considered the highlighted material, they can easily see what kinds of organizational and substantive change they need to make. Highlighting questions they want to ask peers or their teacher also makes it easy for them to get help in the late stages or the process.

Once all of the revision has ended, the student must think about how he or she wants the document to look. Making the document look consistent from page to page, easy to read, harmonious, and unified throughout, the student can show the instructor and peers that he or she took the assignment seriously. Good document design helps students make a good first impression on both peers and the teacher (see Chapter 63 in the *Prentice Hall Reference Guide*).

The first step in designing a document is identifying the genre of the document (essay, report, etc.), the audience for whom it is intended, and the purpose of the document—the same questions a writer asks at the beginning of the writing process. The answers to these questions help determine design, to some extent, but the writer also has some personal choices.

Among these choices are decisions about using visuals, page layout, white space, headings, highlighting, borders and margins, bulleted or numbered lists, colors, and boxed information, clip art, charts, and graphs as well as justifying text, adding headers or footers and choosing an appropriate font (Harris includes information about Web page design in Chapter 63).

Many word processing programs, such as Microsoft Word and Corel WordPerfect, have easy-to-use features that insert charts, graphs, and tables as well as headers and footers. Such page layout software as Adobe Page-Maker and Microsoft Publisher help students to place text and visuals precisely. Graphic design software such as Macromedia Freehand or Adobe PhotoShop can help students create and edit graphics, pictures, and other kinds of visuals. The student must then save these visuals in a format compatible to his or her own word processing system so that they can insert them in appropriate places in the document.

Students will generally find documenting a paper easier than ever. Most word processing programs offer guidelines or templates for the major styles of documentation, especially MLA, APA, and CM. WordPerfect has a template for APA format.

Students love to play with design features on the computer, especially the more unusual typefaces, so teachers need to help them understand which ones are appropriate for the document in question and which ones are the most readable. Fonts are either serif (they have little "feet" at the top or bottom of each letter) or sans-serif (these are without extensions at the top or bottom of the letter). Serif fonts are usually chosen for text because they are more comfortable to read, especially in a long text. One of the most common of these is Times New Roman.

Sans-serif fonts may be more easily read from a distance, so they may be the better choice for charts and signs. They are often used also for headings in documents.

Font sizes are measured in points ranging from six points to seventy-two, but many teachers stipulate a particular size (usually 12-point) to ensure readability as well as to help students write the appropriate amount of text if they have stipulated that an assignment be a certain number of pages.

Harris points out several websites that teachers and students may access for additional help with designing documents: see Online Resources at the end of this chapter in this supplement.

■ USING COMPUTERS TO DO RESEARCH

The sheer wealth of information available to all of us over the Internet means that we must help our students to have access to the mountain of current facts and ideas online if we are to help them keep up with their contemporaries. Our instruction should involve explanations of what the Internet and the Web are, how to use search engines to locate the information they need, how to evaluate the information they find, and how to use information without violating privacy or copyright laws.

UNDERSTANDING THE INTERNET

The Internet is a network of sites found at universities, businesses, research centers, and government agencies worldwide. It is an enormous resource made up of billions of web pages. In fact, sites on the Internet are doubling every year or two.

The best way for students to access the Internet is through The **World Wide Web**, a collection of what are called **Web pages** or **websites**. These interlinked Web pages each have their own **home page**, a catalogue of what the site offers and directions for finding information.

Not a replacement for all library research, the Internet offers more up-to-date information than libraries are able to, so accessing the Internet is especially important for research on current topics.

Students access the Web through a **browser**, a **search engine** that helps them locate the kind of information they are seeking. They need to understand that a **URL** is an address on the Internet that should be typed into the search box of the browser. **URL** is an acronym for "Universal Resource Locator" (Chapters 52 and 53 of the *Prentice Hall Reference Guide* include information on locating and evaluating web content).

Two of the best-known browsers are Netscape Navigator and Microsoft Internet Explorer. Most recent computers will have an icon on the start-up page listing at least one of these among other programs available on that computer. Teachers who want to increase their knowledge of the Internet may find help at a these sites:

➤ "Teaching and Learning on the Web":
(**http://www.mcli.dist.maricopa.edu/tl/index.html**)
➤ *"Bare Bones 101: A Basic Tutorial on Searching the Web."* This site, maintained by the University of South Carolina, offers twenty lessons that include such topics as search techniques, troubleshooting, and evaluation of websites (**http://www.sc.edu/beaufort/library/bones.html**).

PLACES TO BEGIN

Jumping into an Internet search is not the best beginning for most research projects. First, students need to have a general idea of the narrowed topic they want to find out about and some of the key terms that will help in the online search for information. Often a preliminary online search can help students narrow the topic even further, taking an angle that they had never thought of.

Before they can make the best use of online resources, students need to be instructed by the teacher or an information technology specialist in the school's library about the most efficient ways to use keywords to search, the ways to narrow searches, and the ways to use **Boolean operators** to help reduce frustration. Boolean operators are various combinations of words and symbols like *and, or, not,* and *near* and symbols help narrow the search and to stipulate what kinds of related words made of the keyword the student would like to check. Different search engines use variations on these Boolean operators and symbols.

In addition, some keywords can be truncated so that related words containing that root will also be searched if the searcher types in a symbol like *. For example, in some searches * typed at the end of the keyword's root checks for all related words with that root: if the student is searching for information on *communism* and types in the root *comm*, the search will turn up such words as *common, communal, commune,* and *community,* along with *communist and communism.* Many of the terms have nothing to do with the subject of the search, so to avoid such frustrating paths, students must be carefully instructed about using truncation in a search.

Once students are on the Internet, however, they have many other browsers at their fingertips. Among the most popular are these:

➤ *AltaVista*, a fairly comprehensive engine that searches both the Web and news sources: **http://www.altavista.com**

➤ *Excite*, a large database that searches by both subject and keywords: **http://www.excite.com**

➤ *Goto*, which searches by subject and keywords: **http://www.goto.com/**

➤ *HotBot*, searches by keyword and subject: **http://hotbot.lycos.com/**

➤ *Infoseek*, which searches by keyword and subject: **http://guide.infoseek.com**

➤ *Lycos*, which searches by keyword and subject directory: **http://www.lycos.com**

➤ *Northern Light*, which sorts information into requested folders: **http://www.nlsearch.com**

➤ *Webcrawler*, which finds information with either a keyword or subject: **http://www.Webcrawler.com**

➤ *Yahoo*, which searches by keyword and subject directory: **http://www.yahoo.com**

In addition to these basic search engines, the Web offers several that are called **meta-search engines**, because they search several of the browsers simultaneously. Among the best known are these:

➤ *Ask Jeeves* at **http://www.askjeeves.com**

➤ *DogPile* at **http://www.dogpile.com/**

➤ *Highway 61* at **http://highway61.com** (This meta-engine organizes the results from the multiple sites into a unified list.)

➤ *Google* at **http://www.google.com**

➤ *Savvysearch* at **http://savvysearch.com** (This one translates the search term into the appropriate form for each search engine it checks.)

Also available online are many other sites to check out, including those of university libraries, the Library of Congress, and government as well as standard references such as the *Oxford English Dictionary* and encyclopedias. Language students may find help and practice accessing foreign language sites.

Some sites are general; some are narrowed to subject areas. A sampling includes these:

➤ *Encyclopedia Britannica* at **http://www.britannica.com**
➤ *Bartlett's Familiar Quotations* at **http://www.columbia.edu/acis/ bartleby/bartlett**
➤ *Center for Responsive Politics* at **http://www.crp.org**
➤ *How Stuff Works* at **http://www.howstuffworks.com**
➤ *American Statistical Index* at **http://www.fedstats.gov**
➤ *FindLaw* at **http://www.findlaw.com**
➤ *Library of Congress Research Tools* at **http://lcWeb.loc.gov/rr/ tools.html**
➤ *New York Public Library Resource Guides* at **http://www.nypl.org/ admin/genweb/resource.html**
➤ *National Institutes of Health* at **http://www.nih.gov/**
➤ *American Chemical Society's ACS Web* at **http://www.acs.org**
➤ *Math Archives* at **http://archives.math.utk.edu**
➤ *National Academy of Sciences* at **http://www4.nationalacademies. org/nas/nashome.nsf**

School libraries also have databases that include newspapers, periodicals, current business information, book reviews, and many others. These may be available on the library's own network or CD-Rom.

EVALUATING RESOURCES ON THE INTERNET

Researchers with online information must always approach that information cautiously. Knowing what is reliable, what is questionable, and what is downright unreliable comes with experience. New computer users do not realize that almost anyone can put a website on the Internet without regard for its authenticity, fairness, or accuracy. Researchers should always ask these questions of a site:

➤ What is the purpose of this site—to inform, persuade, sell something?
➤ Who is the author of this website and what are his or her qualifications? Does the site offer contact information?
➤ Does the site explain where its information has come from?

➤ How current does the information seem to be?

➤ Is there a bibliography or other list of sources?

➤ How well developed is the site's content, especially when compared to that offered by other sites?

➤ Can you detect any bias in the information that suggests the site has an agenda?

➤ Is the information recent? How often does the site seem to be updated?

The site is more likely to be reliable if it is from an educational or nonprofit organization, government organization, or with Internet addresses ending in *edu*, *org*, and *gov*. Another criterion is whether the author is someone respected and well known in his or her field. We can teach students to learn who is respected by checking out this person in the library's catalogue, reference books, or bibliographies given by other writers in the field. Students should be taught to look for copyright or update dates and sponsor or publisher information. Credible sites generally make publication and sponsorship information clear. Much of what is posted on the Internet may be plagiarized from other sources. Students should learn to be overly cautious and suspicious of all sources on the Internet (refer students to Chapter 53 of the *Prentice Hall Reference Guide* for more information).

Some Internet sites that help with evaluation of online sources are these:

➤ "Thinking Critically About World Wide Web Resources" at **http://www.library.ucla.edu/libraries/college/help/critical/index.htm**.

➤ "Thinking Critically About Discipline-Based World Wide Web Resources" at **http://www.library.ucla.edu/libraries/college/help/critical/discipline.htm**.

➤ "Evaluating Web Resources" at **http://muse.widener.edu/Wolfgram-Memorial-Library/webevaluation/webeval.htm**.

HANDLING COPYRIGHT ISSUES AND PLAGIARISM

Many kinds of dishonesty appear as a result of the openness of the Internet and ease with which students can view their classmates' work and share papers online. However, some resources help teachers cope with these kinds of problems.

In a crowded computer classroom or lab, machines are so close to one another that students can hardly avoid seeing their peers' work on the computer screen. Discussing the problem may help somewhat. However, taking advantage of this proximity may be a better solution. Suggesting that students help one another emphasizes that they are in a community of writers who must help one another.

Teachers should steer clear of assignments that make it easier for students to copy their peers' answers: requiring paragraphs and essays will minimize copying more than fill-in-the-blank, true/false, and multiple-choice assignments.

These days buying a term paper is easier than ever. If a student types in "term papers," he or she has access to thousands of papers from these sources:

> Term Paper & Research Assistance by Collegiate Care

> A1-Termpaper

> Advantage Term Papers

When teachers find papers that they believe to have been plagiarized, they can access several helpful Internet sites:

> **http://www.academicintegrity.org** (This site is by the Center for Academic Integrity.)

> **http://plagiarism.com** (This site is by Glatt Plagiarism Services.)

> **http://chronicle.com/free/v46/i12/12a04701.htm** (This one is called "How to Proctor from a Distance."

> Jungle Page at **http://www.junglepage.com/**

> Plagiarism.org at **http://plagiarism.org/**

> Project Zero: Research Projects: at **http://pzWeb.harvard. edu/Research/Research.htm**

> Web Services Help Professors Detect Plagiarism at **http://chronicle.com/free/v46/i12/12a04901.htm**

> WWW. 2CHEAT.COM at **http://leahi.kcc.hawaii.edu/org/ tcon98/paper/rooks.html**

The freedom of the Internet has also brought thousands of copyright problems and questions, many still unresolved. Teachers must help students understand what kinds of information they need to document and what they must request permission to use. In some cases, teachers need to request permission for their students to access a site.

Generally students may link to any site on the Web that is available to the public. However, Netiquette suggests that you ask permission of every site you plan to send your students to. Some sites, not equipped to handles numerous hits at one time, may crash if all your students sign on at once when many others are also using the site. Although government sites can be accessed without permission, Netiquette suggests that one should ask permission of city, county, and state sites.

Students and teachers must never copy material from a site and post it on their own websites—unless the owner gives permission. Other information about copyright regulations and the Internet is given in Chapter 63 in the *Prentice Hall Reference Guide*. In Chapter 56, Harris also gives general information about avoiding plagiarism.

To learn more about copyright and the Internet, teachers can access this site:

> ➤ "Copyright Office Study on Distance Education" from the U.S. Copyright Office: **http://www.loc.gov/copyright/disted/**

■ GLOSSARY OF BASIC COMPUTER TERMS

Bit—The smallest amount of information read by a computer.

Bookmark—A method of telling the browser to save a particular Internet address so that one can more easily access it again.

Boolean operators—Words like *and, or, but, near* and certain symbols that help users narrow or define keywords for a search.

Byte—Eight bits treated as a unit of information that takes up the space of about one character on a typed page.

Cable modem—A fast modem that uses cable TV lines to connect Internet sites.

CD-Rom—"Read Only Memory," that is, a computer disk that cannot be changed, containing references works. These are available for purchase or for use in libraries.

Cookie—A tiny bit of information left on your computer by a site, especially a commercial site, to help the sender recall your last hit at the site and to enable other websites to see what sites you have accessed.

Cyberspace—The medium where electronic communication over networks occurs.

Download—Copying information from the Internet to your hard drive or a disk.

FTP—"File Transfer Protocol," a way of moving files between Internet sites.

HTML—"Hypertext Markup Language," the code used to create Web pages and to enable users to move from one Web page to another. It includes regular words as well as codes

Hypertext—A document that provides links that allow access to other sites when the user clicks on the links.

Kilobits—The speed of transmitting 1,000 bits per second.

Megabits—A speed of one million bits per second.

Message board—A site where users can post questions or make comments on a particular topic.

Modem (sometimes known as a Dial-up Modem)—a device that uses telephone lines to access the Internet.

Newsgroup—A discussion group among users who post messages for all users in the group.

Operating System—The controlling system for a computer, such as Windows and Mac OS.

RAM—"Random Access Memory." The part of a computer's memory that enables the computer to run programs.

Secure Web site—a site that requires certain protocols, like a password and a user name, for viewing it.

Spamming—sending unsolicited messages to mass mailing lists, often to advertise products or services.

Subject directory—A list of categories of information with links to related websites.

Truncation—listing only the first few letters of a keyword in a search so that the search will also look for closely related terms. The truncation is usually noted by a symbol such as *.

URL—a Universal Resource Locator, a specific address on the Internet.

Virus—A destructive program, often from an unknown source, that can destroy or scramble data or programs. Once imported, computer viruses can spread quickly through your system and can infect any users you send messages to.

Webmaster—A person who maintains the content and operation of a website.

WEB RESOURCES

Web Resources can be found at **www.prenhall.com/harris** under Instructor's Resources

SUGGESTED READING

Anson, Chris M. "Distance Voices: Teaching and Writing in a Culture of Technology." *College English* 61.3 (Jan. 1999): 261–80.

Barksdale, Karl, and John Steffee. *Writing with Computers.* Cincinnati, OH: Computer Literacy Press, 1998.

Beals, Timothy J. "Between Teachers and Computers: Does Text-Checking Software Really Improve Student Learning." *English Journal* 87.1 (Jan. 1998): 67–73.

Benson, Angela, and Elizabeth Wright. "Pedagogy and Policy in the Age of the Wired Professor. *T.H.E. Journal* 27.4 (Nov. 1999): 60–62.

Berzsenyi, Christyne A. "How to Conduct a Course-Based Computer Chat Room: Enabling a Space for Active Learning. *Teaching English in the Two Year College* 28.2 (Dec. 2000): 165–74.

Blair, Kristine L. "Literacy, Dialogue, and Difference in the 'Electronic Contact Zone.' " *Computers and Composition* 15.3 (1998): 317–29.

Chapman, David W. "A Luddite in Cyberland, or How to Avoid Being Snared by the Web." *Computers and Composition* 16.2 (1999): 247–52.

Coogan, David. *Electronic Writing Centers: Computing the Field of Composition.* Stamford, CT: Ablex, 1999.

Crafton, Robert E. "Promises, Promises: Computer-Assisted Revision and Basic Writers." *Computers and Composition* 13.3 (1996): 317–26.

Drechsel, Joanne. "Writing into Silence: Losing Voice with Writing Assessment Technology." *Teaching English in the Two Year College* 26.4 (May 1999): 380–87.

Faigley, Lester. *The Longman Guide to the Web.* New York: Longman, 2000.

Forbes, Cheryl A. "Cowriting, Overwriting, and Overriding in Portfolio Land Online." *Computers and Composition* 13.2 (1996): 195–205.

Hansman, Catherine A., and Arthur L. Wilson. "Teaching Writing in Community Colleges: A Situated View of How Adults Learn to Write in Computer-Based Writing Classrooms." *Community College Review* 26.1 (Summer 1998): 21–42.

Hawisher, Gail E., Sibylle Gruber, and Margaret F. Sweany. *Computers and the Teaching of Writing in American Higher Education, 1979–1994: A History.* Norwood, NJ: Ablex, 1996.

Hewett, Beth L. "Characteristics of Interactive Oral Computer-Mediated Peer Group Talk and Its Influence on Revision." *Computers and Composition* 17.3 (2000): 265–88.

Holdstein, Deborah H. *Computers and Composition.* 2nd ed. Upper Saddle River, NJ: Prentice Hall, 1997.

Huot, Brian A. "Computers and Assessment: Understand Two Technologies." *Computers and Composition* 13.2 (1996): 231–43.

Inman, James, Jeffrey M. Buchanan, Shawn Christian, and Cathryn A. McFaul. "Making Every Voice Count: Constructing on Online Community of Writing Instructors." *Writing Instructor* 16.3 (Spring 1997): 127–35.

Kastman, Breuch, Ann M. Lee, and Sam J. Racine. "Developing Sound Tutor Training for Online Writing Centers: Creating Productive Peer Reviewers. *Computers and Composition* 17.3 (2000): 245–63.

LeCourt, Donna. "Critical Pedagogy in the Computer Classroom: Politicizing the Writing Space." *Computers and Composition* 15.3 (1998): 275–95.

––– and Luann Barnes. "Writing Multiplicity: Hypertext and Feminist Textual Politics." *Computers and Composition* 16.1 (1999): 55–71.

Marshall, James. "Electronic Writing and the Wrapping of Language." *Journal of Philosophy and Education* 34.1 (Feb. 2000): 135–49.

Mauriello, Nicholas, Gian Pagnucci, and Tammy Winner. "Reading Between the Code: The Teaching of HTML and the Displacement of Writing Instruction." *Computers and Composition* 16.3 (1999): 409–19.

Meel, David E. "Email Dialogue Journals in a College Calculus Classroom: A Look At the Implementation and Benefits." *The Journal of Computers in Mathematics and Science Teaching* 18.4 (1999): 387–413.

Moran, Charles. "From a High-Tech to a Low-Tech Writing Classroom: 'You Can't Go Home Again.' " *Computers and Composition* 15.1 (1998): 1–10.

Norton, David W., Matthew Segaard, and Ann Hill Duin. "The HTML Decision-Making Report: Preparing Students for the Information Age Workforce." *Computers and Composition* 14.3 (1997): 377–94.

Pagnucci, Gian S., and Nicholas Mauriello. "The Masquerade: Gender, Identity, and Writing for the Web." *Computers and Composition* 16.1 (1999): 141–51.

Palmquist, Mike. *Transitions: Teaching Writing in Computer-Supported and Traditional Classrooms.* Greenwich, CT: Ablex, 1998.

Peckham, Irvin. "If It Ain't Broke, Why Fix It?: Disruptive and Constructive Computer-Mediated Response Group Practices." *Computers and Composition* 13.3 (1996): 327–39.

Pirto, John. "University Student Attitudes Toward E-Mail as Opposed to Written Documents." *Computers in the Schools* 14.3–4 (1998): 25–32.

Price, Jonathan. "Electronic Outlining as a Tool for Making Writing Visible." *Computers and Composition* 14.3 (1997): 409–27.

Rea, Alan, and Doug White. "The Changing Nature of Writing: Prose or Code in the Classroom." *Computers and Composition* 16.3 (1999): 421–36.

Regan, Alison E., and John D. Zuern. "Community-Service Learning and Computer-Mediated Advanced Composition: The Going to Class, Getting Online, and Giving Back." *Computers and Composition* 17.2 (2000): 177–95.

Selfe, Cynthia L., and Susan Hilligoss. *Literacy and Computers: The Complication Of Teaching and Learning with Technology.* New York: Modern Language Association, 1994.

Sharples, Mike. *Computer Supported Collaborative Writing.* London/New York: Springer-Verlag, 1993.

Shirk, Henrietta Nickels, and Howard Taylor Smith. "Emerging Fair Use Guidelines for Multimedia: Implications for the Writing Classroom." *Computers and Composition* 15.2 (1998): 229–41.

Slattery, Patrick J., and Rosemary Kowalski. "On Screen: The Composing Processes of First-Year and Upper-Level College Students." *Computers and Composition* 15.1 (1998): 61–81.

Sorapure, Madeleine, Pamela Inglesby, and George Yatchisin. "Web Literacy: Challenges and Opportunities for Research in a New Medium." *Computers and Composition* 15.3 (1998): 409–24.

Strickland, James. *From Disk to Hard Copy: Teaching Writing with Computers.* Portsmouth, NH: Boynton/Cook, 1997.

Sullivan, Laura L. "Wired Women Writing: Towards a Feminist Theorization of Hypertext." *Computers and Composition* 16.1 (1999): 25–54.

Sullivan, Patricia, and James E. Porter. *Opening Spaces: Writing Technologies and Critical Research Practices.* Greenwich, CT: Ablex, 1997.

Taylor, Todd W., and Irene Ward. *Literary Theory in the Age of the Internet.* New York: Columbia UP, 1998.

Tobin, Lad. *Using Computers for Collaborative Writing: An Interdisciplinary Project.* Washington, DC: U.S. Department of Education, 1991.

Tornow, Joan. *Link/Age: Composing_in_the_Online_Classroom.* Logan, Utah: Utah State UP, 1997.

Van Hoosier Carey, Gregory. "Rhetoric by Design: Using Web Development Projects in the Technical Communication Classroom." *Computers and Composition* 14.3 (1997): 395–407.

Varone, Sandy. "Voices from the Computer Classroom: Novice Writers and Peer Response to Writing." *Teaching English in the Two Year College* 23 (Oct. 1996): 213–18.

Wienbroer, Diana Roberts. *Rules of Thumb <For Online Research>.* Boston: McGraw Hill, 2001.

Whitaker, Elaine E., and Elaine N. Hill. "Virtual Voices in 'Letters Across Cultures': Listening for Race, Class, and Gender." *Computers and Composition* 15.3 (1998): 331–46.

Wolfe, Joanna L. "Why Do Women Feel Ignored? Gender Differences in Computer-Mediated Classroom Interactions." *Computers and Composition* 16.1 (1999): 153–66.

Yagelski, Robert P., and Jeffrey T. Grabill. "Computer-Mediated Communication in the Undergraduate Writing Classroom: A Study of the Relationship of Online Discourse and Classroom Discourse in Two Writing Classes." *Computers and Composition* 15.1 (1998): 11–40.

PART SEVEN

Answer Key

Exercise 6.1: Proofreading Practice

(1) Office gossip no longer takes place at the water cooler. (2) <u>Companies that are online have a new way to relay gossip</u>, **and** <u>e-mail is the medium.</u> *or* <u>Companies that are online have a new way to relay gossip; e-mail is the medium.</u> (3) <u>Some court cases have made corporate executives rethink policies</u> on transmitting e-mail and destroying old messages. (4) <u>Seemingly harmless conversations between colleagues have been retrieved,</u> **and** <u>this information has been used in sexual harassment cases and other lawsuits.</u> (5) <u>A single employee can store thousands of pages of e-mail messages; however, the mail is not censored or monitored.</u> (6) Consequently, companies are eager for systems that review and spot-check e-mail. (7) <u>Company executives are employing programs that censor e-mail and block messages containing inappropriate material; this monitoring prevents embarrassing situations.</u> (8) CEOs understand that Big Brother has a better view since employees began hitting the Send button.

Exercise 6.2: Proofreading Practice

(1) Cacao beans have been grown in the Americas for thousands of years. (2) They were considered a treasure and were cultivated by the Aztecs for centuries before the Spanish encountered them in Mexico. (3) Hot chocolate became popular in Europe before coffee or tea, and its use gradually spread from Spain and Portugal to Italy and France and north to England. (4) In 1753, the botanist Linnaeus gave the cacao plant its scientific name, Theobroma cacao, the food of the gods. (5) The tree is cacao, the ground bean is cocoa, and the food prepared from it is chocolate, but it bears no relation to coca, the source of cocaine. (6) Most cacao trees grow within ten degrees of the equator. (7) In the late nineteenth century, the Portuguese took the plant to some islands off Africa, and it soon became an established crop in the Gold Coast (modern Ghana), Cameroon, and Nigeria, where the temperature and humidity are ideal for it.

Exercise 6.3: Pattern Practice

Some possible answers are as follows:

1. There are many varieties of chocolate, but all varieties come from the same bean.
2. All varieties are the product of fermentation, and once fermented, beans must be dried before being packed for shipping.
3. Chocolate pods cannot be gathered when they are underripe or overripe, so they are usually harvested very carefully by hand.
4. Dutch chocolate has the cocoa butter pressed out and alkali added, and Swiss chocolate has milk added.
5. Conching influences the flavor of chocolate, for it is the process of rolling chocolate over and against itself.
6. Chocolate is loved by millions of people all over the world, yet some people are allergic to chocolate.

Exercise 7.1: Proofreading Practice

1. is	5. attempts	9. are
2. do not	6. are	10. insist
3. seem	7. study	11. aren't
4. become	8. conclude	12. sets

Exercise 7.2: Pattern Practice

Answers will vary.

Exercise 8.1: Proofreading Practice

(1) If you've ever doubted your child's identity, advanced technology makes it easy and affordable to set your mind at ease. (2) DNA testing, a procedure that determines genetic relationships, is now available to the average person. (3) <u>For a fee of around $500.</u> (4) Previously, DNA testing was used in criminal cases and in custody disputes involving celebrities. (5) <u>When large sums of money were at stake.</u> (6) Now the average person can find out if a child is in fact his or her biological offspring. (7) The procedure is fast and easy. (8) The parent and child need to provide a sample from the inside of the cheek (9) <u>With a cotton swab collecting the tissue that is needed.</u> (10) The sample is then sent to the lab, and an answer can be had within ten days. (11) In some areas, the sample can be sent through

the mail. (12) <u>Instead of being given at the lab.</u> (13) Advanced technology requires responsibility and caution. (14) <u>Especially when a family's happiness is at stake.</u> (15) Many people feel that DNA testing has caused the breakdown of otherwise happy families. (16) <u>Ethical issues involved in the testing.</u> (17) Doctors have been urging labs that offer the testing to encourage counseling for the people involved. (18) Discovering that your child is not your own is a very complex issue. (19) <u>And not a matter to be taken lightly.</u>

Exercise 8.2: Pattern Practice

Patterns given (sample sentences will vary):
1. Independent clause + dependent clause
2. Independent clause
3. Independent clause + independent clause
4. Dependent clause + independent clause
5. Independent clause
6. Dependent clause + independent clause

Exercise 9.1: Proofreading Practice

According to some anthropologists, the fastball may be millions of years older than the beginning of baseball. <u>To prove this point,</u> prehistoric toolmaking sites, such as Olduvai Gorge in Tanzania, are offered as evidence. These sites are littered with smooth, roundish stones not suitable for flaking into tools. Suspecting that the stones might have been used as weapons, anthropologists have speculated that these stones were thrown at enemies and animals being hunted. <u>Searching for other evidence,</u> historical accounts of primitive peoples have been combed for stories of rock throwing. Here early adventurers are described as being caught by rocks thrown hard and fast. <u>Used in combat,</u> museums have collections of these "handstones." So stone throwing may have been a major form of defense and a tool for hunting. <u>Being an impulse that still has to be curbed,</u> parents still find themselves teaching their children not to throw stones.

Exercise 9.2: Pattern Practice

Answers will vary.

Exercise 9.3: Proofreading Practice

(1) The man who was carrying the sack of groceries <u>with an umbrella</u> walked carefully to his car. (2) He <u>only</u> bought a small amount of food for his lunch because he was going to leave town that afternoon. (3) He whistled to his huge black dog <u>opening the car door</u> and set the groceries in his trunk. (4) The dog jumped into the trunk <u>happily</u> with the groceries.

Exercise 9.4: Pattern Practice

Answers will vary.

Exercise 10.1: Proofreading Practice

One of the great American cars was the J-series Duesenberg. The car was created by Fred and August Duesenberg, two brothers from Iowa <u>who began by making bicycles</u> and <u>who then gained fame by building racing cars</u>. Determined to build an American car that would earn respect for <u>its excellent quality</u> and <u>its high performance</u>, the Duesenbergs completed the first Model J in 1928. The car was an awesome machine described as having <u>a 265-horsepower engine</u> and <u>a top speed of 120 mph</u>. Special features of the car were its <u>four-wheel hydraulic brakes and extensive quantities of lightweight aluminum castings</u>. The masterpiece was the Duesenberg SJ, reputed <u>to have a 320-horsepower engine</u> and <u>to accelerate from zero to 100 mph in 17 seconds</u>.

Exercise 10.2: Pattern Practice

Answers will vary.

Exercise 11.1: Proofreading Practice

One possible revision is as follows:
Many people think that recycling material is a recent trend. However, during World War II, more than 43 percent of America's newsprint was recycled, and the average person saved bacon grease and other meat fat,

which <u>they</u> **[he (or she)]** returned to local collection centers. What <u>you</u> <u>would do is</u> **(a person did was)** pour leftover fat and other <u>greasy gunk</u> **(grease)** from frying pans and pots into tin cans. Today, despite the fact that many people are recycling, less than half of Americans' waste is actually recycled. The problem is not to get <u>us</u> **(people)** to save bottles and cans but to convince industry to use recycled materials. <u>There is a concern expressed</u> <u>by manufacturers</u> **(Manufacturers have expressed concern)** that they would be using materials of uneven quality and <u>will</u> **(would)** face undependable delivery. If <u>the manufacturer</u> **(manufacturers)** would wake up <u>and smell the coffee</u> **(this phrase can be omitted)**, they would see the advantages for the country and <u>bigger profits could be made by them</u> **(the bigger profits they could make)**.

Exercise 12.1: Proofreading Practice

Some possible revisions are as follows:

1. One way to relax is to grab a bowl of popcorn, put your feet up, and watch football on television for two hours.

2. Computer science is a field of study in which you learn how to program computers.

3. One of the most common ways to improve your math is to hire a tutor.

4. The next agenda item we want to look at is the question of finding out the cost of purchasing decorations.

5. His job consisted mainly of handling repetitious assembly line tasks.

Exercise 12.2: Pattern Practice

Answers will vary.

Exercise 13.1: Proofreading Practice

One possible revision of this paragraph is as follows:

Although most people think of pigs as providers of ham, bacon, and pork chops, they also think of pigs as dirty, smelly, lazy, stupid, mean, and stubborn. However, there's more to pigs than this bad press they've had, so we should stop and reevaluate what we think of pigs. (2) President Harry Truman once said that no man should be allowed to be president who does not understand hogs. This lack of understanding indicates inadequate appreciation for a useful farm animal. (3) Some people are discovering that pigs make excellent pets. (4) In fact, because pigs have been favorite characters in children's fiction, many people fondly remember the cartoon character Porky Pig and Miss Piggy, the Muppet creation, as well as the heroic pig named Wilbur in E.B. White's *Charlotte's Web*. (5) Clubs for people who keep pigs as pets are now not just on farms, although pigs have long been favorite pets of farm children, who are likely to be fond of animals. (6) People with pigs as pets report that their pigs are curious, friendly little animals that are quite clean despite the "dirty as a pig" saying. However, pigs, which are not very athletic, also have a sweet tooth. (7) Pigs can be interesting pets and useful farm animals to raise.

Exercise 13.2: Pattern Practice

One possible paragraph is given here:
Although plastic used to be considered a cheap, shoddy material, it is taking the place of many materials. In addition to cars made of plastic, there are also boats, airplanes, cameras, fishing rods, watches, suitcases, toothpaste tubes, and plates made of plastic. Plastic, which has replaced the glass in eyeglasses, the wood in tennis rackets, and cotton and wool in our clothing, seems new but has been with us for a long time. Celluloid, which is a nearly natural plastic, was developed in 1868 as a substitute for ivory in billiard balls. However, celluloid proved to be too flammable. Now, because new types of plastic, such as glow-in-the-dark plastic, have mushroomed, the use of plastics has steadily increased. By the mid-1970s, in fact, plastic had become the nation's most widely used material.

Exercise 14.1: Proofreading Practice

1. 14a; 14b
2. 14c; 14f
3. 14f
4. 14e
5. 14e
6. 14d; 14c
7. No error

Exercise 14.2: Pattern Practice

One suggested revision is as follows:
(1) Recently, analysts have paid more attention to how the year 2000 will affect computers. (2 and 3) The Y2K panic revolves around the idea that systems won't work when the year turns from 1999 to 2000 because the computer will understand "00" as 1900 and could cause major chaos. (4) The problem is expected to affect the majority of bank accounts, telephone services, utilities, and food supplies. (5) It seems that most experts

expect computers to crash. (6) The problem was actually discovered over fifty years ago, but no one wanted to address a problem that was fifty years in the future. (7) Consequently, companies are racing against the clock to rid their systems of the Y2K problem.

Exercise 15.1: Proofreading Practice

The largest ocean liner of its time set sail for New York in April 1912. This now-famous <u>ship</u>, (2) the Titanic, never finished <u>its</u> voyage. (3) <u>It</u> (3) hit an enormous iceberg halfway through the trip and caused the 2,227 passengers to head for the lifeboats. <u>Then</u>, (4) within hours, the mammoth <u>vessel</u> (2) plunged beneath the icy Atlantic Ocean. <u>Next</u>, (4) the *Titanic* (1) broke in two and fell to the bottom of the ocean. <u>It</u> (3) was seen by explorers only from a distance and was untouched until 1986, when a team of researchers entered the <u>boat</u> (2) and explored it. <u>Eventually</u>, (4) a small piece of steel brought back from one of the expeditions was examined to determine whether this material played a part in the sinking of the <u>ship</u> (2). <u>Later</u> (4), researchers tried raising a portion of the <u>ship</u> (2) from the bottom of the ocean, but <u>it</u> (3) was too heavy and fell underneath the water once again. <u>In time</u>, the <u>ship</u> (2) <u>itself</u> (3) will disintegrate, but the fascination with the *Titanic* (1) will remain.

Exercise 15.2: Proofreading Practice

One suggested version of paragraph 4 is as follows:
Caring for houseplants requires some basic knowledge about plants. For example, the plant should be watered regularly and its leaves should be cleaned. Moreover, since spring and summer bring a special time of growth, the plant can be fertilized then. In addition, the plant can be repotted, but the diameter of the new pot should be only two inches larger than the pot the plant is presently in. Some plants can be put outside in summer; however, some plants cannot. In sum, if you are familiar with basic requirements for houseplants, you will have healthy plants.

Exercise 16.1: Pattern Practice

One suggested version of paragraph 4 is as follows:
While scientists neglect whistling, amateurs and hobbyists do not. There are whistling contests all over the United States, where accomplished whistlers whistle classical music, opera, jazz, Broadway show tunes, polkas, and even rock-and-roll. People whistle very differently. Some people pucker

their lips, while others use their throat, hands, or fingers to produce whistling sounds that resemble the flute. There are several advantages to whistling: it is a happy sound, whistlers never lose their instrument, their instrument doesn't need to be cleaned or repaired, it costs nothing, and it is easily transported. Because whistling is hard to explain, it is something you pick up either at a young age or not at all.

Exercise 17.1: Proofreading Practice

(1) For a long time psychologists <u>have</u> **wondered** what memories <u>are</u> and where they <u>are</u> **stored** in the human brain. (2) Because it <u>is</u> the basis of human intellect, memory <u>has</u> **been studied** intensely. (3) According to one psychologist, memory <u>is</u> an umbrella term for a whole range of processes that <u>occur</u> in our brains. (4) In particular, psychologists <u>have</u> **identified** two types of memory. (5) One type <u>is</u> **called** declarative memory, and it <u>includes</u> memories of facts such as names, places, dates, and even baseball scores. (6) It <u>is</u> **called** declarative because we <u>use</u> it **to declare** things. (7) For example, a person <u>can declare</u> his or her favorite food <u>is</u> fried bean sprouts. (8) The other type <u>is</u> **called** procedural memory. (9) It <u>is</u> the type of memory **acquired** by repetitive practice or **conditioning**, and it <u>includes</u> skills such as **riding** a bike or **typing**. (10) We <u>need</u> both types of memory in our daily **living** because we <u>need</u> facts and <u>use</u> a variety of skills.

Exercise 17.2: Pattern Practice

(1) To learn more about memory, a psychologist <u>studies</u> **(studied)** visual memory by watching monkeys. (2) To do this, he <u>uses</u> **(used)** a game that <u>requires</u> **(required)** the monkey to pick up a block in order to find the food in a pail underneath. (3) After a brief delay the monkey again <u>sees</u> **(saw)** the old block on top of a pail and also <u>sees</u> **(saw)** a new block with a pail underneath it. (4) The new block now <u>covers</u> **(covered)** a pail with bananas in it. (5) The monkey quickly <u>learns</u> **(learned)** each time to pick up the new block in order to find food. (6) This <u>demonstrates</u> **(demonstrated)** that the monkey <u>remembers</u> **(remembered)** what the old block <u>looks</u> **(looked)** like and also what <u>distinguishes</u> **(distinguished)** the new block. (7) The psychologist <u>concludes</u> **(concluded)** that visual memory <u>is</u> **(was)** at work.

Exercise 17.3: Proofreading Practice

1. learn
2. begin
3. are
4. become
5. has studied
6. may represent
7. took
8. hopped
9. was going
10. concludes
11. sees
12. would not see
13. would conclude
14. failed

Exercise 17.4: Pattern Practice

Last year, St. John's wort <u>was</u> one of the many herbal supplements advertised in magazines and news reports as an alternative remedy for treating anxiety and depression. This herb <u>had</u> been around for hundreds of years, since before the dawn of antidepressants. Many depressed people <u>took</u> medications such as Prozac, but research <u>revealed</u> that herbal treatments <u>were</u> also effective. A person who <u>experienced</u> anxiety or depression <u>might have benefited</u> more from an herbal remedy than from a drug that <u>caused</u> side effects. Antidepressants often <u>caused</u> side effects such as weight gain, lack of interest in sex, and insomnia. Herbal remedies such as St. John's wort <u>might have had</u> no side effects. Many people who <u>had</u> tried this remedy <u>said</u> that they <u>enjoyed</u> life more and <u>were</u> anxiety-free. Experimenting with an herbal remedy <u>was</u> not harmless; however, like a drug, an herbal remedy <u>was</u> capable of causing permanent damage.

Exercise 17.5: Proofreading Practice

(1) Fun and unique training programs <u>await</u> (**active**) this year's college graduates. (2) Interactive computer simulations <u>are</u> (**active**) a good method for training the Nintendo generation. (3) The realization by corporate trainers that new employees in the 21-to-30 age group <u>performed</u> (**active**) best when interacting with a computer or video game <u>led</u> (**active**) to the invention of these special training programs. (4) Designers were informed (**passive**) that it is important for an employee to be comfortable when new material and methods are being presented (**passive**). (5) "Play the game and learn the trade" <u>is</u> (**active**) the motto of many companies recruiting young college graduates. (6) The transformation brought about (**passive**) by interactive training systems <u>is</u> (**active**) just beginning.

Exercise 17.6: Sentence Practice

Here is one possible revision:
Marc Prensky <u>founded</u> (**active**) an interesting company called Corporate Gameware. He <u>noticed</u> (**active**) that younger employees <u>performed</u> (**active**) well using interactive games, and he <u>thought</u> (**active**) they <u>could learn</u> (**active**) skills such as customer relations, company policies, and troubleshooting client problems through this method rather than from a training manual. Some business schools and the military <u>are using</u> (**active**) interactive software. Studies <u>show</u> (**active**) that this approach works. Employees <u>like</u> (**active**) this method, they <u>are</u> (**passive**) better <u>trained</u> (**passive**), and the training <u>requires</u> (**active**) less time. Confident employees <u>stay</u> (**active**) at jobs longer, and they <u>like</u> (**active**) coming to work.

Exercise 18.1: Proofreading Practice

It is a sad fact of life that what some people call the "everyday courtesi<u>es</u>" are disappearing faster than finger bowl<u>s</u> and engineer<u>s</u>' slide rule<u>s</u>. People in movie theater<u>s</u> carry on loud conversation<u>s</u> on cell phones, older people on bus<u>es</u> rarely have anyone get up and offer them a seat, and few shopper<u>s</u> bother to offer thank<u>s</u> to a helpful salesperson. Some people say that courteous way<u>s</u> seem to have lingered longer in small town<u>s</u> than in big cit<u>ies</u> and that some region<u>s</u>—notably the South—cling more than other<u>s</u> to some remaining sign<u>s</u> of polite behavior. But more often we hear complaint<u>s</u> that courtesy is declining, dying, or dead. Says one New York executive, "There's no such thing as umbrella courtesy. Everybody's umbrella is aimed at eye level." And a store owner in another city says that short-tempered waiter<u>s</u> in restaurant<u>s</u> and impatient salesclerk<u>s</u> in stores make her feel as if she's bothering them by asking for service. Common courtesy may be a thing of the past.

Exercise 18.2: Proofreading Practice

Among the people who are most aware of the current lack of everyday politeness are airline flight attendant<u>s</u> and newspaper advice columnist<u>s</u>. Says one flight attendant, "Courtesy is almost zero. People think you're supposed to carry all their bag<u>s</u> on and off the flight, even when you have dozen<u>s</u> of other passenger<u>s</u> to attend to." One syndicated advice columnist notes that courtesy is so rare these day<u>s</u> that when someone is kind, helpful, or generous, it is an event worth writing about to an advice columnist. Some teacher<u>s</u> blame television's poor example, especially the many rude detective<u>s</u> who shove people around, bang down door<u>s</u>, and yell in people's face⁵. Too many of our current movie hero⁵⁵ are not particularly gallant, thoughtful, or polite. As a psychologist recently noted, it is hard to explain to young people what good manner⁵ are when they don't see such behavior on their television⁵ or movie screen⁵.

Exercise 18.3: Pattern Practice

Foreign tourist⁵ who travel in the United States often notice that American⁵ are not as polite as person⁵ from other countr⁽ⁱᵉˢ⁾. Tourist⁵ from Europe, who are used to more formal manner⁵, are particularly offended by American⁵ who immediately call tourist⁵ by their first name⁵. Impoliteness in the United States extends even to object⁵. An English businessperson noted that in America public sign⁵ issue command⁵: "No Smoking" or "Do Not Enter." In England, such sign⁵ would be less commanding: "No Smoking Please" or "Please Do Not Enter." American⁵ can also be rude without meaning to be. As a Japanese visitor noticed, the nurse who led him into the doctor's office said, "Come in here." In Japan, the visitor noted, nurse⁵ would say, "Please follow me." Foreign tourist⁵, unfortunately, have a variety of such stor⁽ⁱᵉˢ⁾ to take back to their countr⁽ⁱᵉˢ⁾.

Exercise 18.4: Pattern Practice

Answers will vary.

Exercise 19.1: Proofreading Practice

Have you ever wondered how people in the entertainment industry choose what you and <u>me</u> **(I)** will see on television, read in books, and hear on CDs? Some producers and publishers say that the executives in their companies and <u>them</u> **(they)** rely on instinct and an ability to forecast trends in taste. But we consumers cannot be relied on to be consistent from one month to the next. So market researchers constantly seek our opinions. For example, they ask <u>we</u> **(us)** moviegoers to preview movies and to fill out questionnaires. Reactions from <u>we</u> **(us)** and our friends are then studied closely. Sometimes, the market researchers merely forecast from previous experience what you and <u>me</u> **(I)** are likely to prefer. Still, some movies fail for reasons that the market researchers cannot understand. When that happens, <u>who</u> **(whom)** does the movie studio blame? The producer will say that the director and <u>him</u> **(he)** or <u>her</u> **(she)** did all they could but that the leading actor failed to attract an audience. Sometimes, though, <u>us</u> **(we)** moviegoers simply get tired of some types of movies and want more variety.

Exercise 19.2: Pattern Practice

Answers will vary.

Exercise 19.3: Proofreading Practice

Some possible revisions are as follows.

1. No error.
2. Parents who educate their children at home do so because home schooling is good for <u>the children</u>.
3. Many parents believe that each child is an individual, and <u>a child's</u> educational needs are best met by <u>his or her parents</u>.
4. A mother who home-schools <u>her son</u> claims it has brought the family closer and increased his self-confidence.
5. Other parents believe that the public education system in this country is in need of repair, and <u>legislators</u> need to do something about <u>public education</u>.
6. Some states have made it very easy for a parent to start educating <u>his or her children</u> at home.
7. In Montana, a parent may remove <u>his or her</u> child from school simply by registering with the superintendent.
8. <u>The ease with which a parent can take a child out of the school system</u> is a cause for concern among educators.
9. Many school districts are in favor of a formal system of accountability for parents when they take their children out <u>of public school</u>.
10. Consequently, the increase in home schooling will require a comprehensive study of the best method to monitor <u>students'</u> achievement.

Exercise 19.4: Proofreading Practice

One possible revision is as follows:

<u>They</u> **(Doctors)** have been saying for years that <u>prevention</u> **(cancer prevention)** is the most effective defense against <u>cancer</u> **(the formation of cancerous tumors)**. The four major killers are breast, prostate, colon, and lung cancers, and the United States has more of <u>them</u> **(cases of these cancers)** than any other country. It is now the responsibility of every person to educate <u>themselves</u> **(himself or herself)** about cancer prevention. For example, some fats are said to be good for the prevention of cancer, and some fats are known to be dangerous. <u>These</u> **(Good fats)** are flaxseed and

olive oils, as opposed to coconut and corn oils. Furthermore, vegetables like broccoli and tomatoes have cancer-fighting chemicals that <u>they</u> (**doctors**) recommend. Exercise is also a factor in the fight against cancer because an obese person places <u>themselves</u> (**himself or herself**) at a higher risk for the disease. Through education and awareness, <u>we</u> (**Americans**) can fight cancer.

Exercise 19.5: Pattern Practice

Sentences will vary; some examples are as follows:

1. The man and the woman ran quickly, and they seemed to be out of breath.
2. All the students in the room read their notes.
3. Jane is the person who is dating my brother.
4. Even though a customer likes a particular dress, she may ask about return policies before buying it.
5. Each of the contestants read his or her favorite poem for the competition.

Exercise 20.1: Proofreading Practice

What will life be like for the child born in the United States in the year 2020? <u>Informed</u> historians have <u>diligently</u> researched what will <u>surely</u> be in store for these youngsters. First, it is expected that children born in the year 2020 will live twice as long as those born in 1910. They will enjoy a <u>more affluent</u> lifestyle and better health than their baby-boomer grandparents. <u>Conveniently</u>, children will be able to eat broccoli Jell-O instead of the actual <u>despised</u> vegetable. They will join an <u>enormously</u> inflated population of 375 million people, with the majority living in California, Texas, and Florida. Larger homes will be squeezed onto smaller lots, and an abundance of homes will be for sale as older homeowners begin to retire. The more <u>academically-inclined</u> person born in the year 2020 will have to pay $320,000 for a year at Harvard. There will not be a <u>really</u> big change in methods of child-rearing. Parents will struggle with the same child-rearing dilemmas that consumed the latter part of the twentieth century. In fact, a child is a child and faces the same challenges no matter what year he or she is born.

Exercise 20.2: Pattern Practice

Answers will vary.

Exercise 20.3: Proofreading Practice

Maintaining ⟦a⟧ clear complexion, salvaging **a** unusually bad semester, and decorating ⟦a⟧ dorm room are among the topics treated in one of the magazine world's fastest-growing segments, magazines for college students. This market is fueled by advertisers eager to reach **a** untapped market of 12 to 13 million college students with **an** large disposable income and **a** earning potential of many billions of dollars after graduation. Most college magazines are quarterlies, distributed free at a campus newsstand or by direct mail as ⟦an⟧ insert in the college paper. While profits are high, there is some criticism that these magazines are merely **a** advertising vehicle and do not focus on substantive issues, such as taking ⟦a⟧ close look at student loan programs or attempting **a** honest appraisal of racism on campus.

Exercise 20.4: Pattern Practice

Answers will vary.

Exercise 20.5: Proofreading Practice

A new sport, already popular in Canada and sweeping across the United States, is indoor box lacrosse. It is a <u>faster</u>, <u>more furious</u>, and often more brutal version of the field game of lacrosse. Box lacrosse is indeed an exciting game, as it is <u>speedier</u> and <u>rougher</u> than ice hockey but requires the kind of teamwork needed in basketball. Scores for box lacrosse are <u>higher</u> than those for field lacrosse because the indoor game has a <u>smaller</u> playing area with <u>more</u> opportunities for scoring. The team in box lacrosse is also <u>smaller</u> than field lacrosse; there are only six people on a side in the indoor game instead of the ten people on a conventional field lacrosse team. In addition, box lacrosse is played on artificial turf in ice-hockey rinks, and the sticks are <u>shorter</u> and <u>thinner</u> than conventional field lacrosse sticks. Almost anything goes in this rough-and-tumble indoor sport.

Exercise 20.6: Pattern Practice

Answers will vary.

Exercise 21.1: Proofreading Practice

The next time you are stuck <u>with</u> **(in)** traffic, look toward the sky. You might be puzzled <u>on</u> **(about)** the birds flying south for the winter. The management of human traffic could <u>of</u> **(have)** been solved hundreds of years ago if we had patterned our behavior on migratory birds. Researchers interested <u>about</u> **(in)** migration have noted that, due to the flocking system, birds do not crash into each other or go astray. This theory was published <u>to</u> **(in)** *Physical Review* about four years ago. The theory refers <u>of</u> **(to)** the behavior of gases and liquids and the idea that a bird flock behaves like a liquid being poured <u>onto</u> **(into)** a glass. If one drop of liquid or one bird deviates from the course, the rest remains intact. Researchers hope this information will help engineers to design spaces that allow people to flow smoothly <u>among</u> **(from)** one area to the next and avoid bottlenecks <u>upon</u> **(on)** the road. <u>Within</u> **(In)** the future, when you "flock" <u>on</u> **(to)** the beach, spare a thought <u>to</u> **(for)** those feathered friends.

Exercise 21.2: Pattern Practice

1. on
2. with; to
3. with or about
4. of; to
5. of
6. as

Exercise 22.1: Proofreading Practice

(1) <u>Humans</u> are unique in preferring to use the right hand. (2) Among other animals, each <u>individual</u> favors one hand or another, but in every species other than humans, the <u>split</u> between the right and the left hand is even. (3) Only <u>humans</u> seem to favor the right hand. (4) Even in studies of prehistoric people, <u>anthropologists</u> have found this preference. (5) For example, in ancient drawings over five thousand years old, most <u>people</u> are shown using their right hands. (6) This <u>evidence</u> suggests that <u>handedness</u> is not a matter of cultural pressures but perhaps of some genetic difference. (7) Although <u>left-handedness</u> seems to run in families, <u>it</u> is not clear how hand <u>preference</u> is passed from one generation to the next.

Exercise 22.2: Pattern Practice

Here are some possible answers:
1. Greedy credit card companies
2. companies
3. Naïve students
4. unsuspecting parents
5. credit card issuers
6. These conscientious companies

Exercise 23.1: Proofreading Practice

(1) <u>Finding a place for our garbage</u> **1** is a problem as old as human beings. (2) On the Pacific coast there are <u>large, round shell mounds</u> **5** where for centuries Indians <u>had been discarding</u> **3** the bones and clamshells that constituted their garbage. (3) When people gathered together <u>in cities,</u> **4** they hauled their waste to the outskirts of town or dumped it <u>into nearby rivers.</u> **4** (4) In the United States the first municipal refuse system was instituted in Philadelphia, <u>a well-organized city.</u> **6** (5) Here slaves were forced to <u>wade into the Delaware River</u> and toss bales of trash into the current. Eventually <u>this dumping into rivers</u> **1** was outlawed, and people looked for new solutions to the garbage problem. (7) Municipal dump sites, <u>unused plots of land far away from houses,</u> were <u>a frequent answer.</u> **5** (8) But the number of landfill sites <u>is decreasing</u> **3** as many dumps are closed because of health hazards or because of cost. (9) America, <u>a land of throwaway containers and fancy packaging,</u> clearly faces a garbage problem, <u>a problem without any obvious answers.</u> **6**

Exercise 23.2: Pattern Practice

1. Verb phrase
2. Phrase that is the subject of the sentence
3. Phrase that comes after a linking verb and completes the subject
4. Phrase that tells more about the subject
5. Verb phrase
6. Phrase that gives added information about the verb
7. Phrase that gives added information about another element in the sentence

Exercise 24.1: Proofreading Practice

(1) For years, strange noises, <u>which would start in June and last until September,</u> (**clause**) filled the air around the waters of Richardson Bay, <u>an inlet of water near Sausalito, California.</u> (**phrase**) (2) The noise was heard in the houseboats, <u>especially those with fiberglass hulls,</u> (**phrase**) moored along the southwestern shore of the bay. (3) <u>The noise was usually described as a deep hum like an electric foghorn or an airplane motor.</u> (**clause**) (4) The noise, <u>which would start in late evening,</u> (**clause**) would continue until morning, <u>ruining people's sleep.</u> (**phrase**) (5) <u>During the summer of 1994</u> (**phrase**) <u>the hum was unusually loud and stirred investigations.</u> (**clause**) (6) Suspicion initially centered on a nearby sewage plant, <u>which was suspected of dumping sewage at night when no one would notice.</u> (**clause**) (7) Other people thought there were <u>secret Navy experiments going on.</u> (**phrase**) (8) An acoustical engineer, <u>studying the mystery sound for months,</u> (**phrase**) kept thinking he would find the answer, <u>but he didn't</u> (**clause**). (9) Finally, a marine ecologist identified the source of the hum as the sound of the plainfin midshipman, <u>a fish also known as the singing toad.</u> (**phrase**) (10) <u>The male's singing</u> (**phrase**) was the sound everyone heard, he said, <u>though some people still suspect the sewage plant.</u> (**clause**)

Exercise 24.2: Pattern Practice

1. 3	3. 2	5. 2
2. 2	4. 1	6. 2

Exercise 24.3: Proofreading Practice

(1) The tiny lichen is an amazing plant. (2) It can survive in an incredibly difficult environment <u>because it can do things no other plant can do.</u> (**adverb clause**) (3) The lichen, <u>which can anchor itself on a bare rock by etching the rock's surface with powerful acids,</u> (**adjective clause**) grows into the pits that it burns out. (4) <u>Because lichens grow in cold climates above the tree line,</u> (**adverb clause**) they are frozen or covered by snow most of the year. (5) Unlike the cactus in the desert, the lichen has no way of retaining moisture. (6) Because of this, the sun dries lichens into waterless crusts during the day.

(7) <u>When there is a drought,</u> (**adverb clause**) lichens may dry out completely for several months. (8) Even under ideal conditions their total daily growing period may last only for an hour or two <u>while they are still wet with morning dew.</u> (**adverb clause**) (9) The lichen, <u>which may take</u>

twenty-five years to grow to a diameter of one inch, **(adjective clause)** can live for several thousand years. (10) These amazing plants are able to live in all sorts of difficult places, but not in cities because the pollution may kill them. **(adverb clause)**

Exercise 24.4: Pattern Practice

Answers will vary.

Exercise 24.5: Proofreading Practice

Kwanzaa, (which is an African American holiday celebrated from December 26 through January 1), did not originate in any one of the 55 African countries. When the festival was first introduced in 1966, it was designed as a ritual to welcome the first harvests to the home. Dr. Maulana Karenga, (who created the festival), was responding to the commercialism of Christmas. Similar to Hanukkah, Kwanzaa uses candles as symbols of the holiday. The seven principles that the candles represent are unity, self-determination, responsibility, cooperative economics, purpose, creativity, and faith. The seven candles, (which are red, black, and green), remind participants of the seven principles and the colors in flags of African liberation movements. Gifts are exchanged, and on December 31, participants celebrate with a banquet reflecting the cuisine of various African countries. Kwanzaa has become an important American celebration.

Exercise 24.6: Pattern Practice

1. 3	5. 2	9. 2
2. 3	6. 1	10. 1
3. 1	7. 3	
4. 1	8. 4	

Exercise 25.1: Proofreading Practice

(1) Art fraud, a widespread problem, is probably as old as art itself. (2)
(N)
Fourteenth-century Italian stonecarvers who wanted to deceive their buyers
(E)
copied Greek and Roman statues and then purposely chipped their works

so they could peddle them as antiquities. (3) Today forgers, <u>who have</u>

<u>become specialists in different kinds of fraud</u>, produce piles of moderately
(N)
priced prints, paintings, statues, and pottery. (4) The people <u>whom they</u>
(E)
<u>defraud</u> are usually beginning or less knowledgeable collectors. (5) These

people, <u>who can usually afford to spend only a few thousand dollars at</u>
(N)
<u>most for a work of art</u>, have not developed a skilled eye for detecting fraud.

Exercise 25.2: Pattern Practice

Answers will vary.

Exercise 26.1: Proofreading Practice

1. CX	5. CP-CX	9. CX
2. CX	6. S	10. S
3. CP	7. CX	
4. I	8. CP	

Exercise 26.2: Pattern Practice

Answers will vary.

Exercise 27.1: Proofreading Practice

An inventor working on a "flying car" says that traveling several hundred miles by commercial airplane is a fairly inefficient way to get around. First you have to drive through traffic to the airport, and then you have to park your car somewhere in order to board a plane. You fly to another crowded airport outside a city, but then you have to take another automobile to your final destination in town. A more practical solution would be a personal commuter flying vehicle. The inventor, working in a company supported by several government agencies, has developed a vertical takeoff and landing vehicle that has the potential to allow everyone to take to the air. The vehicle can take off and land vertically, and it travels five times faster than an automobile. The most recently developed model looks more like a car than a plane; however, it operates more like a cross between a plane and a helicopter. Above 125 mph in flight, it flies like a conventional plane, and below 125 mph, it maneuvers like a helicopter. It has a number of safety features, such as six engines; therefore, it can recover if it loses an engine while hovering close to the ground.

Exercise 27.2: Sentence Combining

Answers may vary; here are some possible sentences:

- **(1 & 2)** The personal commuter flying vehicle now being designed has room for four passengers, yet it can fly roughly 850 miles per tank of fuel at a cruising speed of 225 mph.

- **(3 & 4)** The vehicle can rise above 30,000 feet, or it can also hover near the ground.

- **(5 & 6)** According to the inventor, it has taken two decades of theoretical studies to design the vehicle's shape, but it has also taken ten years of wind-tunnel tests to achieve the aerodynamic shape.

- **(7 & 8)** Government officials foresee an entire transportation network in the future based on the personal flying vehicle, so there will have to be automated air traffic control systems for these vehicles.

- **(9 & 10)** The technology for controlling these vehicles already exists, and it will create electronic highways in the sky.

Exercise 27.3: Proofreading Practice

(1) A recent study showed that small cars are tailgated more than bigger ones, such as SUVs and vans. (2) Moreover, the drivers of subcompact and compact cars also do more tailgating themselves. (3) In the study, traffic flow at five different locations was observed, and various driving conditions were included, such as two-lane state roads, four-lane divided highways, and so on. (4) In all, more than 10,000 vehicles were videotaped. (5) Although subcompact and compact cars accounted for only 38 percent of the vehicles on the tape, their drivers were tailgating in 48 percent of the incidents observed. (6) In addition to having done all this tailgating, these drivers were the victims of tailgating 47 percent of the time. (7) Midsize cars made up 31 percent of the cars on the tapes but accounted for only 20 percent of the tailgaters and 24 percent of the drivers being tailgated. (8) Having considered various reasons for this difference, the researchers suggest that drivers of other cars may avoid getting close to midsize cars because of the cars' contours. (9) Because midsize cars have more curves in their sloping backs and trunks, people may have more trouble seeing around them.

Exercise 27.4: Pattern Practice

1. C	3. B	5. C
2. B	4. C	6. A

Exercise 27.5: Proofreading Practice

(1)The recently introduced television rating system is designed to provide parents with a method of monitoring the shows that children watch. **(E)** (2)The system, which was introduced in 1999, **(N)** operates using a rating scale that flashes in an upper corner of the television screen. **(E)** (3)However, **(N)** the parent is responsible for watching carefully when a child is viewing television programs. (4)For example, **(N)** a very young child would not know what the symbols represent. (5)An older child who knows what the symbols represent **(E)** may choose to ignore them if a parent is not present. (6) Experts agree that the system is not without faults. **(E)** (7)Many parents feel that the television industry should forgo the rating system and remove sex and violence from television shows. **(E)** (8)Proponents of the system, mainly directors of television networks, **(N)** state that parents have the option of restricting television viewing for their children. (9)The subject matter of television programming is not a new debate. (10)However, **(N)** the rating system adds another dimension to this topic, which will continue to concern parents and the owners of television networks. **(N)**

Exercise 27.6: Pattern Practice

Answers will vary.

Exercise 27.7: Proofreading Practice

(1)Imagine not being able to recognize the face of your sister, your boss, or your best friend from high school. (2)Imagine looking into a mirror, seeing a face, and realizing that the face you see is totally unfamiliar. (3)Though this may sound impossible, a small number of people do suffer from a neurological condition that leaves them unable to recognize familiar faces. (4)The condition is called prosopagnosia and results from brain damage caused by infection or stroke. (5)Many people with this problem who have been studied have normal vision, reading ability, and language skills. (6)They know that a face is a face, they can name its parts, and they can distinguish differences between faces. (7)But only through other clues—hearing a familiar voice, remembering a specific feature like a mustache, hearing a name, or recalling a particular identifying mark such as an unusual scar—can the people who were studied call up memories of people they should know. (8)Researchers studying this phenomenon have found evidence suggesting that the step leading to conscious recognition of the face by the brain is somehow being blocked.

Exercise 27.8: Pattern Practice

Answers will vary.

Exercise 27.9: Proofreading Practice

(1)Online shopping is the easiest, fastest way to shop! (2)If you are a person who hates noisy, crowded stores, especially during the holidays, go online to browse, comparison-shop, and even bid on hard-to-find items. (3)Among the best buys on the Internet are fine vintage wines, some clothing, CDs, popular books, and children's electronic toys. (4)Mail-order retailers such as Eddie Bauer, L.L. Bean, and Lands' End all have informative, interesting shopping sites. (5)The sites provide colorful, realistic illustrations of merchandise along with stock availability of colors and sizes. (6)For example, instead of running from store to store to price a white cotton shirt in your size, you can quickly obtain this information by checking online sites. (7)However, buyer beware! (8)You must know prices to be able to determine whether you are getting a fair deal. (9)Add the shipping and handling fees to find out whether you are getting a bargain. (10)If the total price equals the price at your local mall, an online purchase saves you the time spent traveling to the store and waiting in line with tired, cranky shoppers, only to find a tired, cranky salesperson at the register. (11)Now, you can be tired and cranky from shopping in the privacy of your own home.

Exercise 27.10: Pattern Practice

Answers will vary.

Exercise 27.11: Proofreading Practice

(1)In addition to its Web site (http://www.gpoaccess.gov/cgp), the United States Government Printing Office has a paper catalog of thousands of popular books that it prints. (2)If you'd like a copy of this catalog, write to the Superintendent of Documents, Government Printing Office, Washington, DC 20402. (3)There are books on agriculture, business and industry, careers, computers, diet and nutrition, health, history, hobbies, space exploration, and other topics. (4)To pay for the books, you can send a check or money order, but more than 60,000 customers every year set up deposit accounts with an initial deposit of at least $50. (5)Future purchases can then be charged against this account. (6)There are also Government Printing Office bookstores all around the country where you can browse before buying. (7)They do not stock all 16,000 titles in the inventory, but they do carry the most popular ones. (8)For example, if you live in Birmingham, you can find the Government Printing Office bookstore in Roebuck Shopping City, 9220-B Parkway East, Birmingham, AL 35206. (9)There are other bookstores in Cleveland, Ohio, and Jacksonville, Florida.

Exercise 27.12: Pattern Practice

Answers will vary.

Exercise 27.13: Proofreading Practice

(1)There is hope for infertile couples who want to have a child with genetic material from both parents to have a baby. (2)A fertility specialist who does research at New York University has developed a technique that adds an infertile woman's genetic material to a donor egg. (3)Says one woman undergoing fertility treatments,"This gives hope to women who want a natural child." (4)Dr. Jamie Grifo talked about the procedure, called oocyte nuclear transfer, with reporters. (5)"The purpose of this is to give more options to infertile women," he said, "but the procedure remains expensive." (6)Not many pregnancies have occurred yet, but the doctor tries the process on women who are willing to pay for it. (7)Previously, a woman using a donor egg to become pregnant would have no genetic link to the child. (8)"Now," says the doctor, "a child conceived using this procedure would actually contain genetic material from three people," the father, the mother, and the donor. (9)That the genes will come from the mother's nucleus and will determine how the child looks and acts is comforting for an infertile woman. (10)As with all research, ethical questions have been raised, but the research team maintains that this process is for infertility purposes, not for cloning purposes. The process continues to promise to be a major breakthrough in the area of infertility research.

Exercise 27.14: Pattern Practice

Answers will vary.

Exercise 27.15: Proofreading Practice

Although the dangers of alcohol are well known, and have been widely publicized, there may be another danger that we haven't yet realized. Several controlled studies of drunken animals have indicated to researchers, that in an accident there is more swelling and hemorrhaging in the spinal cord, and in the brain, if alcohol is present in the body. To find out if this is true in humans, researchers studied the data on more than one million drivers in automobile crashes. One thing already known is, that drunks are more likely to be driving fast, and to have seat belts unfastened. Of course, their coordination is also poorer than that of sober people, so drunks are more likely to get into serious accidents. To compensate for this, researchers grouped accidents according to type, speed, and degree of vehicle deformation, and found that alcohol still appears to make people more vulnerable to injury. The conclusion of the study was, that the higher the level of alcohol in the person's body, the greater the chance of being injured or killed. In minor crashes, drunk drivers were more than four times as likely to be killed as sober ones. In average crashes, drunk drivers were more than three times as likely to be killed, and in the worst ones, drunks were almost twice as likely to die. Overall, drunks were more than twice as likely to die in an accident, because of the alcohol they drank.

Exercise 27.16: Pattern Practice

Answers will vary.

Exercise 28.1: Proofreading Practice

Although teachers commonly use tests to grade their students' learning, taking a test can also help students learn. People's memories seem to be more accurate after reading some material and taking a test than after merely reading the material with no testing. In fact, studies have shown that students who take several tests learn even more than those who take only one test after reading material. Although everyone's ability to memorize material generally depends on how well the material was studied, scientists' research does indicate that test taking aids memory. The type of test is also important because multiple-choice exams help us to put facts together better while fill-in-the-blank questions promote recall of specific facts. These questions' ability to test different types of learning suggests that teachers ought to include different types of tests throughout the semester.

Exercise 28.2: Pattern Practice

Answers will vary.

Exercise 28.3: Proofreading Practice

Dance clubs used to be for dancing, but that was before moshing and crowd surfing became popular. Young adults flock to dance clubs and concerts to enter mosh pits, which are masses of flailing guys who wave their arms and slam into each other. "It's a way of communicating and having fun," said one mosher. However, there's more to this activity than meets the eye. What's supposed to be fun has turned into a liability for club owners. Recently, a young man died from head injuries after crowd surfing during a concert. His parents sued the club owner for negligence and inability to control the crowd. The lawsuit even alleges that the bouncer pushed the young man off the stage and caused him to fall and hit his head. The owner claims that "it's mosh at your own risk." In fact, many concert producers and club owners have been putting disclaimers on the back of tickets. Another owner claims, "You're responsible for yourself out there." Some bands request that fans refrain from moshing, but others encourage this dangerous behavior. It looks as if there will continue to be a core group of moshers, but to reduce liability, club owners are hoping for a resurgence of ballroom dancing.

Exercise 28.4: Pattern Practice

Answers will vary.

Exercise 28.5: Proofreading Practice

In the 1990's, the use of standardized tests, such as the SAT's for high school juniors, came under scrutiny. Critics said that these commonly used tests did not reflect a student's ability, nor did they project a level of success in college. In the 1970's and 1980's, the SAT's were the primary factor for entrance to college. A movement to consider other factors such as GPA's, activities, and the interview began after educational leaders explored the merits of alternative assessment. Alternative assessment evaluates the whole student and frowns upon ranking the number of A's on a transcript and

GPA's. However, the SAT's are an American institution, and thousands of high school students are still subjected to this procedure each spring. Perhaps in the future the SAT's will be a thing of the past.

Exercise 28.6: Pattern Practice

Answers will vary.

Exercise 28.7: Proofreading Practice

Mention the words *day care* to working parents and a collective sigh can be heard. There is a shortage of reliable day-care centers in the United States, and the situation is not improving. In fact, it's getting worse. The need for child-care workers and centers has increased because of the number of mothers returning to the work force, including woman who reenter after having children. In major cities such as New York City and Los Angeles, it's not uncommon to find high rates of women working outside the home. One working parent said, "I'll pay a high price to know my child's care is excellent, but I can't even find child care near my home." Many parents accept positions in companies simply because the companies offer on-site centers for day care. Other companies offer some type of reimbursement to employees paying for child care. "The best situation," says one parent, "is to have a family member care for your child." However, parents agree that this is usually not possible because many families live far apart. The need for affordable, reliable child care will continue to grow.

Exercise 28.8: Pattern Practice

Answers will vary.

Exercise 29.1: Proofreading Practice

Even before children begin school, many parents think they should take part in their children's education and help the children develop mentally. Such parents usually consider reading to toddlers important; moreover, they help the children memorize facts such as the days of the week and the numbers from one to ten. Now it is becoming clear that parents can begin helping when the children are babies. One particular type of parent communication, encouraging the baby to pay attention to new things, seems especially promising in helping babies' brains develop; for example, handing the baby a toy encourages the baby to notice something new. Some studies seem to indicate that this kind of activity helps children score higher on intelligence tests several years later. Parents interested in helping their babies' brain development have been encouraged by this study to point to new things in the babies' environment as part of the parents' communication with their babies; thus, their children's education can begin in the crib.

Exercise 29.2: Pattern Practice

Answers will vary.

Exercise 29.3: Proofreading Practice

In the not-too-distant future, when airline passengers board their flights, they will be able to enjoy a number of new conveniences;, such as buying their snacks and drinks from onboard vending machines;; being able to take showers, use exercise machines, and sleep in beds;; and making hotel and car-rental reservations from an onboard computer. Such features are what aircraft designers envision within the next few years for passenger jets. Their plans, though, may not be realized until much further in the future, if ever. But the ideas reflect the airline industry's hopes. If fare hikes continue and ticket prices stabilize, passengers may begin choosing different airlines on the basis of comfort, not cost; if that happens, airlines will have to be ready with new and better in-flight features. A Boeing Company executive says that "cabin environment will be a major factor;"; that is, designers must make the cabin so attractive that it will offset lower fares on other airlines. The problem, however, is added weight caused by some of the suggested features;, such as; showers, exercise areas, and more elaborate kitchens. Added weight will mean that the plane consumes more fuel;, thus driving up the price of the ticket. Still, some carriers, determined to find answers, are studying ways to use the new services to generate more passengers and more income;, particularly in the area of advertising-supported or pay-per-use high-definition entertainment.

Exercise 29.4: Pattern Practice

Answers will vary.

Exercise 30.1: Proofreading Practice

When the Apollo astronauts brought back bags of moon rocks, it was expected that the rocks would provide some answers to a perennial question; : the origin of the moon. Instead, the moon rocks suggested a number of new theories. One that is gaining more supporters is called : the giant impact theory. Alan Smith, a lunar scientist, offers an explanation of the giant impact theory: "Recently acquired evidence suggests that the moon was born of a monstrous collision between a primordial, just-formed Earth and a protoplanet the size of Mars." This evidence comes from modeling such a collision on powerful supercomputers. The theory proposes the following sequence of events: (1) as Earth was forming, it was struck a glancing blow by a projectile the size of Mars; (2) a jet of vapor then spurted out, moving so fast that some of it escaped from Earth and the rest condensed into pebble-sized rock fragments; and (3) gravitational attraction fused this cloud of pebbles into the moon. Several reasons make some scientists favor this theory, ; for example, it dovetails with what is known about the moon's chemistry, and it explains why the moon's average composition resembles Earth's. Another lunar scientist says, "We may be close to tracking down the real answer."

Exercise 30.2: Pattern Practice

Answers will vary.

Exercise 31.1: Proofreading Practice

Remember Silverton wine coolers? Silverton, like hundreds of other products that appeared in the same year, was pulled from the shelf after it failed to gain a market. "Silverton didn't seem to have any connotation as a cooler," explains G. F. Strousel, the company's vice-president in charge of sales. Every year new products appear briefly on the shelf and disappear, and established products that no longer have (X) customer appeal (X) are canceled as well. (X)Either way, (X) experts say, (X) the signs that point to failure are the same. (X) Companies looking to cut their losses pay attention to such signs. In a recent newspaper article titled "Over 75% of Business Ideas Are Flops," T. M. Weir, a professor of marketing, explains that products that don't grow but maintain their percentage of the market are known as "cash cows," and those that are declining in growth and in market share are called "dipping dogs." Says Weir, "Marketers plot the growth and decline of products, especially of the dipping dogs, very closely." According to several sources at a New York research firm that studies new product development, **(X)** the final decision to stop making a product is a financial one. **(X)** When the **(X)** red ink **(X)** flows, the product is pulled.

Exercise 31.2: Pattern Practice

Answers will vary.

Exercise 32.1 Proofreading Exercise

For health-conscious people who cringe at the thought of using a toothpaste with preservatives and dyes, there are alternative toothpastes made entirely from plants. One brand of these new, all-natural toothpastes advertises that its paste includes twenty-nine different herbs, root and flower **(X)** extracts, and seaweed. Some of these toothpastes have a pleasant taste and appearance, but the owner of a San Francisco health-food store decided not to carry one brand because it is a reddish-brown paste. "When squeezed from a tube, it resembles a fat earthworm," she explained. She prefers a brand made of propolis, the sticky stuff bees use to line their hives, and myrrh. Another brand, a black paste made of charred eggplant powder, clay, and seaweed, is favored by the hard-core macrobiotic group. This interest in natural toothpastes may be cyclical, explains the director of an oral health institute. He recalls a gray-striped, mint-flavored paste from the Philippines that sought to capitalize on a spurt of interest several years ago. It was a big **(X)** seller for a few months and then disappeared.

Exercise 32.2: Pattern Practice

Answers will vary.

Exercise 33.1: Proofreading Practice

Several years ago the nation's print and broadcast media joined with advertising agencies to launch a massive media campaign against drugs. Some, like ABC-TV, announced that they would donate prime-time T**(X)**V**(X)** spots, but CBS Inc., while agreeing to cooperate, announced its intention to continue to commit funds for campaigns for other public issues such as AIDS prevention. James R. Daly, a spokesman for the anti-drug campaign, said, "We are glad to see other companies joining in to help the campaign."**(X)** For example, the Revlon Co. donated the film needed for TV spots, and in Washington, D.C., a group of concerned parents volunteered to do additional fund-raising. In the first two years of this media campaign, more than $500 million was raised. Says Dr. Harrison Rublin, a leading spokesperson for one of the fund-raising groups, "One thirty-second ad aired at 8 p.m. is ten times more effective than a hundred brochures on the subject." **(X)**

Exercise 33.2: Pattern Practice

Answers will vary.

Exercise 33.3: Proofreading Practice

Recent research has found that the heat can kill you. Two meteorologists exploring weather patterns for the second half of the twentieth century found that the frequency of heat waves increased substantially from 1949 (?) to1995. The deaths of six hundred people in a 1995 Chicago heat wave prompted the researchers to examine the effects of heat on society. The main question of the researchers was whether hot and humid weather that occurs at night is dangerous. Subsequently, the team did find that prolonged periods of hot weather that last through several nights have the most profound effects on people, especially the elderly. A nursing home administrator asked the researchers, "What precautions should be taken when the heat is extreme?" These knowledgeable researchers responded, "Extreme summer heat affects people's health more than other types of weather. The elderly should drink plenty of fluids and remain indoors during the hottest part of the day." With proper precautions, the deaths of countless people from extreme heat can be avoided. With all the TV campaigns, though, is it really necessary to keep repeating these warnings in the twenty-first century?

Exercise 33.4: Pattern Practice

Answers will vary.

Exercise 33.5: Proofreading Practice

At the end of winter, when gardeners are depressed from the long months indoors, plant catalogs start flooding the mail. **(X)** In large type, the catalogs blare out their news to hungry gardeners. "Amazing! **(X)**" "Fantastic! **(X)**" "Incredible! **(X)**" The covers always belong to some enormous new strain of tomatoes. "Bigger Than Beefsteaks!" or "Too Big to Fit on This Page!" they yell. Even the blueberries are monsters. "Blueberries as big as quarters!" the catalogs promise. All you do, according to these enticing catalogs, is "Plant 'em and stand back!" **(X)** On a gloomy February afternoon, many would-be gardeners are probably ready to believe that this year they too can have "asparagus thicker than a person's thumb!" **(X)**

Exercise 33.6: Pattern Practice

Answers will vary.

Exercise 34.1: Proofreading Practice

If you love to shop for clothes but hate fitting rooms, there is a new invention that can eliminate trying on clothing in stores. Surprisingly, scientific researchers—not tailors—have developed a body scanner that measures a person's body. Going to stores to try on clothes could be an outdated practice; you could do it all at home. The body scanner is shaped like a photo booth and contains infrared lights that measure more than 300,000 points on the body. This invention, which is really an electronic tailor, is in the development stage. The team expects that the scanner will be ready for use soon—but not in the next year. Potential customers—such as the leading London fashion designers—are anxious for the product to gain final approval. The prediction is that custom clothing will really fit like a glove. Online shopping for clothes may also become easier—but not soon.

Exercise 34.2: Pattern Practice

Answers will vary.

Exercise 34.3: Proofreading Practice

I have kept a journal since I entered college. In this journal, I have recorded my favorite poems and/or their significance in my life at the time I read them. I enrolled in a poetry course for fun because I was a biology major and poetry was not often recited in lab. Of course, I opted for the pass/fail grading system because I feared that my scientific mind would not yield memorable poetry. I think the poem that I will remember forever is "I never saw a Moor" by Emily Dickinson. The first stanza is familiar to almost everyone:

I never saw a Moor--
I never saw the Sea--
Yet know I how the Heather looks
And what a Billow be.

I have heard these lines again and again since taking the college poetry course. It is the second stanza that is less familiar. The first two lines of the second stanza contain the theme of the poem: "I never spoke with God/Nor visited in Heaven--". These are the two lines I wrote about in my journal. In fact, the journal is filled with lines from the poetry of Emily Dickinson.

Exercise 34.4: Pattern Practice

Answers will vary.

Exercise 34.5: Proofreading Practice

Medical doctors have announced a new finding that Alzheimer's patients are demonstrating remarkable abilities in painting. Alzheimer's (also known as dementia) is a degenerative brain disorder that affects the part of the brain responsible for several functions: (1) social skills, (2) verbal communication, and (3) physical orientation. Neuropathologists (doctors who study brain disorders) have found that this disease may not affect visual thinking. (Some famous artists including Willem de Kooning and Vincent van Gogh may have suffered from Alzheimer's disease.) This study could lead to new and innovative treatments for Alzheimer's disease patients.

Exercise 34.6: Pattern Practice

Answers will vary.

Exercise 34.7: Proofreading Practice

One medieval Christian celebration was called the Feast of the Ass. According to John Smith, a Middle Ages scholar, "At one time this was a solemn celebration reenacting the flight of the Holy Family [Mary, Joseph, and Jesus] into Egypt. It ended with a Math [*sic*] in the church" (*Christian Celebrations* [New York: United Press, 1995]: 23). The festival (started in the fourteenth century by the tribune, a group of church elders) became very popular as it transformed into a humorous parody in which the ass

was led into the church and treated as an honored guest. Historians claim that the members of the congregation all brayed like asses. The church abandoned the celebration in the fifteenth century, but it remained popular for years.

Exercise 34.8: Pattern Practice

Answers will vary.

Exercise 34.9: Proofreading Practice

The last two lines of Archibald MacLeish's poem "Ars Poetica" (written in 1924) are often quoted as his theory of poetry. "A poem should not mean /But be," he wrote. In his notebooks, he expanded on this statement: "The purpose of the expression of emotion in a poem is not to recreate the poet's emotion in someone else... The poem itself is a finality, an end, a creation."

G. T. Hardison, in his analysis of MacLeish's theory of poetry ("The Non-Meaning of Poetry," *Modern Poetics* 27 [1981]: 45), explains that "when MacLeish says the poem 'is a finality, an ending [*sic*],' he means that a good poem is self-sufficient; it is, it does not mean something else. One might as well ask the meaning of a friend or brother."

Exercise 35.1: Proofreading Practice

Melbourne, a City in Australia, is the site of the World's tallest building. The Building has 120 stories and contains offices and apartments. Construction started in the Spring of last year. The Building surpassed petronas towers in Malaysia as the tallest Building. The Malaysian Building became the Tallest Building in 1996 when it took the title from the Sears Tower in chicago. The Melbourne building is now twice the size of the city's previous tallest structure, but developers assured citizens that it did not look out of place. The developers' aim was to build a "Beautiful and appropriate building" for the city of Melbourne. "We will create a new landmark for our city," Said the chief developer. He also claimed, "The people of the city are proud of this accomplishment."

Exercise 35.2: Pattern Practice

Answers will vary.

Exercise 36.1: Proofreading Practice

The fluctuations in the stock market affect investors and job hunters alike. In times of high unemployment, business school graduates will find that the <u>Master of Business Administration</u> may not guarantee a job after graduation. The volatile stock market often causes downsizing in investment firms such as Merrill Lynch, Prudential, and Morgan Stanley. But graduates had no problem landing a position starting at <u>$64,500</u> on average. The recruitment process is fairly constant at prestigious schools such as Georgetown University in Washington, D.C. However, students from the top schools will most likely obtain positions but at a lower salary than previously offered. Students in less prestigious schools in the <u>United States</u> are more worried about finding a position. There can be two or three positions to fill in a company where in the past there would be ten or twelve positions. Worried students network to find internships that may lead to positions. An unpredictable market is a sign that not every MBA student can automatically expect a lucrative job.

Exercise 36.2: Pattern Practice

Answers will vary.

Exercise 37.1: Proofreading Practice

In the <u>twenty-first</u> century, many historians are reflecting on the events that shaped the latter half of the <u>twentieth</u> century. The center of many important events of that century was <u>1600</u> Pennsylvania Avenue, Washington, D.C. Baby boomers remember President John F. Kennedy, who was assassinated in the year <u>1963</u>. Another former resident of the White House, Richard M. Nixon, will be remembered for the Watergate hearings, which dominated television programming for a long, hot <u>seventies</u> summer. Many people recall turning on Channel 2, 4, 5, 7, or 11 and finding Watergate on every station. Ronald Reagan brought the country "Reaganomics" and a new sense of patriotism. George H.W. Bush promised a "kinder, gentler nation" and promised not to raise taxes. Then came William Jefferson Clinton. Even more than those before him, the <u>forty-second</u> president of the United States gave historians much to argue about in trying to evaluate his accomplishments.

Exercise 37.2: Pattern Practice

Answers will vary.

Exercise 38.1: Proofreading Practice

The Internet is considered a mass medium, according to articles in magazines like <u>Time</u> and <u>Newsweek</u>. In elections, the Internet was used as a new genre to lasso voters as candidates established Web sites. A poll of voters for the television show <u>20/20</u> revealed that 82 percent of voters regularly use a computer at home or work. The <u>New York Times</u> reported that California was the first state to use the Internet for political purposes and was quickly imitated by Florida, Texas, South Dakota, and Wisconsin. The sites generally include information on a candidate, photos from the campaign trail, and methods to send in contributions. Voters obtain addresses for the sites from campaign literature and television commercials. While some political experts conclude that this is a less costly campaign method and highly effective for raising funds, others think that having to access a site is a deterrent. The fact remains that print and television advertisements reach more voters and may not be replaced by the Internet. One political consultant observed, "There are more people watching <u>Good Morning America</u> and listening to the radio on the way to the office than visiting political Web sites." Voters feel the Internet provides options. A voter interviewed about the sites stated, "<u>Vive la différence!</u>"

Exercise 38.2: Pattern Practice

Answers will vary.

Exercise 39.1: Pattern Practice

Turkish people <u>don't</u> think of St. Nicholas as having reindeer or <u>elves</u>, living at **the** North Pole, or climbing down chimneys with gifts on <u>Christmas</u> Eve. <u>Except</u> for a twist of history, Santa Claus might well speak Turkish, ride a camel, dress for a <u>warmer</u> climate, bring gifts of oranges and tomatoes, and appear on December 5 instead of Christmas Eve. According to the story of the Turkish church about his <u>background</u>, Nicholas was the <u>first</u> bishop of Myra, on the coast **of** Turkey. Turkish scholars say he was known far and wide for his <u>piety</u> and charity. He was killed around <u>A.D.</u> 245, and after his martyrdom, on December 6, <u>tales</u> of his good deeds lived on. His <u>fame</u> was so great that in the eleventh <u>century</u>, when the Italian branch of the Catholic church began a drive to bring to Italy the remains of the most famous saints, <u>thieves</u> stole most of Nicholas's bones from the church tomb in Turkey and took them to a town in <u>southern</u> Italy. "Nicholas" was abbreviated to Claus, and "St. Nick" became Santa. Since there are no <u>documents</u> or records of the original Nicholas of Myra, some scholars doubt his existence. But others are convinced there really was a St. Nicholas, even if he didn't have reindeer or live at **the** North Pole.

Exercise 39.2: Proofreading Practice

Diwali is a five-day Hindu festival often referred to as the Festival of Lights. During this time, homes are cleaned from ceiling to floor and the windows are opened to recieve **(receive)** Lakshmi, a Hindu goddess. The Hindu people beleive **(believe)** that Lakshmi is the goddess of wealth. The cheif **(chief)** beleif **(belief)** is that wealth is not a corruptive power but is considered a reward for good deeds in a past life. The festival begins with a day set aside to worship Lakshmi. On the second day, Kali, the goddess of strength, is worshipped. The third day is the last day of the year in the lunar calendar. On this day, lamps are lighted and shine brightly in every home. Participants are encouraged to remove anger, hate, and jealousy from their lives on the fourth day. On the final day of the festival, Bali, an anceint **(ancient)** Indian king, is recalled. The focus of this day is to see the good in others.

Exercise 39.3: Pattern Practice

Here are some possible sentences:

1. There are eight days of Hanukkah.
2. If a vein is cut, it will bleed.
3. I did not receive the package in the mail.
4. His conceit was evident when he posed for the photographers.
5. To deceive another person intentionally is wrong.
6. I could get no relief from the pain even though I took the aspirin.
7. A driver must yield the right of way at certain intersections.
8. The field was full of beautiful flowers.
9. Some people believe in guardian angels.
10. My niece looks just like her father, who is my brother.

Exercise 39.4: Proofreading Practice

Last week, Michael planed **(planned)** to have his bicycle repaired, though he admitted that he was hopping **(hoping)** he had stopped the leak in the front tire with a patch. Even though he concealled **(concealed)** the patch with some heavy tape, he found that he had to keep tapping **(taping)** the patch back on the tire. Yesterday, when Michael looked at the bicycle

on the way to his first class, he could see that the front tire had become flatter than it should be because it was <u>lossing</u> **(losing)** air. With no time to spare, he <u>joged</u> **(jogged)** off to class, resolved that he would take the bicycle to a shop that afternoon.

Exercise 39.5: Pattern Practice

Here are some possible sentences:
1. The gymnast <u>flipped</u> and twirled during the floor exercise.
2. My favorite actor is <u>starring</u> in the film.
3. The impatient woman <u>tapped</u> her foot while waiting for the bus.
4. <u>Shopping</u> is a favorite activity of many Americans.
5. The baby <u>napped</u> peacefully in her father's arms.
6. Some scientists claim that global warming is <u>occurring</u> in the world.
7. I <u>preferred</u> to go to the theater, but we went to dinner instead.
8. The author <u>omitted</u> a paragraph from the introduction of the book.
9. She <u>unwrapped</u> the gift enthusiastically.
10. The boss <u>regretted</u> firing the employee.

Exercise 39.6: Pattern Practice

Answers will vary.

Exercise 39.7: Pattern Practice

1. rising, guiding, coming
2. likely, surely, truly
3. careful, useful, stressful
4. continuous, courageous, nervous
5. desirable, noticeable, knowledgeable

Exercise 39.8: Pattern Practice

1. trays	7. merciful	13. loneliness
2. apologies	8. funnier	14. varied
3. allied	9. monkeys	15. ninetieth
4. steadying	10. burial	16. studious
5. accompanying	11. likelier	17. prettiness
6. studying	12. stories	18. employer

Exercise 39.9: Proofreading Practice

1. foxes   11. women
3. companies   12. freshmen
4. latches   13. passers-by
8. brothers-in-law   15. hooves

Exercise 39.10: Proofreading Practice

1. affects	8. any way	15. passed
2. too	9. than	16. assistance
3. quiet	10. by	17. all right
4. any one	11. it's	18. fourth
5. envelope	12. stationary	19. cite
6. everyday	13. all together	20. their
7. advice	14. may be	

Exercise 40.1: Proofreading Practice

One possible revision is as follows:
In the curricula of most business schools, the study of failure has not yet become an accepted subject. Yet average business <u>students</u> need to know what <u>they</u> should do when a business strategy fails and how <u>they</u> can learn from <u>their</u> mistakes. Even the <u>chairperson</u> of one Fortune 500 company says that the average <u>business executive</u> can learn more from (~~his~~) mistakes than from (~~his~~) successes. Yet the concept of studying failure has been slow in catching on. However, a few business schools and even engineering management majors at one university in California now confront the question of how anyone can recover from <u>his or her</u> mistakes. Student papers analyze how a typical failed entrepreneur might have managed <u>his or her</u> problems better. Sometimes, perceptive <u>students</u> can even relate the lessons to <u>their</u> own behavior. One of the typical problems that is studied is that of escalating commitment, the tendency of a manager to throw more and more (~~of his~~) financial resources and <u>personnel</u> into a project that is failing. Another is the tendency of the hapless executive not to see that <u>an</u> idea is a bomb. For this reason, computers are being enlisted to help <u>executives</u>—and <u>their</u> superiors—make decisions about whether <u>to</u> bail out or stay in. The study of failure clearly promises to breed success, at least for future <u>business executives</u> now enrolled in business schools.

Exercise 40.2: Pattern Practice

Answers will vary.

Exercise 41.1: Proofreading Practice

One possible revision is as follows:

Researchers note a growing concern among psychologists that as more working parents entrust infants to day-care centers, some of these babies may face psychological harm. The researchers' findings focus on children younger than eighteen months old left in day-care centers more than twenty hours a week. Researchers say that for children at that formative age, day-care seems to increase the feeling of insecurity. One of the foremost researchers says he isn't sure how the increased insecurity happens, but he guesses that the everyday stress a child undergoes resulting from separation from the parent can be a contributing factor. Studies of infants who spend long periods each week in day-care have shown that more of these infants exhibit anxiousness and hyperactivity. These findings challenge the older view that day-care does not harm a young child.

Exercise 41.2: Pattern Practice

Answers will vary.

Exercise 41.3: Proofreading Practice

The Ford Motor Company has developed a method of testing automobiles for different age groups. In a nutshell, Ford has designed a suit that makes the crash tester feel as old as the day is long. In order for the tester to experience empathy for aging customers, the suit dims vision, weakens muscles, and makes the tester feel stiff as a board. One tester states, "I'm thirty-two years old, but this gear suits me to a T because it helps me do my job." Testers wear the suit while getting in and out of vehicles, buckling the seat belt, and driving in reverse. Ford hopes that vehicles designed for aging consumers will sell like hotcakes. Many senior citizens feel that they are ignored in the competitive market of automobile sales. One senior says, "We are virtually ignored in the car market, so it is good to see cars designed for senior citizens. It's better late than never." With the success of Ford's designing techniques, many other manufacturers will be jumping on the bandwagon.

Exercise 41.4: Revision Practice

One possible revision is as follows:
The Ford Motor Company has developed a new method of testing automobiles for different age groups. In short, Ford has designed a suit that makes the crash tester feel like a senior citizen. In order for the tester to experience empathy for aging customers, the suit dims vision, weakens muscles and makes the tester feel stiff. One tester states, "I'm thirty-two years old, but this gear is ideal because it helps me do my job." Testers wear the suit while getting in and out of vehicles, buckling the seat belt, and driving in reverse. Ford hopes that vehicles designed for aging consumers will sell well. Many senior citizens feel that they are ignored in the competitive market of automobile sales. One senior says, "We are virtually ignored in the car market, so it is good to finally see cars designed for senior citizens." With the success of Ford's designing techniques, many other motor companies will imitate them.

Exercise 42.1: Dictionary Practice

Answers will vary depending on what dictionaries are used.

Exercise 42.2: Writing Practice

Answers will vary.

Exercise 42.3: Proofreading Practice

One possible revision is as follows:
The technology called MP3 has altered the way consumers buy their favorite music. Companies sell music and musicians use this <u>new technology</u> to market songs directly to consumers, bypassing agents, record companies, and distributors. <u>Consumers</u> use a special recording device to download the best <u>music</u> off the computer. Consumers are able to copy and store music on home computers or on a portable music player, such as an iPod. Music industry <u>executives</u> are <u>nervous about this new device</u>. <u>They</u> are afraid they <u>will not make as much profit</u>. The Recording Industry of America Association warns that many illegal copies of certain artists' work will <u>appear</u>. The RIAA is concerned for the artists and the royalties they lose because of this technology. The artists, consumers, and record companies can all <u>benefit</u> from this new technology if they <u>are careful at the start</u>. The old days of buying CDs are almost gone.

Exercise 42.4: Pattern Practice

Here are some possible revisions:

1. **Revised to a more formal tone:**

   An appropriate measure would be to exert pressure on automobile manufacturers and force them to increase the fuel efficiency of the current models, which consume excessive amounts of gasoline.

2. **Revised to a more formal tone:**

   However, a more rapid method of reducing fuel consumption would be to increase taxation on gasoline.

3. **Revised to a less formal tone:**

   People interested in protecting the environment are also asking for tighter limits on smokestacks pouring out sulfur dioxide, a major cause of acid rain.

4. **Revised to a more formal tone:**

   However, states currently producing high-sulfur coal are expressing concern about the resulting damage to their economies.

Exercise 42.5: Pattern Practice

Some possible answers are as follows:

General	Specific	More Specific
1. music	song	Star-Spangled Banner
2. book	novel	Jane Eyre
3. animal	parrot	macaw
4. clothes	pants	blue jeans
5. field of study	physics	astronomy
6. machine	saw	chain saw
7. car	sports car	Porsche
8. plant	violet	African violet
9. place of business	grocery store	fruit and vegetable market
10. athlete	baseball player	catcher

Exercise 42.6: Revision Practice

Answers will vary.

Exercise 42.7: Pattern Practice

Possible answers are as follows:

Most Positive	Neutral	Most Negative
1. puppy	canine	mutt
2. law-enforcement officer	police officer	cop
3. economical	inexpensive	cheap
4. ornate	embellished	garish
5. replica	copy	counterfeit
6. scholar	intellectual	egghead
7. uncompromising	determined	stubborn
8. apprehensive	scared	paranoid
9. explanation	reason	excuse
10. chatty	talkative	gabby

Exercise 44.1: Proofreading Practice

When people from other countries <u>will visit</u> **(visit)** the United States, they find a bewildering variety of words that can be used for the same thing. In some parts of the United States, a salesperson will <u>asked</u> **(ask)** the customer if she <u>would want</u> **(wants)** the item in a "sack." In other places, the salesperson might ask, "Did you <u>wanted</u> **(want)** this in a 'bag'?" It is hard for tourists who don't understand to <u>bring up it</u> **(bring it up)** when they don't know whether there is a difference. Or a tourist may ask, "<u>May</u> **(Can)** I take this metro to First Avenue?" in a city where the underground train is called "the subway." If I <u>was</u> **(were)** one of those tourists, I <u>could</u> **(would)** always keep a dictionary in my pocket to use when the situation <u>calls it for</u> **(calls for it)**.

Exercise 44.2: Proofreading Practice

1. to encourage
2. talk
3. will learn
4. asking
5. to talk
6. to respond / responding (both are correct)
7. to have / having (both are correct)
8. must be

Exercise 44.3: Proofreading Practice

Answers will vary.

Exercise 46.1: Proofreading Practice

(1) When students <u>are</u> looking for part-time work, one difficulty <u>they</u> <u>face</u> is that they want the job to be after class hours. (2) Another difficulty for students is that <u>they</u> want the job to be near their school so that <u>they</u> don't have far to travel. (3) But that means <u>there</u> are many students who want to work at the same time and in the same area of **a** town. (4) The competition for the jobs that exist **it** causes too many students to be unable to find work. (5) Some counselors ~~they~~ tell their students to try looking for jobs that have flexible hours or for work that **it** can be done at home. (6) <u>It</u> is also worth trying to look farther away from the campus.

Exercise 47.1: Proofreading Practice

1. Americans	8. consumer	15. stores
2. goods	9. policies	16. week
3. society	10. mall	17. credit
4. malls	11. stores	18. United States
5. outlets	12. receipt	19. items
6. stores	13. prices	20. supermarket
7. clubs	14. shoppers	

Exercise 47.2: Proofreading Practice

Answers will vary.

Exercise 48.1: Pattern Practice

Sentences will vary, but the adjectives should appear in the following order:

1. six famous old sports stars
2. her favorite old Hispanic song
3. a new German steel knife
4. a strange small square box
5. nine large yellow balls

Exercise 48.2: Proofreading Practice

One of **the** most interesting physicists of last century was Richard Feynman. He wrote **a** best-selling book about his own life, but he became even more famous on television as **a** man who was **a** member of **the** team that investigated after **an** accident happened to *Challenger*, **the** space shuttle that crashed in 1986. People watched on television as he demonstrated that **a** faulty part in **the** space shuttle probably caused **the** accident. Feynman's greatest achievement in science was **the** theory of quantum electrodynamics, which described **the** behavior of subatomic particles, atoms, light, electricity, and magnetism. **The** field of computer science also owes much to **the** work of Feynman. Many scientists consider Feynman to be one of **the** geniuses of **the** twentieth century.

Exercise 49.1: Proofreading Practice

(1) Table tennis used to be a minor pastime <u>at</u> **(in)** America, but a <u>little</u> **(few)** years ago it began to develop into an important sport. (2) Newcomers to the United States from countries such as Nigeria, Korea, and China, where table tennis is a major sport, have helped the United States become a respectable contender <u>at</u> **(in)** world competition. (3) <u>Much</u> **(Many)** new residents who are very good <u>in</u> **(at)** this sport have brought their skills to this country. (4) Now there are specialized table tennis parlors where players play <u>in</u> **(on)** tables with special hard surfaces. (5) Players no longer use <u>some</u> **(any)** sandpaper paddles. (6) Instead, <u>much</u> **(many)** paddles are made of carbon fiber and have special coatings <u>in</u> **(on)** the hitting surface. (7) <u>At</u> **(In)** the past, America was often <u>on</u> **(in)** last place in international competitions. (8) But now, with many strong players, often born <u>at</u> **(in)** China, the United States is beginning to win.

Exercise 49.2: Proofreading Practice

Answers will vary.

Exercise 51.1: Proofreading Practice

Many drivers prefer to put premium gas in their tank because they think they will get better mileage or more power from their car engines. They may also be following instructions in their owner's manual. Also, they want to avoid engine knock. So when they go to the gas station, they often choose premium gas without realizing that they don't require that extra octane. Too many drivers today are paying unnecessarily high prices for premium gas when their cars don't need it. In fact, engineers, scientists, and the federal government say there's little need for premium. Engines designed for regular fuel don't improve on premium and sometimes run worse. And today's engines designed for premium run fine on regular, too, their makers say, though power declines slightly. When drivers want to save money, it's wise to ignore the ads and get regular octane gas instead.

Exercise 54.1: Writing Practice

Answers will vary.

Exercise 55.1: Writing Practice

Answers will vary.

Exercise 56.2: Proofreading for Plagiarism

Many students today wonder if a college education is really worth the effort and expense. Tuition has gone up over the last few years, and many students need to work or take out loans if their parents cannot help to fund their college years. But as college education is definitely worth it, in terms of both learning more about the world and earning a higher income later on. College offers students the opportunity to learn about many different subjects, such as history, philosophy, biology and business management, and a college education can result in being better off financially later on. While the average student leaves college roughly $17,000 in debt, he or she will make roughly $1 million more over a lifetime than someone who has not gone to college. So, while no one wants to graduate and face a large debt that has to be paid off, that college degree will help the person to earn much more and to pay off that debt.

Exercise 56.3: Writing Practice

Student paragraph with added citations:

Another important concern in city planning is to formulate proposals to eliminate or reduce problems caused by automobiles. "Cities with streets designed for cars instead of people are increasingly unlivable" **(Lowe 56)**, for cars cause congestion, pollution, and noise. Providing more public transportation can reduce these problems, but it is not likely that city dwellers will give up owning cars. Therefore, solutions are needed for parking, which already uses up as much as 20 to 30 percent of the space available in downtown areas **(Lipperman 99)**, and for rush hour traffic, which now extends to more than 12 hours in Seoul and to 14 hours in Rio de Janeiro **(Lowe 57)**. Pollution, another urban problem caused partly by cars, needs to be controlled. Automobile emissions cause lung disorders and aggravate bronchial problems **(Lipperman 108)**. In addition, noise from automobiles must be curbed. Noise has already has become a health problem in cities such as Cairo, where noise levels are already ten times the acceptable standard for human health **(Lowe 57)**.

Works Cited format:
Lowe, Marcia D. "Rethinking Urban Transport." *State of the World*, 2001. New York:
     W.W. Norton, 2002.
Lipperman, Irwin. *Planning for a Livable Tomorrow.* New York: Nathanson Press, 1992.

Exercise 56.4: Paraphrasing and Summarizing Practice

Answers may vary; sample paragraphs are as follows:
Paragraph 1 Summary
The NRA is one of the nation's most powerful lobbying groups. Backing their arguments with the Second Amendment, they seek to protect the right to own a gun. They claim that most gun owners are responsible while gun crime, they claim, is the doing of criminals. The NRA argues that existing laws must be better enforced rather than creating new gun control laws, since criminals will always find ways to get guns.

Paragraph 1 Paraphrase
The NRA was first organized in 1871 as a gun safety group but has become the most important player in current gun control debates. The NRA argues that the Constitution guarantees a right to bear arms, so the NRA seeks to protect that right. They claim that people who own guns obey the law and only use guns for hunting or, if necessary, for self-defense. The NRA does admit that many crimes are committed with guns and that many children are killed each year, but they have always argued that "guns don't kill people; people kill people." The NRA argues that new gun control laws won't prevent a criminal from acquiring a gun, but better enforcement of existing laws might.

Paragraph 2 Summary

Groups which oppose the NRA and argue for stricter controls on gun ownership counter that having guns in a home actually increases the likelihood that they will be used in a violent manner, often against friends or relatives, or that they will be a factor in the accidental shooting of children.

Paragraph 2 Paraphrase

Those who oppose the NRA and argue for stronger gun-control laws claim that having guns on hand for self-defense does not prevent crime. NRA opponents have lobbied for stricter controls on gun ownership on the grounds that when a gun is accessible, events can escalate to violence more quickly. In fact, studies have shown that guns purchased for self-defense more often are used to kill relatives and friends than to kill intruders. In addition, guns kept at home often are responsible for the accidental shooting of children.

Exercise 58.1: Proofreading Practice

1. Schlosser, Eric. *Fast Food Nation.* Boston: Houghton Mifflin, 2001.
2. Cather, Willa. "Paul's Case." *Literature and the Writing Process.* Ed. James Torrell and Martin LeBeau. Upper Saddle River: Prentice Hall, 1999. 264-76.
3. John Hockenberry, "The Next Brainiacs." *Wired.* Aug. 2001: 94-105.
4. Sragow, Michael. "Brilliant Careers: Francis Ford Coppola." *Salon.com* 19 Oct. 1999. 3 August 2001 <http://www.salon.com/people/bc/1999/10/19/coppola/index.html>

Exercise 58.2: Pattern Practice

1. Oates, Joyce Carol. *Blonde: A Novel.* Hopewell: Ecco, 2001.
2. Evans, Mari. "I Am a Black Woman." *Literature: An Introduction to Reading and Writing.* Ed. Edgar V. Roberts and Henry E. Jacobs. Upper Saddle River: Prentice Hall, 2001. 821.
3. Lapham, Lewis H. "The American Rome." *Harper's Magazine.* Aug. 2001: 31-38.
4. Zernike, Kate. "And Now a Word From Their Cool College Sponsor." *New York Times on the Web* 19 July 2001. 20 August 2001 <http://www.nytimes.com/2001/07/19/nyregion/19COLL.html>